POLITICAL CORRUPTION IN MEXICO

POLITICAL
CORRUPTION
IN MEXICO

The Impact of Democratization

STEPHEN D. MORRIS

LYNNE
RIENNER
PUBLISHERS

BOULDER
LONDON

Published in the United States of America in 2009 by
Lynne Rienner Publishers, Inc.
1800 30th Street, Boulder, Colorado 80301
www.rienner.com

and in the United Kingdom by
Lynne Rienner Publishers, Inc.
3 Henrietta Street, Covent Garden, London WC2E 8LU

Library of Congress Cataloging-in-Publication Data
Morris, Stephen D., 1957–
    Political corruption in Mexico : the impact of democratization /
Stephen D. Morris.
       p. cm.
    Includes bibliographical references and index.
    ISBN 978-1-58826-680-4 (hardcover : alk. paper)
    1. Political corruption—Mexico. 2. Mexico—Politics and
government—2000–   3. Democratization—Mexico. 4. Political
culture—Mexico. I. Title.
    JL1229.C6M73   2009
    320.972—dc22

                                           2009002534

British Cataloguing in Publication Data
A Cataloguing in Publication record for this book
is available from the British Library.

Printed and bound in the United States of America

    5 4 3 2 1

*To those in Mexico
who struggle to create an accountable,
just, and transparent polity*

Corruption is a cancer on the Revolution. . . . It is no secret that the police abuse their authority.

—President Luis Echeverría, 1972

You govern or you do business. . . . The public charge should not be the spoils for anyone.

—President Miguel de la Madrid, 1983

It is not easy to fight against corruption, I know, we all know, but there is no other option: we attack it or it consumes all of us like a social cancer that penetrates and destroys everything.

—President Vicente Fox, 2001

Contents

Tables and Figures

Tables

Figures

Preface

Corruption represents a sort of back door into the fundamentals of politics. For years the topic has intrigued me, and I have become increasingly convinced of its centrality. For a time, I shifted my analytical attention to questions of political reformism and Mexican national identity. But repeatedly, events and people conspired to pull me back to the topic.

The election of Vicente Fox in 2000 and his announcement of a high-profile anticorruption program crystallized the central theoretical question addressed in this book: the impact of democratization on corruption in Mexico. During the Fox *sexenio,* I had the opportunity to develop my analysis—working with some of the top Mexican scholars who study corruption, collecting extensive data, and interviewing a host of public officials. In 2003, Arturo del Castillo, formerly of the Centro de Investigación y Docencia Económica (CIDE), graciously invited me to Mexico to participate in a seminar sponsored by the Escuela Iberoamericana de Gobierno y Política Pública and CIDE, where I presented a paper on state-level changes in corruption. During that meeting, I began to develop a relationship with del Castillo, who was quickly becoming one of the leaders in corruption research in Mexico, and with Manuel Alejandro Guerrero of the Universidad Iberoamericana. I also worked with Vladimir Juárez, a CIDE graduate student at the time, who over the years and subsequent visits to Mexico would provide substantial feedback on my research, help arrange numerous interviews with public officials, and grant me access to his *diplomado* on accountability. In the course of these visits I also met with Eduardo Bohórquez, the executive director of Transparencia Mexicana, who not only generously granted me time to discuss the critical work of that organization, but also provided needed survey data. I am thankful to my colleagues for sharing their time, insights on corruption in Mexico, and, especially, their friendship. I also met with a number of officials over these years from the Office of the Comptroller General, the Ministry of Public Function, and other ministries, including Aliza Chelminsky, Carlos Jaso, Mauricio García, Xavier Ponce de León, Yossef Meraz, and Rogelio Treviño. I greatly appreciate their willingness to candidly share their thoughts and assessments.

In the United States, a number of colleagues have aided my efforts. John Ackerman (now at the Universidad Nacional Autonoma de México), Chris Blake, Richmond Brown, Roberto de Michele, Sam Fisher, Dan Gingerich, Michael Johnston, Joe Klesner, Chappell Lawson, Claudio Lomnitz, Mitchell Seligson, and Matthew Taylor all facilitated my understanding of the topic and provided much-needed feedback on ideas, drafts, and statistical analyses. I am very grateful for their friendship, collegiality, and assistance. I would also like to thank the anonymous reviewers for their helpful comments and the editorial staff at Lynne Rienner Publishers for their diligence. Jason Cook's editing deserves special commendation. I am also grateful to the University of South Alabama for providing internal grants that allowed me to travel to Mexico to conduct interviews and to attend various conferences. And I am forever grateful to my wife, Celina, and my grown children, David and Tania, for putting up with my *inquietud* regarding corruption and my fascination for everything Mexican. Of course, despite the contributions and assistance from all these good people, I alone am responsible for the content and analysis presented here.

Finally, I beg that no one conclude from this analysis that I believe Mexico is unique (or unlike the United States) in suffering corruption. I have immense respect for the many people in Mexico, both inside and outside the government, who battle corruption on a daily basis and struggle to create accountability and transparency. *Ojalá* their dreams and efforts will create a better tomorrow for the nation.

—*Stephen D. Morris*

1

Political Corruption and Change in Mexico

Scandals, anecdotes, official reports, the rhetoric of politicians, sur-veys, scholarly analyses, and even popular legend all indicate that corruption pervades Mexico, spanning the country, the layers of government, and the years. According to Transparency International's 2005 Global Corruption Barometer, 31 percent of Mexican households paid bribes during the year. Estimates suggest that the country devotes 9–12 percent of its gross domestic product to bribes (Morales 2001), that small and medium-sized businesses spend US$43 billion annually to cut bureaucratic red tape (*SourceMex* August 17, 2005), and that 10 percent of spending on public contracts goes to corruption (Reyes 2004b). Such patterns clearly pervert the public's image of politics and politicians. When asked in an Encuesta Nacional de la Cultura Política (ENCUP) survey in 2001 what word came to mind upon hearing the term "politics," the most common response was "corruption"—the first reply by 21 percent of those surveyed and the second reply by another 13 percent. Capturing what continues to be a prevailing sentiment, Anthony DePalma (1996) once asserted, "Corruption is not a characteristic of the system in Mexico . . . it is the system." About a decade later, José Martínez, author of *CONALITEG–Vamos México: Corrupción de estado, el peón de la reina*, called corruption Mexico's "national sport" (cited in Avilés 2004).

Writing in the late 1980s, I pointed to Mexico's unique authoritarian political system to explain the underlying causes, consequences, and patterns of corruption plaguing the country (Morris 1987, 1991).[1] Rooted in a structural theory linking corruption to the relative balance of state and social forces, I argued that the dominance of a single political party—the Partido Revolucionario Institucional (PRI)—the informal, meta-constitutional powers of the president, the ban on reelection, the weak and submissive legislative and judicial branches, the ineffective workings of federalism, and the government's extensive corporatist and clientelist controls over society crippled the formal mechanisms of accountability and rule of law, fostering instead a pattern of corruption that actually contributed to the regime's longevity. Among the effects, the structural imbalances enabled the president to use corruption to cement the ties wedding the political elite, reward those abiding by the informal rules of the game and punish those who did not, and even co-opt those potentially threatening the system. Through the manipulation of the legal charges of corruption and periodic, ritualistic anticorruption campaigns or social cleansings, the president even used the allegations of corruption to purge his political enemies and garner legitimacy, while simultaneously disassociating his administration from those of his predecessors. This helped renew popular faith in the government and the ideals of the Mexican Revolution, and nurture the government's reformist credentials just enough to manage the pace and the demands for political change (*gatopardismo,* or engaging enough change to remain the same; see Morris 1995).

Since the time of that analysis, however, Mexican politics have changed dramatically. On the heels of important mayoral triumphs in the early 1980s and amid the debt-induced economic crisis of the "lost decade," opposition parties, led by the Partido Acción Nacional (PAN), slowly but surely began to wrestle control of state executive and legislative offices from the once hegemonic PRI. By the mid-1990s, the PAN, along with the center-left Partido de la Revolución Democrática (PRD), the party born from the dramatic split within the upper ranks of the PRI in 1987 and Cuauhtémoc Cárdenas Solórzano's challenge in the fraud-ridden presidential election of 1988, controlled almost half of the nation's unicameral state legislatures and gubernatorial seats, making divided government and real, meaningful electoral competition the norm in vast parts of the country. After pushing through electoral reforms in 1994 and 1996 that eliminated the PRI's and the government's grip over the electoral process itself—reforms triggered in large part by the legitimacy crisis arising from the controversial 1988 election and the mounting social and political pressures—the PRI lost its majority in the Chamber of Deputies in 1997, extending divided government and partisan competition to the federal level. Three years later, in Mexico's "long-awaited surprise," not only did the PRI lose the presidency (which might have happened anyway in 1988), but also, more significantly, the outgoing president, Ernesto Zedillo (1994–2000), accepted the defeat and relinquished power: the *coup de grace* of the long-reigning PRI *gobierno.* For many, the victory of the PAN's charismatic Vicente Fox in July 2000—on his birthday at that—stood as the crowning achievement of Mexican democratization, placing Mexico onto a new and long sought after path.[2] For others, the nation still had a long way to go to achieve true democracy, including the battling of entrenched corruption.

Throughout this protracted process of growing electoral competition and democratic opening, the level and scope of societal pluralism expanded (Eisenstadt 2004). The number and autonomy of civic organizations, many once controlled by the government through a variety of co-optive, clientelistic, and corporatist mechanisms, skyrocketed to well over 50,000 by 2006. The crisis-induced austerity and neoliberal reforms of the period eliminated many of the controls (carrots and sticks) the government once used to discipline the press, business associations, labor unions, and social organizations, as well as the spoils once available to satisfy public officials and maintain elite unity. Throughout the 1990s, as more and more autonomous organizations leapt onto the political stage, they increasingly cast their sights on such issues as human rights, clean elections, and corruption, exerting greater influence over society and the state in the process. Demands for accountability grew exponentially. The press in particular conquered new freedoms during the period (Lawson 2002), while business, now forced to compete in ever more open and competitive markets under neoliberalism, began to break free of the sort of government manipulation it had experienced under the policies of state-led, import substitution industrialization. Even within the government itself, the monolith began to crumble as key institutions like the Central Bank, the Federal Electoral Institute, and the Supreme Court began to take on a degree of autonomy unknown in the past, cutting further and deeper into and checking the power of the once omniscient executive.

This triple play of heightened electoral competition, divided government, and pluralism strengthened the power and the role of the legislature, the judiciary, state and local governments, and society vis-à-vis the president and the federal government. At the same time, it shifted the locus of political conflict away from the executive, the bureaucracy, and the PRI, where it had been under the old regime, toward elections, political parties, Congress, the courts, and specialized agencies. Indeed, the presidency of Fox (2000–2006) abruptly revealed how presidential power in contemporary Mexico had sprung almost entirely from the PRI's electoral hegemony rather than from any real, constitutional powers of the president (Nacif 2004; Rivera 2004). In short, by the dawn of the twenty-first century, the primary features of Mexican politics that had marked the twentieth century—one-party rule, *presidencialismo,* corporatism, authoritarianism—had come to an end.

The watershed election of Fox in 2000 and the defeat of the PRI reflected in large measure the declining legitimacy of the PRI: a decline stemming in part from decades of corruption. So, by the close of the century, what had once seemingly functioned to solidify the political elite and even contribute to regime stability, arguably had come to play a role in undermining that stability (see Morris 1999). Voters increasingly came to associate the PRI with corruption—and, indeed, many still do—making the historic 2000 vote a popular rejection of the corruption of the past and a cry for change. At the same time, by empowering a non-PRI president, the watershed election forged a unique opportunity to take on the entrenched interests of the system and the corruption of the past. Not only did Fox stress corruption as a major campaign issue as well as the theme of change, but as his first act as president he appointed an intersecretarial committee charged with developing and coordinating a broad-based anticorruption program. The country clearly seemed poised for change.

In some ways, of course, a new president promising to fight corruption was hardly novel. Throughout the twentieth century, Mexican presidents had ritualistically pursued high-profile anticorruption campaigns upon taking office, purging corrupt officials from the past and promoting reforms (see Morris 1991). The new drive led by Fox, however, unfolded in a strikingly distinct political, institutional, and even international context. Not only did Fox hail from a different political party and thus enjoy a weaker base of support within the government than had his predecessors—no entrenched interests to protect—but by the time he took office the topic of corruption had become a "hot button" issue as well. Owing to the work of the Berlin-based nongovernmental organization Transparency International, a new post–Cold War reality, new approaches to issues of governance within the World Bank and the International Monetary Fund, the development of cross-national data on a phenomenon difficult to define and even more difficult to measure, and a flood of research beginning in the mid-1990s, the study of corruption by this time was enjoying a remarkable boom worldwide (see Johnston 2005). This global context nurtured concerns in Mexico about the nation's high levels of corruption, strengthened societal pressures to address the issue, and even provided Fox with an orthodox strategy to fight it. The new emphasis on corruption also encompassed international anticorruption conventions—the 1996 Organization of American States treaty against corruption and the 1997 Organization for Economic Cooperation and Development antibribery treaty, both signed by Fox's predecessor, and the 2003 United Nations treaty against corruption, signed by Fox—and even US assistance. Operating within this climate, Fox packaged a new anticorruption campaign that would touch every agency within the federal government and impact state and local governments. The campaign would produce fundamental legal reforms designed to enhance the public's access to information, create a merit-based civil service, and develop programs in schools, universities, and businesses targeting Mexico's pervasive culture of corruption.

The contrast with the not too distant past is stunning. When I first began research on corruption in the late 1980s, during the highly touted "Moral Renovation" campaign of President Miguel de la Madrid (1982–1988), the topic enjoyed scant scholarly or political attention both in Mexico and beyond. Whole texts on Mexican politics omitted any reference to this ubiquitous dimension of the political system, while international institutions, owing to the Cold War climate of the day, were reticent to approach the topic, or even prevented by their mandates from doing so. In some ways, the topic of corruption was taboo. Today, by contrast, a host of Mexican government agencies and scores of Mexican scholars, journalists, and political activists—in a manner similar to the international trends—focus intense attention and analysis on the matter, producing massive reports and detailed studies, some even risking their lives to uncover and report on official wrongdoing. Recent years have brought forth multiple public opinion surveys dealing with corruption (some of which are used and analyzed in this book), serious scholarship delving into the underlying nature of corruption in the country, whole courses and *diplomados* on corruption and accountability at the nation's top universities, high-profile public and political debates, a societal discussion on ethics and morality, public service announcements promoting ethical values, and a general crescendo of consciousness across the nation about the presence of and particularly the pernicious consequences of corruption. Among its effects, this growing public consciousness—coupled with the "long-awaited" defeat of the PRI—heightened the public's expectations of Fox's anticorruption initiatives, raising the political stakes and the bar in the process.

These incredible political and economic developments in Mexico crystallize the fundamental questions steering this study: What effect have these changes—political, structural, institutional, and perhaps even cultural—had on political corruption in Mexico? Has democracy, by itself or together with Fox's high-profile anticorruption campaign, been effective in altering the level and pervasiveness of corruption? If not, why not? Is there less corruption today than in the past? More specifically, have the prevailing patterns of corruption found in Mexico shifted because of the political changes? And finally, how has the Calderon administration, elected in 2006 amid controversy, taken up the anticorruption challenge during its initial years? This study attends to these queries by exploring the nexus linking these twin issues of change: the changes in the political context and the changes in corruption.[3]

The Broader Questions

In a phrase, Mexico has democratized (though it has transited along its own rather unique path). Hence, the broader, theoretical question addressed here centers on the impact of democracy and democratization on political corruption. At a very general level, theory predicts that democracy reduces corruption (Johnston 1998; Rose-Ackerman 1999). It does so through both structural and institutional as well as ideological and cultural mechanisms. At the structural and institutional level, democracy restrains the behavior of the elite by holding them accountable for their actions (i.e., making officials answerable for their behavior and subject to some form of sanction for behavior deemed unsatisfactory) (Etzioni-Halevy 2002, 233; Mainwaring and Welna 2003; O'Donnell 1994, 1998, 2003).[4] This includes, above all, elections—a critical tool of vertical accountability—which allow the general public a means, albeit crude, to hold their elected officials answerable and to reward good behavior and punish bad (Downs 1957; Rose-Ackerman 1999, 127–142). It also includes basic freedoms (press freedoms, freedom of expression), a second mechanism of vertical or societal accountability, which allow citizens, the press, and autonomous social organizations to collect and expose information on public officials independently of the government, to lobby for policy changes, to engage in open public debate, and to operate unfettered by government intervention (Adserá, Boix, and Payne 2003; Brunetti and Weder 2003; Smulovitz and Peruzzotti 2000). Democracy also embraces key mechanisms of horizontal accountability whereby government monitors itself. This occurs through autonomous auditing mechanisms within the government as well as through shared powers and checks and balances across the various branches of government. Through such horizontal mechanisms, democracy structurally seeks to "pit ambition against ambition" so as to control and check the behavior of the elite, as James Madison famously noted in *Federalist Paper* no. 51 (see also Laffont and N'Guessan 1999).

In addition to its structural and institutional effects, democracy also works to curb corruption by way of its ideological and cultural foundations. The philosophical, normative discourse informing the institutions of democracy privileges basic notions of equality and justice, of citizenship, and of openness and accountability: values clearly antithetical to corruption. The very essence of democracy holds that government should serve the interests of the people (popular sovereignty), that the people have a fundamental right to know about the affairs of state in order to fulfill their role as citizens, and, as such, that the rulers are fundamentally answerable to or accountable to the people (Dahl 1998; Warren 2004). Democracy thus nourishes popular demands and pressures for good government and for justice—forces driving efforts to detect and punish corruption—while raising, at the same time, the threshold of intolerance toward those within government who violate the law (Shirk and Ríos Cázares 2007, 7). The very idea of democracy itself, in short, lofts the issue of corruption high atop the political agenda.

Viewed from a slightly different angle, democracy heightens the importance of corruption because corruption constitutes a threat to democracy. By converting collective goods into personal favors, corruption undermines the provision of justice (Johnston 2005). By denying citizens access and a role in determining collective decisions and actions, corruption disempowers people (Warren 2004). By distorting and crippling government responsiveness to popular demands, corruption undermines the meaning of citizenship and the rule of law. Even the perception of corrupt politicians and institutions erodes the foundations of trust essential to democracy (Warren 2004). In a sense, then, corruption and democracy represent opposing forces, one embodying the philosophical ideal of taming corruption and ensuring equal justice for all—a government for the people, rather than for the rulers—the other threatening to undermine the very meaning and existence of democracy itself.

Yet, despite such rational and parsimonious (and clearly a bit romantic, liberal, and normative) arguments suggesting that democracy inhibits corruption, theory and empirical research suggest a much more complex relationship. Susan Rose-Ackerman (1999, 127–142) emphasizes that while democratic competition, federalism, and checks and balances may potentially lower corruption, these may not necessarily be effective; much depends, she stresses, on the precise structures of electoral and legislative processes, and the methods of campaign finance, among other ingredients: the devil's details. Exploring the failure of electoral competitiveness and democratization to lead to accountable governance in rural Mexico, Jonathan Fox (2007, 9) similarly points to the need to look beyond the conventional institutions of political accountability. Findings at the empirical level lend support to this unclear pattern. On the one hand, cross-national studies by Alberto Ades and Rafael Di Tella (1997a, 1997b), Aymo Brunetti and Beatrice Weder (2003), and Daniel Lederman, Norman Loayza, and Rodrigo Soares (2005) confirm a statistically significant inverse relationship between the two, with nondemocratic countries exhibiting higher levels of corruption than democratic nations, though the relationship may be nonlinear (Monitola and Jackman 2002). Other studies also show corruption to be negatively linked to key factors associated with democracy, like a merit-based civil service system (Rauch and Evans 2000), a free press (Brunetti and Wender 2003; Lederman, Loayza, and Soares 2005), the free circulation of newspapers (Adserá, Boix, and Payne 2003), transparency (La Port et al. 1997), rule of law (Brunetti and Weder 2003), federalism (Treisman 2000), and economic development and openness (Ades and DiTella 1997a, 1997b; Goldsmith 1999; Graeff and Mehlkop 2003; Mauro 1995, 1997; Johnston 1998; Monitolla and Jackman 2002; Xin and Rudel 2004). And yet, many question the robustness of these results, particularly as they relate to new democracies and developing countries (Treisman 2007). Studies by Abdiweli Ali and Hodan Isse (2003), Charles Blake and Christopher Martin (2006), John Gerring and Strom Thacker (2004), Johann Lambsdorff (1999), Lederman and colleagues (2005), Gabriella Monitolla and Robert Jackman (2002), Martin Paldam (2002), Daniel Treisman (2000), and Xiaohui Xin and Thomas Rudel (2004), indeed, all fail to confirm any direct correlation linking democracy and corruption when controlling for a range of variables. Instead, these studies suggest that only a longer exposure to democracy tends to lower the level of corruption, not democracy per se, though the robustness of these results has also been questioned (Treisman 2007). This means, quite simply, that it takes time for democracy to have the desired impact on corruption (Lederman, Loayza, and Soares 2005; Serra 2006; Treisman 2000).[5] Such findings, moreover, relate merely to perceptions of corruption rather than to real corruption, a point explored more fully later.[6]

Based on this consensus finding—that democracy does seem to reduce corruption, but only over time—it seems fruitful to distinguish democracy (a state) from democratization (a process) and to differentiate their effects on corruption.

Though cross-sectional (static) research suggests that democracy may *eventually* lead to a reduction in corruption (at least based on the current state of democracy worldwide), the link is clearly not automatic. As Rose-Ackerman (1999, 226) notes, "Corruption cannot be expected to wither away just because a reform government has taken power." This suggests, at least theoretically, that corruption may actually increase during the process of democratization or at best remain unchanged before it falls at some point in the future. And indeed, analysts highlight how in the years following the celebrated return to democracy in the 1980s in Latin America, corruption actually increased (or, as most would concede, failed to fall appreciably as theoretically predicted) (Weyland 1998; Geddes and Neto 1992, 1998; Brown and Cloke 2004, 2005). Or as Mark Robinson (1998, 2) concludes, "Democratic structures have proved markedly ineffective in curbing the spread and tenacity of corrupt practices in developing countries."[7]

Explanations for what was originally a theoretically surprising outcome— an increase rather than a decrease in corruption following a return to democracy in Latin America—vary, but two broad processes seem to be involved. One process entails the emergence of corruption stemming from democratization itself, what I call "new corruption." This occurs through a variety of mechanisms. At a broad level, democratization, by its very nature, implies a state of rapid change, of flux in the political rules and practices. This fluid and less predictable environment itself, according to Jens Andvig (2006), facilitates an increase in corruption at least in the short term as people take advantage of unclear rules, muddled lines of authority, and tentative accountability mechanisms. In addition, democratization creates new rules for institutions and new means of acquiring and exercising power and wealth, conditions that also open new opportunities for corruption. Indeed, many of the explanations for the rise in corruption accompanying democratization and neoliberal economic reforms in Latin America in the 1980s and 1990s seem to refer to cases of "new corruption." Luigi Manzetti (1994) and Luigi Manzetti and Charles Blake (1996), for instance, contend that the emergency economic situation and desperate need for neoliberal reforms in the face of deep economic crisis prompted an increase in presidential discretionary powers that opened up new and unique opportunities for corrupt gain: an explanation pertinent to the corruption scandals involving Presidents Carlos Andrés Pérez, Carlos Menem, and Fernando Collor de Mello in Venezuela, Argentina, and Brazil. Others point to the impact of economic liberalization on the boom in money laundering, contraband, and drug trafficking (Whitehead 2002) or the impact of economic reforms on reducing the scope and role of the state's regulatory controls or even the pay of bureaucrats (Brown and Cloke 2005, 604; Van Rijckeghem and Weder 2001; DiTella and Schargrodsky 2003). Others refer to the new emphasis on elections (Skidmore 1999; Zovatto 2000), the new rules regarding party and electoral systems that have forced candidates and parties to seek alternative means to finance their campaigns (Geddes and Neto 1992, 1998; Skidmore 1999; Rehren 1997), the institutional framework of presidential systems and federalism, and the rise of neopopulism to explain the rise of corruption. In Brazil, for example, Barbara Geddes and Artur Neto (1992, 643) attribute the increase in corruption in the early 1990s to the 1988 constitution and the electoral laws, which hampered "the ability of the executive to a) build coalitions, and b) assure the loyalty of his or her supporters in Congress." Kurt Weyland (1998) and Laurence Whitehead (2000a, 2000b, 2002) underscore the rise of neopopulist leaders and the breakdown of intermediate institutions to explain the recent bouts of corruption. In all these cases, corruption arises from the political and economic changes accompanying democratization.

Other scholars, by contrast, pinpoint the continued weakness of political institutions designed to inhibit corruption, despite rather than because of democratization (Fabbri 2002; Fleischer 2002; Mainwaring and Welna 2003; Santoro 2004; Rodrigues 2004; Subero 2004). In this second process involving, for lack of a better term, "old corruption," democratization can be seen as incomplete or partial and indicate that the development of certain aspects of democracy—like the contestation of power and popular participation—may advance at a pace far quicker than that for other aspects of democracy, like the rule of law or accountability (Fox 2007; Guerrero 2004). With the lagging of these key institutions, including a lag in the development of a more democratic political culture, a new democracy may be unable to address both the traditional (authoritarian holdover) as well as the newer forms of corruption. Analyses in this vein document a vast array of weak or nonexistent institutions in the region designed to provide horizontal accountability across governmental institutions (e.g., few checks and balances in executive legislative-relations, a politicized or overwhelmed civil service, underfunded or nonexistent oversight institutions, insufficient legal frameworks, a weak judiciary). At the same time, mechanisms of vertical accountability between citizens and their governments remain weaker than needed to effectively curb corruption (e.g., limited press freedoms, weak civil society, unrepresentative parties, and limited governmental transparency in which access to government activities is restricted or even kept secret).[8] In their analysis of the continued high levels of corruption in Latin America, Silvia Colazingari and Susan Rose-Ackerman (1998) stress the lack of constraints on government power, an economic system dominated by a small number of families and firms, the lack of independent prosecutors, the use of public ethics laws to help silence the press, and the lack of administrative oversight. A critical shortcoming is the lack of prosecution for official wrongdoing. Indeed, impunity—corruption's evil twin—remains remarkably high throughout Latin America. Despite the many cases of exposed corruption dominating media coverage, prosecutions remain rare (see Chapter 4 for data on the Mexican case). Erecting and perfecting the mechanisms of accountability—including an independent judiciary, a well-paid civil service, a media able and willing to investigate corruption, and interest groups dedicated to the reduction of corruption—thus remain serious challenges standing in the way of democracy's mature ability to control corruption.

Drawing this distinction between the impact of democracy (lowering corruption in the long term) and the impact of democratization (potentially increasing corruption in the short term) on corruption helps crystallize the primary theoretical problem addressed in this study. Analyzing how recent political and institutional changes in Mexico have affected corruption should provide some insights into the nature of the early struggle to forge effective democratic institutions that seek to control corruption. What I find particularly intriguing here is the dialectical nature of this process: while the emergence of democracy (democratization) heightens societal attention to and condemnation of corruption, a necessary condition perhaps to marshaling the resources needed to battle corruption, the presence of corruption tends to undermine legitimacy and the public's satisfaction with the new democracy. This debilitates popular support for the government and undermines the people's faith precisely in those institutions needed to establish the rule of law and strengthen the mechanisms of accountability. As we see in the case of Mexico, the public considers corruption an important problem facing the country, feeding low levels of satisfaction with democracy. Taken to its logical conclusion, this means that just as democracy carries the potential to curb corruption (in the long term at least), corruption has the potential to undermine democracy or, more precisely, prevent it from developing to the point needed to effectively curb corruption over time. After all, if democracy does curb corruption over time as studies seem to suggest, then it is not time that does it, but rather the nature and course of democratic development.

While the impact of democratization on corruption constitutes the primary theoretical question addressed here, two related theoretical queries also arise. The first centers on understanding the conditions that make reform possible. This peripheral question is particularly important in dealing with corruption due to the centrality of the politician's paradox posed by Barbara Geddes (1994). Since those in positions of power (whether politicians making decisions, or bureaucrats implementing those decisions) tend to benefit from corruption, then why would they pursue or abide reforms that go against their own interests? Why (or under what conditions) would politicians or bureaucrats relinquish their discretionary authority? This important paradox contextualizes Manuel Alejandro Guerrero's conclusion (2004) regarding the current situation in Mexico. He contends that it is much more difficult to alter the way power is exercised because of the dominance of the political elite, whose interests would be severely limited if this were to happen, compared to altering how power is won and lost.

Recent studies lay out a host of factors that impact on the possibility of successful reform, though few focus specifically on anticorruption. R. Kent Weaver and Bert Rockman (1993, 465, cited in Franco-Barrios 2003, 8) suggest, for example, that reforms are possible where a newly empowered elite wants to consolidate its power or where old elites, fearing a loss of power, want to manipulate the rules to hang on to power. Ben Schneider and Blanca Heredia (2003) conclude that reforms are more likely when there exists a convergence between the executive and legislature (a willingness to work together) and a cohesive party system where the legislature backs presidential reforms as opposed to a fragmented party system, centralization, and a more cooperative relationship between executive and labor. David Arrellano Gault and Juan Pablo Guerrero Amparán (2003, 171–172) contend that the likelihood of reform is weakened when the high-level bureaucracy is integrated into the political system, and that the greater the competition in elections and parties, the greater the likelihood that the bureaucracy is more concerned with administrative rather than political affairs. Others highlight the role of leadership itself and the style of packaging and offering reforms. Adam Przeworski (1995, 81, cited in Hiskey 2003, 109), for instance, contends that "policy styles matter . . . consultation and concertation may serve to improve the technical quality of reform programs [and] discussion and negotiation may serve to build political bases of support for the particular reform strategy."

Recent studies of judicial and administrative reform in Mexico provide some insights into the study of reform. Analysts offer a number of explanations of the sweeping judicial reforms in the mid-1990s under President Ernesto Zedillo. These include the notion that PRI government leaders pushed reforms in the face of intense political competition as a sort of insurance policy to help protect them and their policies in case they were to lose executive power in the future, or, alternatively, as a way of creating a neutral arbiter to decide conflicts among the elite. In another approach, reforms were designed to increase political legitimacy for the government, and thereby to stave off pressures and manage the pace of change (Beer 2006; Carbonell 2004; Fix-Fierro 2003a, 251–252). Kenneth Mitchell's studies (2001, 2005) of the reforms of the massive social program Conasupo under President Carlos Salinas, however, find that it was not the electoral, competitive pressures that prompted Salinas to overhaul the program, but rather a desire to shift power away from traditional, clientelistic sources toward more technocratic-oriented decision-makers. The changes, Mitchell notes, were undertaken only after competitive pressures softened following the midterm election in 1991. In this book, I am interested in understanding the conditions that shape the ability of the political elite to work together to institute reforms to curb corruption, the ability of the various actors to promote and implement anticorruption measures, and the forces that undermine such efforts.

The second closely related theoretical query centers on the limits of structural and institutional explanations of corruption and the role of culture in our thinking on corruption. The institutional approach is clearly the most prominent theoretical approach in the booming corruption literature today. This approach embraces rational choice assumptions that see laws and institutions as channeling rational individual behavior, and assumes that if built properly, these structures can push that behavior into acceptable avenues, hence limiting corruption. It envisions corruption as a behavioral response to the opportunities and risks that rational actors (officials, bureaucrats, and citizens) face, and assumes that individuals seek to maximize their self-interest by extracting illegal rents, violating campaign finance laws, paying bribes, and the like, if the chance of getting away with it outweighs the likelihood of detection and punishment. Even so, questions arise as to just how far such an approach can go in explaining corruption and particularly the issue of change. Looking at the case of Mexico may provide some insights into this debate. If reforms eliminate certain loopholes and reduce one form of corruption, but corruption simply pops up somewhere else—like squeezing a balloon—then arguably the underlying causes of corruption may remain intact. What role might culture have, then, in shaping corruption and the impact of reforms?

The Current Approach

This exploration of corruption and change in Mexico deviates from prior studies in two ways. First, the emphasis here is on change. This means that the task is not so much to look at the overall level or patterns of corruption in Mexico or to compare Mexico to other countries (though such analysis is sometimes employed in the empirical sections of this study), but rather to assess how corruption has actually changed in recent years, which in turn means less concern with explaining the existence of corruption in Mexico (the primary focus of Morris 1991) and greater attention to explaining its dynamics. This approach departs from most research on corruption, which concentrates on the causes and consequences of corruption and tends to neglect change. With their focus on reducing corruption, Transparency International and others have assembled a good collection of reports on specific programs throughout the world, including a library of reports on "best practices," but there remains a lack of comprehensive case studies looking in detail at changes in the nature of corruption and the efforts of governments to fight it. In short, we know much about the causes and consequences of corruption, but relatively little about what works and what does not work in fighting it, and under what conditions (Manion 2004 offers an important exception). Given the struggles of new democracies to battle corruption and the confusing and countervailing tendencies for democracy to both reduce and yet increase corruption and magnify the exposure of corruption (Johnston 2005), attention to the issue of change is critical.

This study also deviates from prior studies by disaggregating corruption into three dimensions: perception, participation, and pattern. Analysis of corruption has always faced severe methodological handicaps.[9] In short, it is difficult to measure a phenomenon that by its very nature is obscure, illegal, and hidden. If we cannot confidently measure corruption, then it becomes difficult to determine clearly if it has changed. Despite a variety of efforts over the years to quantify corruption using objective measures (Correa 1985; Della Porta and Vannucci 1997, 1999; De Speville 1997; Eker 1981; Hill 2003; López Presa 1998; Meier and Holbrook 1992; Morris 1991; Rehren 1997; Schlesinger and Meier 2002; Spector 2005; Whitehead 1989), such efforts confront a host of problems. Instead, subjective measures of corruption have gained substantial scholarly acceptance in recent years, feeding a wave of empirical research and comparative studies. Such subjective measures of corruption rely largely on perceptions of corruption. This approach measures the level or the amount of corruption an individual believes to exist. Samples and questions vary. They may examine the opinions of business executives, country experts, development officials, or citizens with questions ranging from the general (e.g., levels of corruption in the system or among politicians) to more specific institutional levels (e.g., levels of corruption within the judiciary, the bureaucracy, the police). The widely used Corruption Perception Index, produced annually by Transparency International, for example, draws on a series of polls by various organizations gauging the perceptions of businesspeople and country analysts, both resident and nonresident. Meanwhile, measures by such organizations as Latinobarómetro, the World Values Survey, or the Latin American Public Opinion Project (LAPOP) depict the opinions of citizens (see Appendix A for comparative data).[10]

At an intuitive level, what better way to determine if corruption exists within a country than asking those who deal with the system on a daily basis. After all, it is rather difficult to get those involved to admit to any wrongdoing. Even so, the use of perception to measure corruption has its problems. Foremost among these, the perception of corruption is not the same thing as corruption itself, as most analysts readily admit (Seligson 2004, 2006). One (perception) centers on general beliefs about the nature of the system and the assumed behavior of others; the other (corrupt activity) entails actual behavior and observation. Moreover, as John Bailey (2009) notes, the perception of corruption is an extremely broad concept and potentially conflates corruption with sentiments and opinions about government or politicians generally or even with the nature of humankind.

Though many acknowledge that perception is not the same thing as actual corruption, few have explored the relationship linking the two. Though there are plausible theoretical arguments going in both directions, explored in Chapter 6, empirical analysis suggests that the two may be largely unrelated (Morris 2008). This means that the two can and may move in different directions, stem from unique sets of factors, and shoulder different effects. It is certainly feasible, especially during democratization, for a perceived increase in corruption to occur while actual corruption remains unchanged or even falls. With a freer press and more intense political competition, more exposures of corruption and more intense scandals may arise, feeding the perception that corruption is climbing, neither of which may relate to changes in the actual levels of corruption.

Distinguishing perception from what I call "participation" in corruption does not mean that perception is unimportant. Quite the contrary: in politics, as they say, perception is everything. Apart from its still undefined though limited impact on actual participation in corrupt acts, the public's perception of corruption may be an important ingredient within the broader political culture, reflecting the effects of recent changes in the political system. The widespread perception of corruption and distrust of the system, moreover, may complicate the task of fighting corruption by undermining social capital or citizen participation. Perception of corruption may also affect feelings of regime legitimacy.

With this distinction in mind, it is important to stress that much of what we know based on recent empirical research on corruption relates more to perceptions of corruption than to actual corruption, as alluded to earlier. In other words, the multiple empirical studies demonstrating statistically significant correlations about the causes of corruption and its impact on economic performance, respect for political institutions, and regime legitimacy, tell us much about the causes and consequences of the *perceptions* of corruption—since this is the measure these studies employ—but little per se about corruption itself. This is a shortcoming in the research and a continuing challenge. Mitchell Seligson (2004, 2005, 2006), in particular, has sought to overcome this problem by using measures of corruption based on participation in corrupt acts, or what he calls "victimization rates." I use a similar approach here.

In addition to the problem of separating perception of corruption from actual corruption—perception versus participation—many also criticize existing measures of corruption for being one-dimensional and failing to differentiate the many different types of corruption that exist.[11] According to Michael Johnston (2005, 20), the normal measures of corruption tend to emphasize bribery and neglect nepotism, official theft and fraud, and conflict of interest problems. Clearly, one blanket measure of corruption within a country says little about what types of corruption the country suffers from or the nature of change. Such a blanket measure, moreover, shrouds changes among specific types of corruption. In order to overcome this limitation, the third dimension of corruption studied here is the pattern of corruption. This refers primarily to corruption's location within the system (political versus bureaucratic; federal versus state and local; particular areas within the bureaucracy), the direction of influence (bribery versus extortion), and the actors involved (citizens versus elite; politicians and party leaders versus bureaucrats). Differentiating the patterns of corruption means moving beyond the simple question of whether corruption has increased or fallen in recent years, to focus on how different types of corruption may be changing in different directions. In addition, by differentiating shifting patterns, it is possible to find that the growth of certain types of corruption may play a much greater role in shaping overall perceptions of corruption, despite the reduction in other forms of corruption, or that the growth of certain types of corruption may have more pernicious effects on the political system than other forms of corruption.

Thus the overall approach of this study centers on the impact of recent political and institutional changes on changes in popular perceptions of corruption, participation rates or actual corrupt activity, and the types or patterns of corruption. Two analytical steps are involved: first, to describe the political and institutional changes and to hypothesize about the effects these may be having on each dimension of corruption—perception, participation, and pattern; and second, to assess empirically the changes in each of the three areas as partial tests of the hypotheses.

Analyzing Moving Targets

Venturing real answers to these guiding research questions is trickier than it appears, for three reasons. First, the tools used to gauge corruption generally and changes in corruption specifically are still rather crude and rudimentary. Second, the multifaceted nature of the phenomenon complicates the drawing of clear conclusions. And finally, it is inherently difficult to assess trends and take into account potential lag times. To begin with, any analysis of a transition exhibits a combination of forces and factors. This means that while we may find, on the one hand, numerous changes in recent years that seem to strengthen the forces of anticorruption, it may be difficult, based on polls, news reports, official cases, or even public scandals, to show conclusively that these measures have been effective at reducing the level of corruption in the country. Such a finding, however, does not necessarily mean that the reforms have failed, only that they have yet to bear fruit. Moreover, many changes in Mexico remain at an initial stage of implementation. This means that there may be potential for substantial change in the coming years, and that it is just too early to tell based on the data available. Indeed, it remains open to debate whether polls are even a useful tool for detecting change in the short term. Johnston (2005, 215), in fact, warns against the use of opinion-based indexes to gauge change, suggesting that the better approach is to look at aspects of government that create incentives and disincentives for corruption. Is the government, for instance, reducing the number of bureaucratic steps? Indeed, some contend that changing corruption takes decades and generations, not years. If so, that leaves us with an even more difficult analytical task: trying to determine whether recent reforms even put the country on the right track. Given these problems, in the concluding chapter I attempt to lay out some alternative means of interpreting the evidence presented here.

Organization of the Study

The study begins by examining how recent political changes in Mexico have impacted the perceptions of, participation in, and patterns of political corruption. Chapters 2 and 3 discuss the broader structural political changes in Mexico. Chapter 2 focuses on the state itself, highlighting the weakening of the presidency, the growth of horizontal checks, the transformed role of elections, and the changing locus of political struggles. It analyzes how these changes have created both new opportunities to check corruption and new opportunities to engage in it. Chapter 3 focuses on structural changes in the state-society relationship, exploring the weakening state, the growth of civil society organizations, and the strengthening of new vertical mechanisms of accountability. It similarly examines the impact these changes are having on the occurrence and reporting of corruption. Both chapters show how, owing to these structural changes, corruption has enjoyed far more attention by both state and nonstate actors than at any time in the past.

Chapter 4 shifts attention to the anticorruption reforms under President Fox. This includes the legal reforms, the changes in bureaucratic organization and operation, and the government's efforts to promote integrity and ethics, to incorporate social organizations into the anticorruption fight, and to heighten popular consciousness and alter Mexico's political culture. It also highlights the areas largely untouched by the reforms. As with the discussion of broader structural changes, this chapter differentiates the potential impact of these efforts on corruption in terms of perception, participation, and pattern. The chapter also offers a general assessment of the Fox anticorruption initiatives based on official and unofficial evaluations and official data from the government regarding its efforts. The concluding section briefly profiles anticorruption during the initial years of the Felipe Calderon government.

Following the examination of the structural and institutional changes and discussion of their variable impact on corruption, the study next takes an empirical look at political corruption based on an analysis of multiple surveys conducted over the period. Chapter 5 focuses on perceptions of corruption in Mexico. It looks at whether, according to popular opinion, things have really changed, and it explores factors associated with popular perceptions of corruption and change and the impact of these perceptions. Chapter 6 then uses polling data to look at participation rates or actual experiences with corruption. Building on the earlier chapter, attention focuses on the relationship linking perceptions and participation as well as the underlying causes and consequences of participation in corruption and change. Chapter 7 then examines the shifting patterns of corruption in Mexico. Using both quantitative and qualitative approaches, this chapter explores whether the types of corruption and their location within the political system have changed in response to the new structural and institutional conditions. The chapter reflects on different types of corruption in the polling data, the pattern of press coverage of corruption, citizens' complaints to the government, and data on the sanctioning of public officials.

Chapter 8 turns to a discussion of the question of culture. It briefly explores the literature linking corruption to culture and the controversies over the role of culture in the literature. It then proceeds to explore the broader political narrative in Mexico to help contextualize popular views on corruption and the difficulties of reform. As such, it seeks to offer a broader view on corruption that incorporates both the institutional and the cultural approaches.

The concluding chapter returns to the guiding theoretical questions presented here, discussing the dynamics of corruption, the impact of democratization, and the continuing political and analytical challenges facing Mexico. Two appendixes complement the analysis. Appendix A presents cross-national data comparing corruption in Mexico to other countries. Appendix B offers brief information on political scandals during the period. The cases themselves provide deeper insights into the nature of corruption in Mexican politics.

Notes

1. Defining corruption has always been difficult, and no single definition can seemingly surmount the barrage of analytical challenges (for a taste of the definitional debate and quandary, see Nye 1967; Heidenheimer 1970; Johnston 1996; Scott 1972; Philip 1997, 2002). Most scholars cite and accept Joseph Nye's vintage definition (1967) of political corruption as simply the abuse of public power for personal gain. Longtime corruption scholar Michael Johnston (2005, 11) defines it a bit more precisely, as the "abuse of a trust, generally one involving public power, for private benefits which often, but by no means always come in the form of money." For my objections to the standard definition—particularly the inclusion of personal interests—see Morris 1991, 4–5.

2. For general treatments on political change taking place during this period, see Aguilar Camín 1990; Aguilar Rivera 2006; Camp 2007; Chand 2001; Eisenstadt 2004; Fox 2007; Greene 2007; Luken Garza and Muñoz 2003; Magaloni 2006; Middlebrook 2004; Morris 1995; Peschard-Sverdrup and Rioff 2005; Williams 2001. On the historic 2000 election, see Domínguez and Lawson 2004.

3. A number of studies have explored the impact of rising electoral competition in Mexico, particularly at the subnational level. Victoria Rodríguez (1997) and Victoria Rodríguez and Peter Ward (1995), looking at the first half of the 1990s, for instance, found that newly elected democratic local governments tended to emphasize efficiency and transparency. Caroline Beer's study (2003, 21) at the state level found "that increasing electoral competition strengthens representative institutions in ways that decentralize power away from the national executive and improve the separation of powers and therefore has significant consequences for accountability and the rule of law." Caroline Beer (2004) also found that states with higher degrees of electoral democracy enjoyed lower levels of human rights violations. Matthew Cleary and Susan Stokes (2006) demonstrated that the more democratic the state, the higher the level of institutional trust

and respect for the rule of law and the lower the levels of trust in politicians and reliance on clientelism and personal favors; yet they found increased democracy to be unrelated to perceptions of corruption. A study by Carlos Moreno-Jaimes (2007, 150)
similarly uncovered no link between electoral competition and the quality of municipal services (specifically, water) from 1990 to 2000. He concluded: "There is no evidence supporting the proposition that electoral competition has improved the relative
levels of service coverage in Mexican municipalities." Instead, he found that "demand
factors" like literacy, socioeconomic wealth, and higher rates of voter participation were
driving improvements.

4. On the concept of accountability, see also Przeworski, Stokes, and Manin
1999; Schedler, Diamond, and Plattner 1999; Smulovitz and Peruzzotti 2000. On accountability in Mexico, see Fox 2007.

5. Daniel Treisman (2007) finds that the nonlinear relationship disappears when
looking just at countries that became democratic after 1950.

6. Other factors that correlate at the cross-national level with high levels of perceived corruption include lower levels of development (La Porta et al. 1999; Ades and
Di Tella 1997a; Treisman 2000, 2007); economic openness and competition (Ades and
Di Tella 1999; Sandholtz and Koetzle 2000; Sandholtz and Gray 2003; Gerring and
Thacker 2004); political decentralization and federalism (Treisman 2000; Goldsmith
1999; Kunicová and Rose-Ackerman 2005; Gerring and Thacker 2004); presidentialism versus a parliamentary system (Panizza 2001; Gerring and Thacker 2004; Lederman, Loayza, and Soares 2005); and low levels of female legislators or ministers
(Swamy et al. 2001; Dollar, Fishman, and Gatti 1999) or Protestant population (La
Porta et al. 1999; Treisman 2000). Chapter 8 provides more extensive discussion of the
cultural factors associated with corruption at the cross-national level.

7. Michael Johnston (2005, 5) contends that no one really knows if corruption
has increased: a disclaimer that rests largely on the many methodological problems. On
the problems of using data to conduct longitudinal analysis, see Kaufmann, Kraay, and
Mastruzzi 2006; Treisman 2007, 220.

8. In many cases, people working to curb corruption, by investigating, reporting,
or prosecuting corrupt officials, face strong pressures. Threats and actual killings of
journalists investigating corruption and drug trafficking are all too common (see Faundes 2002).

9. Measuring political corruption—a necessary step to rigorous empirical analysis—has long been problematic and, despite the proliferation of indexes in recent years,
remains so (see, for instance, Del Castillo 2003; Knack 2006; Lambsdorff 2005; Sampford et al. 2006; Treisman 2007; Soreide 2006).

10. Damarys Canache and Michael Allison (2005) examine the relationship between the perceptions of corruption by "experts," as measured by the Corruption Perception Index, and those of citizens, as measured by the World Values Survey. Generally,
they find the two more closely linked where the level of political interest of the individual is high.

11. Corruption takes a number of forms and patterns and represents a broad and
amorphous concept. Various typologies exist. Corruption can be distinguished by type
(e.g., bribery, kickback, graft, embezzlement, nepotism, favoritism, conflict of interest)
or the institutional location of the behavior. Most scholars draw distinctions between
corruption in the private sector and corruption in the public sector. Within the latter—
known as political corruption—distinctions are further drawn between upper-level corruption ("grand corruption"), involving presidents, ministers, members of Congress,
governors, and other high-ranking officials and usually large sums and onetime transactions, and lower-level corruption ("petty corruption"), involving civil servants or the

police and small transactions. This distinction overlaps roughly with a related distinction based on location within the policy process where "political corruption" tends to refer to corruption occurring at the policymaking stage, normally involving the violation of second-order norms (the often unwritten norms determining how politicians should make decisions, like justice, fairness, and impartiality), whereas "bureaucratic corruption" encompasses policy implementation and relates to the violation of first-order norms (the written rules and laws that are the product of politicians' decisionmaking) (Bardhan 2006; Scott 1972; Warren 2004). Even within these two broad arenas, it is still possible and useful to classify corruption by simple reference to the institutional location within the political system where it occurs (e.g., judicial, executive, legislative, partisan, electoral, police). A final distinction points to the direction of influence. Running in one direction, societal groups may use bribery or other devices to capture or colonize the state, illegitimately influencing state policies, and thereby turning that segment of the state into a tool serving specialized interests rather than those of the broader society. I refer to this form of corruption generally as "bribery." Such state capturing contrasts with situations where a powerful state or sectors of the state use (and abuse) state power to demand and capture rents from private actors. It is quite different when drug traffickers, for instance, have half the police on their payroll and doing their bidding (something akin to the privatization of the police) than when the police shake down petty thieves and extort citizens for real or imagined offenses. I refer to this latter form of corruption as "extortion."

2

The Impact of New Politics

Studies of political corruption focus particular attention on the structure of the state and state-society relations. At the level of the state, research links corruption to noncompetitive politics, limited civil liberties, big government, concentrated political power, weak mechanisms of horizontal accountability, the absence of checks and balances, the lack of an independent judiciary, and a strong state, among other factors. At the societal level, studies associate corruption with a weak civil society, low levels of interpersonal trust and social capital, an aversion to law, and shallow mechanisms of social or vertical accountability (e.g. Adserá, Boix, and Payne 2000; Brunetti and Weder 2003; La Porta et al 1997, 1999; Lederman, Loayza, and Soares 2005; Kunicová and Rose-Ackerman 2005; Montinola and Jackman 2002; Gerring and Thacker 2004; Serra 2006; Treisman 2000, 2007).[1]

Throughout much of the twentieth century, Mexico sported a relatively strong state with powers firmly concentrated in the presidency, set amid a weak society co-opted and captured by the state's authoritarian web. This arrangement fostered high levels of corruption, a weak rule of law, and a generalized "culture of corruption." However, over the past two decades or so, Mexico has undergone a fundamental redistribution of power and a restructuring in the relations among state institutions and state and society.[2] Such changes have empowered new players, created new veto points, redefined the functions and the boundaries of state institutions, weakened once well-established informal institutions and rules (thereby exposing the underlying weaknesses in the formal rules), and frayed the bonds of elite unity, producing a fluid and rather ambiguous political climate. Mexico, in short, has transited from a once "strong state" whose strength rested largely on informal rather than formal institutional mechanisms (facilitated in large part by corruption) and elite unity—the subject of my earlier analysis (Morris 1991)—toward a rather "weak state" characterized by a withering of the informal mechanisms within a context of limited rule of law and elite polarization.

This chapter explores these changes in the Mexican state and examines their impact on corruption. It shows that while the changes have fed greater demands for accountability and fostered the beginnings of stronger institutional checks on corruption, the simultaneous elimination of past informal controls amid a rapidly changing institutional setting have also created new opportunities for corruption, and at the same time have facilitated a continuation of key authoritarian (and highly corrupt) enclaves from the past. Discussion begins with a look at the changing nature of elections and the rise of multiparty competition, followed by a review of the weakening of the presidency vis-à-vis elections, Congress, the bureaucracy, the judiciary, and state and local governments. Chapter 3 continues this analysis of the state-society balance, focusing on changes within Mexican society and state-society relations.

Avoiding Monoliths

Before exploring inside this state-society framework, it is important to make explicit a nonmonolithic view of both the state and society. Most observers easily acknowledge this point with respect to the state and no longer view it as one sole entity. In the analysis of corruption, this simply means that while certain parts of the state may be engaged in corrupt acts and abuse of power, other parts of the same state may be working to assert oversight, uncover and sanction the abuses of power, or promote preventive reforms. Rather than representing a sole, unified actor, the state thus represents the site of intense conflict, of battles pitting state agencies, interests, and individuals against one another. Such intrastate conflicts, in fact, play out inside each bureaucratic agency almost daily, with those pursuing the general interests of the organization often battling personnel from the *órganos internos de control* (OICs) who struggle to promote the anticorruption interests of the comptroller general. The Comisión Nacional de Derechos Humanos (CNDH) illustrates this arrangement even better, with one "hand" of the state human rights apparatus working primarily to identify abuses committed by another "hand" of the state (Silva 2007, 187–188). Increasingly, personnel from the different segments of the same state represent different experiences and different backgrounds: distinct bureaucratic cultures and political interests.

Of course, a monolithic view of society is equally problematic. In terms of its anticorruption role, civil society does not represent a unified entity or actor struggling to hold officials accountable or to oppose corruption (a rather romantic notion of society). Sectors or groups within society are often involved in efforts to create pressures to hold government accountable and to expose corruption, but others within society collude secretly with state officials to engage in corrupt transactions and exchanges. Indeed, corruption usually involves transactions between state and societal interests working in league together. The facile implication, as we will see, is that an increase in societal autonomy and social capital can have variable effects on corruption.

Moreover, in envisioning the multifaceted nature of both state and society within the corruption equation, it is important to think in terms of the various networks and webs that link the two. State forces battling other state forces in the fight against corruption may ally and work closely with civil society organizations doing the same. Indeed, many consider such societal support critical in fighting crime, establishing the rule of law, battling corruption, and building accountability, even to the point of co-governance (Ackerman 2003, 2004; Fox 2007; Peruzzotti and Smulovitz 2006; Reames 2007, 128; Shirk and Ríos Cázares 2007, 5). Likewise, just as the state cannot handle the struggle alone without the support of civil society, neither can civil society develop the tools of accountability alone without the support and cooperation of portions of the state. Civil society, too, looks to and relies on state allies and institutions to help address its problems with other state institutions. Similarly, corruption—the target of anticorruption initiatives—also works through strategic state-society alliances and networks. Operating in the shadows, certain societal groups work with parts of the state to acquire influence, or particularistic, tangible opportunities for wealth that they cannot otherwise obtain through legal means.

Mexican Democratization

Mexico's democracy did not emerge from the demise of the old system, a celebrated elite pact, or a foundational election as occurred in so many countries during democracy's celebrated "third wave" (Huntington 1991); instead, it evolved gradually, over time, in a lengthy, protracted process. Nor did all the component parts "democratize" at an equal pace or, for that matter, even democratize. As Manuel Alejandro Guerrero (2004) explains in *México: La Paradoja de su Democracia,* while the forms of coming to power have become far more open and democratic, this is not the case for the exercise of power (which remains more closed and authoritarian). Indeed, the multiple political changes marking this lengthy process have not taken place in any simple linear fashion; rather, they have played off one another in a rather complex, interactive dynamic of political reformism. Changes in the electoral fortunes of the once hegemonic Partido Revolucionario Institucional (PRI), for instance, helped pave the way for a shift in power away from the executive, but such electoral changes themselves grew out of the diluting of the president's ability to control the electoral process. Decentralization of power away from the federal government to the states and even the judiciary similarly reflect not only the product of the rising opposition and declining power of the president, but also the political strategies of PRI presidents seeking to protect rather than relinquish power. In fact, many of the structural and institutional changes discussed here occurred prior to the onset of full democratization—if (and only if) one uses the year 2000 to mark that critical juncture. Because of this intriguing dynamic, it is important to view the structural changes discussed here holistically, and recognize their mutual causal linkages. Of course, it is necessary to separate them out analytically, so I begin with Mexico's hegemonic party and the changing role of elections.

The Changing Nature of Elections and Corruption

The political party established by President Plutarco Elías Calles from the seat of power in 1929 to solidify and protect the power of the "Revolutionary Family" (and his own power, to be sure) did precisely that, maintaining a monopoly hold over elections and the government for over seven decades. In a strategic melding of party and government (known in Mexico as the *pri-gobierno*), the PRI's dominance at the polls guaranteed the party's full control of almost all the levers and layers of government. The control of government, in turn, gave it the tools to favor itself and ensure its continued electoral hegemony. The government used public resources to nurture clientelist relations, feed the PRI's vast political machine, and outspend any challengers; it crafted and implemented the rules governing political parties and elections to favor the PRI and disfavor opponents (e.g., gerrymandering, overrepresentation of the PRI, the creation of satellite parties), including regulations making it exceedingly difficult if not impossible to "prove" electoral fraud; and it manipulated governmental policy to channel support through "official" organizations aligned with the party (Molinar 1991; Morris 1995). Because of the centrality of the party's lengthy electoral hegemony to Mexico's unique authoritarian system, I begin this exploration of political change and corruption by focusing on the changing nature of elections.

If the PRI's dominance at the polls and the use of a biased state to support itself worked harmoniously, then the gradual dismantling of this system had to take place in unison. From one side of the choir, the PRI's electoral support softened during the period as voters increasingly turned to opposition parties, including the center-right Partido Acción Nacional (PAN), and the center-left Partido de la Revolución Democrática (PRD) after its formation in 1989, to register their demands and their frustrations.[3] Though the independent PAN had operated since the 1940s, drawing support from a swath of urban middle-class and Catholic voters in certain geographic regions, it was really only after the onset of the economic crisis in 1982 (and the end of decades of sustained economic growth known as the "Mexican Miracle") and the subsequent dismantling of the state-led model of import substitution that the PAN began to ratchet important electoral victories. When the PRI government acknowledged these victories, as occurred in the early 1980s and throughout much of the 1990s, it gave PAN-istas a strategic foothold in government from which to further contest the PRI's power and legitimacy. In the early 1980s, opposition parties, particularly the PAN, began to wrest control of key municipal governments, mainly in the northern and western portions of the country, and in 1989 the party won its first gubernatorial seat in Baja California.[4] Within a few short years, as this pattern rapidly unfolded, the opposition forced divided government onto a majority of the nation's thirty-two states (thirty-one plus the federal district)—a pattern facilitated by Mexico's mixed majoritarian and proportional representation electoral system—and garnered control of almost half the nation's gubernatorial seats. In 1997, the PRD dislodged the PRI from its historical grip over the Mexico City government—until then the mayor of Mexico City was a presidential appointee—while the opposition collectively extinguished the PRI's majority control of the Chamber of Deputies. Three years later, the PAN stripped the PRI of the ultimate prize, the presidency.

From the other side of the chorus, the *pri-gobierno* was slowly losing its hold over the electoral process. As electoral competition increased, opposition parties pushed not just to sway voters and win posts like any normal party, but also to pressure the government to end its unfair and biased support of the PRI and actually permit free and fair elections. As part of this approach, the opposition often staged massive protests accusing the government of engaging in electoral fraud, to deny its victory at the polls. This tactic often forced the government to "reconsider" the election outcome in order to restore stability and normalcy. Through this path, common throughout the middle to late 1980s and early 1990s and referred to as "second-round" voting in Mexico, the opposition negotiated additional seats in the government and real democratic reforms that would help set the stage for future electoral victories (Eisenstadt 2004). Through this tactic of contesting the government's democratic credentials, the opposition left it with few options but try to slow and manage the process of democratic opening while protecting some of its privileges.

Gradually, however, these reforms whittled away at the *pri-gobierno*'s control over the process and eventually ended the unfair advantages accorded the PRI. Through a series of critical reforms in 1990, 1994, and again in 1996, the government, usually working with the opposition, created what would eventually become a truly autonomous electoral body, the Instituto Federal Electoral (IFE), giving it broad, sweeping powers to design and run elections, police the political parties, and monitor publicly financed electoral campaigns. Equipped with a substantial budget and run by "citizen counselors" beginning in 1994, with parties and government representatives reduced to nonvoting status, the IFE significantly eclipsed the power of the president and the central government over elections (Middlebrook 2004, 6; Córdova and Murayama 2006; Gómez Tagle 2004).[5] The electoral reform of 1996, in particular, coupled with a subsequent Supreme Court decision, furthered this tendency by making the Tribunal Electoral del Poder Judicial de la Federación (TEPJF) more autonomous and giving it sweeping powers to rule on electoral disputes and even overturn state and national election results.[6]

The product of early democratization, these electoral institutions, particularly the IFE, rapidly acquired substantial credibility in the public's eyes, laying the institutional groundwork for freer and fairer elections and a reduction in the older forms of electoral fraud. Alternation in power in 2000 solidified much of the IFE's legitimacy, though controversies surrounding the 2006 presidential election would cut into that legitimacy somewhat (Elizondo Mayer-Serra 2006, 87; see also Eisenstadt 2007; Córdova and Murayama 2006; Gómez Tagle 2004; Lehoucq 2003; Middlebrook 2004; Rosas, Estévez, and Magar 2005).[7] The 2006 election, at minimum, as Jonathan Fox (2007, 4) points out, demonstrates that electoral democratization does not proceed in a linear fashion.

Among the many consequences of growing electoral competition in Mexico during this time was a fundamental change in the nature and role of elections. Under the old regime, elections served less as a vehicle for recruiting officials—since for all practical purposes they were already selected by the PRI leaders, especially the president—and more as a device to legitimize the revolutionary party, renew popular faith in the principals of the Mexican Revolution, mobilize supporters, test the capacity of aspiring politicians to deliver the vote, and acquaint the country with the president's hand-picked successor. With the changes during the 1980s and 1990s, however, elections increasingly became the primary vehicle for selecting political leaders, the trajectory of the politically ambitious, and, consequently, the site of intense political conflict. These changes thus shifted power not only to opposition parties—even smaller parties now have some leverage to broker deals with larger parties—but, alas, to the voters and, as we will see, the Congress.[8]

These electoral trends have had multiple effects on the underlying patterns of political corruption. First, the end of the biased state and more specifically the creation of the IFE crippled some of the older forms of electoral corruption once considered widespread. The blatant and unlimited use of state resources to support campaigns, the manipulation of vote tallies, the forged voting identification cards and precinct records, the shaved voting rolls, ad infinitum, are all somewhat more difficult to carry out and are generally thought to be less common today than in the past. These are far from extinct to be sure, particularly at the state and local levels. Still, by organizing and training citizens to conduct and observe elections, by developing a sophisticated system of tamper-proof voter identification cards, by crafting a system of public vote-counting with substantial checks and oversight, and by monitoring the activities of the political parties and campaigns through rigorous reporting requirements and investigative powers, the IFE has done much to reduce this pattern of "old corruption." In a few short years, as Loreno Córdova and Ciro

Murayama (2006, 215) contend, "Discussion of the trustworthiness of the Mexican electoral system is behind us."

Second, the heightened role of elections and growing electoral competition has politicized the issue of corruption, pushing it high atop the political agenda (Davis, Camp, and Kenneth Coleman 2004). In that the logic and rhetoric of democracy—ritualistically reified during elections by both candidates and voters—emphasizes accountability and the simple notion that government should work for the benefit of the people and not the rulers, the issue of corruption plays an important role in shaping the views and behavior of voters and candidates. Citizens now possess a blunt instrument they can use to fight back, rewarding those considered more capable of serving the public interest and punishing those deemed less capable. Now that their vote has some meaning, voters are more likely to vote against the party perceived as corrupt or against candidates tarnished by accusations of corruption. At the same time, competition alters the behavior of candidates, prompting them to redesign their appeals and strategies (Beer 2003; Guerrero Gutiérrez 2002). Competition, for instance, alters the expected returns of exposing the corruption of others (or even accusing them) and the costs of one's own (exposed) corruption, particularly when it erupts into a public scandal. This has had different effects on different parties and politicians. For the once hegemonic PRI, the increasing electoral competition diminishes the comfortable margins that had once allowed it to abide the corruption of its members, forcing it to select better candidates, and even to get out in front on the anticorruption issue. It has also made it more difficult to keep the lid on corrupt behavior. Locked into the battle of its political life, corruption by the 1990s had become a political liability for the party, making the combating of corruption an ingredient in its struggle to regain popular legitimacy and compete; hence, as we will see, the PRI played a central role in supporting and even leading many of the anticorruption reforms of the period. For the opposition, of course, underscoring the widespread corruption, assailing corruption's pernicious impact on society, and portraying the *pri-gobierno* as thoroughly and irredeemably corrupt, became the leitmotif of its electoral and political campaigns. Even beyond the election, elected representatives would carry this anticorruption rhetoric with them into office. They would make frequent allegations of wrongdoing by their opponents, demand investigations, open public inquiries, and attack the corruption of the prior regime. This politicization of corruption is further enhanced, according to Benito Nacif (2005, 23), by the proportional representation system in Mexico, which increases the level of competition among the parties and hence the degree of horizontal accountability exercised by Congress.[9]

Adding to this tendency, increasing electoral competition weakens the degree of unity among the political elite.[10] This feeds accusations and outings of corrupt behavior from within. When the PRI constituted, for all practical purposes, the only game in town, discipline and secrecy prevailed. After all, abiding by the informal rules of the game, including keeping quiet about the corruption of others, was crucial to one's career and fortune, as according to the Mexican saying *"cada quien tiene cola que le pise"* (roughly: everyone has a something to hide). With various parties with a credible chance to win already enjoying seats in government, and direct appeals to voters being decisive in the outcome, such informal rules lose their effect. Many of the scandals in recent years emerged precisely from the eruption of divisions among the elite, something exceedingly rare in the past. A substantial share of the information regarding Raul Salinas in the mid-1990s, records of PRI's illegal spending in the gubernatorial race in Tabasco in 1994 and 1997, information on the military's involvement in drug trafficking in the late 1990s, the secret recordings of bribes in the 2004 video scandals, and the accusations against one of the top candidates for the PRI's presidential nomination in 2006, for instance, all stemmed from information leaked by former allies.[11] The admission by the former mayor of Tuxtla Gutiérrez, Chiapas, of the diversion of more than 1 million pesos (US$125,000) from state coffers to finance presidential campaigns through ghost organizations created by the state congress, speculation that General Jesús Gutiérrez Rebollo might name names in the investigation, including, according to reports in *La Reforma,* those of at least six governors tied to drug trafficking, and even mutual accusations by the Supreme Court and the attorney general's corruption office, all illustrate the impact that elite divisions can have (see *La Reforma* August 7, 1997; *Mexico Update* nos. 135–136, 1997).[12] Partisan splits add even more gasoline to the flame. Complaints regarding the illegal activities of "Amigos de Fox" during the 2000 presidential election came most stridently from the PRD, while intense pressure to investigate the Pemexgate scandal came from the PAN's delegation.

By feeding accusations of corruption and public and official attention to the issue, these tendencies arguably have a more immediate and direct impact on the public's overall perception of corruption than they do on the other dimensions of corruption (participation and pattern). Above all, the politicization of corruption—replete with more political attention to the issue, more revelations of wrongdoing, greater public and political sensitivity, and the like—can all nurture the sense that corruption has increased, even dramatically so, and that little is actually being done about it by the government regardless of the underlying reality. Even effective measures that help identify corrupt activity, with or without sanctions, can feed the perception that corruption is on the rise by simply drawing public attention to the matter. Such perceptions of increased corruption can easily outpace the impact that these changes may be having on the real levels of corruption within the system (participation).

Even so, the greater electoral conflict and partisan competition in Mexico, though potentially making corruption more of a liability for politicians, at the same time increases the political stakes and hence the potential use of new forms of corruption to help candidates and aid their campaigns. Guerrero (2004, 186) contends that those who come to power now face a zero-sum game in competing for the spoils of the system. Controlling the influence of money is a particular problem in democracies where ideas of political equality prevail (Córdova and Murayama 2006, 18). The greater the stakes and the competition, in short, the greater the likelihood of employing illegal campaign contributions, of not reporting or underreporting donations and campaign spending to the IFE, of creating patronage deals and new and old forms of clientelism, of vote-buying and other types of electoral-related corruption designed to help put a candidate over the top. This is especially true at the lower levels, where intense electoral competition may encourage candidates and campaign workers to test the limits of the law or exploit its limited enforcement, and even dampen the likelihood that their superiors will punish them. Indeed, given the broader context of poverty and inequality that pervades Mexico, renewed patron-clientelism, facilitated by corruption, becomes a distinct possibility.[13] José Velasco (2005, 72) in fact argues that enhanced electoral competition has led to the greater use of authoritarian practices to gain votes.[14] Sergio Aguayo refers to the use of "new, much more sophisticated forms of vote-buying" in the 2006 election (cited in Fox 2007, 349). An empirical study by Federico Estévez, Beatriz Magaloni, and Alberto Díaz-Cayeros (2002) also shows continued use of clientelism despite the increase in electoral competition.[15] Though the authors find clientelism more prevalent in hegemonic municipalities where competition is low, bipartisan competition nonetheless prompts politicians to resort to clientelism as a way to hedge their risks. Many raise concerns about the use of illegal drug money in campaigns both to launder the funds and to support candidates.

These tendencies thus suggest a pattern of "new corruption" in Mexico—a seemingly more modern form of electoral corruption, illustrated by an array of recent corruption scandals. Election-related scandals include the lottery scandal, the Caminos y Puentes Federales (CAPUFE) scandal, the Carlos Ahumada bribery scandals (video scandals), and allegations that the Partido Verde Ecologista de México (PVEM) was selling local *regidores* positions,[16] among others (see Appendix B). Two of the major scandals of the period, both stemming from the 2000 election, which ended the PRI's reign of power, also reflect a new sort of election-related corruption: the Amigos de Fox and Pemexgate cases. These high-profile cases both involved unreported or illegal campaign contributions to the presidential campaigns of Vicente Fox and PRI candidate Francisco Labastida Ochoa and, consequently, the surpassing of campaign spending limits.

Pemexgate centered on the hidden transfer of over 500 million pesos (US$53 million) from the state-owned oil company Petroleos Mexicanos (PEMEX) through its labor union, the Sindicato de Trabajadores Petroleros de la República Mexicana (STPRM), to the PRI presidential campaign as well as simulated or rigged raffles. Despite a year of intense speculations, hearings, rulings, and negotiations in 2002, the Procuraduría General de la República (PGR) (attorney general) never officially prosecuted anyone. The government eventually dropped the initial money-laundering charges against PEMEX and union officials because of lack of evidence. The PRI, perhaps strategically, publicly touted the affair as politically motivated, accusing Fox of engaging in a witch-hunt. They promised obstructionism in response: "It is not possible for us to heed [Fox's] call to unity while also facing a series of false accusations" (*SourceMex* September, 18, 2002). Nonetheless, the IFE, operating within its power to determine violations of the electoral law, fined the PRI more than 1 billion pesos (US$97 million) for failing to report a like amount diverted from PEMEX: the largest fine in history and the equivalent of the federal financing the PRI would have received in 2003 and half its 2004 allocation (*SourceMex* March 19, 2003).

The Amigos de Fox case reflected a similar though somewhat more sophisticated pattern of channeling and laundering unreported funds into the coffers of the Fox presidential campaign, through a series of special interest political action committees (primarily the Asociación Civil Amigos de Fox and El Fideicomiso para el Desarrollo y la Democracia en México). In this case, the IFE's oversight committee, the Comisión de Fiscalización, uncovered a parallel financial structure for the campaign. It found that the PAN-PVEM alliance supporting the Fox campaign failed to report 99 million pesos (US$10 million); spent beyond the campaign spending limit; violated individual donation caps; received funds illegally from foreigners, businesses, and the public (legislature); engaged in payments to third parties for media that was unreported; and failed to respond to IFE inquiries for clarification. In all, the IFE could not identify the sources of funding of 77 million pesos (US$8 million) (Córdova and Murayama 2006, 159). Again, no one was punished for such activities and the PGR exonerated the principals of any wrongdoing in the financial scandal. Even so, in October 2003, the IFE ordered the PAN-PVEM coalition to pay a fine of 545 million pesos (US$48.7 million) (*SourceMex* October 15, 2003).

In some ways, these two period-defining cases, particularly the Amigos de Fox case, illustrate the strides made in recent years in the levels of transparency and accountability. Facing stiff resistance to obtain information from the Comisión Nacional Bancaria y de Valores (CNBV) and the Secretaría de Hacienda y Crédito Público (SHCP), the IFE battled through the courts to obtain bank records and financial information. After more than two years, the Supreme Court upheld the ruling of the electoral tribunal that bank secrecy laws should not be an obstacle to the IFE's investigations. Though occurring after the election, the historic significance of the fines to the PRI and Fox's Alliance for Change are important. "For the first time political parties supporting a presidential campaign were sanctioned, even having won, these sanctions were applied. And this is very important." Above all, the Amigos de Fox case showed that "not even the President of the Republic and his party could be beyond the reach of the law. This is not an insignificant fact in a country with a long tradition of abuses of power" (Córdova and Murayama 2006, 190, 214).

Of course, while competitive elections enhance the efforts of money to influence politics via campaigns, the IFE seeks to battle this growing trend. It learns and adapts, but the level of impunity for wrongdoing remains high.[17] Aided by the reforms in the mid-1990s, the IFE has made tremendous strides in ensuring greater transparency, instituting strict reporting requirements for the parties, and eliminating certain patterns of corruption. It has sought to close loopholes and the *lagunas* that remain, and to adapt and reign in the activities of the parties. Nonetheless, problems remain. The IFE lacks authority to regulate private media and government expenditures during campaigns.[18] It lacks the tools to fully monitor campaign spending and, above all, does not have the power to sanction individuals, only to levy financial penalties and, in the extreme case, cancel a party's registration (Schatz, Concha, and Kerpel 2007, 207). It cannot prosecute government officials, party members, or citizens (Ackerman 2003, 7). According to José Antonio Crespo, "We are not vaccinated against electoral corruption and cases like Pemexgate and Amigos de Fox can be repeated." Crespo predicted that in 2006 Mexico could have a repeat of "the dance of the millions, the scandals, the overspending of the campaigns, the improper purchases of media space" (Ramírez Cuvas 2005).[19] Moreover, many have questioned the neutrality of the IFE, noting the revolving door between the IFE and Congress and the political nature of the votes. Looking at the votes cast from 1996 to 2005, Guillermo Rosas, Federico Estévez, and Eric Magar (2005), for example, find that the citizen councilors behave essentially as party watchdogs representing the interests of the parties that sponsored their appointments. The electoral tribunal (the TEPJF) has also been accused of subjective and possibly party-driven decisions over the past several years, particularly in the cases of Tabasco (2001) and Colima (2004). Moreover, its powers remain limited and dependent on the executive (Eisenstadt and Poire 2005). Interestingly, despite having fined all the parties for various irregularities—not just for Pemexgate and Amigos de Fox—the IFE has not been able to clean up the image of the political parties. In fact, as we will see, political parties continue to enjoy the lowest rankings in terms of public credibility and are still widely considered one of the most corrupt institutions in the country.[20]

The changing nature and outcome of Mexican elections in recent years have had an even more profound effect on the country, totally refashioning the Mexican state and state-society relations. As the PRI's electoral monopoly slowly dwindled, there occurred a dramatic shift in the distribution of power among state institutions and a recrafting of relations among them. The president lost much of his dominance over the political system, bringing to an end a major pillar of the old regime, *presidencialismo,* while the power, autonomy, and roles of Congress, the bureaucracy, the judiciary, and even state and local governments expanded.

The Restructuring of the Mexican State

Executive-Legislative Balance

Perhaps the greatest reduction in presidential authority in recent years stems from the president's new relationship with Congress (Casar 2000; Nacif 2004; Rivera Sánchez 2004; Weldon 2003). The presence of the opposition and, particularly, the onset of divided government in 1997, effectively undermined the three major ingredients that once fed the meta-constitutional powers of the Mexican president: unified government, party discipline, and presidential leadership over the party. As Benito Nacif (2005, 8) categorically states: "With the emergence of divided government, a lengthy period of presidential dominance over Mexican politics was brought to an end." In practical terms, beginning in 1997 the president could no longer dictate the terms of legislation or budget figures to Congress, which until then was simply a rubber-stamp organ, or block it from exercising its oversight powers. The president retains significant powers to be sure, including the power to initiate legislation and a partial veto power—though the latter's use and limits remain somewhat constitutionally questionable—and perhaps a cultural predisposition emphasizing presidential leadership.[21] But there are real limits on presidential power now, making the Mexican presidency relatively weak by Latin American standards (Mainwaring and Shugart 1997; Weldon 1997). So in contrast to his predecessors, Fox was forced to negotiate legislation with Congress, suffered major setbacks when some of his important reform initiatives were defeated—like the fiscal reform of 2001—and at one point was even denied permission to travel abroad. Nonetheless, Fox did enjoy a relatively high success rate in getting legislation through the 2000–2003 Congress, including important anticorruption reforms, as discussed in Chapter 4. In fact, according to Nacif (2005, 34), the amount of presidential legislation approved during Fox's tenure was actually the same as before.

Divided government, to be sure, also strengthened Congress—though the weakening of the presidency and the strengthening of Congress are not synonymous (Ugalde 2000a). The increasing autonomy of Congress, now that the president no longer exercises control through party discipline, has led to a dramatic increase in the number of bills introduced by opposition parties, a reduction in the overall number of presidential initiatives (Nacif 2005, 9), and a strengthening of congressional oversight. Since 1997, no party alone has been able to block or stall efforts to investigate corruption or prevent Congress from using its power to force members of the government, though not secretaries of state, to appear before it and answer questions (Rivera Sánchez 2004). Congress is also freer to establish and even strengthen institutional checks on the power of the executive and the bureaucracy, to curb the president's discretionary authority, and review and audit administrative regulations and bureaucratic actions.

As with elections, these changes in the executive-legislative relationship have had multiple and varied impacts on the nature and patterns of political corruption. One positive effect of a stronger and more autonomous Congress has been greater oversight and controls on government spending—important ingredients in strengthening horizontal accountability. Though Congress has long held the power to audit and issue reports on federal spending—the Ley Organica de la Contaduria Mayor de Hacienda (Law of Treasury Accounting) dates back to 1978—this power remained limited in practice because of the PRI's majority control of the Comisión de Vigilancia within the Chamber of Deputies: a situation that effectively prevented the divulgence of any irregularities or the investigation of uncovered problems (Martínez Miranda 2000). As opposition presence grew, however, so too did the role of congressional audits and the autonomy of the congressional auditing agency. Even during the PRI's control of the committee, the opposition began using its influence to at least uncover and publicize irregularities, though little more. In 1995, for example, the Comisión de Vigilancia, which for the first time in its history included members of opposition parties, conducted a series of audits of the 1994 federal budget that uncovered 3,089 irregularities and diversions of funds (*La Jornada* September 27–28, 1996, cited in *Mexico Update* no. 92, 1996). Similar audits of the large governmental program Solidarity uncovered over 45 million pesos (US$5.9 million) in missing funds (*El Financiero* October, 7 1996, cited in *Mexico Update* no. 93, 1996). With divided government and the end of the PRI's majority control, such trends expanded considerably. Reflecting the growing level of democratization, Congress passed constitutional changes in 1997, actually designed by President Ernesto Zedillo, that strengthened the autonomy and the powers of its auditing agency, turning the Contaduria into the Auditoria Superior de la Federación (ASF) (see Guerrero Gutiérrez 2002). The reforms made the ASF responsible for reviewing revenues, spending, and the use of public resources, and for even assessing the achievement of program objectives. It also gave the agency greater powers to audit any branch of government, to review federal funds used by states and municipalities and autonomous organs, to determine who was responsible for the irregularities, and to issue sanctions once it determined damages (Martínez Miranda 2000). A 2002 Supreme Court decision further granted the ASF the power to obtain confidential bank information, while a 2004 reform expanded the agency's power by permitting audits of the hundreds of public *fideicomisos,* or trusts (*Atlatl* no. 19, 2004, 8). In 2002, for instance, the ASF conducted 24 audits on performance, 129 on compliance, 60 on public works and physical investment, 3 on systems, 21 on federal funds executed by federal entities, 47 on federal funds exercised by municipalities, and 52 special audits (SFP 2005a, 36). As of 2004, the government had acted on 90 percent of the *informes* issued by the ASF. According to Marisela Martínez Miranda (2000), "The constitutional reforms as well as the powers of the ASF represent an advance in the accountability process in our country."[22]

At the same time, Congress placed greater controls on government spending, limiting in particular many of the discretionary powers once enjoyed by the administration. In 1999, for example, Congress abolished the *"partida secreta"* (secret fund), the multimillion-dollar account presidents had long used unfettered. It also established rules that set the maximum levels of spending that can occur when income increases and declines, created new rules preventing the executive from spending more than approved in salary negotiations, and eliminated the ability of the executive to transfer funds with discretion to the states (see Guerrero Gutiérrez 2002). In recent years, Congress has also played a more pivotal role in negotiating budget items and asserting much greater control over the purse, even shifting funds from presidential priorities to its own.

Consistent with such oversight powers, Congress has also sought and obtained more information from the executive, while simultaneously beginning to establish the means to collect and analyze information independently of the executive, further facilitating its oversight functions. It now receives detailed, periodic reports on collections and evasions from the tax authority, the Servicio de Administración Tributaria (SAT), and the state of the economy from the Banco de México and the CNBV (Del Castillo 2004; see also Guerrero Gutiérrez 2002; Ugalde 2000b). In addition, the Congress has created a permanent professional staff for congressional committees and established the Center for the Study of Public Finances and the Office of Parliamentary Services, the Center for Social and Public Opinion Studies, and the Permanent Unit for Training and Education for members of the parliamentary service (Rivera Sánchez 2004, 282). The Center for Social and Public Opinion Studies, for instance, has produced detailed reports on corruption and contraband in the textile sector (Ochoa León 2005) and examined the impact of corruption on the lack of confidence in society (Arellano Trejo 2005).

In addition to its greater legislative and auditing roles, the end of presidential dominance has also freed Congress to conduct its own investigations into government corruption. Though Congress lacks the authority to prosecute officials, it does have the power to strip their immunity *(fuero),* and it can publicly pressure the administration to open criminal investigations. Soon after the 1997 election, which brought opposition control to Congress, for example, a host of congressional committees on budgeting and public accounts exposed the practices of self-loans, loans to ghost companies and clients, illegal contracts, and irregular procedures within the national development bank, in some cases filing official charges against those responsible (Acosta Córdova 1998).[23] The Chamber of Deputies' investigation of Conasupo uncovered evidence of ghost purchases, irregular privatizations of public enterprises, the paying of below market price for products, the sale of black-market powdered milk, and the fraudulent importation of beans unfit for human consumption, as well as cover-ups and widespread favoritism in the agency (see *Siglo 21* June 25, 1996, 4–5). The opposition in Congress also took steps to impeach the governors of Morelos, Tabasco, and Yucatán in the late 1990s, and pressured for the removal of the governors of Puebla and Oaxaca in 2006 on charges of corruption, violation of human rights, and abuse of authority.[24]

Such oversight includes investigations into questionable spending even under Fox. Following revelations by the ASF of irregularities of more than 1.2 billion pesos (US$120 million) between 2001 and 2004 in Fonden, the natural disaster relief agency, the Senate conducted special hearings (*Milenio* December 5, 2005). During the Fondengate scandal, members of the opposition accused Fox of the diversion of over 1 billion pesos (US$93 million) in federal disaster assistance funds to help PAN candidates (*SourceMex* October 12, 2005; see also *La Jornada* January 18–19, 1998, cited in *Mexico Update* no. 156, 1998; Monge 1998). Congress also conducted a special investigation into alleged influence peddling by the Bribiescas, the sons of the first lady, Marta Sahagún, and Fox's stepsons. According to Jesús González Schmall, chair of the committee that conducted the investigation, the Bribiescas used the presidential jet, entertained guests at the president's ranch, closed off national monuments and then brought in Brazilian girls on cruise ships, and were leaked privileged information from the bank rescue agency to profit in the real estate market (Latin American Regional Report, Mexico and NAFTA August 2006). Investigations into eight companies with ties to the Bribiescas prompted harsh attacks by the president and first lady against members of Congress. Many saw the profits enjoyed by the Bribiescas as part of a broader pattern that included Marta Sahagún's questionable handling of funds in the charitable organization Vamos México (see Appendix B). Whereas the Towelgate scandal tarnished the president's image in the early days of the *sexenio,* lingering allegations of influence peddling by the Bribiescas and impunity seriously hounded the administration during the latter years.

Indeed, demands for investigations have come from a wide range of congressional committees. A February 2004 document by the Environmental and Natural Resource Committee, for example, demanded that the internal auditor of the Secretaría de Medio Ambiente, Recursos Naturales y Pesca (SEMARP) make progress on the investigations into corruption in the granting of hunting licenses. The document described how the agency had allegedly granted 93,000 permits illegally (cited in Arellano 2005). Deputy Miguel Alonso Raya, chair of the Social Security Committee, conducted a press conference to denounce a network of corruption involving personnel from the Instituto de Seguridad y Servicios Sociales de los Trabajadores del Estado (ISSSTE), banks, and others that allowed workers of the institute to withdraw their funds from retirement accounts without having met the requirements. He also demanded that authorities conduct an investigation into the matter, prompting the ISSSTE to acknowledge the problem and change the rules to prevent such anomalies in the future (Arellano 2005). Congress even set up a special committee to investigate the mining accident in Pasta de Conchos in February 2006 and the role of key officials in covering it up.[25]

The September 12, 2005, congressional appearance by the secretary of Función Pública, Eduardo Romero, before joint congressional committees illustrates Congress's more aggressive role toward corruption. Members of Congress not only criticized the secretary for the overall lack of progress in the administration's struggle against corruption, but also pressed him on a number of specific cases (e.g., Fonden and Bribiescas; see Appendix B). They assailed the agency's lack of progress on its implementation of the new civil service reform, and demanded an investigation into the Pasta de Conchos mining accident in Coahuila and the falsification of education titles (Cámara de Diputados, *Boletín* no. 2601, 2005).

While the strengthening of the mechanisms of horizontal accountability and the curbing of presidential powers work to curtail corruption, the impact of these changes has been limited and, in some ways, disappointing. Civic Alliance president Sergio Aguayo, for instance, predicted that the three-year period 1997–2000, following the end of the PRI's majority, would be "rich in scandalous revelations that . . . will serve to clean up Mexico" (quoted in *Siglo 21* July 16, 1997). He envisioned official investigations and public hearings into the unresolved cases of Raul Salinas, Conasupo, the assassination of PRI presidential candidate Luis Donaldo Colosio in 1994, the privatization of state enterprises, and corruption by state governors like Roberto Madrazo of Tabasco and Victor Cervera Pacheco of Yucatán. Yet the reality was quite different; most of these cases remain unresolved and those responsible unprosecuted. Part of the failure of Congress to exert greater and more effective oversight powers relates to its own institutional weaknesses. The absence of reelection, which undermines ties to constituents, and the centralization of power in the parties' leadership, together weaken the legislature's mechanisms of vertical accountability, cutting into its ability to offer a counterweight to presidential authority (Fox 2007, 36; Middlebrook 2004, 25). This also prevents individual legislators from developing expertise. As noted, Congress is just beginning to develop a more professional staff to assist in its effort to assert checks and balances, and to establish truly independent sources of information and analysis. Even with investigative powers, Congress nonetheless still has limited powers to prosecute officials for corruption and must depend on the administration, specifically the Secretaría de la Función Pública (SFP) and the PGR, for legal action.

A further weakness of congressional powers of accountability relates to the continued weaknesses of the ASF. Among the shortcomings, the congressional entity looks at only a small fraction of the overall budget, operates under a two-year lag in reviewing accounts, and even after making recommendations must rely on Hacienda and the SFP to levy fines and impose sanctions. The ASF completed its *informe* for the 1999 budget, for example, in September 2001, while in 2004 the ASF conducted less than 400 audits (Cámara de Diputados, *Boletín* no. 2601, 2005). In 2005, members of Congress complained that there had still not been any action on ASF reports since 2001, prompting accusations of impunity and cover-ups (Garduño 2005; Martínez Miranda 2000).[26]

The polarization and gridlock inherent in divided government have also worked not only to make governing difficult, but also to inhibit and weaken the pursuit of anticorruption measures (Guerrero 2004). Throughout the Fox *sexenio,* the PRI controlled the largest voting bloc in Congress. This severely constrained Fox's ability to act, somewhat ironically, according to Carlos Elizondo Mayer-Serra: "The president who came to power with the expectation of change had little political room to effectively make change." Indeed, Fox initiated fewer constitutional changes during his first two years in office than Ernesto Zedillo, Carlos Salinas de Gortari, Miguel de la Madrid, and José López Portillo (Elizondo Mayer-Serra 2006, 77). Such pressures made reforms targeting corruption, particularly corrupt officials from the PRI, especially problematic. Luis Moreno Ocampo, former head of Transparency International in Argentina, captures the essential political dilemma: "You can announce a fight against corruption, but you have to govern, too. . . . And governing is easier if you don't question corruption" (cited in Rosenberg 2003). Diane Davis (2006, 58) in particular points to this factor, as well as the growing intensity of intrastate and bureaucratic conflicts, to explain the government's failure to effectively curb police corruption. This suggests that while competition may help expose corruption, it may also make it difficult for politicians to work together to pass meaningful reforms. Indeed, one result of such polarization is much talk and little action. As Héctor Aguilar Camín (2006, 17) avers, "We have democratic politics of much discussion and few substantive agreements." Luis Ugalde (2001, 30), more dangerously, contends that the reduction in presidential power creates a vacuum that itself sets the stage for new forms of corruption: "Today the risk facing Mexican democracy is not an all-powerful president who in the past dominated the other powers, but rather the risk of a paralyzed presidency incapable of governing."

The growing power of Congress also opens opportunities for corruption within the institution itself. When Congress exercised limited political power, the prospects for conflict of interest among legislators, the development of influence markets by lobbyists, and outright bribery of members of Congress remained rather limited, as did the tools to detect such abuses. After all, why bribe members of Congress if they have limited or no say over policy? A strengthening of Congress, however, enhances members' influence and hence makes them potentially more "bribable" (Valverde Loya 2002), yet the institutional rules to prevent such abuses of power have yet to catch up to this new reality.[27] The Ley Federal de Responsabilidades prevents public servants, including members of Congress, from interfering in matters in which they have a personal, family, or business interest, and from lobbying the government within a year of leaving office. Yet according to John Ackerman (2008), this law is not enforced against members of Congress who systematically violate it by legislating and conducting activities on matters in which they do have a personal or economic interest. Indeed, a study by the Grupo de Ética, within the Chamber of Deputies, shows that the Mexican Congress lags most other congresses in the region in terms of its internal rules and procedures regarding internal ethics. According to the study, as of 2008, only 83 of the 500 deputies had signed the internal code of ethics, the Compromiso de Ética de los Diputados Federales. The Grupo de Ética, now inactive, went on to offer a host of recommendations, including the creation of a committee on ethics, transparency, and accountability that would be charged with maintaining, applying, and guaranteeing the fulfillment of the ethics code and handling complaints (*Milenio* March 23, 2008).

In March 2004, noting continuing problems of corruption, senators from all three major parties proposed the establishment of a special committee to focus on creating a more efficient instrument to fight corruption among the ranks. The committee devised a packet of constitutional reforms as well as reforms to the laws governing Congress and public officials that would define conflict of interest, regulate the outside activities of legislators, strengthen sanctions for influence peddling, restrict immunity, and create a register of legislators' activities before joining Congress and their outside incomes. The reforms would allow members of Congress to continue working in their profession, but not work on legal cases against the state, engage in sales to the state, or consult or provide other services to the state. The reforms would also limit immunity in cases of flagrant violations and just to officials elected by the people, thereby eliminating *fueros* for secretaries of state (*Atlatl* no. 14, 2004, 4). This packet of reforms, known as the Ley Anti-Diego, was approved by the Senate in April 2007, but has since been held up in the Chamber of Deputies.[28]

Executive-Bureaucratic Balance

In addition to Mexico's reforging executive-legislative relations, a fundamental change has also taken place in the role of the bureaucracy and its relationship to the executive. Under the PRI-dominated system, the state's massive administrative apparatus constituted the primary site of political struggle and elite negotiations. It was here where corporatist and clientelistic forces bargained with state officials over the details of policy and where the president and the party brokered state resources and official favors in exchange for loyalty and support (Guerrero 2004, 84; see also Arellano Gault and Guerrero Amparán 2003). As such, the bureaucracy constituted the very foundation of presidential power and was consequently highly politicized, focusing more on protecting the PRI's and the president's power than on the efficient delivery of services to the public (Hill Mayoral 2005; Sánchez González 2004). As part of this social pact, a certain level of corruption was tolerated as bureaucrats enjoyed the spoils of power in return for their support of the system. "This lower level corruption was not only tolerated as part of the informal compensation that this type of bureaucracy enjoyed, but it was also possibly encouraged and protected from the upper reaches of the administration" (Guerrero 2004, 99). As former attorney general Antonio Lozano Gracia (2001, 18) so aptly put it, it was a government of friends, not of laws.

Two important mechanisms have been at work to redefine the nature and role of the bureaucracy in recent years. First, the growing political competitiveness among parties and the shift in decisionmaking authority toward elected officials have worked to push for the depoliticization of much of the bureaucracy. Pressured to produce results to attract voters, politicians at all levels began to see the bureaucracy more as the site for the delivery of services rather than the site of political bargaining and discretion. Presidents, similarly, became more interested in improving conditions and thus improving the work of the administration to show the public real results, rather than using the administration as a political tool. Among the parties as well, there arose an incentive to have a public administration that was politically neutral (Hill Mayoral 2005). As the political battle lines were being redrawn, societal demands for change were increasingly taken not through the bureaucracy, but rather through Congress and, as we will see, even the courts. Much of this political restructuring came in the form of legal restrictions on the discretionary powers of the bureaucracy, more oversight, and other administrative reforms, as well as through a decline in bureaucratic forms of corruption (these trends are discussed in detail in Chapter 4).

Second, the watershed election of 2000 produced a temporal rupture in the control of the executive, giving the country a president with virtually no real ties to or entrenched interests within the bureaucracy and the prior administration. As José Juan Sánchez González (2004, 443) contends: "Upon the PAN's winning of the presidency, the fusion of the political elite and the upper public administration was broken, forever separating the PRI from the bureaucrats." This systemic decapitation meant that the new president not only had fewer friends and allies in the former government to protect, but also actually stood to gain much needed credibility by pursuing past abuses and past abusers. Since the bureaucracy had operated largely to protect and promote the interests of the PRI, and since Fox had no reason to maintain or protect such a system, alternation freed the new president, theoretically at least, to engage in sweeping administrative reforms. Seeing the bureaucracy therefore as the site of much needed change, the president could focus on moves to depoliticize the bureaucracy and reorient its actions to the delivery of government services, including nonpartisan management of government social programs such as Oportunidades, as shown by Jonathan Fox (2007, 334), as well as extensive efforts to introduce new management techniques and improve bureaucratic efficiency and performance.

One major indication of this shift toward a more depoliticized bureaucracy was the creation and strengthening of independent, autonomous, and more professional agencies within the administration, many of which predate alternation in political power, including accountability institutions such as the ASF and IFE as well as the CNDH, the Banco de México, the Instituto Federal de Acceso a la Información (IFAI), and a host of other regulatory bodies. Although many of these began as dependent, weak, and underfunded agencies, during the 1990s most expanded their autonomy, strength, and impact as the political transition proceeded (Ackerman 2003, 3).[29] The CNDH, for instance, which handles complaints of police abuse and carries out investigations, remained under executive control from its establishment in 1992 until 1998, when the Senate assumed control (see *SourceMex* October 7, 1998, June 30, 1999). Though it exposes abuses and issues public recommendations, it is unable to prosecute abuses (Schatz, Concha, and Kerpel 2007, 206). A World Bank study similarly finds that the regulatory agencies in Mexico are rather weak and unable to serve as independent checks on the behavior of large business interests (Guerrero, López-Calva, and Walton 2006, 18). Nonetheless, underlying all of these trends is a much more Weberian view of bureaucracy, the development of islands of embedded professionalism, and the restriction of politics to the policymaking stage and away from the stage of policy implementation.[30] These agencies also provide the framework for the development of new co-governance arrangements and for the nurturing of a unique bureaucratic culture.

These same changes, however, have also prompted a new source of structural resistance to change that severely complicates efforts at anticorruption reform. On the one hand, the end of the informal, social pacts linking the bureaucracy and social organizations to the *pri-gobierno* threatens the livelihood and privileges of these groups. Though no longer having to demonstrate loyalty to the president's pet party, these groups nonetheless have sought to protect their privileges and interests as they redefine their relationship with the government. Bureaucratic resistance to change has thus become common. One clear illustration of bureaucratic resistance to anticorruption efforts involves the Mexico City government. In March 2002, after the government completely suspended the issuance of licenses and auto permits in one vehicular control office in Mexico City because of widespread corruption, the union of Mexico City government workers threatened a general strike. In the Miguel Hidalgo delegation alone, some 300 workers demanded reincorporation into their original areas (García Rojas Castillo 2004, 6n). Noting the problems in Mexico City, Tina Rosenberg (2003) stresses not only the difficulties in taking on unionized municipal workers, but also that the budgets and mandates for comptroller and city council auditors are meager. Similar resistance to change can be found throughout the vast bureaucracy.

At the same time, the political rupture ended the president's ability to discipline the bureaucracy and corporatist organs. The tools once used by former

PRI presidents to reward and punish bureaucrats, union leaders, and others are no longer at the president's disposal. This largely freed the organizations from such top-down controls—accountability to the president—broadening the latitude for internal corruption. With less control than in the past, corrupt union officials in particular are in a sense freer in some ways to exploit union members. Arguably, unions now have to be more accountable to members because of growing levels of pluralism, but the mechanisms of grassroots control have remained limited. In fact, according to Arturo Alcalde (2006), workers are denied secret ballots to select their union leaders and the right to see their own contracts. Unions continue to operate opaquely.

Some of this resistance lay behind the failure of the Fox government to go after the corruption and abuses of former officials. Despite lofty campaign promises, Fox failed to prosecute many officials from the past. Shying away from a full-fledged truth commission, the government appointed a special prosecutor for the crimes of the past following the CNDH's confirmation in 2001 of government involvement in disappearances in the 1960s and 1970s. Yet the special prosecutor did not enjoy much cooperation, particularly from the military (Schatz, Concha, and Kerpel 2007, 206). In the end, despite a few arrests of generals and failed efforts to prosecute former president Luis Echeverría, the government offered its final report with limited fanfare (see Appendix B).

Executive-Judiciary Balance

Like the bureaucracy, the Mexican judiciary historically operated to sustain the authoritarian system as a pillar of presidentialism. Subordinate to the executive, the judicial system featured exceedingly weak rule of law and low levels of accountability (Domingo 2000; Magaloni 2003; Taylor 1997). Presidents not only operated unfettered by the judiciary, but they could also use and misuse the law itself to favor friends and supporters and to punish opponents. This pattern extended from the very top—the Supreme Court—all the way down through the lower courts, the peripheral judiciary bodies of the *ministerio público* (public prosecutor) charged with investigation and prosecution, and the judicial police. Widespread impunity and corruption sustained this system of political subordination. According to Pilar Domingo (2000, 706), in Mexico the judiciary "has fallen considerably short of the criteria for rule of law, independent judicial review and control of the legality and constitutionality of the acts of the power-holders." "Not only do they allow crime to go unpunished because of their incompetence," Beatriz Magaloni and Guillermo Zepeda (2004, 194) add, "but in some instances they have actually been 'captured' by criminals."

Political changes have altered the structural relationship, though its impact on corruption, especially at the lower levels, varies. Unlike in other realms, however, major reforms to the judiciary began well before the PRI's loss of power, or, as Silvia Inclán Oseguera (2004) stresses, before actual democratization. Though prefaced by a 1987 constitutional reform that gave the Supreme

Court and the federal judiciary more power and laid out some rather minimal guidelines for local judiciaries and judges (López-Ayllón and Fix-Fierro 2003, 317), real reforms took place in 1994 under President Ernesto Zedillo. "Designed to set the tone for a presidency that intended to take law and order, corruption and impunity seriously" (Domingo 2000, 730), Zedillo's reforms—his first major act as president—fundamentally redefined the role of the judiciary.[31] Among their far-reaching effects (the reform altered twenty-seven articles in the Constitution), the reforms dissolved the twenty-six-member Supreme Court and reduced it to eleven members, its original size; changed the nomination process to make the Court more independent of the PRI and increased the term of appointment from six to fifteen years (Kossick 2004); broadened the Court's jurisdiction over constitutional cases, giving it a limited form of judicial review and the power to decide what cases it would hear;[32] and established a separate entity, the Judicatura, charged with administering the courts and creating a judicial civil service system (Fix-Fierro 2003a). Two additional reforms in 1996 incorporated the Federal Electoral Tribunal into the judiciary and vested it with the power to invalidate state and municipal elections and the power to review the constitutionality of federal and state electoral laws, measures that helped foster greater confidence in elections and further depoliticized electoral controversies.[33]

In horizontal terms of balancing the power of the executive, including the potential to curb corruption, the new powers of the Court gave it a much greater political role. Conflicts once channeled into other areas of the political process were now being resolved by the courts. "Today, the judicial branch should also be recognized for its significant role in ultimately defining the rules of the game as they apply to the law as well as to society" (Cossio 2005, 123). The courts have decided on the constitutionality of local electoral laws, of single trade unions in public agencies, of the Chapter 19 binational panels of the North American Free Trade Agreement (NAFTA), of financial and jurisdictional conflicts between different levels of government, of extradition treaties, and of the intervention of the armed forces in public security (López-Ayllón and Fix-Fierro 2003, 317). In a striking contrast to the past, the courts have even struck down presidential initiatives, demonstrating their political independence. In the first constitutional controversy presented by Congress, in September 1999, for example, the Court sided with the Chamber of Deputies and ordered that the executive provide access to information about the trust fund operated by Banca Union in connection with the Fondo Bancario de Protección al Ahorro (FOBAPROA) banking crisis. Later, the Court invalidated two decrees by Fox, one that allowed companies producing electricity to sell excess production to the Comisión Federal de Electricidad (CFE) without going through a public auction, and one that exempted the beverage industry from a special 20 percent tax on sweeteners produced in Mexico and imported from the United States (Inclán Oseguera 2004). Empowered by Article 97 of the Constitution, the Supreme Court even launched investigations into government actions during the 1995 massacre of peasants in Aguas Blancas, Guerrero, and repression in Acteal in 1997 and in Atenco and Oaxaca in 2006 (Domingo 2000; Latin American Regional Report, Mexico and NAFTA, July 2007).

In vertical terms as well, the creation of the Judicatura and other internal changes within the judiciary have strengthened internal oversight and enhanced the level of professionalism. A number of potentially important changes have occurred in this area. One centers on the recruitment and the monitoring of federal judges. Before 1995, there was virtually no transparency within the judiciary and no competition-based culture of accountability (Kossick and Minutti Z. 2007). The Supreme Court was responsible for monitoring and controlling federal judges, which individual judges did through *visitas*. Yet seldom were judges subject to any disciplinary measures or dismissed for bad behavior, because the justices tended to take care of the judges whom they had originally appointed. The 1994 reforms, however, eliminated this clientelistic and largely opaque structure (Domingo 2000). First, they changed the way judges are selected. Having laid out the general principles and requirements for a career in the judiciary in 1995 (Cossio 2005, 120), the reforms required that selection of district judges take place, beginning in 1999, by means of competitive exams (Domingo 2000). Second, the reforms eliminated the use of *visitas* and instead created a more independent monitoring agency within the Judicatura called the Visitaduría Judicial, and also gave the federal courts the power to review the formal decisions of the *ministerio público* not to prosecute (Magaloni and Zepeda 2004, 175).[34]

One factor that has strengthened professionalism with the judiciary—and that has potentially lowered levels of corruption (Beer 2006; Domingo 2000)—is increased pay. From 1999 to 2003, the judiciary enjoyed a substantial increase in salary, becoming the best-paid branch within the government. Average salaries of MN$222,603 (US$23,000) per month in 1999 climbed to MN$502,567 (US$48,000) by 2003. "No other branch of the Mexican government has similar average salaries" (Inclán Oseguera 2004, 159).

Consistent with their new powers and functions, the courts have become much more "public."[35] As politicians and members of society began to turn to the courts to resolve political questions, the courts emerged from the obscurity that characterized their operations in the past. In terms of "social accountability," judges, the courts, and their rulings are now part of the political debate (Fix-Fierro 2003a, 262). Increasingly, political groups within society, including the Asamblea Popular de los Pueblos de Oaxaca in 2006, have used the courts as one strategy to pursue their political demands. "The increasing orientation of social expectations toward the law can be interpreted as a sign of the growing autonomy of the legal system vis-à-vis the political system" (Fix-Fierro 2003a, 254).

What is commonly referred to as the judiciary in Mexico encompasses more than the courts; it also includes the *ministerio público,* the judicial police, the public defenders, and the nation's prison system. These institutions, however, generally fall under the constitutional authority of the executive, not the judiciary per se, and as such are examined in Chapter 4. The hope, of course, is that the increasing autonomy of the courts will resonate downward throughout this complex system, strengthening the rule of law and hence the checks on corruption. Historically, however, the courts have long been considered a "network of ineffectiveness and corruption that can trap and process very few criminals" (Carbonell 2004, 8), featuring exceedingly high levels of discretionary authority, impunity, and corruption. Though the federal courts can now review formal decisions by the *ministerio público* not to prosecute, the prosecutor still enjoys a virtual "monopoly over investigative and prosecutorial actions"—an "enormous legal discretion [that] promotes arbitrariness" (Magaloni and Zepeda 2004, 175; Zepeda Lecuona 2007). In that nine out of ten suspects brought to trial are convicted, it is clear that the incredibly high levels of impunity—only 3 percent of criminal suspects go before a court—are not the result of a lenient judiciary, but rather the failures of law enforcement institutions (Zepeda Lecuona 2004). The few suspects who are brought before a court are either those who are caught in the act, or those who are "unable to bribe authorities in prosecutors' offices to secure their release" (Magaloni and Zepeda 2004, 176). Indeed, most analysts attribute the high levels of impunity to "the ineffective behavior of the police and the public prosecutor and . . . their inability to investigate and prosecute a significant proportion of the reported crimes" (López-Ayllón and Fix-Fierro 2003, 303; see also Carbonell 2007; Silva 2007; Zepeda Lecuona 2004, 2007).

Clearly, the broader criminal justice system plays a central role in the corruption equation. As Benjamin Reames (2007, 118) notes, "Police forces must function effectively and fairly for the legal system to do the same." At the broadest level, the lack of effectiveness to prosecute and punish those who violate the law—the excessively high levels of impunity within society—feeds the widespread perception in Mexico that "laws and regulations are not enforced" (López-Ayllón and Fix-Fierro 2003, 301). As such, the system nurtures a lack of respect for the rule of law and adds to the tendency for citizens to expect corruption from others and to engage in it themselves. At a more specific level, this impunity extends to the investigation and prosecution of corruption as well as sanctioning. Effective accountability demands not only having public officials explain their actions, but also having a judiciary capable of sanctioning wrongdoing. Failure to punish corrupt officials does nothing to discourage corrupt activity, while simultaneously nurturing the widespread perception of corruption. In addition, the criminal justice system itself is the site of high levels of corruption—from police and the *ministerio público* to judges and prisons. Indeed, the system encompasses the state institution that has the greatest interactions with the public and that, according to numerous by polls, is the site of the most bribery and also the site of significant drug-related corruption:

the police. Such high-profile infiltration of the criminal justice system greatly shapes popular perceptions of corruption.

Despite the potential for these reforms to reduce corruption by crippling the protection that judges once provided to the executive and the corruption within the lower ranks of the judiciary itself, or even to strengthen the rule of law, there is limited evidence that the changes in the judiciary-executive relationship have had much of an impact. Magaloni and Zepeda (2004), for instance, contend that the changes affecting the Supreme Court have had limited impact on people's lives. Indeed, such changes have done little to curb the perceived levels of corruption within the judiciary. A 2002 UN report estimated that more than half of attorneys and judges in the Mexican justice system were corrupt, and that civil matters could not be processed in some states without the payment of a bribe: "The transformation process since 1994 has been slow, and impunity and corruption appear to have continued unabated" (*SourceMex* April, 17, 2002).[36] Indeed, the Judicatura, according to Arturo Del Castillo (2004, 2), despite greater power to monitor and enforce, has been "inefficient when it comes to initiating investigations." Robert Kossick and Rubén Minutti (2007, 306), for example, note that no federal judge or magistrate has ever been sanctioned for corruption. Sara Schatz, Hugo Concha, and Ana Kerpel (2007, 197), by contrast, find the climate of legal change positive, "but tempered against long-standing challenges that will complicate and sometimes hinder the process of reform." Both society's control and politicians' control over agents of law enforcement also remain weak, making judicial power and the police ideal authoritarian enclaves (Magaloni 2003, 278). In her analysis of police reform, Diane Davis (2006, 55) notes that, "despite the clear resolve by Mexico's leaders to undertake police and judicial reform, the pattern of success has been mixed, especially when measured by degrees of public confidence."

Yet some analyses suggest positive changes in this area extending outward from increasing electoral competition and alternation in political power. Caroline Beer (2006), for instance, sees potentially greater accountability within the judiciary because of recent changes. In an analysis of state-level data, she finds a statistical correlation linking the overall perception of corruption with confidence in the application of justice and the judicial budget. She also finds that states with more competitive elections spend more on the judiciary. Magaloni and Zepeda (2004) similarly find less crime in states where the opposition has been in power for longer periods. Both studies suggest that growing competition translates into more improved performance of the judiciary, and a growing respect for the rule of law.

One major change is in the area of perception. In the past, police corruption took place in exchange for their loyalty in arresting and harassing counterrevolutionaries. The PRI government was able to keep the worst abuses out of the public eye by reshuffling assignments. Democratization in the 1990s, however, put an end to these cover-ups, "catapulting problems of impunity and public insecurity into the public limelight and unleashing a floodgate of citizen hopes about reversing the problem" (Davis 2006, 65). As seen in other venues, democratization here raises the bar of expectation while exposing more real and imagined corruption and making the issue itself more important.

This area thus supports evidence of both continuity and change. The lack of effectiveness of reforms, as suggested by the aforementioned 2002 UN report and the persistence of these authoritarian enclaves, indicates a continuation of the past patterns of corruption. Yet Sergio López-Ayllón and Hector Fix-Fierro (2003, 319), among others, argue that the problem within the criminal justice system lies more in the direction of change than in the persistence of the old system, suggesting the development of perhaps new forms of corruption. Davis (2006, 58) argues, for example, that the political changes—decentralization and power sharing—have created new and more intense intrastate and bureaucratic conflicts that have paralyzed government and legislative efforts to enact effective police reforms. As a result, she contends that the current problems are not due to legacies of the past, but rather to the interorganizational conflicts created by recent reforms.

In 2007, following the Fox term, the government passed yet another major constitutional reform of the judiciary. The measure, which took effect June 19, 2008, after having received support from the required majority of states, includes changes to ten articles of the Constitution and envisions a sweeping change in two particular areas. First, the reform will totally transform the judicial system by mandating public hearings, oral arguments, presumption of innocence, an accusatorial system, cross-examination, and transparency. The reform will fundamentally alter the inquisitional system now in place, eventually end the veil of secrecy encasing judicial matters and the paper-based system, and introduce a layer of accountability into the judiciary. Second, the reform will limit the role and the discretionary authority of the *ministerio público*. Rather than making initial determinations of guilt and innocence and working with the judge to investigate and present evidence, the *ministerio público* will focus only on presenting the state's case before a neutral judge and even face direct opposition from an empowered defense. The measure has a long transitory time, eight years, however, and the accompanying statutes and regulations remain pending. Even so, many believe that the changes will alter the conditions that give rise to high levels of corruption, largely by allowing for greater scrutiny of judicial decisions and accountability (*SourceMex* March 12, 2008).[37]

State and Local Governments

As with the changing functions and relations between institutions at the federal level, democratization has also fundamentally altered the relationship between federal institutions and those at the state and local levels. Above all, democratization in Mexico has gone hand in hand with decentralization of power and a refocusing of many of the nation's political struggles to the state and local arenas (see Cornelius et al. 1999; Willis, Garman, and Haggard 1999; Rodríguez 1997; Rowland 2003).[38] Through programs stretching back to the strengthening of municipal governments in the early 1980s, and all the way up to the decentralization of education, health, and other social policies in the 1990s, the decentralization of power has brought a shift in the distribution of resources and decisionmaking authority to state and municipal officials (Díaz-Cayeros 2004, 207). The impact of these changes on corruption, once again, varies.[39]

One view contends that by shifting the implementation of government programs closer to the people, decentralization operates to reduce the incidence and likelihood of corruption. According to this widely held view, by moving programs down to the local level, where citizens are more able to observe the actions of public officials firsthand, corruption becomes difficult to hide and relatively easy to control. Citizen groups at this level can exercise more oversight and a greater role in controlling the implementation of public policies. At the same time, federalism can add an effective layer of accountability, with state governments providing a check on the power of the federal government. This logic leads many international institutions to stress decentralization as part of an anticorruption strategy (Campbell 2003; López-Cálix et al. 2009).

Yet decentralization can also enhance the opportunities for corruption. First, decentralization of government programs shifts control of resources and discretionary authority to state and local officials. By itself, this move heightens the range of opportunities for corruption and expands the access points for others to influence policy through illegal means. Whether such moves result in more corruption, however, depends on the levels of internal controls within the states themselves. Second, the decentralization of programs weakens or undermines prior centralized controls. The decentralization that came with the reforms of 1997, for instance, eliminated the role of the federal government in ensuring transparency and accountability in government programs, thereby enhancing the potential for corruption at the local level.[40] Capturing this danger, Valverde Loya (2002) warns that decentralization may result in simply the "decentralization of corruption." According to Adriana López Monjardin, the 1999 reform of Article 115 of the Constitution did not provide any advance in terms of citizen participation or accountability. Instead, "the program keeps the transparency discourse, but does not specify how to put it into practice" (cited in Fox 2002, 110). Federal judicial reforms, in like manner, did not force any changes at the local level and, according to Hector Fix-Fierro (2003a, 2003b), constitute the site of greater judicial corruption associated with "buying an opportunity to be heard" rather than "buying a verdict." Compared to the federal courts, state courts have been severely neglected (Magaloni and Zepeda 2004). Fewer institutional limitations, for instance, explain municipal failures to develop credible anticrime policies: "despite shifts in politics and formal rules, Mexican local governments appear to have progressed little in terms of policy approaches to crime control and prevention" (Rowland 2003, 440, 444). A report by the Organization of American States cites weak whistle-blower protection laws and a lack of programs and strategies to inform society about the results against corruption and transparency at the state level (SFP 2006). Generally, the pace of decentralization has been greater than the development of oversight and control mechanisms. Most agree that the federal bureaucracy has tighter systems of bureaucratic control (audits, accountability systems, etc.) than do most state and particularly municipal governments. Indeed, Davis (2006) points to the role of decentralization and power sharing in undermining the rule of law.

In addition to eliminating some of the formal controls, decentralization has also eliminated the informal presidential controls over the states: controls exercised in the past by PRI presidents over PRI governors and PRI-controlled state legislatures. Though clearly a factor in the authoritarian power of the president, presidents often used these controls to prevent governors from going too far in exploiting the resources of their states.[41] The shift in power has thus left governors and other local officials with a broader range of authority and greater discretion, crafting what Manuel Guerrero (2004, 124–125) refers to as the *"feudilizacion del poder."* No longer tied to the president or dependent on presidential favor, this frees groups or individuals to operate for themselves rather as "men of the system."[42] Recognizing this danger, Wayne Cornelius (1999, 12, 14) notes how deconcentration of power can strengthen authoritarian elites in the periphery, acknowledging Mexico's "new federalism" as a "double-edged sword." In that state governors are no longer answerable to the president, this frees them to use state resources to create their own political machines and intimidate local mechanisms of accountability. Though governors are subject to federal laws regarding money laundering, drug trafficking, and federal funds, the level of corruption within the states now goes beyond the once disciplinary reach of the president, even as once exercised through informal means. Indeed, recent years have witnessed a range of accusations against governors, who have at times been able to hide behind federalism to prevent prosecution. In describing the breakdown of internal PRI discipline, Todd Eisenstadt (1999, 269–270), for instance, notes how President Zedillo failed in his efforts to remove the governor of Tabasco, Roberto Madrazo, amid charges of extensive corruption, and how "corrupt local political bosses prevailed" by using the new federalism to "shield themselves from sanctions."[43] Summarizing these tendencies, Luis Carlos Ugalde contends that corruption at the state level is actually worse today, despite the "good intentions at the top of the administration," because "states have more money to spend, more autonomy than before and no supervising" (cited in Reyes 2004).

In many ways, decentralization means that much of the corruption in Mexico corresponds to local dynamics. However, at the state level, competition, democratization, institutional development, and social capital—factors contributing to corruption—all vary. As has taken place at the national level, increased competition has politicized the issue of corruption at the state level, prompting new state and local administrations to expose the corruption of their predecessors, promise to clean up the delivery of public services, and craft reforms, but again this varies widely.[44] Cross-state comparisons show that the greater the level of electoral competition within the state, the better the selection of candidates for public office, even within the PRI, the more responsive and autonomous the legislature (Beer 2003), and the greater the respect for rule of law and trust in institutions (Cleary and Stokes 2006), all suggestive that democratization may help lower the incidence of corruption. But despite such findings, these same studies have failed to show any significant impact of these changes on perceptions of corruption. Jonathan Fox (2002), for example, shows that levels of social accountability vary. In states where social accountability is low, such as Chiapas, the level of corruption is higher, while in states with higher levels of social accountability, such as Oaxaca, the level of corruption is lower. Empirical analysis of all thirty-two entities shows that states with higher levels of democracy and alternation in power have had, if anything, only a slightly better record at reducing corruption than states with less electoral and political competition or states that are still dominated by the PRI (see Morris 2009).

Indeed, progress at reform and fighting corruption at the state level varies, making it difficult to assess the overall impact of decentralization on corruption. Though states tend to copy federal reforms and trends—like the freedom of information law and the establishment of judicial councils and formal judicial careers (Fix-Fierro 2003a, 247)—the design and impact of such changes varies tremendously.[45] Examples of actions by state and local governments in their fight against corruption are numerous, with such state and local programs and local news dominating press reports on corruption in Mexico. Assessing the impact of local policies and programs on corruption, however, is much more difficult.[46] The biggest problem in most states and municipalities involves the police and drug trafficking. In responding to these many trends, the federal government has attempted to bolster and coordinate local reforms against corruption through a variety of programs, including the arrest of whole police departments, the militarization of the war on drugs, and other such efforts. Chapter 4 discusses these and other initiatives.

Finally, decentralization can potentially strengthen the mechanisms of accountability, with states serving a role in holding the federal government accountable. Yet according to Fox (2007, 339), the divisions of the national elite and their need for political support from those who control subnational authoritarian regimes have undermined the development of this accountability mechanism.

Conclusion

Writing in the late 1980s, I attributed the widespread political corruption in Mexico to a fundamental imbalance between the power of state and the power of society. Part of the exorbitant power of the state reflected the centralized control exercised by the president over personal opportunities for political advancement. With the PRI's electoral victory ensured, the president's control over nominations to elected and even nonelected public office—even to the point of hand-picking his successor through the *dedazo* (see Langston 2006)—guaranteed a rubber-stamp Congress, a weak judiciary, a subservient bureaucracy, pliable state and local governments, and weak rule of law. This authoritarian structure—downward accountability—facilitated corruption, particularly the misuse of state power to extort the citizenry, which in turn eased the operation of the system by rewarding those who supported it.

This chapter has explored the weakening of the state and the dismantling of this system owing to changes internal to the state: internal divisions within the government, the weakening of the presidency, the creation of checks and balances across institutions, and the shifting locus of political struggles. The shift away from the federal executive, the PRI, and the bureaucracy, toward elections, parties, Congress, the judiciary, and state and local entities, has had varied effects on perceptions and levels of corruption. Analysis shows that while these changes have clearly focused greater attention on corruption, bolstered demands for accountability, and fed the development of stronger institutional checks, the simultaneous elimination of past informal controls amid a rapidly changing institutional landscape has also created new opportunities for corruption and even facilitated the continuation of authoritarian (and corrupt) enclaves. Table 2.1 summarizes the variable effects of these changes on corruption.

On the other side of the state-society equation lies society. The changing nature of societal power in recent years, with the shift away from the state and toward more autonomy, has had variable impacts on perceptions of, participation in, and patterns of corruption.

Notes

1. As pointed out by an anonymous reviewer, much of the literature on corruption to date fails to consider the impact of transnational criminal organizations as a corrupting influence on the state. This is particularly relevant to the case of Mexico.

2. One indication of the extent of political change in Mexico in recent years is that between 1982 and 1996 almost 80 percent of the federal laws were newly enacted or extensively amended, with many of the changes dealing with the electoral system and the organization and power of the Congress and the federal judiciary (López-Ayllón and Fix-Fierro 2003, 290, 295).

3. On the PAN and its role in Mexican democratization, see Ard 2003; Middlebrook 2001; Mizrahi 2003. On the PRD, see Bruhn 1997; Garrido 1993.

4. This statement always has to be qualified, since the party technically won at least one if not more gubernatorial elections before 1989. The distinction, of course, is that 1989 was the first time the gubernatorial victory was officially recognized. On the rise of the opposition parties see, for example, Ard 2003; Bruhn 1996; Garrido 1993; Loaeza 1999; Mabry 1973; Shirk 2004; and Wuhs 2008.

Table 2.1 Impact of State Structural Changes

Nature of Change	Impact on Corruption	
	Inhibiting Factor	Facilitating Factor
More competitive elections	Allows voters to throw out corrupt officials and reward reformers; candidates quick to expose corruption of opponents	Increase in marginal returns to illegal campaign activity; vote-buying, new clientelism
Autonomous electoral body	Checks on elections, parties, and campaigns; lessens likelihood of electoral fraud	Growing partisanship in the electoral body
Austerity and economic restructuring	Fewer resources, fewer regulations to exploit; economic crisis reduced public tolerance	Fewer resources or personnel to fight corruption; end of informal controls; greater need to supplement income
Weakening of president vis-à-vis Congress	Less discretion of president and executive; pressures to depoliticize bureaucracy; more transparency	President must negotiate and compromise to pass needed reforms; difficult to pursue corrupt officials of the past without undermining needed support from parties
Strengthening of Congress vis-à-vis president	Checks on presidential and executive actions; more transparency	Members of Congress more "bribable"
Divided government	Must work together to protect interests and create more objective arbiters	Difficult to pass reforms
Alternation in power	New president not tied to entrenched bureaucratic interests; free to pursue past corruption	President has limited control over bureaucracy; more difficult to institute reforms
Political empowerment shifted toward elections, Congress, courts, and state and local governments, and away from president, executive, bureaucracy, and the PRI	Depoliticization of bureaucracy; focuses less on protecting the power of a particular party and more on its own interests; more transparency and horizontal checks	Multiplies the points of access to policy influence; fewer centralized controls
Weakening of president vis-à-vis judiciary	Less discretion of president and executive; more transparency	More decisionmaking power in judiciary, which operates with less transparency
Strengthening of judiciary vis-à-vis president	Checks on presidential and executive actions	Judiciary more open to political influence
Creation of Judicatura	More effective oversight of judges and prosecutors	Weak oversight
Decentralization	Less discretion of federal executive	Fewer controls and less oversight (varies by states)

5. Prior to 1993, the electoral authorities enjoyed limited oversight. The parties had no obligation to disclose information on the origin or use of resources. The IFE received and reviewed reports but had no powers to investigate. The 1996 reforms gave the Comisión de Fiscalización (oversight committee) broad authority to ensure that funds going to parties and campaign spending were in conformity with the law. It gave the committee sweeping powers to establish an accounting system for the parties, to police their conduct, to demand detailed information, to order audits and inspections, to initiate investigations, and to monitor television and radio during campaigns (Córdova and Murayama 2006, 33–35).

6. Part of the assertion of judicial independence vis-à-vis the executive relates to the power of appointment. Prior to the 1996 reforms, magistrates were appointed solely by the president. Today, lower-level judges are named by the Supreme Court, while the magistrates of the Court are appointed by the president and Congress. In December 2000, the Court, for the first time, overturned the gubernatorial election in Tabasco (Schatz, Concha, and Kerpel 2007, 207–208).

7. The controversies and accusations surrounding the 2006 presidential election tarnished the stature and credibility of both the IFE and the electoral court (see Crespo 2007). One poll, conducted in November 2006 (four months following the election), found that 29 percent of those who supported Felipe Calderon believed that there had been fraud, whereas 50 percent of those who supported Andrés Manuel López Obrador felt there had been fraud (Crespo 2007, 44; see also Rubio and Jaime 2007). Another poll, in 2006, revealed that confidence in the IFE fell from 74 percent before the election to 56 percent afterward (Galán 2006).

8. It is important to note that, despite the changing nature of elections and the fortunes of the PRI, support for the once dominant party has remained rather consistent and surprisingly durable (Middlebrook 2004, 7).

9. Corruption research suggests that accountability is lower in proportional representation systems, particularly in closed-list proportional representation systems such as Mexico's (see Kunicová and Rose-Ackerman 2005; Persson, Tabellini, and Trebbi 2003; Treisman 2007).

10. Jonathan Fox (2007, 63) highlights the role of divisions among the elite as one key to construction of basic citizenship rights.

11. In Tabasco, the official internal documents of Roberto Madrazo's 1994 state campaign were given anonymously to PRD leader Andrés Manuel López Obrador. They showed conclusively that the PRI spent 237 million pesos (US$24 million) on the campaign, far surpassing the limit prescribed by the state electoral law.

12. Calculations of US dollar equivalents are based on information from Economagic.com: Economic time series page. Where a particular month and year are specified, the calculations refer to the exchange rate at that time. If reference is made simply to multiple months or years, I use the prevailing rate at the midpoint of the time period. All US dollar equivalents are rounded.

13. On this tendency throughout Latin America, see Vilas 1997.

14. Looking at the social and partisan correlates of vote-buying in Mexico during the 2000 election, Wayne Cornelius (2002) found that 26 percent of survey respondents received gifts from parties or candidates. In an earlier study, Silvia Gómez Tagle (1987, 21–24) found that as competitiveness increased, so too did the share of impugned votes, from 46 percent of districts in 1979 elections to 62 percent in 1985.

15. Jonathan Fox (2007, 42) refers to clientelism as a form of "reverse accountability" in that state and party create mechanisms to control behavior of citizens.

16. The PRD and the PAN demanded that the IFE investigate the sale of candidacies for *regidores* by an official of the PVEM in the state of Mexico. According to PRD national leader Leonel Cota, the PVEM has become a family business: "The business

of politics in the state of Mexico is the best business, city council members earn more than 100 thousand pesos monthly, to distribute among their clientalist sectors: the politicians earn whatever that want in the state of Mexico, there are no limits" (*Milenio* September 25, 2005).

17. A 2002 report suggested that only 3 percent of electoral crimes are ever investigated, meaning a 97 percent level of impunity. Acknowledging the problems, the special prosecutor for electoral crimes (a post created in 1994) stated that it is important to apply heavy and exemplary punishment in order to gain the confidence of society, so that society will denounce electoral irregularities. He also noted that electoral crimes mainly occur in poorer areas (*El Universal* August 1, 2002).

18. In June 2008, the Chamber of Deputies approved reforms to the Código Fiscal de la Federación to eliminate bank secrecy in the oversight of political parties, a major hurdle in the investigations following the 2000 election. The reform will also give officials thirty days to respond to requests for information (*Milenio* June 20, 2008).

19. One of the irregularities exposed following the 2006 election was the existence of 281,000 campaign spots (out of a total of 751,000) that the parties did not claim to have sponsored or paid for in their report to the IFE.

20. One neglected area involves the spending of political parties for normal operations. In a report looking at party spending for perhaps the first time, *Proceso* in 2002 (August 22) revealed the excessive spending of party leaders and the lack of transparency.

21. The Constitution claims that the president can only veto measures passed by both houses of Congress, leaving open the question as to whether he can veto budget items that come only from the Chamber of Deputies.

22. In June 2007, for instance, the Comisión de Vigilancia recommended that the ASF conduct 141 audits, reviews, and inspections of the 2006 budget. The recommendation also included a request for evaluation of the internal auditing agencies and their effects on combating corruption, inefficiency, and transparency (*El Milenio* June 6, 2007).

23. A similar pattern marked the PRD's assumption of power in the federal district. Within weeks of taking office in January 1998, the new administration released details of corruption under the prior administration, including the existence of ghost workers, the rechanneling of construction materials to private persons, the double payment of public works contracts, the granting of city concessions without following appropriate procedures, the underuse of budgetary resources, and the illegal use of ecological reserves by individuals or groups. Further investigations found irregularities amounting to some 5 billion pesos (about US$625 million). A month later, information from the accounting office of the PRD-controlled Legislative Assembly revealed even more irregularities in the operation of the city government.

24. Even after gaining majority control in the Chamber of Deputies, the PRI's continued control of the Senate helped it block opposition efforts to remove corrupt officials. In 1997, the opposition took steps to oust the governors of Morelos (Jorge Carillo Olea), Tabasco (Roberto Madrazo), and Yucatán (Victor Cervera Pacheco) on charges of corruption and violations of the Constitution. After the six PRI members walked out, the PAN and PRD members of the subcommittee of the Comisión de Gobernación y Puntos Constitucionales voted 7–0 to support impeachment proceedings against Cervera and Madrazo. The subcommittee charged Madrazo of violating three clauses in the Constitution through his actions to block investigations into a campaign financing scandal stemming from his 1994 gubernatorial election, and accused Cervera of violating a constitutional clause that prohibits a chief executive from serving more than six years in office (Cervera had been appointed in 1995 to complete the term of former governor Dulce Maria Sauri and then ran for reelection). But since legal action requires the vote of both the Chamber of Deputies and the Senate, the accusations went nowhere (*SourceMex* April 22, 1998).

25. On June 13, 2007, it was reported that the deputies would request sanctions against the secretary of economy, Eduardo Sojo Garza-Aldape, former president Fox, and union leader Napoleón Gómez Urrutia for protecting acts of negligence by Grupo México (*Milenio* June 13, 2007).

26. The duplication of efforts and institutional division here cloud the lines of accountability. Governmental audits are conducted not only by the ASF but also by the SFP, which conducts far more audits than does the ASF. In 2004, whereas the ASF conducted fewer than 400 audits, the SFP conducted 5,013 (according to Secretary Romero's September 12, 2005, appearance before Congress). The ASF remains highly critical of the internal audits, and some members of Congress argue that the SFP should relinquish its auditing role in favor of the ASF. According to federal deputy Victor Infante, the twenty observations conducted by the SPF provide clear evidence that Fox's fight against corruption failed, and that the "results lack credibility" (transcript).

27. According to Jeffrey Weldon (2004, 133), a "true revolution" in parliamentary organization and procedures began to take shape only during the fifty-seventh legislature (1997–2000). The Centro de Investigación y Docencia Económica (CIDE) began investigating transparency and accountability within the Chamber of Deputies in 2004. It highlighted high levels of impunity within the institution, contending that members do basically what they want.

28. On June 15, 2007, the president of the Comisión de Vigilancia, alleging the presence of 500 ghost workers in the Chamber of Deputies, publicly demanded more oversight and accountability in Congress. He called this a *"herencia negra"* from the days of PRI control (*Milenio* June 15, 2007). The following day, representatives of the PAN and others denied the existence of the ghost workers (*Milenio* June 16, 2007).

29. John Ackerman (2003, 12–15) explains the success of the IFE in terms of "active legitimation" and "embedded professionalism." Active legitimation stems from and reflects the close linkage between the IFE and civil society during the formation and operation of that state agency. Embedded professionalism, in turn, stems from the existence of meritocratic recruitment and promotion and the IFE's strong institutional location within government.

30. Despite advances in legal, organizational, and procedural areas, as well as technology, during lengthy periods of administrative reform (1970–1982) and modernization (1984–2000), Mexico never truly instituted a Weberian model and maintained patrimonial bureaucracy. According to Rafael Martínez Puón (2002, 6), the country "still has pending issues and enormous deficiencies to overcome."

31. On the judicial reforms, see Beer 2006; Carbonell 2004; Davis 2006; Domingo 2000; Inclán Oseguera 2004; Magaloni 2003; Magaloni and Zepeda 2004; Taylor 1997; United Nations 2002.

32. Judicial review can be conducted only within thirty days of a law's publication, and only the attorney general, either house of Congress (with 33 percent approval), and the state legislatures (with 33 percent approval) can challenge a law (Taylor 1997).

33. Budget numbers provide one indication of the growing strength of the judiciary relative to the executive. As demonstrated by Guillermo Cejudo and Laura Sour (2007), spending on the judiciary more than doubled in real terms, as a proportion of the federal budget, from 1999 to 2006, from 0.59 percent to 1.13 percent.

34. Michael Taylor (1997, 160) sees the creation of the Judicatura as one step forward and two steps back: positive in the sense of increasing the autonomy of the judiciary, but negative in that the membership of the institution raises old questions about the lack of trust and respect for the judiciary.

35. The courts have also become far more transparent than in the past. Sessions of the Supreme Court are now broadcast on *Canal Judicial* and recorded. The court has also installed an Observatorio Ciudadano de la Justicia Federal with the participation

of social organizations like Iluminemos México to provide oversight and feedback (Carrasco Altamirano 2008).

36. In one particular case, Bell Helicopter filed charges in March 2003 against civil judge Justino Ángel Montes de Oca Contreras, alleging that in February 2002 he issued a sentence that condemned Bell to pay US$16 million as part of case brought by Transportes Aereos Pegaso against Bell. The case, however, was plagued with irregularities, like a failure to study the evidence presented by Bell. Although the Fiscalía de Servidores Públicos (Special Prosecutor of Public Servants) handled the case, it remained unresolved. Bell then sought an *amparo* (injunction) to determine a period for the ministerio público to resolve the investigation ("100 jueces bajo investigación" 2006).

37. The constitutional reforms will also strengthen the government's power and discretion in confronting organized crime, including an extension to eighty days of the period that the government can hold an individual without charge. Some see these measures as creating a potential for abuse (see interview with John Mill Ackerman, "Big Changes to Mexico's Judicial System: NPR," at http://www.npr.org/templates/story/story.php?storyid=91684101&sc=nd&sc=emaf; see also *Diario Oficial* June 18, 2008).

38. Mexico's power concentration index—a composite measure of the geographic spread of revenues among levels of government and the partisan shares of elected offices among different levels of government—developed by M. De Swan and Juan Molinar Horcasitas (2003), fell from a score of 90 before 1997, to 77 in 1997, and to less than 50 after the 2000 election. According to Fabrice Lehoucq (2007), state and municipal governments now spend a larger share of government revenues and engaged in more lobbying of members of Congress than in the past. Governors, in particular, have become key players, creating more veto players and thus making structural reforms more difficult.

39. Jonathan Fox (2002) shows that the decentralization reforms in 1997 increased resources going to the larger municipalities, but weakened the accountability mechanisms.

40. Zedillo created a budget line to provide federal funds to states for education, health care, and social infrastructure (Middlebrook 2004, 28).

41. Under the old system, the government gave state officials access to patronage channeled through federal bureaucracies, and part of the deal was informal tax exemptions protected by the local authorities (Díaz-Cayeros 2004, 228). On the operation of federalism under the old system, see also Bailey 1994; Rodríguez and Ward 1995.

42. The cases of Arturo Montiel in Mexico, Ulises Ruiz Ortiz in Oaxaca, and Mario Marin Torres in Puebla point to the ability of governors to create authoritarian and corrupt enclaves. See Appendix B.

43. In the 1994 Tabasco election, federal authorities eventually backed down in the face of substantial PRI resistance. PRI campaign records indicate that the candidate spent over US$50 million, grossly surpassing the legal limit (Eisenstadt 1999, 280).

44. During the 1990–2001 period, 51 percent of all municipalities enjoyed alternation of parties in power on at least one occasion (Moreno-Jaimes 2007, 141).

45. A 2002 study indexing fiscal federalism and accountability found that only twelve of the nation's thirty-one states made budget information public. It nonetheless noted improvements in recent years, pointing out that before 1995 all states were like *"cajones cerrados"* (closed drawers) (*Atlatl* no. 5, 2002, 3). By July 2004, twenty-three states had adopted their own version of a transparency law (Merino 2007, 32). Of course, by 2008, all states provided such rights in compliance with the constitutional reforms of 2007. Even so, as Merino (2007, 19) notes, "there have been problems of institutional design, operational difficulties, and differences in legal viewpoints." Today, these laws battle an administrative culture that is resistant to public scrutiny. The process takes time and requires that the government first designate an agency to oversee the creation of a strategy and supervise the entities of the executive. Later, the state government

must designate an *enlace* (liaison) in every secretariat and decentralized agency, while at the same time promoting knowledge of the law. The federal government recommends that the agencies in charge conduct an analysis of the state entities and inventory the information (*Atlatl* no. 6, 2003, 1–2). On state access to information laws, see IFAI 2007 and Merino 2007.

46. Examples of anticorruption initiatives by local governments are far too numerous to discuss in any detail here. Three examples suffice. In the first, Rigoberto Garza Faz (PRI), the former interim mayor of Reynosa, Tamaulipas, and a city council member, announced a contest for the best video, audio, or photograph revealing an act of corruption, promising a monthly award of 5,000 pesos (US$550) to the five best works, with the money to be taken from the corrupt officials' own salaries (*La Reforma* February 19, 2001). In another example, the government of the city of Puebla took what it described as drastic steps to curb corruption in February 2002 by ordering traffic police to wear neon-green vests covered in antibribery slogans. The vests bore a picture of a crocodile whose gaping jaws represented a huge *mordida* (bite or bribe). Beneath that picture were slogans such as "violations are free" and "honesty has no price." The idea, a local spokesperson said, was "to make citizens equate the crocodile with the end of *mordidas* and realize they don't have to allow traffic cops to extort money from them." Police disliked the tacky vests and felt that they undermined their authority. City hall, in contrast, said police were only upset because "many of them are going to see their extortion income dry up considerably" (*EFE* February 21, 2002). Finally, the government of the violent border city Tijuana, Baja California, installed closed-circuit cameras in local police stations and jail cells in June 2002 to reassure the public that its officers were not taking bribes or torturing suspects and prisoners. Reportedly, the cameras were to broadcast images twenty-four hours a day on a public website (*Associated Press* June 8, 2002).

3

Changing State-Society Relations

This chapter continues the analysis of structural changes, exploring recent changes in civil society and state-society relations, and their impact on corruption. From one end of that equation, we find a weakening of the Mexican state resulting from both the deconcentration of power as well as the loosening (in some cases abandonment) of its corporatist and clientelist controls over society. From the opposite end, we see a thickening or strengthening of civil society, an increase in the scope of societal demands and the intensity of public pressures placed on the government, and the conquering of political space left open by a retreating and diminished state (Fox 2007). The impact of these changes on corruption has varied. In many cases, the trends have had a positive effect, broadening the level of pluralism, inciting social consciousness, and creating organizations that seek to impose standards of accountability on the government. Michael Layton (*El Universal* July 9, 2007, cited in Pardinas 2007), in fact, attributes the major institutional changes in Mexico in recent years precisely to the work of civil society organizations. Jonathan Fox (2007, 334) similarly credits "the independent media, civil society organizations, and social movements" for keeping issues of transparency and accountability on the agenda. Yet in other cases, the effects have been problematic, such as when criminal organizations or civic organizations and social movements challenge governmental authority and seek particularistic solutions to their problems, filling the geographic and societal vacuum left by the retreating state. Discussion of these changes and their impact on corruption centers first on the press, followed by a broader focus on civil society organizations. Attention also focuses briefly on the challenges posed by the underlying political culture and the structure of civil society itself, prefacing somewhat the broader analysis of political culture found in the penultimate chapter.

The Press

Throughout much of the twentieth century, the Mexican press served as a pillar of support for the *pri-gobierno* (Hughes 2006; Lawson 2002). This arrangement derived from a combination of corporatist and clientelistic control mechanisms (the Ley Mordaza, direct subsidies, secret payments to journalists, etc.), the long-term legitimacy of the political system, and norms within the journalistic profession (Hughes 2006, 51). As well, the complicity of the media not only constituted an important factor in the system's remarkable stability and longevity, but also helped the regime keep the lid on corruption. Yet a wide range of changes in recent years have fundamentally altered the nature of the press and its relationship to the state and society. At one level, the mechanisms of state control eroded. Due in large part to the economic crisis, the government sold the company providing subsidies for newsprint, cut back on advertising, and curtailed the customary payoffs to individual reporters (Acosta Silva 2004; Reyes 2004; Rosenberg 2003), though this practice has not disappeared entirely (Laufer 2004, 138–150). The emergence of opposition governments also undermined the traditional authoritarian model, contributing to the changing of the norms of media-state relations (Hughes 2006, 40).

At another level, the industry itself changed. Journalists and specific newspapers developed a new sort of civic-minded professionalism, spurred in part by changes within society, becoming more competitive, autonomous, and critical of government, public officials, and policies (Hughes 2006, 6). Part of the process of change in newspapers started at the individual level with diffusion of new ideas about the role of the press: views that conflicted with continuation of the hegemonic system (Hughes 2006, 38). As Sallie Hughes (2006, 4) notes, such changes had an important impact on Mexican democratization: "By giving voice to oppositional messages that challenged the PRI's monologue, the civic-oriented press eroded autocrats' ability to shape political reality through the control of information and national symbols in the mass media."

A freer press has had a formidable impact on corruption. At one level, a more civic-minded press has become an active player in exposing and denouncing corruption. Indeed, much of the flood of allegations of corruption and scandals in recent years stems from reports in the national press. In June 2001, for instance, using publicly available information on public procurement, the press revealed that President Vicente Fox had spent lavishly on linens for Los Pinos, striking a blow to the credibility of the president (and his anticorruption reforms) (see Appendix B). In August 2002, the press exposed, for the first time, the excessive amounts and limited transparency behind the financing of political parties. The critical weekly *Proceso* (August 22, 2002) presented a detailed list of irregularities, calling this an area hitherto neglected, but one that should be considered part of "democratic transparency." In 2004, the media again played the lead role in publicizing a series of video recordings of officials of the Mexico City government and the leader of the green party (the Partido Verde Ecologista de México [PVEM]) accepting payoffs and bribes (see Appendix B). For the first time, the public saw officials accepting bribes on national television. The press has even begun to employ investigative techniques to expose corruption. In an example unique in the history of Mexico, Grupo Reforma conducted an undercover investigation in the state of Mexico to see how easy it was to pay a bribe to obtain an auto verification sticker. The investigative group worked with a mechanic to make sure a car could not pass the test, and then took it to various locations. In virtually every case, the group was able to pay bribes and obtain the permits (Padgett 2002).

The foreign press has also become far more active in exposing Mexican corruption. The *Miami Herald* and the *New York Times* in particular played pivotal roles in uncovering detailed information regarding the hidden millions of Raul Salinas, his ties to important business leaders and drug traffickers, and the possible involvement of his brother, the former president, as well as other corrupt activities (see Haro Bélchez 1998).[1] Britain's *Financial Times* took the lead in raising allegations of the mishandling of funds and the misstatement of finances in the organization Vamos México and the role of the first lady, Marta Sahagún, in using her position to promote the charitable organization (*Source-Mex* March 10, 2004).

Not only has a more independent media emerged that seeks to "uncover and follow up on scandalous incidents" (Lawson 2002, 139), but the press now also provides a ready outlet for the various reports on corruption and related activities of other social organizations. Indeed, an interactive process has unfolded. As Hughes (2006, 6) notes, "Mexico's civil journalism was influenced by the awakening of civil society and simultaneously stimulated its development." The press has helped organize conferences on corruption and exert pressure itself on the government for reform. This is particularly true of a new generation of newspapers like Mexico City's *Reforma* and even a new generation of television programming on the duopoly Azteca and Televisa. The press today is far more apt to cover the activity of civic organizations like Civic Alliance or Transparencia Mexicana, reprint accusations and reports of corruption that come from outside the country, and even follow up on accusations leveled by political leaders. In July 2001, for example, Grupo Reforma sponsored a panel composed of academics, business leaders, and government officials who examined the impact of corruption on the private sector. According to the panel's report, the presenters showed how corruption has a detrimental impact on development and investments and thus emphasized the need to "convince others of the advantages that can be obtained from acting in a legal and transparent manner" (*El Mural* July 2, 2001).[2]

As an interest or advocacy group, the press has also become more directly involved in the struggle against corruption. As described by Greg Michener (2005), representatives from the investigative group Grupo Reforma as well as from newspapers *La Jornada* and *El Universal* played key roles within Grupo Oaxaca in drafting, mobilizing public support for, and pressuring the administration to adopt the Access to Information Law in 2002. Together with a group of academics, representatives of these newspapers negotiated directly with the administration the terms of the new law and mounted a full-fledged public campaign to support its adoption.

In discerning the impact of these changes on corruption, two types of changes are notable. First, there has clearly been a reduction in some of the older patterns of corruption within the industry. Payments to journalists (the *embute*), the corrupting use of advertisements and paid insertions *(gacetillas),* and the politically determined distribution of newsprint have lessened considerably. This represents a decrease in a type of "old corruption." Second, the press now plays a more important role in shaping perceptions about politics and politicians, and about corruption. The media dramatizes and personalizes politics, and like the media in the United States, focuses significant attention on personal scandal rather than the system itself. Among the consequences, this foments societal pressures for quick action, and tends to reinforce the public's views regarding corrupt politicians, especially when the institutions seemingly fail to respond or are slow to respond to the allegations. According to Adrián Silva Acosta (2004, 17): "The media's influence has generated the dramatization of politics, its personalization and, consequently, undermines the procedures and the time that traditional democratic political institutions—the executive, courts, congress—require to process suspects or the facts, thus altering or threatening the credibility and legitimacy of the political order."

This suggests a mixed result. While the former trend points to a decline in actual participation in corruption, the latter trend arguably contributes more to the perception of an increase in corruption and the perception of the failures of government to do anything about it.[3] Even so, by increasing the likelihood of being exposed, a more aggressive press can play a key role in diminishing the actual levels of corruption among politicians (Chapter 7 explores the role of the media as it relates to the patterns of corruption and the overall discourse developed by the press).

The situation is not one of complete independence, autonomy, or a full break with the government or the past, of course (Reyes 2004; Laufer 2004). Such ruptures are rare. Hughes (2006), for instance, depicts a hybrid system composed of civic-minded, free-market, and adaptive authoritarian newsrooms. Advertising is still used at times to gain sympathetic coverage (Reyes 2006) and many state governments still exercise pressures and controls over reporters and editors. Reports still exist that the members of the press accept bribes for favorable coverage and that television and radio even charge for interviews.

Reportedly, the president of television station Azteca tried to blackmail the government by threatening to report on a story on the bank bailout if the government did not rescind a prior fine for fraud (Center for Public Integrity 2005). The use of legal action against reporters based on rather strict and often abused libel and slander laws also continues as a form of controlling the press. In October 2002, for instance, eight journalists of *Norte de Juarez* faced legal action after reporting on the existence of favorable contracts to campaign contributors by Partido Revolucionario Institucional (PRI) governor Patricio Martínez. Even the first lady has taken such legal action, suing Argentine journalist Olga Wornat and *Proceso* for stories about her sons' alleged influence trafficking and use of insider information on real estate deals.

Even more disturbing is the danger faced by journalists who report on certain types of activities. It is risky for journalists to expose wrongdoing, blow the whistle, or dig around in the wrong places. The crusading weekly *Zeta* of Tijuana, founded in 1980, has a reputation not only for reporting on government corruption and drug trafficking, but also for suffering the consequences. *Zeta*'s cofounder was assassinated in 1988, and his partner was the victim of an assassination attempt in 1997 that left him permanently injured (his bodyguard was killed); in 2004, the editor of *Zeta*, Francisco Ortiz Franco, was killed (Laufer 2004, 138–139, 141). Overall, from 2000 to 2005, sixteen journalists lost their lives, prompting the organization Reporters Without Borders to classify Mexico as the most dangerous country in Latin America. According to its 2006 annual report, "impunity reigns despite apparent efforts by the federal government" and "organised crime, often linked with corrupt local officials, is the main reason for worsening press freedom in Mexico."[4] Even so, this figure is less than the numbers killed during the *sexenio* of Carlos Salinas (forty-six) and Ernesto Zedillo (twenty-four) (Center for Public Integrity 2005). For obvious health reasons, journalists often exercise self-censorship as a result.

Civil Society

As with the press, recent political and economic changes have also wrought a dramatic increase in the power and presence of civil society, mirroring changes taking place within the state. In the past, most major societal organizations were co-opted into a top-down corporatist relationship extending from either the PRI or the state (see Brachet-Marques 1995; Cook, Middlebrook, and Molinar Horcasitas 1994; Grayson 1998). The PRI incorporated the nation's major labor, peasant, and popular organizations into its organizational structure: an arrangement that enabled the party—more specifically the president—to selectively and strategically distribute the spoils of monopoly power ("elected" and administrative positions within the government, roles in the implementation of policy, state resources, opportunities for corrupt gain, protection against prosecution) among the organizations and their leaders. Presidents used these multiple carrots and sticks to discipline organizations, often pitting one against another in the process (see Morris 1995). According to the unwritten pact, the mass organizations tendered unquestioned loyalty to the PRI and the president, mobilizing votes for the PRI during elections, and limits on their political autonomy in exchange for some control over their own internal affairs, government protection against rival or dissident groups or against prosecution for assorted violations of the law, and a role in shaping and implementing public policy: slices, in other words, of the fruits of power. For other organizations in society, corporatist controls extended outward from the state rather than the party. Through such compulsory chamber organizations as the Confederación de Cámaras Nacionales de Comercio (CONCANACO), the Confederación de Cámaras Industriales (CONCAMIN), and the Cámara Nacional de Industria de la Transformación (CANACINTRA), business interests worked directly with the executive rather than via the PRI, exchanging a share of autonomy for favorable policies, guaranteed profits, and protection against foreign economic interests and labor (see Shadlen 2004; Thacker 2000). The press, as noted, was also effectively controlled through a range of subsidies and policies from the state (Lawson 2002). This arrangement, according to Fox (2007), created a top-down form of accountability.

Within this corporatist framework—and feeding it perhaps, or more likely, nurtured by it—there existed an underlying political culture characterized by a lack of confidence in the ability of formal public institutions to perform as designed, low levels of trust in politicians and one another, limited respect for the rule of law, and a certain tolerance, perhaps, toward political corruption. In one 1995 survey, for instance, 71 percent of those questioned agreed that it was acceptable to take advantage of official positions, provided the official did not exaggerate and that the benefits were shared (*Este País* no. 92, 1998, 57).[5] The public was right, of course: rights were rarely effective, and the law was only selectively applied. This meant that opportunities, rights, the law, benefits, and the like, rested largely on personal relationships, clientelistic networks, favors, and onetime bargaining arrangements. Rather than strictly dictating behavior, the law served instead as a point of reference for negotiations (Guerrero 2004, 122), or as former attorney general Antonio Lozano Gracia (2001, 18) so aptly characterized it: the government operated as a government not of laws, but of friends. As such, a sort of "culture of corruption" prevailed wherein everyone expected corrupt behavior by others and saw engaging in corruption as the only way to function and survive (Morris 1991). This culture found expression through such popular sayings as *"el que no transa, no avanza"* (one who does not cheat, does not advance) and *"con dinero baila el perro, y sin dinero uno baile como perro"* (with money the dog will dance, and without money one dances like a dog). Indeed, José Aguilar Rivera (2006, 102) refers to this lack of confidence in politicians as a legacy of authoritarianism and the birthmark of Mexican democracy.[6]

Yet during the past decade or so, Mexican civil society organizations have become far more numerous, more active, more autonomous, and more focused on the pursuit of political and social rights. In so doing, civil society has not only untied many of the corporatist knots that once constrained it, but has also begun to openly question predominant values of the political culture and the nature of Mexican politics, and to offer new ideas on the role of society and the state. These developments have taken place in conjunction with the economic and political transformations marking the period, changes that have shaped the course of Mexican democratization and contributed to the creation of key accountability mechanisms (Fox 2007).[7]

The economic crisis that erupted in 1982—and continued intermittently for the next two decades—had a profound effect on the country. It left millions without jobs or struggling to make a living in the burgeoning informal market, and increased the rates of poverty and inequality. The economic crisis also— along with the earthquakes of 1985—awakened civil society (Middlebrook 2004, 11). Societal groups emerged to pool scarce resources to try to make ends meet, to protest the high cost of living and high interest rates on loans, and to demand government attention to their needs and to the rising levels of crime and insecurity associated with economic decline. At the same time, the economic situation forced government to curtail public spending and, eventually, embrace far-reaching neoliberal structural reforms.

Both these measures—austerity and neoliberal restructuring—fundamentally altered the state's controls over society, leaving the state without the "fruits"—the regulations, the funds, and the programs that it had long relied upon to discipline these groups—to reward its friends and punish its enemies—thus crippling the government's ability to engage in what Alan Knight (1996, 223) once referred to as "chequebook peacekeeping." In short, the traditional means to co-opt social actors were no longer available (Olvera 1997, 109). The power of PRI-controlled organizations, like labor unions, both within the party and vis-à-vis other societal groups, dwindled in the face of such changes. Even national business, now freed (or abandoned) to compete on its own against foreign business, found itself freer to voice its interests and mobilize politically, with many of its members bolstering the ranks of the Partido Acción Nacional (PAN).

In addition to these economic changes, changes in the political environment—increasing electoral competition, opposition victories, signs of PRI's vulnerability, divided government, and the opening of pluralistic boundaries (discussed in Chapter 2)—furthered this expansion of civil society. During the late 1980s and 1990s, tens of thousands of civic associations emerged across the country in response to the political and economic situation. Convergencia de Organismos Civiles por la Democracia, which emerged in the shadow of the fraud-ridden 1988 presidential election, for example, triggered a wave of coalitions, networks, and individual nongovernmental organizations (NGOs) that came to view democracy and political reform "as a proactive solution to many of the nation's . . . problems" (Bailey 1998, 7). Even the ending of compulsory membership in chambers of industry by judicial decision in 1996 prompted diversification within the private sector (Luna 2004). Together, these new movements "made the regime's authoritarian character visible and publicized democratic values as something genuinely new in Mexican political culture" (Olvera 1997, 118). In 1994, Alianza Civica—a coalition of over 400 NGOs and academics—extensively analyzed the electoral campaigns to reveal the gross inequality of resources, press coverage, and television time favoring the PRI. For the first time, they coordinated wide-scale efforts to monitor the election, inviting in foreign observers to complement the thousands of national observers. The documentation of these injustices deeply cut into the PRI's and the government's democratic credibility, and fed the chorus of demands for real reform (Olvera 1997, 115).

Accompanying and feeding this wave of civil society activity, one finds the emergence of a new discourse within the political culture. People began to openly question the government and criticize the president, something once considered taboo (López de Nava, Cano, and Gutiérrez Viggers 2004). Demands for effective rule of law, in particular, "become a mantralike phrase in public discourse" (Fix-Fierro 2003a, 241). Moreover, as Jonathan Hiskey and Shaun Bowler (2005) show, as electoral competition increased, individuals' perceptions about the fairness of the system and of elections, and their willingness to participate, changed; but because of the underlying distrust toward politicians and public institutions, this new consciousness and discourse developed a sort of Manichean dimension to it. On one face of the coin, society rejected and disregarded virtually all aspects of the state. According to Fernando Escalante Gonzalbo (2006, 27), "a new 'standard of purity' [emerged] that demanded opposition to the government, the party and the state as a sign of being against corruption and backwardness." On the coin's opposing face, the public saw civil society as pure and as the site of authentic democratic voices (Escalante 2006, 33). This view, wrapped up in the verb *"ciudadanizar,"* privileged citizen control and empowerment as the preferred pathway to counter the corrupt state, address societal problems, and establish the rule of law. Thus, according to Alberto Olvera (1997, 118), civil society became a "new moral power." This underlying view, in turn, would feed and shape many of the democratic reforms of the period. The reforms of the Instituto Federal Electoral (IFE), in particular, stressed complete citizen control through the empowerment of citizen counselors. This view also underscored a certain optimism regarding the role of civic society.[8]

These changes—the weakening of the state (amid its discrediting) and the strengthening of society (with its crediting)—have had variable effects on the nature of corruption. At one level, the activities of civil society organizations have created a growing consciousness among the people regarding the rights of citizenship and the proper role of government. Consequently, certain civil society organizations have taken on a more direct role in demanding accountability, fighting corruption head on, exposing wrongdoing, collecting and disseminating information on the operation of government, and mobilizing pressures for change (Valverde Loya 2002). As Claudia López de Nava, Claudia Cano, and Leticia Gutiérrez Viggers (2004) note, there has emerged in Mexico a plural and open society that not only is willing to question the government, but now also has the tools to evaluate its performance and sanction wrongdoing. Best known for its role in monitoring elections during this early and critical period in the struggle, Alianza Civica also mobilized the struggle early on against corruption. Following the 1994 presidential election, for example, it established a program called Adopt an Official to help promote governmental accountability. Adopting the president, it acquired information—following a lengthy and expensive court battle and stiff resistance—about his salary (hitherto unknown) and about his (once) "secret" funds routinely used over the years to provide multimillion-dollar bonuses to cabinet-level officials (Bailey 1998, 10). Revealing that, since 1983, presidents had spent over US$1 billion in this manner was a decisive first step in reining in this practice. In 1997, Congress eliminated the secret fund.[9]

Similar examples abound at the local level. Work by Fox (2002, 2007), for instance, shows a clear link between participation and accountability in rural Mexico. Simply stated, the greater the social participation in the making of decisions for local projects, the greater the level of accountability. The fight against corruption in the state of Morelos, for example, a battle that led to the arrest of a handful of officials and the resignation of the governor, revolved in large part around the work of the grassroots organization Civic Cause (Ferriss 1998). In February 2002 in Monterrey, civic organizations together with the local government staged a "Caravan for Honesty" to help bring attention to the struggle against corruption. Reportedly, 3,000 people and 500 vehicles participated in the event, including Francisco Barrio (Secretaría de la Contraloría y Desarrollo Administrativo [SECODAM]) and the rector of the Instituto Tecnológica de Estudios Superiores de Monterrey (ITESM; also known as Tec de Monterrey). Meanwhile in Empalme, Sonora, as part of the national program Municipios por la Transparencia, a group of youths took to the streets and to government offices to hand out information about government services and the costs of *trámites* (bureaucratic procedures), and to help citizens process their complaints (see SECODAM's *Para Leer Sobre Transparencia* no. 6, 2002).

Examples of Mexican NGOs working to hold government accountable have become numerous.[10] Helena Hofbauer (2006) details the case of NGOs (Consorcio para el Diálogo Parlamentario y la Equidad; Equidad de Género, Ciudadanía, Trabajo y Familia; Fundar: Centro de Análisis e Investigación; Grupo de Información en Reproducción Elegida; Letra S; Sida, Cultura y Vida Cotidiana; and Salud Integral para la Mujer) working together to investigate and expose a series of budget irregularities in the publicly funded private agency Provida. Facilitated by the new transparency law (see Chapter 4), the group conducted its own audit and found excessive spending on public relations paid to a firm with close ties to the organization; the importation of overpriced medical equipment; and numerous procedural violations in the allocation of funds. The NGOs unveiled their citizen audit at a press conference in June 2004 and launched a public campaign demanding transparency and accountability. These demands enjoyed the support of 700 NGOs across the country. They also demanded that the Ministry of Health explain its reasons for financing the private organization, and that the government conduct an official audit and draft legislation to prevent similar transgressions in the future. In response, Congress demanded that the health minister explain the use of the 30 million pesos (US$2.6 million) and speed up an official audit. Soon after, the ministry requested the return of the 30 million pesos from Provida and canceled its contract. Within a year following its efforts, government audits were conducted, the Senate examined the matter, and the Secretaría de la Función Pública (SFP) removed the three officials at the head of the ministry. The case itself is important for two precedents. According to Hofbauer (2006, 45), "This was the first time CSO's followed a misallocation of resources and its corrupt expenditure throughout the entire budget process." In addition, the case established a legal precedent: this was the first time the government applied the Law of Responsibilities against an individual who made an unlawful use of public resources (see case of Jorge Serrano Limón in Appendix B).[11]

While accountability has become a key demand of many within civil society, the organization Tranparencia Mexicana, Mexico's chapter of Transparency International, focuses solely on the issue of corruption. Though small groups such as the Mexican Anticorruption League began operation in the mid-1980s (see *Mexpaz Bulletin* no. 22, May 18, 1995), it was not until the establishment in 1999 of Tranparencia Mexicana that such organizations took on a much larger political and public role. Chaired by Federico Reyes Heroles—the editor of *Este País* magazine—and featuring an impressive array of academics, such as David Ibarra, Olga Pelicer, and Luis Rubio, social activists like Sergio Aguayo of Alianza Cívica, and former government officials such as former attorney general Sergio García Ramírez and former Supreme Court justice Ulises Schmill, Tranparencia Mexicana set out in 1999 "to strengthen the fight against corruption" through a wide range of high-profile activities. Seeking to foment the public's consciousness on corruption and infiltrate the political agenda, Tranparencia Mexicana has sponsored substantive research and academic conferences on this once neglected issue. In November 1999, together with the US embassy, for instance, Tranparencia Mexicana organized what was perhaps Mexico's first conference on the subject, "Transparency and Corruption: Trends in Mexico": an event that featured some of the world's foremost experts. In May 2000, with assistance from the Ford and McArthur Foundations,

Tranparencia Mexicana brought together forty-three specialists, academics, state workers, and others to discuss and identify specific policy strategies to promote transparency and fight corruption. The result—a ten-point action plan—was published in October and presented to all the presidential candidates, including Fox (*La Reforma* October 11, 2000). The eighty-six-page document sought to provide a policy map for the Fox administration to fight corruption.[12] In addition, Tranparencia Mexicana has designed and conducted massive opinion polls on corruption including the Encuesta Nacional de Corrupción y Buen Gobierno (ENCBG) in 2001, 2003, 2005, and 2007 and the Indice Mexicano de Reputación Empresarial in 2004, calculating perceptions of corruption concerning over 130 companies, and has undertaken a study on the supplying of medicines in the Instituto Mexicano de Seguro Social (IMSS) (*Boletín Informativo* no. 17, 2006). Through its *Boletín Informativo,* Tranparencia Mexicana also seeks to educate the public on the nature of corruption, efforts to fight it, and resources on the topic. With significant credibility and increasingly recognized as the primary social interlocutor on the subject, Tranparencia Mexicana has also become active in providing real oversight.[13] It officially reviewed Mexico's implementation of the Convention on Combating Bribery of Foreign Public Officials (the antibribery treaty of the Organization for Economic Cooperation and Development [OECD]), signed in 1997;[14] and from 2001 to 2005 managed over twenty integrity pacts overseeing public procurement processes within the government (Transparencia Mexicana 2005, 43–44).

In addition to NGOs, other civil society actors like Mexican universities and academics have also taken on a new and more decisive role against corruption. Often working in conjunction with the government, international institutions, and groups like Tranparencia Mexicana, academic institutions have organized symposiums and forums on corruption, sponsored research and academic competitions, developed *diplomados* (seminars) for students, business, and public officials, and collaborated on efforts to measure corruption.[15] Since 2001, for example, the Universidad Nacional Autonoma de México (UNAM) has cosponsored an annual research competition on transparency and corruption, with the first prize worth 125,000 pesos (US$12,000) in 2008. The ITESM, in cooperation with the government and funding from the World Bank, teaches "Open and Participatory Government": a four-hour online course directed at public officials (see http://www.ruv.itesm.mx/portal/promocion/ds/dtbg/; *El Mural* July 29, 2001). In late 2001, the government reported that more than 1,500 public workers had already taken the course, helping to train them in "values, efficiency, and quality of service provision" (*El Universal* July 12, 2002).[16] The ITESM also conducted a cycle of conferences titled "Ethics Is Good Business" for consultants, entrepreneurs, and experts on business ethics (see SECODAM's *Para Leer Sobre Transparencia* no. 4, 2001), as well as the program "Governing Municipalities Without Corruption" to develop strategies to fight corruption at the local level (*Atlatl* no. 5, 2002, 4), and designed and conducted a major poll, the Encuesta de Gobernabilidad y Desarrollo Empresarial (EGDE), that gauges the level of business participation and perceptions of corruption (*Atlatl* no. 3, 2002, 1–2). Mexico's preeminent business school, the Instituto Panamericano de Alta Dirección de Empresa (Panamerican Institute for High Business Direction, Universidad Panamericana, IPADE), for its part, has taught a series of courses to five groups of high-level officials titled "Managing Directive Processes and Information." The Universidad Iberoamericana similarly agreed to develop a model program for training public servants of various agencies with the objective of creating a culture of service, honesty, transparency, and accountability (see SECODAM's *Para Leer Sobre la Transaprencia* no. 1, 2001). Even beyond training for officials, SECODAM (now the SFP) signed an agreement with the organization the Asociación Nacional de Universidades e Institutos de Educación Superior (ANUIES) to incorporate the study of ethics and corruption into college curricula. In a separate accord, eleven universities agreed to put together specialized codes of honor for their accounting and administration programs.[17]

In addition to such programs, scholars from these and other institutions such as the Centro de Investigación y Docencia Económica (CIDE), as well as NGOs, including CEI Consulting and Research, created by former CIDE scholar Arturo del Castillo and now headed by Vladimir Júarez, plus a variety of new think tanks, have produced innovative and in-depth studies on corruption. Four NGOs conducted a study of eighteen municipalities in Nuevo León, Zacatecas, Morelos, Chihuahua, and Veracruz in 2002, "Ciudadanos por Municipios Transparentes," exploring citizens' relationship to local government, the channels of interaction, and access to information (*Atlatl* no. 6, 2003, 3). A group called aregional.com has assembled a series of indexes measuring mechanisms of fiscal accountability and levels of transparency among the states. Its "Indice de Federalismo Fiscal y Rendicion de Cuentas," for example, shows Michoacán to be the most transparent (*Atlatl* no. 5, 2002, 3).[18] During the 1990s, academics and civil organizations produced studies reflecting concerns about the police in Mexico City, documenting systemic corruption throughout the institution (see de la Barreda Solórzano 1995; Comité de Abogados 2001, cited in Silva 2007, 182). Of the various studies and consulting work performed by CEI, one such study gauges the impact of the government-sponsored film *Cineminutos por la Transparencia* on viewers (Corduneanu, Guerrero, and Rodríguez-Oreggia 2004). Another, "La Tipificación de los Delitos de Corrupción en México," analyzes the impact of sanctions on corruption based on state-level data.[19] Indeed, in striking contrast to the past, Mexican scholars have ushered in a flood of research, contributing to the literature both inside and outside the country, while igniting intense student interest.

Transnational organizations—governmental and nongovernmental alike—often working in conjunction with local NGOs and providing financial and technical support, have added to these societal pressures upon the Mexican government (and support for those within the government promoting account-ability) (on binational linkages of NGOs, see Fox 2000; Keck and Sikkink 1998). Through various mechanisms, the World Bank and the International Monetary Fund, both prominent players in the global initiatives against corruption, have helped the Mexican government to adopt transparency and accountability reforms. The World Bank, for instance, has funded research at UNAM, sponsored seminars and training initiatives, and worked closely with Mexican officials to develop appropriate policies. Transparency International has also pressured the government for change. In fact, President-Elect Fox met with Transparency International president Peter Eigen after the election to discuss the need for a major assault on corruption (*La Reforma* July 31, 2000). With Mexico's signing of the Organization of American States (OAS) anticorruption convention in 1996, the OECD antibribery treaty in 1999, and the UN Convention Against Corruption in 2003, the Mexican government has not only committed itself to reforming its laws and developing an integrative anticorruption program, but also opened itself up to periodic reviews and assessment by follow-up committees. Groups such as the OAS Committee of Experts, for instance, document and assess Mexico's progress in complying with the terms of the OAS convention. Such reviews are important in holding the government more accountable, providing an independent source of information on its role in battling corruption, and focusing public and political attention on the issue. The OECD treaty, which obligates Mexico to establish mechanisms to prevent, detect, and sanction public officials, businesses, and third parties that offer or receive bribes during the course of international business, similarly requires Mexico to present an annual report (*Atlatl* no. 18, 2004, 2).[20]

The US government, through the Bureau for International Narcotics and Law Enforcement Affairs (BINLEA), the State Department, and the US Agency for International Development (USAID), also sponsors a wide range of programs designed to help battle corruption in Mexico. These include programs to promote professionalism among police and prosecutors, criminal experts, curricula in public schools to promote respect for the law, and programs to promote drug awareness, as well as conferences, seminars, studies, and training for bureaucrats. The projects Atlatl and Innovación México promoted a vast array of activities in Mexico, including the symposium "Consturyendo un Gobierno Honesto y Transparente" in November 2001 and "Mexico Contra la Corrupción" in April 2002; various workshops on measuring corruption, developing integrity programs and codes of conduct, and training managers, auditors, and journalists (*Atlatl* no. 1, 2002, 4–5); courses on techniques for investigating and detecting fraud in November 2001 and a special conference in Las Vegas for internal auditors in 2002; collaboration in the production of the film *Cuando sea grande* (When I grow up); and technical advice on evaluating institutional structures and designing internal anticorruption programs. Innovación México also sponsors courses emphasizing efficiency and the effectiveness of institutions, and even works with Congress through its Comisión de Vigilancia (*Atlatl* no. 15, 2004, 1). The United States has also worked directly with state governments and civil society. For example, it worked with personnel of Ógrano de Fiscalización Superior in Nayarit to design a preliminary evaluation of the latter's structure and organization, and it prepared a diagnostic study of the functioning of the Auditoria Superior in the state of Campeche. USAID also provided financing to civil society initiatives focused on transparency and public integrity, including, for instance, development of the Foro Mensual Anticorrupcion with CIDE, and copublication, with the civic organization Libertad de Información México A.C., of *Decálogo del marco normativo del derecho de acceso a la información pública:* an evaluation of eighteen state and federal laws as of June 2004 on access to information (*Atlatl* no. 20, 2004). Through Project AAA, USAID also sponsored the publication of *Atlatl* (a general newsletter providing information on the government's battle against corruption) and for a few years offered a news-clipping service.

In sum, because of these vast changes within society and the state-society relationship, the issue of corruption attracts far more attention and corrupt acts are more readily exposed than in the past. Clearly, government behavior is subject to a much higher degree of public scrutiny (Valverde Loya 2002), and such pressures are critical in holding the government accountable.[21] Of course, those demanding accountability and exposing wrongdoing—as with the press—often face severe obstacles and resistance. Alianza Civica, as noted, battled for years to expose the multimillion-dollar secret spending of the president, just as others continue to battle to expose corruption. In a study of civil society activities in Ciudad Juarez, Kathleen Staudt and Irasema Coronado (2007, 349) highlight the difficulty civic activists face in their quest to obtain political accountability, including threats, harassment, and intimidation.

Yet, while such changes help expose corruption, and presumably help root it out, they also reduce tolerance levels, feed expectations of change, and thus enhance the overall perceptions of corruption in the country. This, in large part, makes perceptions of corruption and popular evaluations of government performance a moving target. Fernando Escalante Gonzalbo (2006), for instance, notes how the suspicion of fraud under the PRI became so intense that the public expected all the corruption to miraculously end once the PRI was defeated. When these expectations proved to be unrealistic, the situation generated cynicism and a reinforcement of the notion that all politicians are corrupt.

While much of the anticorruption activity of civil society focuses on government and public officials, it also targets the morals and ethics of the Mexican culture (Caiden, Dwivedi, and Jabbra 2001, 5). According to Fox (2007, 50), "social movements and NGOs that do focus on transforming political cultures make an especially important contribution to horizontal accountability" by changing expected standards of behavior. Indeed, the view that Mexican culture plays a critical causal role in shaping corruption informs many of the efforts by civil society, and, as we see in the next chapter, by the government, to fight corruption. After noting that a majority of Mexicans (55 percent) respond to rules in "the most brutal and primitive way" (to avoid punishment) and only 15 percent truly understand the values of rules in themselves, Federico Reyes Heroles (1999), the president of Tranparencia Mexicana, stated: "Without the solid foundations of a culture of lawfulness, institutional reforms will always be weak. Needless to say unless a culture of respect towards lawfulness is implanted, popular corruption problems will prevail." Reyes Heroles then proceeded to blame the "problem of perception"—wherein everyone takes for granted that others will be corrupt—for actually facilitating corruption, a situation, he contended, that could be broken by identifying areas of honesty to serve as reference points, thereby restoring trust in institutions.[22]

Such arguments—attributing corruption to the culture and sense of social ethics—have become quite commonplace in Mexico. Ronén Waisser (2002), for example, attributes corruption in Mexico to "the scarcity of an ethical culture in the education system, the impunity, the lack of governability, as well as the absence of norms of integrity acquired within the workplace." The preface to the 2001 EGDE poll, sponsored by the Tec de Monterrey, makes a similar point: "Although corruption involves primarily the public sector, this phenomenon is not exclusively its responsibility, such that the fight against it cannot center only on actions directed at the government. Civil society and the private sector also gravitate, through various actions, around the problem of government corruption and, therefore, are an undeniable part of the solutions to preventing and tearing it apart." During a colloquium analyzing surveys of the political culture, José Woldenberg, director of the IFE, echoed this cultural argument: "The matter is of concern because no democracy can firmly sustain itself without a citizen base that is well informed about public matters. . . . [I]t is worth asking if democracy is possible without politicians, legislators, and parties that enjoy such respect" (*El Universal* August 15, 2002).

It is within this broader context that many of the organizations involved in the struggle against corruption are playing a major role in promoting ethics, anticorruption initiatives within their own ranks, education, and a more participatory culture. The Instituto Mexicano de Ejecutivos de Finanzas (IMEF), for example, agreed, in collaboration with SECODAM, to provide information to its members about best practices, and to work to improve the quality of the public services they receive. IMEF has also promised to present detailed proposals for reforms to the government. The Federación de Colegios, Institutos y Sociedades de Valuadores, in a similar accord, agreed to include in its plan of study aspects regarding professional ethics, while the Federación de Colegio de Ingenieros Civiles de la República Mexicana has agreed to elaborate and apply a code of conduct among its members. The Barra Mexicana Colegio de Abogados (Mexican Bar Association) also signed on to promote a code of ethics among its members, to organize conferences and workshops on ethics, and to promote throughout the country's law schools a professional culture of ethics. The Barra also agreed to work with SECODAM to offer a *diplomado* (seminar) on corruption and strategies to fight it. Similarly, the Cámara de la Industria de la Radio y la Televisión (CIRT) agreed to promote and diffuse measures to fight corruption and to promote the free flow of information. It also agreed to channel complaints and denouncements from the population. CONCAMIN promised to channel complaints and proposals from its members and to work with universities to train future business leaders in the area of ethics. CANACINTRA agreed to collect the codes of ethics of companies and to sensitize business to the importance of ethics. The Confederación Patronal de la República Mexicana (COPARMEX) guaranteed to promote a culture of honesty in relations between its members and the government, to elaborate official codes of conduct and train its members in ethics, and to create a commission on ethics in business. CONCANACO signed an accord promising to promote honesty and transparency in its dealings with the government. Even the business magazine *Expansión* signed an agreement to publish articles on the subject, to make public its code of conduct, to create a section on ethics in business, and to publish a list of businesses that perform well in the area of ethics (SECODAM, Comunicado de prensa, No. 092/2001). The business association Consejo Cordinador Empresarial (CCE), for instance, along with the stock market and the Mexican Institute of Executives, created a committee in 1999 to develop a code of best corporate practices (see http://cce.org.mx, cited in *Atlatl* no. 18, 2004, 8). In this same realm, IPADE, in a study of 500 businesses, showed that half of Mexican corporations have a code of conduct, but that only 17 percent of these codes are actually observed (see http://www.ipade.mx/eps, cited in *Atlatl* no. 5, 2002, 5). For its part, the civil association Libertad de Información (see http://limac.org.mx) focuses on corruption in education. Through a program called Monitoring Institutes of Higher Education, it examines the level of transparency within the nation's universities (*Atlatl* no. 10, 2004, 2). The Guadalajaran university Instituto Tecnológico y de Estudios Superiores de Occidente (ITESO), meanwhile, has collaborated on the publication (now in its second edition) of a manual on transparency and accountability for NGOs.

Given these strong cultural concerns, many groups prioritize education to strengthen the people's sense of responsibility (López Presa 1998, 116). According to Reyes Heroles (1999), civic education and the promotion of a new ethics within society gets at the "root of the problem." Even Woldenberg concluded his statement on civic culture by emphasizing the role of education: "The civic culture, the assimilation of democratic citizen practices and attitudes, are strengthened above all in the schools" (*El Universal* August 15, 2002). Consequently, many programs focus on education. Together with SECODAM and the IFE, the Consejo Nacional para la Cultura y las Artes (CONACULTRA), for instance, conducted a drawing contest for children titled "Goodbye to

Cheating" (Waisser 2002). In 2001, CIDE, SECODAM, USAID, and ANUIES, along with UNAM, sponsored the first annual essay contest—Certamen Nacional de Ensayo sobre Transparencia, Rendición de Cuentes y Combate a la Corrupción en México—in which 231 contestants participated. The contest continued into its eighth year with new sponsors. A range of groups (Cinemark, the World Bank, Fundación Telemex, Kodak, and Labo Filmes) also came together with SECODAM to produce the film *Cuando sea grande,* a short movie about a five-year-old boy facing a string of ethical challenges (*Notimex* August 28, 2002). Meanwhile, Tranparencia Mexicana worked with the Children's Museum in Mexico City to elaborate a program providing kids with tools to fight corruption (Reyes Heroles 1999).

In addition to highlighting the importance of morals and education, this new thinking also attacks the inactivity of society and thus calls for a more participatory culture. José Octavio López Presa (1998), for example, is quick to criticize a culture that discourages people from filing complaints or holding the government accountable. He points to the need to create mechanisms to facilitate the people's involvement in denouncing corruption and the need to involve professional organizations in promoting codes of ethics within their particular areas. According to Catherine Bailey (1998), the activities of these groups are helping to foster a culture of citizenship, though most recognize this as a slow, grueling, and nonlinear process (Fox 2007).

The Flip Side?

Despite these positive trends, a somewhat darker side to this transformation in state-society relations exists. The breakdown of the state's informal mechanisms of control, the decline in state resources, and the already-existing weak rule of law have all made it difficult at times for the state to assert its interests or those of the broader society when dealing with civil society. This opens opportunities that feed corruption, though a different pattern of corruption than that associated with the former authoritarian regime. At the same time, the weak state and weak societal support for rule of law undermine broader societal efforts to curb corruption or cooperate with state institutions in developing practices of accountability. This forces societal groups to seek new particularistic and clientelistic favors with government officials.

A number of areas illustrate the impact of the weakening of the state on corruption. Though neoliberal reforms have opened spaces for the private sector, its conduct now goes virtually unchecked. Corruption in the private sector, according to many, is widespread, though less known than corruption in the public sector. Privatization itself opened opportunities for corruption and the collusion of state and private sector forces (Clifton 2000a, 2000b; Teichman 1996; Valverde Loya 2002; Weiss 1996). The privatized banking sector, for instance, constituted the site of numerous confirmed irregularities. Reviews and audits of the bailout of the Fondo Bancario de Protección al Ahorro (FOBAPROA) revealed a wide range of fraudulent loans and questionable practices, while surveys describe routine bribes to government officials, particularly at the local level (CEE 2002; CEESP 2007).

One of the more pernicious effects of neoliberalism and democratization has been in terms of the opportunities provided for drug trafficking and money laundering: growth areas with widespread consequences for corruption. According to José Velasco (2005, 99), the weakening of the state has contributed to the growth of criminal organizations in many ways. First, the declining capacity of the state to control the economy has brought greater opportunities for alliances between legal and illegal businesses. Second, the reduction in state revenues has made illegal money more attractive to public officials. The growing inability of the state to enforce the rule of law and address growing crime has also fed the growth of this industry. Even the cutting of state subsidies to rural areas, the liberalization of the agriculture sector, and the elimination of the collective farms have pushed peasants toward the production of illegal drugs (Velasco 2005, 99).

The growth of drug organizations in concert with the weakening of the state has significantly enhanced the ability of the former to capture state agencies and personnel through massive payoffs (see Paternostro 1995). This relatively new pattern of corruption accompanying recent changes in Mexico (described in Morris 1991) has become perhaps the most visible and most sinister pattern of corruption facing the nation today. This is certainly the view of the US government: "The main threat to Mexico is the level of corruption that drug traffickers can use to disrupt and neutralize law enforcement authorities and that makes it next to impossible for the Mexican government to regain full control of its police apparatus" (Rocha 2005, 213). Indeed, drug traffickers have established the best routes by corrupting law enforcement authorities (Rocha 2005, 211).[23] Moreover, the growth of drug trafficking, coupled with the decline of the state and weak rule of law, has facilitated a spiral of crime, violence, and related corruption. This fosters a striking paradox: during the years of greatest electoral opening and change in Mexico, the country has witnessed a severe deterioration in the capacity of the state to enforce the rule of law (Chapter 4 examines aspects of the police and efforts to fight this pattern of corruption).[24]

As described in Chapter 2 with respect to state and local officials, the demise of the PRI-led system ended many of the centralized controls and left local officials largely free to construct their own clientelistic networks and corrupt schemes. In a similar manner, the end of the PRI-led system and presidential power has meant the end of the informal clientelistic controls that once shaped the patterns of corruption in state-society affairs. In the past, centralized power occupied the core of clientelistic relations. Presidents could discipline public officials and the leaders of civic organizations who overstepped the bounds of acceptable behavior. The deconcentration of power and the weakening of the state in recent years, however, have frayed the clientelistic ties and undermined the informal order provided by these corporatist arrangements (Elizondo Mayer-Serra 2006, 51). This has ripped open various power vacuums wherein, first, the state finds it increasingly difficult to exercise its authority over societal groups. This gives groups freer rein to operate largely as they please, creating or maintaining authoritarian and corrupt practices internally. The breakdown of centralized though informal controls, for instance, has left labor unions—whose internal operations remain opaque and, according to many indications, highly corrupt—largely unregulated (Rendón Corona 2001).[25] Moreover, the breakdown of controls diffuses power, creating multiple points of access to influence policy, often through corrupt means. In a sense, the weakening of the state has "decentralized" clientelistic relations; rather than central control, these relations have passed to new actors in different spaces and regions (Guerrero 2004, 160). A comment often heard is that corruption now is more disorganized than in the past, that under the PRI system, at least you knew who to pay to get things done. Such changes suggest a type of proliferation of corruption. Third, and closely related, the new situation forces social organizations into a more fluid and ambiguous situation in which they must mobilize their resources and battle a decentered and fragmented state in an effort to redefine and reforge their pact with authority. Here, the weakening of the state means that it is less capable of dictating the terms of state-society negotiations. As Manuel Guerrero (2004, 74) argues, the state "has become ever weaker within a setting in which the rules of the game, which are still predominantly informal, [are] now without a central agent capable of establishing the terms and forms of negotiation and exchange."

The power vacuums left by a weakening state, however, go even further. Unable to enforce old mechanisms of control or establish the new rules of engagement or the rule of law, the state has been unable to enforce order or pursue its broader policy objectives. A weak state becomes easy prey to organized groups capable of violating the rights of others, kidnapping officials, blocking roads, engaging in violent resistance, and the like, all in pursuit of their own particularistic demands. In many cases, these groups resort to disruptive and even illegal activities to press their demands. Guerrero (2004, 121), for instance, notes an increase in the number of closures of highways by protest groups from 404 in 2000 to 513 in 2002 and 442 in 2003. Under such conditions, the logic of negotiations with the government centers not on law, but on politics as groups negotiate special, clientelistc privileges with the state. This has the effect of privatizing the state, since it operates at the service of these groups. In this context, as José Aguilar Rivera (2006) notes, growing social pluralism undermines and weakens democracy rather than strengthening it; he refers to this as the "dark side" of social capital (see also Levi 1996). This same situation finds communities taking the law into their own hands in an effort to fill the void left by a diminished state. Bernardo González-Aréchiga (2007) notes that between 1987 and 2001 there were almost a hundred cases of lynching across the country: an alternative to the incapacity of the institutions to punish and render justice. This reflects above all the lack of faith in the police and the lack of confidence in the criminal justice system.

From the point of view of society, two effects are important. First, the levels of distrust of politicians and the state are such that they undermine the public's cooperation with the state. Citizens, for example, fail to support the efforts to increase state revenues that are needed to engage in state reforms, because, as Aguilar Rivera (2006, 108–109) contends, "the abuses by the police, the corruption, the extortion and other arbitrary acts contribute to the citizens' view that taxes represent a confiscation of their income." This same lack of trust also prevents society from working with the state cooperatively to fight corruption or participating politically. State-society cooperation, as alluded to earlier, is considered critical in creating virtuous circles of accountability (Fox 2007, 337). As Diane Davis (2006, 80) highlights with regard to police reform: "The real obstacle is the inability of state and citizens to join together in the struggle to restore trustworthiness and accountability to the system of policing." Caroline Beer (2006) also points to the vicious cycle at play: citizen pressure is necessary for government accountability, and yet without concrete gains, citizens become further alienated from their democratically elected officials.

Second, this situation complicates the spread of civic consciousness and the development of social capital. The growth of crime, corruption, confrontations in the streets, and the like, all tend to undermine social capital and trust (Parás 2007), pushing many to seek protection through clientelistic dealings with politicians, the state, or even organized crime. Citing polling data, Guerrero (2004) contends that the political culture remains disposed to maintaining clientelism because of this difficult setting. Sergio López-Ayllón and Hector Fix-Fierro (2003, 286) similarly contend: "There is not enough social support for the rule of law in the external legal culture, mainly because of the prevalence of group interests and social networks over individual rights, values, and merits. . . . [T]here is an incipient and insufficient internalization of the meaning and consequences of the rule of law in social practice." Or as Miguel González (2006) posits, the time of the unwritten rules is over, but the culture lives on.

Some point to the highly unequal structure of Mexican society—the large gap between rich and poor—as nurturing this culture and thus feeding corruption. Indeed, cross-national studies show an interactive relationship, with inequality feeding corruption and corruption worsening the distribution of resources (Anderson and Tverdova 2003; Paldam 2002; Shleifer and Vishny 1993). Inequality increases "the probability that large sectors of the population will remain vulnerable to political coercion, clientelist domination, and violence of different kinds" (Middlebrook 2004, 41). Indeed, poverty is a crucial determinant in clientelism and the use of such devices to garner political support (Eisenstadt and Lemarchand 1981; Estévez, Magaloni, and Díaz-Cayeros 2002; Kitschelt, Mansfeldova and Markowski 1999; Lemarchand 1972; Schmidt et al. 1977; Scott 1972). Moreover, inequality constrains opportunities for political participation, weakening the mechanisms of vertical accountability; it prevents the development of a concern for others or sense of collective responsibility; and it undermines efforts to establish rule of law. From this perspective, inequality and poverty constitute major obstacles to anticorruption.

Conclusion

Corruption under the unique political system run by the PRI grew out of and took place within a context of a relatively strong, centralized state and a weak, subordinate society. Power was concentrated in the hands of the president, who used his extensive informal powers to maintain discipline within the ranks, rewarding and punishing allies within the PRI, the government, and the social organizations. Yet, as seen in this and the prior chapter, the process of democratization in Mexico has meant a fundamental transformation in the nature of the state and society, with a significant weakening of the state and a concomitant strengthening of civil society. This transformation, in turn, has affected the nature of corruption in a variety of ways: it undermines the top-down structure whereby presidents had used corruption to maintain support and stability; it facilitates the greater exposure of corruption as politicians and officials compete for public support and the press gains latitude; it cuts social organizations off from their dependence on government, preventing blackmail from government, while freeing them to mobilize against the government and demand greater accountability; it opens more access points whereby citizens can use bribery to influence government decisions; and it opens the way for societal interests to infiltrate and capture state officials or institutions through bribery. The key to the transformation is recognizing that the weakening of the state—centered primarily on the elimination of the informal rules and institutions—merely revealed the underlying weakness of the more formal rule of law. This weakness, in turn, constitutes the basic setting for the forces feeding and inhibiting corruption. It also provides the most critical challenge to efforts within the state and society to establish accountability and combat corruption. It contributes to polarization, to wild accusations of corruption, and to accusations of the use (abuse) of the law itself to harass opponents. It also feeds off the lack of confidence in institutions.

Ideally, progress in fighting corruption and in constructing a more responsive and accountable government should breed greater confidence in state institutions. As confidence grows, citizens are more likely to use the legal system to pursue their demands and then abide by the decisions. There are some signs of this in Mexico. Sara Schatz, Hugo Concha, and Ana Kerpel (2007, 211), for instance, note that "more and more citizens have turned to lawyers to solve, pacify, and even prevent conflicts." Part of the growing power of the courts has been a move toward legalism and legal solutions to problems. Yet many problems are still handled in the streets via confrontation, or side deals, at the margins of the law, while confidence in politicians and institutions, as we will see later, remain dangerously low.

As with its counterpart in the prior chapter, Table 3.1 summarizes the variable effects on corruption of the changes in the power of the state and society. It suggests distinct changes in perceptions of, participation in, and patterns of corruption.

This and the prior chapter have focused on broad structural changes in Mexico and their effects on corruption. Below this level lie institutional factors shaping the opportunities for and risks of corrupt behavior. It is at this level where a series of reforms undertaken by President Fox in response to the broader structural forces have taken place, measures that in most cases are being consolidated and strengthened by Fox's successor, Felipe Calderon.

Table 3.1 Impact of State-Society Structural Changes

	Impact on Corruption	
Nature of Change	Inhibiting Factor	Facilitating Factor
In Society		
Increased press freedoms and professionalization	Ending of state bribes of journalists; greater likelihood of revelations of corruption in the media	Sensationalization creates impression of increasing and deep-seated corruption and the inability of government to respond
Proliferation of nongovernmental organizations	Greater monitoring of government activities; provides a vehicle for demands for better, more effective government	Lack of cooperation with what is perceived as a "corrupt" state
Creation of anticorruption organizations	Promotes consciousness about the nature and impact of corruption; mobilizes public support for reforms; engages in anticorruption practices	May give the impression of growing corruption or government failure to respond
Weakening of corporatist controls	Greater competition forces social organizations to attend to the needs of their members	Ending of informal controls leaves leaders of organizations unrestrained from the top; in context of weak rule of law, organizations mobilize to negotiate particularlistic political solutions with weak government
In State		
Weakening due to deconcentration and decentralization; cutbacks in spending and government controls	Less able to use controls or resources to extort, buy support, or keep corrupt activities hidden	More access points with fewer controls from the top; greater likelihood of state capturing and bribery from powerful societal interest, including drug traffickers

Notes

1. The *Miami Herald,* for example, reported on June 6, 1996, the discovery of an investment fund in Switzerland and tied Raul Salinas to Ricardo Salinas Pliego, who had deposited US$30 million in a Swiss account through his subsidiary Silvestar. On July 11, 1997, the *New York Times* cited recently released intelligence information confirming that Raul and other family members had used confidential information on the sale of banks to make investments, and providing strong hints linking the Salinas family to drug trafficking. A February 1997 report in the *New York Times* tied the governors of the states of Morelos and Sonora to drug traffickers, while the *Washington Times* magazine *Insight* in 1998 cited US Central Intelligence Agency information linking the actual secretary of government to drug traffickers while he served as governor in the state of Sinaloa (cited in "Llega a labastida la sombra" 1998 and Beltran del Rio 1998).

2. The development of awards for investigative reporting also illustrates the new role of the press. The Latin American division of Transparency International along with the Instituto Prensa y Sociedad (see http://ipyspe.org.pe), for example, offer annual awards for best investigative journalism concerning corruption in Latin America and the Caribbean (*Atlatl* no. 5, 2002, 5).

3. Perceptions of crime and insecurity illustrate a similar differential impact. Despite evidence that the increase in crime had leveled off by the time of the Fox government, the perception that crime had increased was widespread (Shirk and Ríos Cázares 2007, 8). This culminated in a massive march against insecurity in July 2004. According to Chappell Lawson (2002), the independent and competitive media played a role in molding citizen perceptions of this increase in violence.

4. See http://www.rsf.org/article.php3?id_article=17426 (and see http://www.rsf .org, in general, for annual reports on deaths of journalists). In February 2006, following an attack on the offices of a local paper in Nuevo Laredo, the federal government named a special prosecutor to handle attacks on journalists (*SourceMex* February 15, 2006).

5. See also the discussion on corruption in "La corrupción" 1996.

6. A best-seller by Germán Dehesa (2002), copublished by Tranparencia Mexicana, provides a fun, satirical look at this culture. The purpose of the work, according to Reyes Heroles in the prologue, is to prompt reflection through humor.

7. In his detailed study, Jonathan Fox (2007, 333) shows that "changes in the balance of power between society and the state in the countryside were driven by long-term cycles of reciprocal interaction between scaled-up grassroots organizations and other institutional innovators." He points, moreover, to the major role of coalitions of allies in society and the state in creating legacies that subsequent movements utilize to forge greater accountability.

8. The strengthening of civil society organizations has often met government resistance. Catherine Bailey (1998, 10), for instance, notes how the state attempted to impede the work of NGOs by refusing to modify the tax laws that were prejudicial to foreign funding, restricting foreign funding, and engaging in public campaigns to denigrate NGOs.

9. See *San Antonio Express-News* November 12 1994, 11A; *La Reforma* August 18, 1995. A report by Civic Alliance titled "Las violaciones al derecho a la información de los mexicanos" details the rigorous and lengthy process in acquiring the information about the president's funds. The ordeal also prompted Civic Alliance to take the lead in pushing for freedom of information legislation.

10. This includes investigations into the work of the legislature. In 2004, for example, the Centro de Investigación y Docencia Económica (CIDE) conducted an investigation into the transparency within the Chamber of Deputies. In November 2001,

Confederación Patronal de la República Mexicana (COPARMEX), a private sector organization, also conducted a study grading legislators (*El Universal* August 4, 2003).

11. Another example involves the creation of a sort of mock citizen trial (Tribunal Ciudadano por la Transparencia y la Rendición de Cuentas) of Luíz Pazos (PAN deputy) and Jorge Serrano Limón (former head of the pro-life group ProVida) on charges of corruption by the social organizations Letra S, Fundar, and Salud Integral para la Mujer. The trial group accused the PAN and the federal government of protecting these officials. The trial's jury included Sergio Aguayo, Alvaro Delgado, and anthropologist Marta Lamas, as well as members of NGOs (*La Jornada* April 5, 2006). More recently, México Unido Contra la Delincuencia mobilized to pressure the government to respond to the wave of violence.

12. The document recommends sweeping reforms to the judicial system, enhanced access and quality of public information, promotion of career civil service in specific areas of the administration, improvement and broadening of mechanisms of accountability, strengthening or creation of new organs for oversight and control, stimulation and enrichment of a culture of legality, improvement of the quality of regulations in public administration, strengthening of the tax system, reform of social institutions, and promotion of an integral approach to fighting corruption.

13. One sign of Transparencia Mexicana's profile comes from its own tally. From June to August in 2006, the national and local press mentioned Transparencia Mexicana ninety-three times. The press in Argentina, Cuba, Guatemala, Spain, and the United States has referred to Tranparencia Mexicana (*Boletín Informativo* no. 17, 2006).

14. Transparency International's February 25, 2000, study of Mexico's implementation of the OECD treaty found a good faith effort to pass legislation to implement the requirements of the treaty, yet noted that the actual scope of the legislation would not be clear until after specific cases had been brought before the courts.

15. As Jonathan Fox (2007, 57) contends, "Associational life does not unfold in a vacuum: state or external societal actors can provide either positive incentives or negative sanctions for collective action."

16. The four-hour course centers on the twelve values highlighted by Fox in his inaugural address. It includes various examples of ethical behavior and ethical dilemmas. The course is not obligatory, however, nor a requirement for advancement or higher pay.

17. Beginning in November 2001, CIDE, together with the Instituto Mexicano de Auditores Internos (IMAI) and Alianza Compromiso, an NGO, sponsored a series of anticorruption forums (*El Universal* August 4, 2003).

18. The organization aregional.com presents an annual measure of transparency of local governments in its transparency of fiscal information index. The index, started in 2003, presents the sum of points given for a state's regulatory framework, program and budgetary framework, and accountability and fiscal statistics. In 2004, it showed Mexico's federal district as having the highest level of fiscal transparency, and Baja California Sur as having the lowest (*Atlatl* no. 6, 2003, 5; *Atlatl* no. 10, 2004, 1).

19. This study finds no relationship between the measures of corruption by state and the sanctions spelled out in state penal codes (*Atlatl* no. 9, 2004, 2).

20. These reports are available at http://www.funcionpublica.gob.mx/code/doctos/informe_fase2/reporte_esp.pdf. The OECD also offers a number of reports relating to corruption and ethics. Its 1996 report "Ethics in Public Service: Matters and Current Practices," for example, provides eight components of "ethical infrastructure," while its 1998 report "Recommendations for Improvement in Ethical Conduct of Public Service" lays out twelve principles for "ethical management of public service" (see OECD 2000, cited in Martínez Puón 2002).

21. This point comes from the experience of promoting human rights. According to Human Rights Watch (1999, cited in Silva 2007, 183), only when NGOs and human

rights commissions have applied pressure are abuse investigations concluded and responsible officers punished.

22. There is no doubt that targeting the culture in the fight against corruption, and promoting popular participation, are objectives shared by the international anticorruption movement and constitute part of the new orthodoxy on corruption. Robert Klitgaard (1988, 58, 186), for instance, points to both the need to change the public's "attitudes toward corruption" and participation as vital in the fight against corruption (see also Klitgaard, Maclean-Abaroa, Parris 2000; Manion 2004). At the level of international activism, Transparency International certainly champions this approach. Its nonconfrontational strategy centers on education and mobilization. According to Fredrik Galtung (2001b, 200), Transparency International's "most focused interest today is on empowering, equipping, and rapidly training a global web of tri-sectoral partners to actively regain control of and responsibility for all their interactions." Strategies such as the integrity pact are designed specifically to cut through the prisoner's dilemma facing business and its competitors, in order to break what Galtung (2001b, 195) calls the "corruption scenario."

23. Examples of drug-related corruption are plentiful. Appendix B provides some examples.

24. On the infiltration of narcotrafficking into electoral campaigns and politics at the state level, see "Bienvenido a la narcopolítica" 2007; Ravelo 2007; "Narcopartidismo 'militante'" 2007.

25. Power within the unions, despite having been curbed by decisions of the courts (*SourceMex* April 25, 2001), remains concentrated (see Rendón Corona 2001).

4

Fox's Anticorruption Reforms

Shifting from the structural to the institutional, analysis now turns to the anticorruption reforms undertaken by President Vicente Fox.[1] Reflecting the dominant institutional approach in the literature and its strong policy orientation, recommendations of institutional changes to battle corruption abound, ranging from "off-the-shelf" diagnostic guides and sample pieces of legislation outlawing conflict of interest or protecting whistleblowers, to "toolkits" crammed with the best practices from around the globe (Transparency International 2002a). Robert Klitgaard (1988), author of one of the earliest texts on controlling corruption, stressed four keys to an effective anticorruption program: (1) prosecute and punish a few top officials to break the culture of impunity, (2) improve bureaucratic systems to reduce discretionary authority and enhance the competitive environment, (3) bolster the incentives for public officials, and (4) involve the public through surveys, educational programs, consultations, and watchdog organizations.

Continuity and Discontinuity: The Historical Context

Before detailing the multifaceted Fox program, it is important first to provide historical context. At one level, Fox was clearly not the first Mexican president to pursue anticorruption reforms (see Morris 1991). In fact, recent Mexican presidents railed publicly against corruption, and pursued many of the tasks recommended by Klitgaard. Presidents Luis Echeverría (1970–1976) and José López Portillo (1976–1982), for example, implemented reforms that strengthened the mechanisms of budgetary control. President Miguel de la Madrid (1982–1988) instituted further controls on the budget, transparency, and the conduct of public servants through his high-profile "Moral Renovation" campaign (Arrellano Gault and Guerrero Amparán 2003). He established the Office of the Comptroller General (Franco-Barrios 2003, 17), instituted a system requiring public servants to declare their assets, reformed the overarching Ley de Responsibilidades to increase the penalties for illicit conduct and broaden its reach to apply to families of public officials, initiated a program of administrative simplification, and created mechanisms for citizens to report on official wrongdoing (Franco-Barrios 2003; Martínez Puón 2002; Sánchez González 2004, 272).[2] In addition, de la Madrid jailed a handful of corrupt officials from the prior administration, including the head of Petroleos Mexicanos (PEMEX), Jorge Díaz Serrano. President Carlos Salinas de Gortari (1988–1994), in turn, pursued a program of administrative simplification that sought to decentralize and deregulate government operations, reduce bureaucratic response times, and eliminate procedures (Franco-Barrios 2003, 18). At the same time, he struck a blow against entrenched clientelistic networks, jailing a number of officials from the prior administration for corruption (see Mitchell 2005).

With a more intense focus on corruption and brandishing the ideas of new public management theory,[3] President Ernesto Zedillo (1994–2000) launched a wildly ambitious public administration modernization program during his term. He sought to derail corruption by (further) simplifying bureaucratic procedures, reducing discretionary authority, promoting a civil service system, improving the culture of service, adopting performance evaluations, and enhancing citizen involvement in decisionmaking (Arrellano Gault and Guerrero Amparán 2003, 161; Franco-Barrios 2003, 5, 19; Martínez Puón 2002; Sánchez González 2004, 369).[4] Zedillo created a program of social *contralorías,* empowering citizens to monitor public works projects, stiffened the penalties for corruption, and strengthened the government's ability to confiscate property during a corruption investigation. Zedillo also changed the name and function of the comptroller's office to the Secretaría de la Contraloría y Desarrollo Administrativo (SECODAM) (Sánchez González 2004, 278), created an elaborate electronic bidding system known as Compranet to handle public procurement contracts in an evenhanded way, instituted a simulated user program (Usuario Simulado) to detect corruption using undercover methods, and even helped organize what was perhaps the first conference on the topic of corruption in Mexico, "Transparencia y Corrupcion: Tendencias en México," held in Washington, D.C., in November of 1999. Zedillo, moreover, penned the Inter-American Convention Against Corruption in March 1996 (ratified May 27, 1997); as well as the Organization for Economic Cooperation and Development (OECD) antibribery agreement in December 1997, thereby signaling Mexico's commitment to work domestically and internationally to fight corruption (López Presa 1998 provides a good overview of the reforms under Zedillo). Zedillo's 1995–2000 "National Program for Public Safety" also targeted entrenched corruption within the criminal justice system. His administration criminalized organized crime and money laundering, raised the salaries of law enforcement officials, improved law enforcement training, fired hundreds of drug agents for accepting bribes, and restructured agencies (Global Integrity 2004; Ugalde 2002).[5]

It is clear from this brief overview not only that such efforts largely failed to curb deep-seated corruption, but also that Fox does not represent a complete break with the past. Fox did not have to cobble together an anticorruption program from scratch, but instead inherited some important anticorruption initiatives (Compranet and Declarnet, Usuario Simulado, administrative simplification) and built on previous national debates on civil service reform and transparency.[6] Even the much heralded transparency law—considered by many as the most important anticorruption development during the Fox years—traces its origins back to the 1977 constitutional reform (Article 6) under López Portillo that granted citizens the right to information. This view of continuity—that envisions Fox as part of a protracted process—fits neatly with the notion of Mexico's gradual political transition. Nevertheless, despite this modicum of continuity, the Fox anticorruption effort remains qualitatively distinct from the efforts of his predecessors because of the underlying political changes. Whereas prior anticorruption campaigns were designed and orchestrated by the heads of the hegemonic political party, unfolded within an authoritarian setting, and sought, among other things, to maintain the hegemony of the Partido Revolucionario Institucional (PRI) and protect the authoritarian regime rather than alter it, Fox led the first anticorruption effort by a democratically elected president with no formal links to the prior authoritarian regime.

Prioritizing Corruption

Recognizing corruption as the PRI's Achilles heel, Vicente Fox, the charismatic, former governor of the state of Guanajuato, routinely denounced the entrenched corruption of the PRI and the cynicism it had bred throughout his presidential campaign, while affirming his steadfast commitment to fight it. In a speech before the National Federation of Lawyers on September 29, 1999, for example, he made clear his understanding of the scope of the problem:

> Corruption is of such magnitude that in public debates, [and] academic discussions . . . it is characterized as an intrinsic component of Mexican political culture; an indelible trait of the national idiosyncrasy; an endemic phenomenon, with deep historic and cultural roots. . . . Corruption is of such magnitude that a part of society believes that all efforts to eradicate it will end up being useless tasks, an unequal and catastrophic confrontation between political will and hard cultural reality. The truth is that corruption has clear origins. The post-Revolutionary regime made corruption a preferred instrument of political control. . . . In the name of the public interest, thousands of officials perpetrated an unknown number of corrupt acts in order to ensure the

survival and reproduction of the political system. . . . The cooptation of dissident groups in return for rewards, the bribing of social and opposition leaders, or the distribution of monetary payments to journalists, all became the signs of the times.

He went on to cast corruption as "a social phenomenon with origins in political and economic arrangements and specific institutions," and promised "to combat corruption without privilege or protections, and without political or partisan vengeance."[7]

Key to conquering corruption was to clarify the abuses of the past and bring to justice those responsible:

Without clarification and, in pertinent cases, the punishment of the illicit acts committed under cover of a system of complicities, it will be impossible to break the enclave of power that chokes the daily lives of Mexicans. It will run the risk of reproducing the old practices in a new context. The investigation into the past should be oriented toward the needs of the future and not a desire for vengeance. Clarification of acts of corruption should proceed with a high sense of responsibility without a witch-hunt or incriminations of a partisan nature. Adequate instruments and precise limits to the amounts and time in which to call those accountable must be defined; and it should proceed with the caution necessary to avoid a generalized climate of suspicion and accusations that frustrate all efforts to reconstruct the credibility and legitimacy of the state, state authorities and its representatives.

What he considered past abuses, subsequent interviews revealed, included the "dirty wars" of the 1960s and 1970s, the connection between power and drug trafficking, "everything that occurred during the *sexenio* of Salinas," and the operation of Fondo Bancario de Protección al Ahorro (FOBAPROA)—the agency that handled the government's bailout of the nation's banking system in the mid-1990s (*La Jornada* October 12, 2000).

During the inauguration, Fox declared corruption a priority of his administration: "The fight against corruption that until now was considered an objective of secondary importance, will, beginning today, have the character of a national priority." He announced the formation of the Comisión Intersecretarial para la Transparencia y el Combate a la Corrupción en la Administración Pública Federal (CITCC), which, he assured, would make anticorruption the responsibility of all agencies of the federal administration, not just SECODAM, and promised to release a statement of his income and properties to create an example of propriety. He also committed members of his cabinet to making similar declarations of holdings, deposit them in a trust, and present the information to SECODAM and any judicial authority requesting it (*La Reforma* January 31, 2001), and made all the members of his team publicly pledge to uphold a new "code of ethics" (*La Reforma* December 1, 2001).[8] The anticorruption rhetoric was thick and contagious throughout the new Partido Acción Nacional (PAN) administration during those early days, becoming a key dimension to the official line of the government.[9]

Policymaking and Coordination

Fox's broad vision for transforming Mexican public administration and fighting corruption, encompassed in Chapter 4 of the 2001–2006 Plan Nacional de Desarrollo, centered on the Agenda de Buen Gobierno. Designed by the Presidential Office for Governmental Innovation, this broad strategy called for a complete reorientation of public management in order to adapt to institutional and efficient criteria rather than political criteria (SFP 2005b, 33). The government, in fact, touted it as "a permanent style of management and reinvention of government" (SFP 2005b, 42). As part of this reform, Fox established the CITCC just three days after taking office, as promised during the inauguration, charging it with elaborating and coordinating policies and actions to combat corruption, strengthening transparency in the federal administration, and conducting annual follow-ups on the programs instituted within the various agencies of the government. An interministerial body, the CITCC incorporated all eighteen secretaries of state, the attorney general, the directors of the various decentralized agencies (SAT, PEMEX, CFE, LyFC, CNA, ISSSTE, IMSS, ASA, CAPUFE, and LOTENAL), SECODAM's undersecretary for citizen attention, and five officials from the president's staff, and was presided over by the secretary of SECODAM. The CITCC reflected a broad-based approach whereby all agencies of the government, not just SECODAM (which in April 2003 became the Secretaría de la Función Pública [SFP]), would take on the task of battling corruption.

During its initial meeting on January 30, 2001, the CITCC agreed that each agency of the government would establish and fund a permanent working group designed to orchestrate and monitor anticorruption efforts within its respective area, comply with the activities and goals of the CITCC, and provide trimester reports to the executive secretary on its advances. Over the course of the six-year term, the CITCC held twelve ordinary and two special sessions, signed thirty-nine cross-institutional agreements (seventeen ongoing) covering a wide range of programs and initiatives, issued a variety of reports on the advances of the programs within each government entity, developed and broadly applied a measure of transparency (the Indicador de Seguimiento para la Transparencia [IST]), and promoted a series of publicity campaigns against corruption. Unfortunately, Fox rarely attended the meetings. The cross-institutional accords ranged from the development of programs throughout the government to recognize and reward public servants for integrity, improve internal regulations, and draft codes of conduct, to an assortment of initiatives to develop electronic procedures and services within the government, evaluate public opinions on the CITCC's honesty, and create integrity systems linking the public and private sectors.[10] Though far too numerous to examine separately, many of the main initiatives are discussed below. The CITCC also created three subcommissions, covering access to information (established in June 2003 to implement measures for compliance with the new law and harmonize criteria within the federal government), improved measures (established in June 2003 to create the methodological tools to measure progress), and compliance with the United Nations anticorruption treaty (established in April 2004 to coordinate implementation of the provisions of the treaty).

Fox's overarching 2000–2006 anticorruption program took the title Programa Nacional de Combate a la Corrupción y Fomento a la Transparencia y el Desarrollo Administrativo. Unfurled at the CITCC's initial meeting, approved during its subsequent meeting in April, and incorporated into the 2001–2006 Plan Nacional de Desarrollo (though it was not published in the *Diario Oficial* until April 2002), the Programa Nacional presents the government's broad, integrative strategy to battle corruption and impunity.[11] Its mission was straightforward: "reduce the level of corruption in the country and give absolute transparency to the management and conduct of the institutions and public servants of the federal public administration." It lays out four objectives, six strategic lines of action, and over thirty initial strategic projects (see Reyes 2004b; Gutiérrez and López de Nava 2004; http://www.programaanticorrupcion.gob.mx/presentacion.html). The four objectives are to (1) prevent and eliminate corruption and impunity, (2) control and detect corruption, (3) sanction corruption and impunity, and (4) improve transparency and engage society. Among the many strategic projects, the Programa Nacional calls for administrative modernization and simplification, electronic government, improved professional and ethical training of public officials, the establishment of a civil service career system, the strengthening of measures and mechanisms to denounce and sanction corruption, the establishment of integrity pacts and the further development of *contralorías sociales,* and greater transparency.

Though the interdepartmental CITCC was established to coordinate policy at the broadest level and enlist the participation of all federal agencies via the working groups or liaisons, primary responsibility for implementing the government's anticorruption initiatives (as well as for overseeing the executive branch and implementing the basic laws governing public officials and public property) resides with SECODAM. According to the Ley Federal de Responsabilidades Administrativas de los Servidores Públicos, SECODAM has the power to investigate, process, and punish corruption within the public administration and shares with the Auditoria Superior de la Federación (ASF) the task of auditing government spending. Though SECODAM can investigate and impose administrative sanctions, it lacks the power to prosecute officials and citizens for corruption. These tasks rest solely with the Procuraduría General de la República (PGR) (attorney general).[12] Generally, SECODAM pursues its mission through two primary mechanisms: central administrative units and internal control organs (*órganos internos de control* [OICs]) located within each department of the federal government, but reporting directly to SECODAM. In 2005, there were 213 OICs within the dependencies of the central federal administration, and 40 *delegados* and *comisarios públicos* assigned to oversee the operations of the semiautonomous state-owned entities.

Objectives of the Anticorruption Program

Objective 1: Prevent and Eliminate Corruption and Impunity

The Fox government saw prevention as the key to its anticorruption strategy, making the catching and punishing of corrupt officials secondary, a view that paralleled the nonconfrontational approach championed by Transparency International. According to the government, the key to prevention was to develop a new "consciousness among the public servants and the citizenry." This, in turn, centered on improved training of public servants, the promotion of ethics, and the creation of a more efficient, modern, and transparent administration (*La Reforma* January 28, 2001).

Critical areas: diagnostics, operational programs, and follow-ups. The initial step of the anticorruption program was diagnostic—to determine the areas where corruption occurred, identify the problems, and design solutions. At its initial meeting, the CITCC charged the working groups within the federal entities with the task of conducting an exhaustive inventory of critical areas and, under the supervision of the secretary of SECODAM, Francisco Barrios, developing operational programs to address them. The operational programs outlined the goals, methods, specific changes, timelines for implementation, and the like, needed to attend to the critical areas. After some delays and even a public scolding by Barrios, the massive diagnostic identified over 2,000 critical areas in 205 federal agencies, more than 5,000 irregular behaviors, and over 7,000 specific improvement measures. The diagnostic revealed such problems as the existence of complex regulatory environments where discretionary and subjective decisionmaking prevailed without enforcement mechanisms or oversight; oversized bureaucratic structures that reduced creativity and productivity; the lack of efficient incentives for good behavior and weak technical and ethical capacities; opaque operations; control mechanisms not oriented to prevention and detection of corrupt systems and acts, but rather to the simple verification of the execution of regulations; among many others (Franco-Barrios 2003, 23–24).

The government carried out a second, less high-profile diagnostic study of risk areas in 2004 in conjunction with the Modelo Integral de Desempeño de Órganos de Vigilancia y Control (MIDO). Conducted by the more than 200

OICs, *delegados,* and *comisarios públicos,* and involving the participation of the CITCC, this detailed program mapped the risk of corruption in 722 services, programs, and processes within 216 institutions based on the levels of risk, discretion, accountability, supply, demand, clients, and so forth, and provided the methodology for the operational programs during 2005 and 2006. A major assessment and planning tool, MIDO seeks to incorporate an anticorruption focus into the improvement of the delivery of services.

Numerous operational programs have been developed, and their sophistication and implementation vary widely across government entities.[13] The CITCC website (http://www.programaanticorrupcion.gob.mx/) presents complete information and periodic reports on all the operational programs within the federal agencies over the course of the *sexenio.* According to Barrio, the initial diagnostic study revealed the greatest problems in two major priority areas, procurement and contraband. In response to the first, SECODAM improved and increased the use of Compranet, the computerized system of soliciting bids for government contracts developed under the Zedillo administration. In the area of contraband, Fox brought together officials in the areas of migration, national intelligence, taxation, customs, the economy, justice, and public security, together with SECODAM secretary Barrio, to create the interinstitutional coordination needed to implement a program focusing on customs and *centros de abasto* (markets). Early crackdowns included the firing and transfer of hundreds of workers from Tijuana to the Mexico City airport.[14] According to Fox: "We want to make clear that this time the federal government is serious in going against contraband and illegal imports that foment informal commerce [black market] and weaken small and medium size industries in the county" (*La Reforma* April 3, 2001).[15]

Building a professional bureaucracy. Arguably the priority within Fox's broad program was the development of a more professional and efficient government. The multiple efforts in this area encompassed the development and promotion of codes of conduct, ethical training, better recruitment techniques, programs of recognition, and above all, the passage and initial implementation of a civil service system in 2003.[16]

Both Fox and Barrios placed great importance on ethics. Rafael Martínez Puón (2002, 19) calls ethics the "backbone" of the "responsibilization" model adopted by Fox. As Barrios suggested: "We have to pursue a situation where ethical themes start becoming an everyday thing in public offices, that we don't just ask whether the law allows something or not, but rather if the subject is ethically valid or not" (*La Reforma* January 28, 2001). To this end, the government published a federal code of ethics for the *sexenio* in 2002, presenting "clear rules so that within the acts of public servants a conduct of dignity prevails that responds to the needs of society and that their conduct is oriented toward the specifics of the case." Used during the swearing-in of the Fox cabinet, the code includes sections on the common good, integrity, honesty, impartiality, justice, transparency, accountability, cultural and ecological arenas, generosity, equality, respect, and leadership.[17] In addition to the adoption of this generic code, the Programa Nacional also called on each public institution to develop its own more specific codes of conduct (*Atlatl* no. 4, 2002, 5).

In its quest to promote a new ethics within the administration, the government emphasized improved training and recruitment. SECODAM signed agreements with the Universidad Iberoamericana and the Instituto Tecnológica de Estudios Superiores de Monterrey (ITESM; also known as Tec de Monterrey) to design and conduct an ethics program for public officials. The ITESM, for example, created a virtual course on ethics with funding from the World Bank called "Open and Participatory Government," noted in Chapter 3. Interestingly, however, the course was not obligatory, nor a requirement for advancement or higher pay (*El Mural* July 29, 2001).

One of the most important anticorruption reforms under Fox was the new civil service law, adopted in April 2003.[18] The product of roughly two years of negotiations and slight modification in Congress, the law established merit as the basis for access to federal employment (Article 2), specified entry requirements (Article 21), and prohibited conflict of interest (Article 11) (*Atlatl* no. 6, 2003, 6). The law applies only to the middle to upper reaches of the administration, however, including the general directors and subdirector, the department chiefs, and the liaisons, representing approximately 62,000 of the 649,000 employees in the federal administration (the remainder are part of the labor union of government workers) (Guerrero 2004, 115; SFP 2005b, 154).[19] The law also eliminated SECODAM, creating the SFP in its place and charging it with the task of creating and operating the new civil service system (Sánchez González 2004, 422–423).

Though the new law took effect in October 2003, implementation has been slow and much is still pending, a factor that diminishes its impact on corruption during the period under analysis. The government did not publish the accompanying implementing regulations until April 2004 (*Atlatl* no. 4, 2002, 3) and these merely set the stage for the elaboration of the official 2004–2006 professional service program, which listed objectives and strategic lines of action, established professionalization and selection committees inside each federal entity (SFP 2005b, 56),[20] and created a computerized system called TrabajaEn to post vacancies, receive applications, and conduct examinations.[21] In May 2004, the Secretaría de Hacienda y Crédito Público (SHCP) and the SFP presented their diagnostic report to Congress, revealing the wide range of problems in the organization of the federal administration, including duplication of services, lack of information, ill-defined missions and purposes, lack of planning and evaluations, nonexistent job descriptions, lengthy processes, an unwieldy and nonsystematic pay structure, and lack of publicizing vacancies (SFP 2005b, 50, 53; see also the SFP's 2004 Encuesta Diagnostico del Servivio Profesional de Carrera survey). In essence, the report crystallized the Herculean task faced by the SFP in creating a truly merit-based, Weberian bureaucracy. By December 2004, the SFP had only certified twenty-nine (out of seventy-three) entities for the program—the first step in allowing merit-based applications—and by August 2006, according to the annual operative program, only 2,354 career public servants had been integrated into the system.[22]

Deregulation and simplification. Another part of fighting corruption and reorienting public management under Fox centered on altering the foundations of public administration itself. Programs designed to improve bureaucratic organization and reform complex procedures sought to shift the focus to the client (the citizen), improve efficiency in the delivery of services, and thereby eliminate the systemic causes of bureaucratic corruption. The government clearly envisioned this as a long-term and slow process: "This has to be part of a multi-year program in which the objective is to have agile, easy and clear procedures. The people must know what requirements they must fulfill and what they can expect from the public offices" (*La Reforma* January 28, 2001).

A wide range of programs and initiatives were nestled within the category of administrative reform. Within the presidency, Fox created the Office of Governmental Innovation to coordinate many of these efforts and, specifically, to shift administration away from one based on "norms" to one based on "results"—a key ingredient in new public management theory. Among its many efforts, the office developed an intergovernmental quality model in which it laid out a series of programs to improve performance. It created an operational quality committee to revise, redesign, and certify agencies, and developed a special quality training program for personnel within the SFP. Part of its effort included gaining ISO certification of certain bureaucratic processes. Together with the SFP, the Office of Governmental Innovation also developed a system of Evaluation and Compensation for Results—a process to review programs to determine whether they actually served a public purpose (*Público* July 31, 2001). It organized committees to improve internal regulations, simplify legal norms, and produce an updated and digital inventory of laws and regulations. It conducted meetings that brought together those making regulations with the users of the services, and drafted a rapid reference guide to help public officials find information on regulations. A program called "Citizen Language" even sought to "translate" the bureaucratic language of regulations into the language of regular citizens, while an integrated system of information on patterns of government reportedly eliminated duplication in 20 percent of all government programs. A major initiative in this effort centered on the elaboration of "letters of commitment to citizens"—also called citizen charters—which lay out in clear language the responsibilities of an agency to the citizen, guaranteeing a certain level of performance. These charters provide citizens with all the information needed to carry out a bureaucratic operation or to obtain a government service, information on how to file a complaint and how to appeal a decision, and even a section titled "What happens if we don't comply?" In 2003 the SFP helped craft eleven such letters and by the beginning of 2005 the total had risen to eighty-four, resulting in greater transparency, a reduction in operational costs, increased productivity, and the development of a culture of quality (SFP 2005b, 83).

Another component of these many "managerialist reforms" was the further development in the use of the Internet and computer technology.[23] Per the fourth line of action within the Agenda de Buen Gobierno, the Fox government built on many of the advances begun under Zedillo's Promap. The project e-México, for example, focused on the diffusion of digital communication centers across the country. The program e-Gobierno, in turn, concentrated on the introduction of computers to handle government work. Examples of e-Gobierno include the Innovation Portal, which promotes government innovation among public servants, and the Citizen Portal, created in 2002 to provide a focus on education, health, employment, housing, and the like, for citizens. Compranet, though developed under the prior administration, was further improved and expanded by SECODAM: "With this process of modernization, Compranet will gradually become an efficient tool contributing to the fight against corruption and will be the principal system of purchases at the global level" (*La Reforma* August 13, 2001). In January 2002, the government also initiated an electronic bureaucracy system, known as Tramitanet with the objective of "bringing the government closer to citizens, retire millions of steps, create a culture of transparency, integrity and efficiency" (*Atlatl* no. 1, 2002, 3). This program permits citizens to consult the Internet to discover the steps to obtain government service and eventually to complete these steps online (CITCC 2002). A similar program for both public servants and citizens known as Normativanet distributes and updates all the legal and regulatory changes (see http://www.normteca.gob.mx).

The Programa Nacional's jurisdiction, like SECODAM's, relates only to the federal government. SECODAM does conduct audits of the spending of federal funds by state and local governments, but not of state funds. Given the process of decentralization in recent years, there is a clear need for greater control and vigilance at the local level. The Programa Nacional thus included coordination with states and municipalities as one line of strategic action. Over the years, SECODAM signed a number of agreements *(convenios)* with states to coordinate anticorruption efforts and provide technical support. The federal government signed agreements with twenty-three states in 2001 as part of a program to strengthen state systems of control and evaluation in order to enhance management, collaboration, and transparency in the fight against corruption, as well as agreements with all thirty-one states to oversee the use of federal funds (SECODAM 2002). Besides facilitating joint action to strengthen oversight systems, the former program also resulted in a catalog of successful experiences in the states (SFP 2005a). The government also inserted a clause into the traditional federal-state coordination agreements that required states to learn about the international treaties on corruption (SFP 2005a), and developed a federal diagnostic program involving the comptrollers of the thirty-two entities (the thirty-one states plus the federal district) to gauge the level of transparency within states (SFP 2006). In addition, the SFP updated its fiscal manual, elaborated a verification guide, and designed an informational system to assist states in conducting oversight. It also formed a permanent committee of state-federal auditors; conducted and coordinated a variety of training programs for states and municipalities (SFP 2005b, 248); and promoted and facilitated the development of Compranet systems at the state level by providing technical support and training for local officials, including *contralorías sociales* and two subcomptrollers elected democratically in a neighborhood assembly. According to the government, over 5,000 *contralorías sociales* were being created every year, with 87 percent of their members receiving training, resulting in a 92 percent level of supervision over public projects using federal funds (SFP 2005b, 248).

Objective 2: Control and Detect Corruption

Despite its emphasis on prevention, the government recognized that controls on corruption were weak to nonexistent and devoted considerable attention to improving its systems of vigilance, internal oversight, and handling of complaints, as well as to developing a legal framework to control corruption. According to the Plan Nacional de Desarrollo:

> The existing mechanisms and control procedures were not oriented toward detecting corrupt practices specifically, but to verifying strict compliance with the law; they lacked mechanisms to allow for the control or improvement of procedures or to make the organization of work more transparent and more efficient in the provision of public services; it put a large emphasis on formal oversight and a corrective focus which has resulted in the irreparable loss of resources. (cited in SFP 2005b, 225)

With this diagnosis, the government stressed the need to "transform the internal organs of control within the dependencies and entities with a preventive focus that concentrates attention on the analysis and improvement of internal controls, in paying proper attention to citizen complaints, and in carrying out audits directed at substantive aspects of public activity and at the results that should be obtained" (cited in SFP 2005b, 225). Or, as Barrio once noted: "We need the auditor to become much more perceptive, canny and not just involved in reviewing paperwork" (*La Reforma* January 28, 2001).

The task of controlling corruption within the Mexican public administration falls primarily to the SFP, and more specifically to its central auditors and the internal oversight organs *(órganos internos de vigilancia),* which include the OICs (SFP officials assigned to each dependency within the federal administration) and the *delegados* and *comisarios públicos* (assigned to the decentralized state entities). The OICs oversee roughly 80 percent of the federal budget (SFP 2005b, 135n) and evaluate and assess the transparency and anticorruption activities within the agency. According to one SECODAM official, strengthening internal auditors is the department's greatest challenge.[24] In an effort to strengthen internal controls, SECODAM intensified the training and oversight of the OICs. Among its various efforts, it contracted with the Instituto Panamericano de Alta Dirección de Empresa (IPADE) to train internal auditors, organized a specialized two-week course on techniques for detecting and investigating fraud in November 2001 (in conjunction with Project AAA of the US government) in order to "form a specialized group of auditors and lawyers to take charge of investigations of crimes against the public treasury and other forms of fraud and corruption," and sent OIC officials from the Secretaría de Gobernación (SEGOB) to a conference of the Institute of Internal Auditors in Las Vegas in January 2002 (*Atlatl* no. 1, 2002, 3, 6). It also sponsored a satellite seminar in 2003 titled "Introduction to Professional Norms and Practices of Government Auditors" (*Atlatl* no. 7, 2003, 1) and even sent internal auditors to the Second National Congress of Internal Auditors in Ecuador in 2004 (*Atlatl* no. 17, 2004, 2). To strengthen oversight of the auditors themselves, SECODAM formed the General Coordination of Commissaries and Internal Comptrollers in 2001 and, according to one report, began giving economic, toxicological, and ethical exams to new auditors in order to keep a close eye on their property holdings (*La Reforma* August 14, 2001).

More broadly, through a program to strengthen internal control launched in September 2001, the government sought to provide not just OICs, but also other officials in the administration, with better information and better tools to foster an ethical environment, to evaluate and recognize risks, and to develop more rigorous control processes. According to its 2002 report, SECODAM strengthened 98 strategic processes of internal control in that year alone (SECODAM 2002). It also increased the number of meetings between *delegados* and *comisarios públicos* and government agencies (1,008 meetings) to evaluate the conduct of government institutions (SECODAM 2002). By 2003, the focus had shifted to establishing a clear set of norms to help superiors and mid-level officials control their respective areas. The government also assembled a guide outlining norms on basic control (including a code of ethics and transparency and anticorruption programs), evaluation of risks, and mechanisms to evaluate internal systems of control. The guide also recommended the use of surveys of clients as an independent check on the activities of agencies (SFP 2005, 215).

At the same time, the SFP introduced a system of external reviews of internal control mechanisms, and even developed a sophisticated tool to measure progress and promote planning. In one part of this system, the SFP contracted members of the Academia Mexicana de Auditoria Integral al Desempeño (AMAID) to conduct an audit to determine if a government agency had well defined and quantified objectives, had developed plans and practices to determine whether goals and objectives match resources, had taken a long-term view of processes, had established goals and strategic indicators and quantitative and qualitative standards, had organized personnel consistently, and had optimized utilization of resources. The auditors, in return, identified the major causes of the problems and defined corrective measures, together with those responsible for the agency (SFP 2005b). In 2004, the SFP selected as part of a pilot program four parastate entities and one decentralized entity for external review.

As part of its enhanced controls, in 2004 the government also established MIDO, alluded to earlier. Crafted by the Coordinación General de Órganos de Vigilancia y Control, MIDO forms the bases for the direction, administration, planning, and evaluations of the OIC and the *delegados* and *comisarios públicos*. Broadly, MIDO seeks to

> guarantee that the *Órganos Internos de Control and the Delegados y Comisarios Públicos* contribute to the reduction of the risks of corruption and of opacity in the federal public administration, as well as to make these measures effective by way of an adequate relationship with the dependencies, entities, deconcentrated organs and the PGR, with a focus on preventive control, a proper vigilance of the public management, and an effective application of corrective measures.[25]

In 2004, MIDO included 26 measures for OICs and 12 for the delegates and public commissions, and the model was administered by 214 OICs and 40 delegates and commissions. Called the "backbone of the SFP" by the government, "MIDO has sought to move from the logic of strict legal compliance to a logic based on results" (SFP 2005b, 234).

Another strategy to strengthen internal controls centered on improving the role and effectiveness of citizen complaints. In fact, the administration sought to create a "culture of complaints," which, it held, depended on four factors: (1) the public having information about its rights and proper procedures; (2) reduced costs of presenting a complaint, including the costs of potential reprisals; (3) the elasticity of demand for the service (if the service is necessary and a monopoly, the greater the likelihood that people will exercise voice); and (4) the effectiveness of the system of handling complaints (Are wrongdoers being sanctioned? Are problems being resolved?). Uncovering a huge backlog of complaints in the system, inefficient attention to complaints, and lack of immediate action, SECODAM created a new office at the subdirector level focused on citizen attention *(atención ciudadana)*. This office, in turn, created two citizen hotline systems, the Sistema Electrónico de Atención Ciudadana (SEAC) and enhanced the previously existing Sistema de Atención Telefónica a la Ciudadana (SACTEL). Improvements have not only made it easier to register a complaint and created a system for the government to use the information more effectively, but also have guaranteed the citizen an official response and reduced the burden on the citizen to provide proof of wrongdoing. In the first year, SEAC handled over 22,000 petitions, including 14,520 regarding complaints and reports, 1,610 regarding irregularities, and 6,708 regarding suggestions (SECODAM 2002). By 2005, SACTEL was operating twenty-four hours a day, seven days a week, was receiving about 137,000 calls a year, and was ISO-certified (SFP 2005b).

Fox also strengthened two internal control mechanisms developed under the prior administration: Declarnet and Usuario Simulado (Simulated User). In accordance with the Ley de Responsabilidades (and an executive order published in April 2002), all public officials and civil servants must provide a statement of net worth (property and income) within sixty days of taking office, an annual update, and a final statement within sixty days of leaving office. Fox broadened this system to include officials not originally covered, and computerized the submission and handling of the statements through Declarnet, providing more effective oversight by auditors and the public (Kossick and Minutti 2007, 306). By 2005, the government had received 261,044 declarations of wealth (SFP 2005a). The Usuario Simulado program is a sort of undercover operation run by the SFP. Started under Zedillo, the use and focus of these operations expanded under Fox. The program operates by two modes. One involves areas where, based on prior investigation, suspicious wrongdoing already exists. Undercover workers from the SFP then simulate an administrative process with the idea of finding solid evidence of corruption using videos and recordings. The other mode entails a simpler—and less confrontational—verification approach, whereby public servants and social service individuals operating undercover solicit government services to verify the quality and transparency of the services. In 2005, the government reported that it had conducted 5,934 inspections of procedures and services through Usuario Simulado (SFP 2005c, 44) and caught 90 public officials engaged in corrupt activities (Cámara de Diputados 2005).

Objective 3: Sanction Corruption and Impunity

The Programa Nacional's third objective centers on sanctioning corruption and ending impunity. Efforts in this area encompass, first, the strengthening of the legal framework and the powers of both the SFP and the PGR, and second, the investigation and sanctioning of corrupt officials from the past and present. Initial efforts included legal reforms to the criminal code in December 2001 and to the Ley de Responsabilidades in March 2002. The former boosted the sentence for influence trafficking and illicit enrichment from three to eight years, and reclassified crimes committed by public servants to felony status, thereby allowing for the imprisonment of the accused until trial rather than guaranteeing their release on bail (*Atlatl* no. 1, 2002, 2). The reform to the Ley de Responsabilidades—known as "Barrio's Law"—similarly strengthened SECODAM's investigative and sanctioning powers. It removed the obstacles of the bank secrecy law, allowed SECODAM broader powers to confiscate property as a precautionary step in its investigations, expanded the time frame to punish corrupt acts, and provided a mechanism for indemnity to individuals suffering damages (*Atlatl* no. 2, 2002, 4). The new law also required SECODAM to keep a registry of civil servants and their declarations of net worth. According to Guillermo Cejudo and Laura Sour (2007, 7), "This new law surpasses the exclusively punitive and *a posteriori* character of the prior laws of responsibility, since it integrates measures to prevent illicit conduct of public servants and establishes norms to develop and apply ethical values on the public's affairs." To bolster the ability of the government to investigate and prosecute corruption even further, in June 2004, the government announced the creation of two special anticorruption prosecutors within the PGR. The first, the Subprocuraduría de Investigación Especializada de Delitos Federales (SIEDF), focuses on cases involving officials from all areas of the federal administration. The second concentrates solely on cases within the PGR itself and works in coordination with the Visitaduría General (internal affairs) of the PGR.

An important component in sanctioning wrongdoing and crippling impunity involves efforts to clarify and pursue past cases of corruption, as promised during Fox's presidential campaign. Many, including Klitgaard, as noted, consider going after those of the past or "frying big fish" critical in terms of sending the proper message to public officials, and gaining credibility and support among the public. During the initial year of the new government, SECODAM enjoyed an extremely high public profile in this regard. Few days passed without it capturing the headlines with allegations of corruption and pledges of pursuit. In January 2001, for instance, it announced that it was conducting audits of Governor Roberto Albores of Chiapas, PEMEX, and the Comisión Federal de Electricidad (CFE) (*La Reforma* January 19, 2001). In March, it removed the head of PEMEX's internal control organ after discovering a triangulated kickback scheme in which companies were providing technical assistance without public bidding. At the same time, SECODAM reported that it had uncovered financial losses totaling 215 million pesos (US$23 million) involving PEMEX and the Instituto Politécnico Nacional (*La Reforma* April 7, 2001). In April, the secretary of economy made headlines by stating publicly what many already knew: that corruption was rampant within PEMEX and that irregularities within the CFE cost over 600 million pesos (US$71 million). Such news provided the occasion for the secretary to call for sweeping legal reforms, including changes to the Ley de Responsibilidades (Morales 2001). In May, SECODAM reported an ongoing investigation into PEMEX for the illegal sale of diesel, having already discovered fraud in PEMEX's 1999–2000 budget (*La Reforma* May 24, 2001). Meanwhile, agency audits dating back to 1997 revealed extensive misuse of federal funds under Governor Albores of Chiapas, including nonexistent public works projects, half-finished projects, and many other irregularities (see Idalia Gómez 2001).

In addition to the various reports and the high-profile crackdown on customs agents noted earlier, other reports spotlighted SECODAM's dramatic and heroic acts against police wrongdoing, misuse of funds in the Ministries of Tourism and Education and the Social Security Institute, and its successful prosecution of a high-ranking national lottery official. In February 2001, for instance, SECODAM filed charges with the PGR against the Policía Federal Preventiva (PFP) for irregularities in the purchase of nine helicopters and three planes during the prior *sexenio* (*La Reforma* February 19, 2001). Three months later, SECODAM audits produced three more cases that it filed with the attorney general for the sale of middle- and upper-level jobs in the PFP (*El Mural* June 26, 2001). In early July, SECODAM captured front-page headlines for detecting more than 440 irregular acts within the Ministry of Education, including the existence of *aviadores,* or ghost workers; "speed money" (bribes paid to speed up bureaucratic processes); and alteration of information: all of this as part of the broader anticorruption project of identifying "critical areas" (*El Mural* July 5, 2001). About a month later, SECODAM filed charges against three directors of the Social Security Institute for the diversion of 14 million pesos (US$1.5 million) of federal funds and the existence of 790 *aviadores.* The investigation also highlighted salary overpayments to 250 workers (*El Público* August 7, 2001). In April, SECODAM reported the removal of the internal comptroller in the Ministry of Tourism and also filed charges against, among others, the recently extradited Oscar Espinosa Villareal, former secretary of tourism and former chief of the Mexico City government (*La Reforma* April 6, 2001). Finally, in June the government fined and sentenced to three years in prison the former head of the national lottery for pilfering over 1 billion pesos (US$109 million) (*El Mural* June 26, 2001). Citing this dimension in the battle against corruption, Barrio in his semester report claimed that by May 2001 the agency had produced seventeen denunciations (eleven administrative and six criminal), that it had detected diversion of funds totaling 957 million pesos (US$105 million), and that fifty-nine officials were awaiting trial. Barrio also mentioned twenty-three cases dealing with the state of Chiapas alone, amounting to more than 174 million pesos (US$19 million) (*La Reforma* May 25, 2001).

Among the "big fish" captured during that initial year was the former governor of Quintana Roo, Mario Villanueva, who was arrested in May 2001 following a lengthy manhunt; as mentioned previously, the former director of the national lottery, who received a three-year prison sentence in June (*El Mural* June 26, 2001), and in August, the extradition of Oscar Espinosa Villareal from Nicaragua for the alleged disappearance of 420 million pesos during his tenure as head of the Mexico City government (*El Público* August 7, 2001) (see Appendix B). Concurrently, the PGR also struck out at corruption within its own ranks. With General Rafael Macedo de la Concha at the helm—the military attorney, who had prosecuted the former head of the antinarcotics department, General Jesús Gutiérrez Rebollo, in the late 1990s for corruption—the PGR uncovered and reported on the sale of jobs in the PGR, the escape of a former delegate of the federal judicial police in Chihuahua, and the resignation of two top officials being investigated for corruption (see Monge and Ravelo 2001). In May 2001, the PGR reported that it had evaluated 866 officials, and sanctioned 287, including 151 firings (*El Mural* May 31, 2001).

One important and high-profile measure to attack past crimes and impunity involved the appointment in early 2001 of a special prosecutor to investigate and prosecute the abuses of past governments, the Fiscalía Especializada para Movimientos Sociales y Políticos del Pasado (FEMOSPP). Adopting this approach rather than a truth commission, the government sought to clarify events surrounding Mexico's "dirty war," particularly the repression of students in 1968 at Tlaltelolco and in 1971 on Corpus Cristi day, and to prosecute those responsible. The effort, however, was slow to produce any results and encountered an assortment of problems and setbacks. In the end, as described below, the results were minimal.

Amid the rhetorical promises of investigating and sanctioning corruption, however, the cases that attracted significant public and media attention were, not surprisingly, often accusations against Fox himself, the first lady, and members of Fox's anticorruption team, seriously undermining the president's and the anticorruption program's credibility. In Chihuahua, the local PRI-controlled state congress, for example, found nineteen irregularities during the reign of former governor Barrio, which they turned over to the state's attorney general, including a case of a bankruptcy of a company dealing with the government. Barrio—the architect of the government's anticorruption effort—dismissed the audits as "political" and the charges as unfounded (Gutiérrez 2001). To be sure, the government never filed formal charges. This minor controversy, however, paled in comparison to the scandal that erupted over the president's exorbitant purchase of household items for Los Pinos, including towels at a cost of 4,000 pesos (US$440) each. Revealed through Compranet—demonstrating a feature of the government's commitment to make the public's business transparent—the scandal forced the president to respond by firing his personal secretary, Carlos Rojas, and forced SECODAM and Congress to promise to audit presidential spending. During this period, the president also faced questions from Instituto Federal Electoral (IFE) investigators regarding foreign finances during his presidential campaign (see discussion of the Amigos de Fox case in Chapter 2 and Appendix B). Later in his term, the president's efforts to prosecute Andrés Manuel López Obrador—member of the Partido de la Revolución Democrática (PRD), mayor of Mexico City, and front-runner in the upcoming presidential election—for obstruction of justice, were widely seen as abusive and politically motivated, though the administration touted them as a demon-stration of his commitment to the rule of law (prosecution for the mayor's ini-tial failure to abide by a lower-court injunction would have prevented him from running for the presidency). Though in the end the president backed down, the affair cut further into the president's credibility and the public's faith in his anticorruption credentials, and prompted the removal of the attorney gen-eral (see Appendix B).

Cases revolving around the first lady, Marta Sahagún, brought Fox's cred-ibility further into question. In 2004, allegations surfaced that Marta had mis-managed funds in the Vamos México charity and had used her position to promote the foundation. Though a nonbinding resolution calling for a congres-sional investigation of Vamos México was introduced, it never prospered (*SourceMex* March 10, 2004). Accusations that Fox's stepchildren—the sons of Marta Sahagún—had brokered government contacts and information into their businesses, prompting a spectacular growth in their level of wealth, further tar-nished Fox's anticorruption image. This case sparked more than one congres-sional inquiry and mutual accusations on the front pages of the newspapers. Many believed that Fox was protecting the Bribiescas (see Appendix B).

Objective 4: Improve Transparency and Engage Society

The fourth objective under the Programa Nacional embraced a vast range of programs and fundamental changes in the nature of governance in Mexico. These centered largely on the adoption and implementation of the Ley de Transparencia—perhaps the single most important anticorruption measure during the Fox regime—as well as the launching of a national agreement, the Acuerdo Nacional para la Transparencia, the establishment of integrity pacts, the further development of *contralorías sociales,* and massive public relations campaigns designed to fight corruption.

Transparency. In recent years, transparency has become synonymous with an-ticorruption, as strenuously promoted by Transparency International, the World Bank, and others. Many hold transparency not only as the key to forging a new relationship between the Mexican government and its citizens, but also as a primary tool for eliminating the shadows where corruption festers. As Secre-tary Barrio emphasized: "To the extent that government management becomes more visible, the less room remains for possible acts of corruption" (*La Reforma* January 28, 2001). According to Jaime López (2002, 4), the main benefit "is that, by way of complete exposure of cases, it permits the proper consciousness and education of citizens about the problem of corruption, generating genuine sentiments of indignation toward the scourge" (on the benefits of transparency, see also Franco-Barrios 2003).

The new Ley Federal de Transparencia y Acceso a Información Pública Gubernamental was published June 11, 2002, and took effect a year later.[26]

Pursuant to Article 6 of the Constitution, which guarantees citizens the right to information, the sweeping reform law declared all information held by the government to be public and hence accessible to all. It gave citizens the right to solicit information and makes each government entity responsible for providing and updating information on structure, functions, goals, objectives, directory of personnel, monthly compensation and benefits, services provided, requirements, forms, budgetary information, results of audits, concessions, permits and authorizations granted, and reports. The law also established a separate, autonomous authority—the Instituto Federal de Acceso a la Información (IFAI), composed of five commissioners named by the president with the consent of the Senate—and made it responsible for publicizing the law, establishing and revising criteria, exercising oversight, training personnel, providing technical support, establishing policies, and resolving controversies when requests for information are denied (*Atlatl* no. 3, 2002, 10).[27] The sweeping reform applied to all aspects of the administration, Congress, and the federal courts, as well as the Comisión Nacional de Derechos Humanos (CNDH), the Bank of Mexico, public universities, administrative tribunals, and all federal entities, though the law gave these entities a year to publish their own criteria.[28] The law furthermore stipulated that the government can classify information as reserved for a period of twelve years for specific exceptions, but only concerning personal information on individuals or matters of national security (SFP 2005b, 141). The courts subsequently confirmed the power of the IFAI, declaring its decisions final and beyond challenge (*Atlatl* no. 8, 2004, 3).

Civil society programs. Under the general direction of the SFP's Unidad de Vinculación para la Transparencia and in accordance to its internal regulations, the Fox government developed a wide range of outreach anticorruption programs targeting society and culture. Striving to break the cycle of corruption, the multiple programs sought to enliven the public's cooperation with its own anticorruption initiatives, help private and social actors improve ethics and their own internal operations, and promote the production and dissemination of awareness-building materials and programs in the field.[29] These programs rested on the widely shared assumptions that "the participation of society is fundamental to prevent corruption" (SFP 2005b, 284), and that popular attitudes and culture play a fundamental role in facilitating corruption (see Chapter 8).

Social pacts formalize state-society cooperation and partnership. The government signed pacts with hundreds of social organizations, ranging from universities and professional organizations to businesses, unions, and political parties. The largest such accord, the Acuerdo Nacional para la Transparencia y el Combate a la Corrupción, was signed in February 2001 by eighty-three political, educational, and labor organizations, including the PRI, Confederación Revolucionaria de Obreros y Campesinos (CROC), Confederación de Trabajadores de México (CTM), and Confederación Nacional de Campesinos

(CNC). This massive accord acknowledged the importance of collaboration in fighting corruption and laid out a series of commitments on the part of both government and society. For their part, the social organizations agreed to (1) refrain from participating in corrupt acts with the government, (2) denounce corrupt acts and oversee honesty in government, (3) collaborate and promote information on programs designed to fight corruption, and (4) strengthen within themselves a culture of ethics that rejects corruption. Jointly, the government and social entities promised to (1) collaborate in the drive against corruption, (2) promote the recognition of honest conduct, and (3) analyze and create agreements in specific areas to avoid corruption and promote transparency in public administration. Participants also agreed to study ethical culture and incorporate that study into their educational plans, improve administrative systems, deregulate, and even promote the phrase *"ya no más mordidas"* (no more bribes) (*La Reforma* February 26, 2001).

Within this broader context, the government contracted with social organizations to monitor government operations and compliance with treaties, to train public officials, and to strengthen research on corruption (many of these joint initiatives are discussed in Chapter 3). Among the many efforts to incorporate civil society into anticorruption was the establishment of *contralorías sociales*. Though created in 1991 as part of Salinas's solidarity program and formalized under Zedillo,[30] the Fox government expanded and strengthened the *contraloría social* program. Through the Sistema Integral de Contraloría Social (SICS), the government helped design models and a forum for citizen control and vigilance, create lines of communication between citizens and government, and train government workers and citizens to use information as a means of democratic participation (SFP 2005b, 251–252). Beginning in 2001, the SFP promoted the use of *contralorías sociales* in large social programs like Oportunidades, Atencion a Jornaleros Agricolas, Apoyo al Empleo, Escuelas de Calidad, and Abasto Rural, among others (SFP 2005a, 33). Similar programs found the government contracting with social organizations for *testigos social* (social testimonials, promoted by Transparencia Mexicana) to oversee and verify that procurement processes were in strict compliance with the law. By the end 2004, Tranparencia Mexicana, La Fundación Heberto Castillo, and La Academia Mexicana de Ingeniería had served as forums for such testimonials (the government published the testimonial procedures on December 16, 2004). The government also contracted organizations such as Tranparencia Mexicana to independently monitor and evaluate its compliance with Organization of American States (OAS) and United Nations treaties.

The government signed agreements with universities to provide instruction to public officials and to promote research on corruption. As noted previously, the ITESM developed and has taught for years an ethics course to public officials. Together with the Instituto Nacional de Administración Pública, the ITESM also created an annual transparency award to recognize best practices in the government. The government also sponsored a variety of conferences and symposiums on corruption, including the November 2001 "Construynedo un Gobierno Honesto y Transparente" and the April 2002 "Mexico Contra la Corrupción,"[31] organized research contests, and signed agreements with the ITESM and Tranparencia Mexicana to develop and conduct studies to measure corruption.

The Fox government also pursued international cooperation in its fight against corruption, often in conjunction with social organizations. Mexico hosted the UN's conference in Merida in December 2003, where the UN Convention Against Corruption was signed (approved by the UN General Assembly in October 2003), signaling its leadership role in the area. Ratified in July 2004, the convention commits Mexico internationally to adopt certain preventive measures to combat and sanction corruption and cooperate with other nations in the pursuit of corrupt officials and the return of stolen proceeds. It also commits the government to undertake periodic assessment of its compliance. The Fox government also continued to work closely with the OAS and the Organization for Economic Cooperation and Development (OECD) to implement the prior anticorruption agreements signed under Zedillo and to participate actively in such organizations as the Network of Government Institutions for Public Ethics in the Americas.

In addition to these efforts, the government also sponsored a wide array of public campaigns and programs to inform and inspire the people, equip them with tools to fight corruption, and fundamentally alter the underlying culture feeding corruption. According to the administration, "it should be kept in mind that the real changes are not in the laws but in the minds" (SFP 2005b, 313). Beginning in May 2001, for instance, SECODAM published twenty-six issues of *Para Leer Sobre Transparencia,* an online newsletter spelling out the activities of the agency and instructions on how to denounce corruption, and providing updates on the activities of Transparency International and recent research on corruption. The government also promoted a massive public antibribery campaign in 2001 (*"ya no más mordidas,"* noted earlier). Joined by 33 companies, 14 newspapers, and 110 OICs, the campaign featured the conspicuous displaying of an anticorruption logo (a crossed out, bitten apple) in offices, on milk cartons, in movie theaters, and on vehicles (see SECODAM's *Para Leer Sobre Transparencia* nos. 1, 4, 2001; CITCC 2002). As part of this massive public relations campaign, PGR personnel even reportedly answered their phones with the greeting: "Say no to corruption, denounce it" (*El Mural* July 18, 2001). The government also assembled a set of online materials called "Do It Yourself: Your Toolbox Against Corruption" to assist citizens interested in fighting corruption. At the same time, the SFP promoted a variety of public information systems that encouraged citizens to file complaints when encountering corruption, offer suggestions, or demand information from the government.

In targeting this underlying culture of corruption, the government also worked closely with business and societal organizations to promote ethics not just in the government, but within society as well. For business, for instance, the government published brochures with such titles as "Transparent Business: Steps Toward Its Construction,"[32] "Ethics Is Good Business," and "Honor Codes: Creation of a Culture of Transparency." It also conducted workshops and courses, created a model of certification, and, together with the Confederación de Cámaras Industriales (CONCAMIN), sponsored an ethics award in industry. Such efforts sought, above all, to "convince [business] about the advantages that can be obtained by acting in a legal and transparent way" (*El Mural* July 2, 2001; see CITCC 2002). Together with the Mexican Bar Association and the Tec de Monterrey, it presented a course in Mexico City and via satellite in September 2004 titled "Combating Corruption: An Integrated Vision" and focusing on practices to prevent corruption in the private, social, and public sectors, including a review of actions taken at the international level (*Atlatl* no. 13, 2004, 3). The 2005 project "Citizen Monitoring" similarly provided a written guide, an Internet site, and a series of workshops for civil society organization (SFP 2005b). Efforts aimed at universities and schools included programs with the National Association of Universities and Institutions of Higher Education and the Ministry of Education to provide materials on ethics, social responsibility, and transparency, courses to teach instructors about these subjects beginning in 2004, and a distance-learning course on the role of universities in promoting the values of transparency and rule of law. The government designed an online learning project on corruption for high school students, a website on corruption solely for children (http://www.adiosa lastrampas.gob.mx), a children's museum, and, together with the National Council of Arts and Letters and the IFE, an art contest for children in 2002 and 2004 (which received over 15,000 drawings) and a story contest in 2003. Together with a host of organizations, the government also produced a brochure titled "Valuable Families: Ideas to Strenghten Values Between Parents and Children," sponsored a series called "Radio-Seconds Against Corruption," and produced the short film *Cuando sea grande* (When I grow up) in 2002, and a series of video spots over the next three years focused on corruption, transparency, and honesty. The short film *Cuando sea grande,* produced by SECODAM together with Cinemark and financed by the World Bank, the Telmex Foundation, Kodak, and Labo Filmes, showcased the ethical dilemmas facing a five-year-old and was shown in more than a hundred theaters across the country (*Notimex* August 28, 2002).

Reforms to the Criminal Justice System

Arguably, the institutions most infected by corruption in Mexico are located within the criminal justice system (according to data from surveys and citizen complaints—see Chapter 7; Parás 2007; Reames 2007; Silva 2007). This includes the various preventive and investigative police forces, the antidrug and anti–organized crime units, special units focused on money laundering, federal prosecutors, the courts, and the prison system. With the exception of the courts, all these institutions fall under the jurisdiction of the executive branch and thus constitute part of the panorama of the Fox anticorruption effort. The head of the transition team on security and justice, for example, reportedly informed the president-elect that corruption was devouring the PGR. He even proposed the elimination of PGR and the creation of a prosecutor's office (Ravelo 2000). Similar reports emphasized the entrenched corruption among the police, who were involved in kidnappings, armed robbery, and extortion, and were also providing protection to criminals and drug traffickers (USG, Bureau of Democracy 2004).

Efforts to root out corruption within the criminal justice system under Fox included various attempts to restructure the institutions, enhance the vetting of new officers and improve training, periodically shift assignments, and massive crackdowns even to the point of using federal authority to take control of local police departments. First, in November 2001, Fox formed the Secretaría de Seguridad Pública (SSP) and brought the Policía Federal Preventiva, created in 1999 under Zedillo, under its jurisdiction, along with the areas of migration, treasury, and highways. At the same time, he disbanded the notoriously corrupt judicial police, the Policía Judicial Federal (PJF), and created three new agencies within the PGR: the Agencia Federal de Investigaciones (AFI), which includes the new judicial police, investigators, and specialists; Agencia Federal Antisecuestros (AFA); and Subprocuraduría de Investigación Especializada de Delincuencia Organizada (SIEDO). The restructuring allowed the government to raise recruitment standards and institute rigorous training procedures for the new AFI officers. The PGR's Center for Confidence Control reportedly reviewed about 10,000 police, investigators, and prosecutors. Though some personnel from the former PJF were forced into retirement (BINLEA 2003), in the end the government recruited many former officers to fill the ranks of the AFI (Velasco 2005, 118) and transferred some to other police units. In 2003, one of the AFI's programs and internal processes received ISO certification (World Bank 2007, 30). Even so, problems continued to plague the federal forces, prompting a second restructuring in January 2003. This time the government dissolved the Fiscalía Especializada para la Atención de Delitos Contra la Salud (FEADS) (the special office against drug trafficking) following the arrest of six agents in Tijuana and the military seizure of FEADS offices in eleven states (the agents were accused of trying to extort US$2 million from a drug cartel in exchange for release of two alleged traffickers and nearly five tons of marijuana). A subsequent change in the Organic Law in August 2003 brought all antidrug units under SIEDO, strengthened the requirements for employment, the standards of conduct, and the procedures for dismissal for corruption, and provided better pay (BINLEA 2005, pt. 1).

Fox also put together a broad judicial reform in March 2004. The proposal sought to strengthen legal protections within the criminal justice system, eliminate the use of confessions except those given before a judge, unify the federal police under the Secretaría de Gobernación, and create an independent prosecution system by reorganizing the PGR to create an autonomous attorney general's office. This office would be in charge of investigating and prosecuting, while the PGR would be responsible for safeguarding the constitutionality and legality of the proceedings. The measure also sought to introduce oral trials, to eliminate much of the opacity of the legal system (Carbonell 2004; García Rojas Castillo 2004). The reforms, however, failed to obtain congressional approval during Fox's term (though a slightly revised package passed in 2008; see Chapter 2). In the face of this defeat, the PGR unilaterally restructured once again, creating two special anticorruption prosecutors (*fiscalías*) dedicated exclusively to handling complaints and conducting investigations of wrongdoing by public officials. One, incorporated within the Subprocuraduría de Investigación Especializada de Delitos Federales (SIEDF) (the special office for investigating federal crimes), was to focus on officials within the federal administration, while the other, incorporated within the Visitaduría General, was to focus on cases within the PGR.

In 2005, Fox referred to the police in terms of "low pay, poor training, a lack of resources, disorganization, corruption, ineffectiveness, lack of public confidence" (Reames 2007, 118). Facing massive social protests over the perceived deterioration in security, Fox established a security cabinet, and created the post of undersecretary for prevention and citizen participation. At the same time, he increased the pay of federal public administrators and the number of training courses, created obligatory human rights courses for personnel in the PGR, and established a new recruitment program by means of examinations among *ministerios públicos,* dismissing those who did not comply with professional standards (Schatz, Concha, and Kerpel 2007, 214).

To fight the growing influence of organized crime over state and local police forces and the rising levels of violence, in the latter years of the *sexenio* the government took the bold measure of arresting entire police departments and using the military to take control of the streets and law enforcement functions. Following a wave of violence that resulted in the deaths of local police chiefs, federal forces took control of Nuevo Laredo, Tamaulipas, in 2006. Such measures prefaced the approach subsequently embraced by Fox's successor, Felipe Calderon, who deployed the military in seven states plagued by violence and organized crime.

Mexico also worked cooperatively with a number of international organizations in its struggle against organized crime and law enforcement corruption, particularly the US government. In 2000, for example, Mexico joined the Financial Action Task Force, adopting international standards to fight money laundering, which opened the country to international assessment mechanisms (BINLEA 2005, pt. 2). The Mexican government also received the support of numerous US government programs promoting the professional development of police, prosecutors, and criminal experts at the federal, state, and municipal levels through the Administration of Justice Project, as well as training in ethics, anticorruption measures, and mid-level management at the PGR and SFP through the Law Enforcement Professionalization program (BINLEA 2004).

Another important approach to root out corruption within the criminal justice system has been to identity and sanction corrupt officials. Early on, both Fox and Attorney General Rafael Macedo announced massive crackdowns on middle- and high-level officials in the PGR and the periodic rotation of judicial police as part of their "National Crusade Against Narcotrafficking and Organized Crime" (*La Reforma* January 24, 2001). Over the years, news of links between military and police officers and drug traffickers peppered the papers,[33] including the role of police in kidnappings and executions.[34] Below the publicity radar, investigations, crackdowns, and firings were relatively common. In August 2002, for example, Macedo reported that the PGR had initiated 400 investigations involving over a thousand public servants in the judicial system and prosecutors in the PGR (see *Notimex* August 29, 2002). By early 2003, Fox claimed to have replaced more than 3,000 corrupt police officers (Global Integrity 2004). From 2001 to May 2004, the PGR conducted more than 1,300 investigations into the possible malfeasance of 2,200 officers, resulting in 418 legal cases against 711 officers (267 prosecutors and 335 AFI agents) (BINLEA 2005, pt. 1). According to a PGR report, between 2001 and 2005, 21 percent of the almost 7,000 agents of the AFI were investigated and, despite the creation of the AFI in November 2001 to eradicate the corruption that permeated the PJF, at least 1,493 agents were investigated and 457 were indicted (*Milenio* December 4, 2005).

Though clearly more pronounced and problematic in terms of its impact on law enforcement, the illicit, corrupt influence of organized crime in recent years has reached well beyond police and criminal justice organizations to include banking officials, state governors and mayors, and perhaps even the presidency itself. In October 2001, for example, the government arrested two high-level banking officials on charges of fraud, money laundering, and extortion: the deputy director of the Instituto para la Protección al Ahorro Bancar (IPAB), Eugenio González Sierra, and the research director of Bancomext, Leon Alberto Schietekat Ballesteros. Allegedly, González and other IPAB employees transferred illicit funds between Mexican and foreign banks and offered to clean up an engineering company's irregular operations through the IPAB bailout system in exchange for a bribe of US$1 million (*SourceMex* October 17, 2001). At the gubernatorial level, the former governor of Quintana Roo, Mario Villanueva Madrid, was at the time the highest-ranking official ever to be accused of drug trafficking and racketeering. Fleeing days before his term ended, he was arrested in May 2001 on charges of providing assistance to drug traffickers—specifically, protecting members of the Juarez cartel—laundering drug profits, and misusing public funds, and was subsequently convicted to six years in prison for money laundering (no convictions on charges of drug trafficking or organized crime) (*SourceMex* May 30, 2001; *SourceMex* March 1, 2000) (see Appendix B). In 2004, allegations surfaced that the governor of the state of Morelos, Sergio Estrada Cajigal (PAN) had allowed the powerful Juarez cartel to use the state as a collection and distribution site. The scandal forced the resignation of two key members of the Estrada administration, the state attorney general and state secretary, and prompted a chorus of demands for the governor to step down (*SourceMex* April 21, 2004). In the case implicating Los Pinos, Nahum Acosta Lugo, the travel coordinator under Fox's private secretary, Emilio Goicochea Luna, allegedly provided insider information to the Sinaloa cartel. According to an investigation by the PGR, the official received a gift from the cousin of drug baron Joaquín Guzmán (*SourceMex* February 23, 2005).[35]

Assessments of Fox's Anticorruption Reforms

Assessing the results of the multifaceted Fox anticorruption program is certainly no easy task. Methodological approaches vary, as do the conclusions to which they lead. As one interviewed official indicated: "We know they are doing things, we know that administrative improvements exist, but from there to say that we are combating corruption or that nothing is happening, we cannot say."[36]

Official Assessments

Official interpretations by Fox and his government were certainly optimistic. In an interview with the magazine *Latin Trade* (May 2006, 32–36) near the end of his term, President Fox proclaimed: "We've closed the door on corruption, and if it does occur it's highly likely that the person will be caught and taken to jail." In fact, according to the Fox government, the various changes achieved spectacular results. In its report to the OAS Committee of Experts in 2005, for instance, the SFP stated that the improved internal controls "prevent civil servants from committing illegal acts." It claimed that by reducing complexities, discretionary authority, and opacity, it had transformed public administration in Mexico and that the new civil service system was beginning to combat "friend-mongering or old boy networks for influence and jobs in the government" (SFP 2005b, 310). It further contended that both government and society now had the tools needed to guarantee efficiency and honesty in the use of public resources. In the words of the SFP secretary during his September 12, 2005, testimony before Congress: "We have reoriented and strengthened the presence of the internal control organs in the federal agencies; we have invigorated a growing level of participation of civil society, the private sector and universities in the creation of spaces of integrity and in the affirmation of values of a social ethic among citizens." The SFP did acknowledge some ongoing challenges, however, noting that change was not easy (SFP 2005b, 309). The SFP admitted that it was struggling to overcome inertia, alter attitudes, create a new consciousness among citizens and public servants, break vicious cycles, and make the new methods understandable and adoptable (SFP 2005b, 309).[37]

In addition to altering the nature of the Mexican bureaucracy, the government also took credit for promoting attitudinal changes within society that helped turn the corner on corruption. As evidence, it pointed to the formation and work of civic organizations like Tranparencia Mexicana, to opinion polls that showed over 90 percent of respondents agreeing that citizens should participate in combating corruption, and to the over 70,000 requests for information made through the Sistema de Solicitudes de Información (SISI) (SFP 2005b).

In support of its efforts, the government frequently paraded the absolute numbers behind its anticorruption efforts, pointing to the total number of improvement programs, audits, and sanctions. Though such numbers do not necessarily guarantee the reduction of corruption, most agree that they do reflect the presence of the necessary tools to fight corruption and that, in absolute terms, they are rather impressive: for example, 2,800 improvement actions in 157 federal agencies, 3,800 electronic bids through Compranet (Franco-Barrios 2003); 29,503 audits and 33,294 administrative sanctions against 25,937 public servants, including 87 criminal prosecutions (Cámara de Diputados 2005); 5,934 inspections of procedures and services through Usuario Simulado (SFP 2005a, 44); and more than 1,493 police agents investigated and 457 indicted for various crimes (*Milenio* December 2, 2005).

Unofficial Government Assessments

Systematic yet unofficial assessments from those within the government also point to some clear signs of progress. In a 2006 study based on extensive interviews of personnel from thirty-nine *unidades de enlace* (liaisons) in charge of maintaining information, and receiving and processing requests for information, in ten secretariats, 80 percent felt that the federal administration was more transparent than in 2003, though only 62 percent agreed that there was complete transparency. Of those interviewed, 61 percent saw the law as guaranteeing transparency, though 51 percent felt that the law was insufficiently applied. Interestingly, only 31 percent said the federal administration was more efficient than in 2001, while 36 percent saw no change and only 36 percent saw public servants as more honest than in 2003 (Juárez Aldan 2006, 67).

In-depth written interviews administered to twenty-two participants in the "Diplomado de Rendición de Cuentas y Combate a la Corrupción"—almost all federal employees—at the Tec de Monterrey campus in Mexico City in the summer of 2006 also revealed clear signs of progress. Most believed that the level of corruption had fallen within their particular areas and within the federal administration generally. Only three felt that corruption had not declined in recent years, and one felt agnostically that it was impossible to know. The most frequently cited reasons for the decline included the new law on access to information, improved transparency, the strengthening of internal controls, the reduction in discretionary authority, the improved work ethic that prevented conduct contrary to the norm, a greater consciousness among civil servants, the development of electronic processes, and improved recruitment. Yet according to many respondents, the public was largely unaware of these advances. When asked about the changing patterns of corruption, most concurred that corruption at the administrative and micro level had declined in recent years, particularly in those areas having electronic services, but that corruption among governors, legislators, autonomous regulatory agencies, police, and the judiciary had increased. As one official noted:

> I believe that the technological advances have helped diminish corruption principally in procedures that have to be done inside government offices (like, for example, in acquiring passports), but I believe corruption has increased among the political elite (primarily members of congress and in public procurement at the local level). . . . Today corruption has different patterns: conflict of interest and the trafficking of influence now occupy a central place.[38]

External Assessments

Many analysts echo at least some of these assessments of change. Adrian Franco-Barrios (2003, 21), for example, deems Mexico "a real example of [new public management] reforms oriented by transparency and anticorruption tasks." Rafael Martínez Puón (2002, 20) similarly finds Mexico's preventive approach more effective than approaches of the past. He contends that at least in certain areas of the administration, the government has achieved much greater levels of professionalization.[39] An assessment by scholars at the Centro de Investigación y Docencia Económica (CIDE) praised the assessment and planning tool MIDO in particular as an important step toward the adoption of new public management. The study concluded that MIDO is congruent and logical, that it begins to break with bureaucratic inertia and to implement a new culture, and that it goes beyond inherited tendencies (cited in SFP 2005b, 241). The OAS also found much to commend, including the promotion of ethics and values through codes of conduct and training, an improved legal structure against conflict of interest and mishandling of resources, and efforts to measure transparency (OAS 2004, 2005). According to the Instituto Mexicano de Auditores Internos:

> The impulse that the Public Function Secretary has given to the implantation of general norms of control in all the dependencies and entities of the federal public administration establishes the bases for the modernization of governmental

control, providing also a clear and strong structure for the leaders and upper
and mid-level managers to fulfill their obligations to be accountable, and promotes transparent public management and establishes a front against corruption. (cited in SFP 2005b, 205)

Many view the civil service reform and the transparency law as monu-
mental triumphs, setting the stage for vast changes in the nature of Mexican
governmental operations in the near future.[40] Roberto Moreno Espinosa of the
Universidad Nacional Autonoma de México (UNAM), for instance, calls the
civil service law a "a watershed . . . that will end . . . the traditional system of
spoils, the so-called patronage system where co-god parenthood, old-boy connections and nepotism have constituted the privileged set of mechanisms and
procedures for the recruitment to fill middle and upper level positions in all
three areas of the government" (SFP 2005b, 66). Elizondo (2006, 77n), in turn,
touts the sweeping transparency law as the greatest advance under Fox. Official information shows that from June 2003 to May 2004, the IFAI received
over 36,000 requests for information, of which the agency responded to 87
percent, with 73 percent of the latter requests approved. The IFAI, in turn, received 1,171 appeals (SFP 2005a, 2005c).[41] Of course, whether transparency
per se translates into a reduction in corruption or an alternation in the patterns
of corruption, including the hiding of information, remains an open matter.

The Mexican government has also received numerous accolades for its
adoption and use of technology within the public administration. In 2003, the
UN classified Mexico as "one of five developing countries with the greatest
determinations to offer transnational services on line to citizens." Two years
later, the UN awarded Mexico its "Award for Service to the Public" in recognition of the contributions of improving public administration using technology (SFP 2005b, 98). The SFP also received recognition from such entities as
the OECD, the Inter-American Development Bank, and the World Bank for
similar advances (SFP 2005b, 91). Information Week Mexico and Ernst &
Young named the SFP one of the top fifty most innovative enterprises in
terms of transparency. Citizen Portal received the 2004 Stockholm Award for
providing 1,450 government services on the Internet (*Atlatl* no. 9, 2004, 5).[42]
That a number of areas within the administration have been ISO-certified also
provides a clear indication of steady improvement.[43]

Many, however, question these positive appraisals. Criticisms range from
general indictments to the identification of more serious problems. Some, for
instance, question the effectiveness of the CITCC owing to its lack of autonomy
vis-à-vis the executive (it is located within the SFP) and its limited resources (it
had one of the lowest budgets and only sixteen staff to attend to 200 institutions
of the federal administration) (Wesberry 2004).[44] Noting that the president himself rarely attended the meetings of the CITCC, one interviewed official felt that
despite its early importance, Fox and other top officials neglected the CITCC

during the later years of the term. In a similar context, some see the Programa Nacional as constrained because of its reliance on projects developed within each individual agency of the government. Such self-monitoring, the essence of the Mexican strategy, is questioned at a very general level by Susan Rose-Ackerman (1999, 163), for example. Indeed, according to one SECODAM official, the quality of the initial diagnostic reports and operational programs varied widely, with some being virtually useless. Jorge Romer León (2005, 20) criticizes in particular the lack of real controls: "It is evident that the most serious problem is perceived at the level of the wrongdoing committed: in the first place, it is difficult to know when there is wrongdoing, and more to the point, when irregularities exist it is difficult to penalize the official responsible." He is particularly critical of the fact that the power to sanction resides within the administration itself (with the SFP and Hacienda concerning fines, and with the PGR concerning crimes), and that the administration is often slow to react.[45]

More pointedly, some analysts see the Fox anticorruption program as superficial, selective, inexperienced, and even disingenuous. One official, for instance, said the government developed the program too quickly and failed to incorporate a clear methodology to measure effectiveness. Noting that, in the area of transparency, Vinculación (UVT) within SECODAM operated with a staff of about eighty to ninety, while the CITCC operated with a staff of only ten to fifteen, this official considered the anticorruption program to be primarily a public relations tactic, and part of the political posturing of Francisco Barrio to become the PAN's presidential candidate for 2006.[46] In addition, key officials in the anticorruption drive, from directors in SECODAM to many of the *enlaces* within each federal agency, had limited experience working in the federal government. They had limited knowledge of procedures and specific departments, knew few of their clients and constituents, failed to establish a working relationship with mid-level officials, and were thus in a tenuous position at best to diagnose the problem areas of corruption, craft operational programs, and effectively implement them. According to one official within SECODAM, what these newly arriving officials had in ambition and political will, they lacked in technical expertise. The strategy's reliance on individuals within each government department and agency compounded this problem.[47] Finally, many questioned the credibility of the president due to allegations of corruption against him, his family, and his government (the Towelgate scandal and allegations of protecting the Bribiescas; see Appendix B).

Perhaps the most cited failure of the Fox administration was the continued high level of impunity, including the lack of prosecutions against former officials. Contrary to campaign promises, the regime shied away from prosecuting any "big fish" or opening exhaustive investigations into the past. As José Crespo (2007, 20) contends, "the accountability page remained blank during the government of Vicente Fox, which did not fail to be paradoxical, since it involved the president with the greatest electoral and democratic legitimacy in the history of Mexico." In the end, despite its case against former PEMEX officials (Pemexgate), the government not only failed to remove the official immunity of Carlos Romero Deschamps and Ricardo Aldana because of the vote of the PRI and PAN, but also failed to garner any indictments; despite promises to go after officials from the Salinas government or examine the irregularities in the bank privatizations and bank bailout, no prosecutions were ever made; and despite bending to pressures to create a special prosecutor to investigate the abuses associated with the "dirty war" (particularly events surrounding the 1968 Tlaltelolco and the 1971 Corpus Cristi student movements), prosecutions were limited to a handful of lower-level officials (see Appendix B).[48] At one point, commentator Denise Dresser even accused Fox of complicity with the former PRI, suggesting that the special prosecutor had been set up to fail (*SourceMex* March 2, 2005).

Assessments of the reforms within the criminal justice system similarly suggest that the vast restructurings and the crackdowns did little to curb the real level of corruption plaguing that sector. Sergio López-Ayllón and Hector Fix-Fierro (2003, 286, 243, 330), for instance, offer a rather skeptical assessment of changes and the chances of success in the area of criminal justice reform, noting that the positive transformations in the legal system over the past three decades have been "somewhat counteracted by negative factors that obstruct and resist change and, ultimately, prevent the rule of law from taking hold in society." They point, for example, to technically poor legislation, low-quality legal training, lack of professionalism, weakness of internal enforcement, formalistic judicial mentality, and a pervasive distrust of legal institutions. "Judges continue to behave very traditionally and formally," while "some bar associations have their own code of ethics, but they do not enforce it." A US government report (US Department of State 2006), for instance, categorically stated that "corruption, inefficiency, and lack of transparency continued to be major problems in the justice system." It noted, for instance, the high levels of corruption in prisons (that "corrupt guards staffed most prisons," that "prisoners often had to bribe guards to acquire food, medicine, and other necessities," and that drug dealers sometimes ran their external criminal organizations from inside). It also noted the involvement of police in "kidnapping, extortion, or in providing protection for or acting directly on behalf of organized crime and drug traffickers" and assailed the exceedingly high levels of impunity.[49] Diane Davis (2006, 55, 73) similarly alludes to the lack of success at reforming police and judiciary: "Despite the clear resolve by Mexico's leaders to undertake police and judicial reform, the pattern of success has been mixed, especially when measured by degrees of public confidence." She attributes the lack of success, in part, to the centralization and the institutionalized legacies of police power. She even suggests that the 2003 restructuring that created SIEDO, rather than curbing corruption, actually "fueled further police corruption" and even drove former police into crime. Analysis by Benjamin Reames (2007) similarly highlights the lack of progress in this sector, referring specifically to the understaffed and underfunded internal affairs division.[50] But in an unpublished study of the police forces in Mexico, Neils Uildriks (forthcoming) finds some indication of change within the ranks. Based on a survey, the researcher found 53 percent of preventive police and 60 percent of judicial police agreeing that corruption had decreased since 2005.[51]

At a more specific level, analysts highlight a wide range of deficiencies,[52] including weak whistleblower protection laws,[53] the lack of a program or strategy to inform society about the results of efforts against corruption and transparency, weak implementation of laws and codes of conduct concerning conflict of interest, the lack of verification of officials' disclosures of wealth, the lack of attention to state and local level corruption (OAS 2005),[54] problems related to public perceptions, inefficient regulations, cultural resistance to change in bureaucracy (Franco-Barrios 2003), and continued pockets of arbitrary power with few checks (Mendoza, García, and Anonales 2005). Others criticize the pace of the reforms. In the initial years, Transparencia Mexicana criticized the limited use of integrity pacts (*El Mural* May 30, 2001), while more recently many observers have pointed to the snail-pace implementation of the new civil service system. Though waxing optimistic, Manuel Guerrero (2004, 115) nonetheless notes the continued challenges: the reform, he notes, is "a great step toward rescuing the public administration from patrimonialism and clientelism, however its full implementation and adoption still face many challenges." Some even question Calderon's application of the new law.[55]

Perhaps even more confounding is evidence that programs designed to foster improved and more efficient services, a culture of ethics, transparency, and anticorruption may actually have had the opposite effect. Business executives, for instance, suggest that the fear within the bureaucracy of the discretional application of the Ley de Responsabilidades and of committing errors have actually paralyzed the bureaucracy. The director of the Centro de Estudios Economicos del Sector Privado (CEESP) survey stated that Barrio and his agency "have generated a climate of terror, of such rigidity, with their attitude of be careful because I am watching you, like Big Brother, that you are always being watched." Claudio X. González, head of the Consejo Mexicano de Hombres de Negocio, added that the federal agencies are not spending their appropriations because of the absence of clear rules from SECODAM regarding public bids and contracts, an opinion shared by the president of CONCANACO (*El Financiero* June 7, 2002).

Another example of distorted outcomes comes from an imaginative study by Isabela Corduneanu, Manuel Guerrero, and Eduardo Rodríguez-Oreggia (2004). In this study, the researchers administered a test to a group of 164 individuals in Mexico City before and after viewing the *cineminutos* films produced by the SFP in its effort to promote the fight against corruption.[56] Amazingly, those who viewed the anticorruption spots were more likely to engage in dishonest behavior, not less likely. In focus group discussions, the authors found that the viewers saw the government as blaming citizens for corruption rather than as taking responsibility and action. The study concluded that the film spots did not correspond to the collective mentality regarding corruption and, rather than facilitating cultural change, reinforced the existing culture of corruption.

Quantitative Evidence

Related quantitative evidence suggests mixed results. A comparison of the multiple opacity measures developed originally by PriceWaterhouseCoopers in 2001 and continued in 2007–2008 by the Milken Institute, for instance, shows some progress in terms of limiting the level of legal and judicial opacity, economic and policy opacity, and accounting and corporate governance opacity, and rather substantial improvement in regulatory opacity and uncertainty and arbitrariness (see Table 4.1). The CEESP survey of Mexican business representatives in 2007 similarly points to some progress. It shows a decline in bureaucratic obstacles, including in the number of steps or days to open a business. The index that ranks business satisfaction with the quality of services provided by the bureaucracy also climbed significantly, from 46.1 in 1998 to 73.6 in 2005. In fact, positive evaluations of the quality of state regulations almost

Table 4.1 Changes in Levels of Opacity and Competitiveness

Opacity Index

	C	L	E	A	R	O-Factor
2001	42	58	57	29	52	48
2007–2008	60	47	47	21	12	37

Sources: PriceWaterhouseCoopers 2001; Kurtzman and Yago 2008.
Notes: C = impact of corrupt practices; L = effect of legal and judicial opacity (including shareholder rights); E = economic and policy opacity; A = accounting and corporate governance opacity; R = impact of regulatory opacity and impact of uncertainty and arbitrariness; O-Factor = composite opacity score.

Global Competitiveness Reports 2001, 2005, 2007 (select indicators)

Indicator	2001	2005	2007
Burden of government regulations[a]	2.4	2.5	2.6
Favoritism in decisions[b]	3.2	2.9	2.7
Extent of bureaucratic red tape	2.5	3.4	(not asked)

Sources: Porter et al. 2002, 2005, 2007; Lopez-Claros 2005.
Notes: a. Scale 1–7: 1 = burdensome, to 7 = not burdensome.
b. Scale 1–7: 1 = usually favor, to 7 = neutral.
c. Question: "How much time does your company's senior management spend working with government agencies/regulations?" Scale 1–8: 1 = less than 10%, 2 = 11–20%, to 8 = 71–80%.

doubled from 1998 to 2005 (Rodarte 2007). Yet data from the World Economic Forum's *Global Competitiveness Report* show limited if any changes over the period, and maybe even a worsening of conditions within the administration. Based on multiple surveys of business executives, it finds that government regulations—despite the simplification efforts and new public management reforms—became slightly more burdensome, that decisions became less neutral, and that the level of red tape increased.

Official data on administrative sanctions and prosecutions, citizen complaints, and budget appropriations also suggest only limited changes over the period, raising questions about both the application of government initiatives and their effectiveness in combating corruption. As presented in Figure 4.1, the number of administrative sanctions against federal workers under Fox, while quite impressive in an absolute sense, was actually less than during the previous government. Whereas under Zedillo the government applied 43,293 sanctions against public officials—mainly for administrative negligence and resulting in simple warnings—it only issued 39,950 under Fox. More specifically, the number of sanctions for the more serious offenses—abuse of authority and bribery or extortion—also fell. During the Zedillo term, SECODAM issued 191 sanctions per year for bribery and extortion, compared to just 127 under Fox.

Figure 4.1 Sanctions of Federal Officials by the SFP

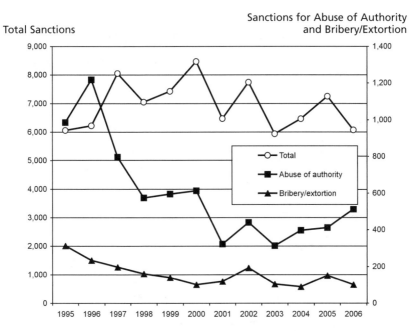

Source: Data provided by the SFP in response to an official request through SISI in 2008.

The number of sanctions applied solely to officials within the PGR—the major actor in terms of law enforcement and the agency with the highest number of cases under the categories of abuse of authority and bribery and extortion— follows a similar pattern. As presented in Figure 4.2, the average number of sanctions fell from 1,048 under Zedillo to 380 under Fox. The average number of sanctions issued for abuse of authority and bribery and extortion similarly dropped from 197 and 31 under Zedillo to 69 and 19 under Fox.

Information obtained from the government spanning the period April 2003 to November 2007 for cases originating in the SFP similarly reveals the limited number of criminal cases. The government handled just forty-six cases over that period. Of these criminal cases, eleven were for *"uso indebido de atribuciones y facultades"* (improper use of attributes of the office), nine were for *"peculado"* (graft), five were for *"enriquecimiento ilícito"* (illicit enrichment), three were for *"ejercicio indebido de servicio público"* (improper performance of public servant), three were for *"ejercicio de abusivo de funciones"* (abuse of authority), one was for *"cohecho"* (bribery), and fourteen were for other offenses, including fraud, falsification of documents, and illicit use of resources. More important, of these forty-six cases, only one had resulted in a sentencing by February 2008. While another two cases stood at the judicial or trial stage, most remained stalled at the investigative stage.[57]

In sum, the data on administrative sanctions leveled by the agency charged with implementing the anticorruption program during the Zedillo and Fox years

Figure 4.2 Sanctions of PGR Officials by the SFP

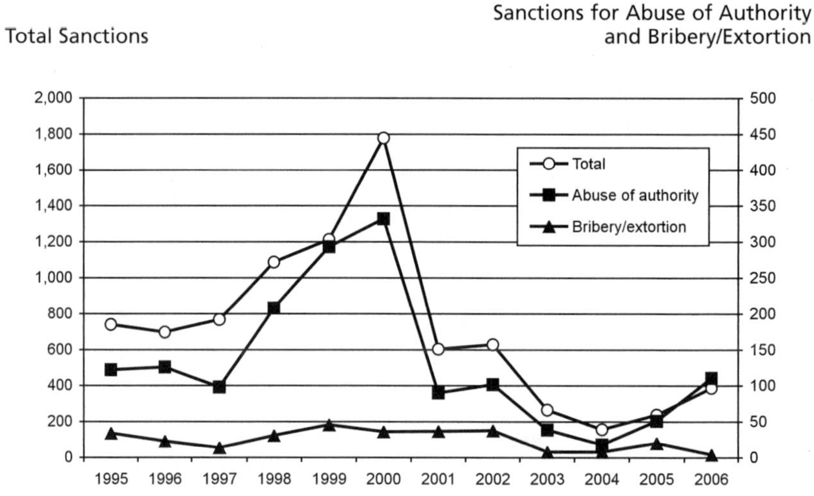

Total Sanctions

Sanctions for Abuse of Authority and Bribery/Extortion

Source: Data provided by the SFP in response to an official request through SISI in 2008.

hardly suggest a massive crackdown on bureaucratic corruption under Fox or a dramatic change in the signals sent to bureaucrats regarding risk. While the data do provide further evidence of the presence of corruption in particular areas of the government and its relative absence in other areas, they do not show a government totally inactive in enforcing the norms of public office. The total number of sanctions does point to a seemingly active level of supervision and horizontal oversight. In fact, from 1995 to 2007, there were 88,286 sanctions applied to public officials. Of these, 11 percent resulted in firings, 21 percent in suspensions, and 24 percent in prohibitions of further employment in the federal government. For charges of bribery and extortion, such sanctions were even more common. Though few officials ever faced anything more than administrative sanctions—criminal charges were quite rare—the pattern leads one to question the effectiveness of these sanctions and the cultural context that might feed abuse of authority and corruption within bureaucratic agencies.

Interpreting such data and trends is not easy, to be sure. What do fewer sanctions really tell us? Even a decline in the number of sanctions, audits, or citizen complaints can be seen as indicating either the success or the weakening of an initiative, just as cases of corruption can be taken as evidence of the existence of corruption or a sign that the tools to identify and prosecute it are working. Arguably, then, the less the corruption, the fewer the sanctions. Mexico's 2005 report to the OAS Committee of Experts (SFP 2005a, 27) adopts this argument, touting the reduction in administrative sanctions, dismissals, suspensions and warnings, internal audits, and complaints received during the 2000–2004 period as an indication of the success of its internal controls and improvements.[58] The administration even hailed the Towelgate scandal, which cut into Fox's credibility and prompted many to question his political will to fight corruption, as proof of the success of its campaign to ensure transparency.

Complementary data from the government on citizen complaints during the Fox term, however, lead one to question this interpretation. Given that 51 percent of all cases that resulted in any form of administrative sanction during the period originated from citizen complaints, with 83 percent of those involving bribery and extortion, citizen complaints clearly play an important role. Yet if corruption were declining during the period, one would expect fewer citizen complaints, a pattern matching the trends seen with the number of sanctions. However, the number of complaints under Fox, after peaking in 2001 and 2002, remained steady from 2004 to 2006 and then climbed dramatically again in 2007 (see Table 4.2).[59] Using citizen complaints as an indirect measure of citizen confidence in the government's anticorruption efforts (see Manion 2004), this decline suggests a growing disillusionment following the initial enthusiasm and optimism, a pattern that becomes even clearer from the public opinion data presented in the next chapter.

In addition to sanctions and complaints, budget figures also raise some doubts about the claims of the administration and the effectiveness of its

Table 4.2 Citizen Complaints of Government Irregularities

	Number of Complaints
2000	2,000
2001	13,801
2002	17,175
2003	14,743
2004	11,596
2005	12,450
2006	12,292
2007	15,458

Source: Data provided by the SFP in response to an official request through SISI in 2008.

anticorruption efforts. From 1999 to 2006, according to Guillermo Cejudo and Laura Sour (2007, 9), the budget for the SFP—the governmental arm in charge of anticorruption—actually fell in both real and relative terms. This is surprising given its role in designing and coordinating the administration's massive anticorruption program and, subsequently, in creating and implementing the massive civil service reform. In fact, as a percentage of federal spending, the SFP's portion fell from 0.082 percent in 1999 to 0.065 percent in 2006. By contrast, other accountability institutions—independent of the federal executive—saw their budgets grow. The budget for the congressionally affiliated ASF, for instance, climbed from 0.022 percent in 1999 to 0.035 percent in 2006, while the budget for the CNDH grew from 0.018 percent in 1999 to 0.036 percent in 2006 (Cejudo and Sour 2007, 15).

Anticorruption Under Calderon

Anticorruption did not enjoy the profile or priority during Felipe Calderon's first two years in office (2006–2007) as it did under President Fox. During this period, the government was involved in a series of key reforms, some initiated under Fox and discussed previously, designed in part at least to enhance accountability and fight corruption. These changes include the constitutional reform (described earlier) elevating access to information to the status of a fundamental constitutional right and establishing principles and criteria for all levels of government; a fiscal reform that, among other changes, obliges all parts of the administration to adopt schemes to evaluate the effectiveness of public spending; a reform extending auditing oversight to include *fidiecomisos* (government trust funds); and major justice and security reforms that over a period of years will, as described in Chapter 3, fundamentally alter the nature of the judicial system, expanding transparency and openness. Generally, these reforms consolidate the gains enjoyed under Fox.

Clearly, Calderon's top priority during this time was drug trafficking, organized crime, and the nation's deteriorating security situation. High profile efforts in this area, however, brought into sharp relief the entrenched corruption plaguing the criminal justice system.[60] Because of the degree of corruption linking local and federal law officials to criminal organizations, Calderon broadened Fox's program of deploying the military to fight drug traffickers.[61] The influx of troops not only destabilized the relationship, but also unleashed an unprecedented wave of violence. One of the earliest tasks of the military was to vet local police departments in an effort to root out corruption, often jailing and disarming local forces (*Milenio* November 28, 2008). At the same time, the government struggled to deal with entrenched corruption within the federal agencies charged with fighting organized crime. In October 2008, as part of a lengthy and ongoing investigation called *Operación Limpieza,* the government revealed that over thirty officials from the justice department's unit fighting drug trafficking, SIEDO, including two senior-level employees, had been systematically leaking information to the Beltran Leyva cartel in exchange for monthly payments of between $150,000 and $450,000. This triggered perhaps the most prominent scandal rocking the new government (*SourceMex* November 5, 2008). In early November, the PFP also announced that it had turned over two of its agents to prosecutors because of their links to drug traffickers, prompting the resignation of the acting director of the PFP (*SourceMex* November 5, 2008). According to Ravelo (2009, 12) penetration of drug traffickers into the government extends to "the entire security and organized crime fighting apparatus, without precedent in the history of the country." In January 2009, the PGR insisted that it would continue the renovation within the PGR with comprehensive reassignments of officials within SIEDO and further investigations (*La Jornada* January 18, 2009). In noting the continuing problem with corruption and its impact, Salvador Vega Casillas, the secretary of FP, called corruption a cancer as serious as nacrotrafficking (cited in *Milenio* November 27, 2008).

In addition to ongoing investigations within the agencies charged with fighting organized crime, the government took measures to strengthen the vetting of police and prosecutors and to restructure law enforcement agencies. In November 2008, for instance, the federal government announced that it would increase the confidence control examinations given to officials to avoid corruption, noting the SSP had conducted 65,000 exams since Calderon took office (*Milenio* November 28, 2008).[62] It also announced that it would broaden the application of such exams to include state and local police (*Milenio* November 27, 2008). To fight corruption, the government also announced yet another restructuring of federal police agencies, this time merging the two federal law enforcement agencies, the PFP and AFI, into one.

It was not until December 2008—two years after taking office—that Calderon formally released his anticorruption program, the "Programa Nacional de Rendición de Cuentas, Transparencia y Combate a la Corrupción, 2008–2012" (*Diario Oficial* December 11, 2008). Building largely on the changes undertaken during the Zedillo and Fox administrations, the anticorruption program seeks to "generate a social culture of accountability, anticorruption and respect for rule of law by way of the transformation in the processes of the federal government and a redefinition of the relationship between State and society."[63] Recognizing the continuing challenges and the new forms of corruption related to organized crime plaguing the nation, the Calderon program lists among its priorities the consolidation of policies of transparency, the strengthening of oversight in the use of public resources and inspections of infrastructure projects, the improvement of the internal norms within the administration, the promotion of a culture of legality and greater societal participation in the administration, greater coordination among anticorruption units, and the combating of corruption within law enforcement agencies. The program spells out specific indicators to gauge progress in promoting these changes and lays out specific action lines. Among the more novel approaches are efforts to strengthen the controls and oversight of officials in the area of security, measures to enhance a culture of legality, including greater involvement of *contralorias sociales* and the simulated user program, and steps to reduce the degree of discretional authority among officials. It is certainly far too early to tell whether these reforms will be implemented or their effectiveness.

Conclusion

Amid deep structural changes at the state-society level, President Fox took office promising a broad assault on corruption. Early on, the first non-PRI president assembled an intersecretarial commission and laid out a multifaceted and integral program to fight corruption. The government diagnosed bureaucratic operations and procedures and designed hundreds of specific improvements to reduce the risks of corruption. It strengthened laws against corruption and the level of internal oversight within the bureaucracy, and promoted sweeping administrative reforms stretching from administrative simplification to the establishment of a merit-based civil service system. It pried open the government through a sweeping transparency law, and orchestrated a massive social campaign to enlist the support and participation of civil society and to promote a more ethical culture and greater respect for the rule of law.

Unfortunately, as Robert Klitgaard, Ronald Maclean-Abaroa, and H. Lindsey Parris (2000, 11) note, "the history of anti-corruption campaigns around the world is not propitious." General assessments of the impact of the Fox reforms vary, with some, including the administration, claiming some important successes, while others raise serious doubts. In some ways, the changes seem to point to a slow yet certain depoliticization of the state administration, the beginning signs of a more professional and merit-based bureaucracy, more rigorous systems of oversight, much greater transparency, and the integration of civil society actors as co-governing partners. Yet the impact of these changes has been slow, selective, and, at times and in particular areas, seemingly undermined by other forces. To be sure, many of the reforms remain in their early stages of implementation, like the civil service reform—and hence their true impact on corruption may take more time to materialize—but some, like the transparency law, have radically transformed the nature of governance in a rather short period of time. In other areas, such as the efforts to sanction officials from the past or clean up corruption within the criminal justice sector, the results have been rather limited.

Such general assessments provide a bridge to an examination of public opinion polls: the people's assessment of change and evidence regarding participation in low-level corruption. The government insists that it has effectively curtailed corruption, particularly within the bureaucracy—the focus of most of the programs within the broader Programa Nacional. What do polls show with regard to the public's experiences in obtaining basic public services? Has corruption, indeed, diminished in these areas as the government claims? Similarly, to what extent has the government's high-profile anticorruption campaign as well as its insistence on positive results influenced or shaped the public's perceptions about corruption? Are citizens, for instance, more likely now to denounce corruption? Are they more likely to trust the system to fight corruption than in the past? In that perception is fundamental to politics, it is important to ask whether the Fox government was able to alter basic assumptions about politicians and government.

Notes

1. In questioning the effectiveness of institutional reforms versus structural changes, a study of corruption in US states by Kim Hill (2003, 626) found no empirical link between corruption and the scope of the anticorruption laws in the state or the law enforcement power. The results suggested "that the transparency and public scrutiny of governmental processes that arise out of democracy and party competition are more important for reducing corruption than are regulatory initiatives directed at that goal."

2. The program of simplification identified 4,876 administrative processes to be targeted, of which 3,315 had been simplified by March 1986 (Sánchez González 2004, 360).

3. New public management reforms have been called "market-based" or entrepreneurial because they rely on market mechanisms. Jan-Erik Lane (2000, 3, cited in Franco-Barrios 2003, 5), for instance, calls new public management "the theory of the most recent paradigm change in how the public sector is to be governed." According to Adrian Franco-Barrios (2003, 6), however, new public management theory does not consider issues of transparency and corruption because it presupposes the absence of corruption, leading him to question whether new public management reforms are even appropriate for developing countries.

4. During this period, an initiative to create a civil service system was introduced and studied in the Senate (Sánchez González 2004, 379). On past efforts to create a civil service reform in Mexico, see Arrellano Gault and Guerrero Amparán 2003.

5. Following the dramatic arrest of General Gutiérrez Rebollo, the director of the Instituto Nacional para el Combate a las Drogas, (in February 1997 for his ties to drug traffickers, Zedillo dissolved the agency and created a special prosecutor for drug

crimes, the Fiscalía Especializada para la Atención de Delitos Contra la Salud (FEADS). Zedillo also oversaw the drafting of an operations manual on detecting and preventing money laundering, and created specialized groups to combat narcotrafficking and money laundering as well as mechanisms through which citizens could report corruption (Ugalde 2002).

6. Despite these historic measures and some progress, past reforms generally failed to transform Mexican public administration, curb the high levels of corruption, improve the public's perceptions of corruption, or instill greater confidence in the bureaucracy or the government (Franco-Barrios 2003; Martínez Puón 2002; Sánchez González 2004). According to Rafael Martínez Puón (2002), Mexico never achieved a Weberian model, and instead maintained a largely patrimonial bureaucracy. Reflecting on this failure, Adrian Franco-Barrios (2003) contends that the programs lacked an integrated vision, a wide-ranging commitment (anticorruption was considered the exclusive task of the comptroller's office), and the means to evaluate public sector performance; and that they failed to incorporate international oversight, relied too heavily on formal and legalistic schemes, and incorporated little societal participation. Many attribute the failure of past efforts to the underlying political context, contending that the reforms, quite simply, reflected the centralization of power under the PRI *gobierno* and that a true transformation would have risked presidential control (Sánchez González 2004, 367, 390; Arrellano Gault and Guerrero Amparán 2003). According to the Fox administration itself, past initiatives failed because of the lack of democracy (SFP 2005b, 15).

7. I suppose it is somewhat ironic that while championing the fight against corruption, the Fox campaign was secretly engaged in an assortment of corrupt practices through its "Amigos de Fox" organization, including laundering funds, establishing ghost companies, foreign financing, and failing to report donations (see Chapter 2 and Appendix B).

8. The code of ethics presented during the inauguration and subsequently taught in the Tec de Monterrey's virtual course concentrated on the following twelve components: common good, integrity, honesty, impartiality, justice, transparency, accountability, cultural and ecological surroundings, generosity, equality, respect, and leadership (*La Reforma* January 26, 2001).

9. While Fox set the tone, he was not the only member of the administration preaching against corruption during this period. The secretary of SECODAM, Francisco Barrio, in striking contrast to his predecessors, enjoyed perhaps more publicity than any other member of the cabinet during the initial years. Frequent speeches, sound bites, presentations, and press releases by the former Chihuahuan governor helped keep the anticorruption campaign plastered on the front pages of the nation's newspapers and uppermost in the minds of the people. Even before taking office, he promised to pursue the Salinas case, and stated that he was studying the anticorruption crusades in Singapore, Hong Kong, Italy, and Colombia (*La Jornada* October 12, 2000). In December 2000 he echoed Fox's call for a new law of public information and by May 2001 claimed that the legislation would be ready within six months (*La Reforma* December 11, 2000, May 2, 2001). In January 2001, Barrio announced the establishment of the CITCC and outlined for the public and the press the broad features of the national anticorruption program (*La Reforma* January 27, 2001). Also in May 2001, he publicly promised to measurably reduce corruption within one year, though, he claimed, the overall strategy envisioned a twenty-five-year period. At the same time, interestingly, he also posited that he would not bend to pressures to create "scapegoats" for publicity: a ready response to his failures to act in certain cases. According to the secretary, "Many times we can intimate that there is something improper. Our challenge, and that of all of society, is to have the elements to prove it. We should remember that the dishonest are shrewd, not stupid" (*La Reforma* May 25, 2001).

10. These cross-institutional accords covered recognition of the integrity of public servants; improvements in internal regulations; the simulated user program; nongovernmental participation in defining the bases for government procurement; publication of the bases for procurements; evaluations of user opinions and perceptions about the honesty and transparency of agencies; public information on the Internet; electronic government procurement systems; codes of conduct; e-procedures and e-services; publication of the results of agencies' anticorruption programs; training of public servants regarding values; selection of public servants based on ethical values and rigorous mechanisms; establishment of integrity agreements between the public and private sectors; review of salaries in critical areas; and establishment and publication of standards for the delivery of public service.

11. The Agenda Presidencial de Buen Gobierno included both the Programa Nacional and the Modelo Estratégico para la Innovación Gubernamental, and was part of the Plan Nacional de Desarrollo, the government's main planning document (Martínez Puón 2002, 17; Franco-Barrios 2003, 33).

12. SECODAM/SFP is responsible for oversight of the federal public administration only. The law establishes separate oversight bodies for the legislative branch (Article 70 of the Constitution and Articles 53, 112, and 113 of the Organic Law of Congress establish the internal comptrollers of the Chamber of Deputies, Senate, and the Judicatura).

13. As one example, the ISSSTE was the first to publicly announce its anticorruption plan, on February 19, 2001. The plan included making public, via the Internet, information on the budget, spending, projects, works, and catalog of services. According to Benjamín González Roaro, "I want to make it clear that we are serious in ISSSTE: That no abuse will be tolerated; that there will be no room for impunity; that any conduct at the margins of the law, any act of corruption, will be pursued and punished" (*La Reforma* February 19, 2001).

14. In April 2001, for instance, SECODAM and the Policía Federal Preventiva discovered a network of corruption and contraband within the customs office and local businesses in Ciudad Juarez, resulting in the immediate firing of twenty-eight officials. More than 300 companies and persons remained under investigation (*La Reforma* April 3, 2001). In May, the government launched a massive operation against workers in the customs office at the Guadalajara airport. This operation uncovered over twenty-four warehouses of contraband material (see Gutiérrez 2001). That same month, the government also cracked down on customs officials at the Mexico City airport. During the period, the new customs director fired eighteen of nineteen station directors while altering the hiring system (Jordan, 2001).

15. This statement by Fox is a bit ironic, since such crackdowns in customs have occurred in the past. Tina Rosenberg (2003), for instance, refers to the blow that Francisco Gil Díaz as assistant secretary of treasury in 1989 dealt to entrenched corruption in customs. Noting that a mafia ran the customs house with the eager participation of airline personnel, government officials, customs agents, truck drivers, and police, Gil Díaz persuaded Congress to change the customs system, instituting such changes as random "stoplights." The government reduced the sixteen customs steps to three, appointed professionals, and conducted surprise inspections. According to the report, Gil Díaz "changed the behavior of customs workers by removing opportunities for theft and bribery and increasing the probability of their being caught." Yet given the results found when Fox took office, it is clear that the problem of corruption either never disappeared or reappeared once vigilance fell. In fact, a congressional report in 2005 pointed out that illegal channels supplied 58 percent of the national clothing market. This included both "bronco" contraband (foreign goods that do not pass customs) and "documented" contraband (foreign goods that enter by false documentation, underreporting, misclassification, or other means to avoid paying taxes or abiding by quotas) (Ochoa León 2005).

16. Cross-national studies by Peter Evans and James Rauch (Evans and Rauch 1999; Rauch and Evans, 2000) find meritocratic recruitment to have the greatest impact on bureaucratic performance.

17. Details on the code of ethics cited above.

18. This was clearly not the first time the government suggested a civil service overhaul. In 1983, the government created the Dirección General de Servicio Civil and the Comisión Intersecretarial de Servicio Civil de Carrera. Though the government sought to incorporate the labor union of federal workers and registered some advances, it suffered numerous setbacks. Presidents Carlos Salinas and Ernesto Zedillo also undertook some efforts to reform the civil service, but these did not go far (Sánchez González 2004, 427).

19. The civil service law does not apply to those working in the office of the presidency, secretaries, department chiefs, subsecretaries, chiefs of staff, unit chiefs, members of the armed forces and members of public security forces, foreign service personnel, education and health workers, contractual workers, and workers who belong to bureaucrats' labor unions.

20. The Comité de Profesionalización is to be composed of the chief of staff of the agency, the director of human resources, and a representative from the SFP. The Comité de Selección is to be composed of the head of human resources, a representative from the SFP, and the immediate supervisor to the position being filled (SFP 2005b).

21. Other improvements included numerous courses on technical capacity along with a published manual to identify and describe technical capacities. According to the SFP (2005b, 61), as of 2005, 22,616 training courses had been given to 177,213 people.

22. During the first phase in the process of recruitment and selection, in 2004, the SFP received over 198,000 applications, from 38,507 applicants and 16,336 participants, in response to public announcements. By the end of 2004, the SFP had made 1,435 appointments through the system (SFP 2005b, 59).

23. Kenneth Mitchell (2005, 379) defines "managerialist reforms" as second-generation reforms whereby the state embraces private sector managerial strategies like decentralization, contracting out, integrated information and budgeting systems, merit-based recruitment and advancement, and results-based incentives.

24. Interview with Aliza Chelminsky, director of SECODAM's Unidad de Vinculación, Mexico City, July 2001.

25. The regulation was published on October 7, 2004. Specifically, MIDO indexes five measures: reduction of risks of corruption, reduction of risks of opacity, institutional performance, perception of performance, and actual performance.

26. Though promised during the inauguration, and incorporated into the Plan Nacional de Desarrollo and the Programa Nacional, the government's proposal for the transparency law was not put forward until late 2001. Moreover, Fox's initial proposal, which positioned SECODAM as the agency to guarantee and enforce the law (*La Reforma* May 2, 2001, May 26, 2001), was overtaken by an initiative developed and promoted by Grupo Oaxaca (a consortium of academics and journalists), as described in Chapter 3 (Michener 2005).

27. In implementing the legislation, the IFAI established liaisons and information committees in each area of the government. The liaisons are responsible for maintaining and updating the information for their specific Internet areas in compliance with the law, and for processing requests for information that come through the IFAI. To handle requests for information, the IFAI created the computerized Sistema de Solicitudes de Información (SISI). Under this user-friendly system, petitioners specify the information requested and the target government agency. This information is then forwarded to the liaison, who has a specific number of days to respond to the request. This initial response can be a request for clarification as to the type of information sought, or a denial based on the fact that the information does not exist or is not within that particular government

agency. SISI not only allows the petitioner to follow the progress of the request, but also informs the petitioner when the information is available. Options exist to receive the information electronically or even by mail. SISI also allows one to consult the fulfilled information requests of others. The IFAI handles appeals of denials of information.

28. Internal regulations for transparency were issued for the Senate in April 2003, for the Chamber of Deputies in May 2003, and for the executive and the judiciary in June 2003 (*Atlatl* no. 7, 2003, 2). On obstacles to access to information within the judiciary, see Kossick and Minutti Z. 2007, 308–309.

29. Recognition of the role of popular attitudes and culture in facilitating corruption and of the need to target programs to alter that underlying culture are indeed among the unique features of the Fox anticorruption drive.

30. From 1995 to April 1998, there were 8,227 citizen "control and vigilance" committees, involving 24,681 citizens (Haro Bélchez 1998).

31. The symposium "Constructing an Honest and Transparent Government," held November 24–25, 2001, at SECODAM and organized by the Comisión Intersecretarial para la Transparencia y el Combate a la Corrupción en la Administración Pública Federal (CITCC) and Project AAA, included presentations by Robert Klitgaard and Bartrand de Specille of the Hong Kong anticorruption commission. The conference "Mexico contra la corrupción," held April 15–19, 2002, and sponsored by SECODAM, the Organization of American States (OAS), the Centro de Investigación y Docencia Económica (CIDE), the Universidad Nacional Autonoma de México (UNAM), the Instituto Federal Electoral (IFE), the Universidad Iberoamericana, and the US Agency for International Development (USAID), among others, included the debut of the film *Cuando sea grande* (When I grow up), various workshops for journalists on integrity programs, codes of conduct, and ways to measure corruption, and special workshops for managers and auditors (*Atlatl* no. 1, 2002, 4–5).

32. This handsome brochure, produced in cooperation with the Confederación de Cámaras Industriales (CONCAMIN) and released in May 2001, informs businesses on specific strategies for avoiding corruption, including information on creating business processes and operations, suggestions on professional practices and ethical conduct, and strategies for working with authorities and others. The document begins with the statement: "Corruption is a social bad that is not limited to government. When there is corruption within a society, it contaminates all spheres of life: business, school, work, government, commerce, etc." (*La Reforma* May 18, 2001).

33. Among the more spectacular stories was the arrest of drug trafficker Delia Patricia Buendia Gutiérrez, also known as Ma Baker, in September 2002. The case revealed how a network of public officials at the federal, state, and municipal levels had protected Ma Baker's criminal organization (*El Universal* August 27, 2002). There were reports that PJF agents had actually picked up cocaine from airplanes and delivered it, and that Ma Baker had sent presents to PGR officials, including to the *padrino* of the Fiscalia Especializada (*Proceso* September 2, 2002). Such revelations also centered on the military. See Appendix B.

34. In 2005, eight AFI agents were arrested for kidnapping, torturing, and possibly murdering members of the Zetas Gulf cartel, as revealed in a graphic video. Five of the agents were subsequently freed because of a lack of evidence. In June, the newspaper *Milenio* went public with the video, which presents an interrogation of four members of Zeta that ended with the execution of at least one of them (*Milenio* December 5, 2005). The videotape even seemed to imply some involvement by former attorney general Rafael Macedo with the Sinaloa cartel (he had resigned in May 2005 following the failure to oust López Obrador) (see also *SourceMex* December 14, 2005).

35. The official was released two months later for lack of evidence. SIEDO maintained the investigation against Acosta for laundering drug profits (*SourceMex* April 27, 2005; *La Jornada* March 26, 2007).

36. The OAS Committee of Experts in 2005 arrived at a somewhat similar conclusion, noting in its report that the information provided by the government "does not make it possible to evaluate comprehensively the results obtained by each of the high-level oversight bodies with respect to the provisions of section 1, 2, 4 and 11 of Art III of the Convention [against corruption]," though it did agree that the information indicated that the oversight bodies had actively pursued their auditing tasks (OAS 2005). The committee similarly found that, though the government had created strong ties with society, the impact of these ties remained unclear. It thus recommended that Mexico adopt better quantitative and quantifiable indicators to help determine the impact of citizen participation.

37. The government documents much of its progress in overhauling public management through the MIDO internal assessment program, described earlier. Among the details, MIDO's intricate assessment measures point to improved perceptions of the OICs from the bureaucrats within their areas of operation (e.g., in 2006, 92 percent of the *órganos internos de control* were evaluated positively by those within the OICs, with 95 percent of bureaucrats expressing a favorable opinion of OIC contributions to reducing the risks of corruption [up from 87 percent in 2004] and 95 percent positively evaluated OIC contributions to lowering the risk of opacity), as well as real improvements in the work of the OICs in contributing to the performance of the agencies they are assigned to. At the end of 2005, the OICs received a rating of 9.32 on a scale of 0–10 (up from 9.17 in 2004) for institutional performance, 9.04 (up from 8.82 in 2004) for implementation of the civil service law, and 8.21 (up from 5.94) for operational performance. Overall, according to the MIDO report, such advances show conclusively "that these organs have successfully achieved a culture of prevention in all areas of their work. This reflects the work and achievements that these agents have deployed, beyond the operative indicators of MIDO, to better orient themselves to understand the nature of the institutional problems and to mitigate the causes of those problems."

38. Even so, problems remain. A superintendent of ten years, for example, noted that corruption in the contracting of services remains a problem, with kickbacks provided to the officials awarding the contracts. He stated that officials who do not go along are forced out of their organizations. He also felt that the failure of the anticorruption programs currently in place relates to the fact that high-level officials participate in corruption. Another critic pointed to the awarding of contracts and services to friends, and to the growth of influence trafficking. Among the continuing problems identified by those voicing positive overall assessments was the continued impunity at the highest levels, the lack of prosecution, the absence of a culture of legality and transparency, the lack of attention to the local level, the slow implementation of the civil service reform, and the ambiguities in the legal framework. According to one individual, Mexico still lacks "a legal culture that teaches and sanctions, an incorruptible ethical attitude and deep convictions of honesty and honor among public officials and citizens that stem from the uncontestable principle that there is no one who misleads without an accomplice."

39. Greater professionalization exists within the following agencies of the government: government statistics and information, education, PGR and PGJDF, National Water Commission, agriculture, IFE, SAT, and foreign affairs (Martínez Puón 2002, 5n).

40. Benjamín Hill Mayoral (2005) notes that there is just one public competition *(concurso)* per year to enter civil service at the lowest level, and that serious problems remain in terms of creating a system of evaluation for thousands of workers.

41. In July 2007, in a further measure to institutionalize freedom of information, changes to Article 6 of the Constitution lifted access to information to the status of constitutional guarantee. The measure forced all levels of government to strengthen and

homogenize their access to information laws according to international standards (Transparencia Mexicana, *Boletín Informativo* no. 20, 2007; see also IFAI 2007, a comparative study).

42. While highlighting early advances and potential, Robert Kossick (2003) also notes a series of infrastructure, technological, legal, and financial obstacles facing the electronic bureaucracy system, known as Tramitanet.

43. In January 2003, SECODAM reported that seven of its processes had obtained ISO quality management certification (http://200.34.175.29:8080/wb3/wb/sfp/prensa_2003). Chesterton Global Solutions (http://www.chesterton.com/corporate/iso) defines the ISO quality management system in the following terms: "Enables an organization to develop a Quality policy and establish objectives and processes which demonstrate its ability to consistently provide product that meets customer and regulatory requirements, and enhances customer satisfaction and continual improvement of the system."

44. Though Robert Klitgaard (1988) supports the idea of an interagency coordinating body like the Comisión Intersecretarial, others, including Tranparencia Mexicana, have stressed the need for greater independence from the executive. According to Peter Williams, the commissioner of Hong Kong's Independent Commission Against Corruption, "To ensure public confidence in the new organization it must be independent of political and executive Administration and responsible directly to the highest authority in the land" (cited in Klitgaard, Maclean-Abaroa, and Parris 2000, 121).

45. Jorge Romero León (2005) contends that the irregularities have been fewer, but more significant.

46. "Off-the-record" comments during an interview with a SECODAM official, July 2001.

47. Barrio took his team from Chihuahua to fill SECODAM. Seven of the top officials worked for Barrio in Chihuahua and the PAN. Only one, Alejandro Torres Palmer, had any previous experience in SECODAM (*La Reforma* January 11, 2001). Indeed, there has been little holdover from the past, feeding the tendency to throw out past programs designed to tackle corruption, and develop new ones. Compranet stands as one important exception to this rule. Interestingly, key officials in the struggle against corruption under Ernesto Zedillo, like José Octavio López Presa, are now involved in the struggle from outside the government.

48. In some ways, Barrio foresaw this outcome, noting in an interview in late February 2001 that while corruption was widespread in the prior administration, there was no way to formally accuse those former officials because of the lack of evidence. He noted that while audits revealed irregularities that "smelled bad," the regulations and laws were so flexible as to allow almost anything, and that the former officials had eliminated the proof of corruption (*La Reforma* February 27, 2001).

49. The content of the 2006 report cited here differs little from the reports by US government agencies in prior years (see BINLEA 2002, 2003, 2004, 2005, detailing the impact of corruption on the drug war).

50. Benjamin Reames (2007, 129) notes that if an official is under investigation, he or she can usually pay off the internal affairs investigating officer.

51. Such assessments generate a sense of déjà vu. Mexico offers a history of efforts to battle corruption among the police and the judiciary with limited results. In 1994, Attorney General Antonio Lozano from the PAN (the first non-PRI attorney general) fired 850 corrupt police, who later returned due to *amparos* (injunctions). In 1996, the PGR fired more than 1,200 staff for corruption or unsuitability (courts ordered that it reinstate some 234). In April 1997, the government dissolved the Instituto Nacional para el Combate a las Drogas (INCD) (following the arrest of General Gutiérrez Rebollo, the head of the organization, who was jailed for conspiring with drug traffickers)

and replaced it with FEADS and the Unidad contra al Crimen Organizado, which were to be staffed by personnel who could pass a vetting procedure. Yet, despite Jorge Madrazo's promises to root out corruption, at the end of his term, 800 police had been fired for corruption, ties to drug traffickers, and consumption of drugs, and their posts had not been filled by new elements. As well, there were 391 people on the payroll who were not present on the job, and all types of irregularities existed ("El crimen organizado" 2000). It was reported that between April 1997 and December 1999, more than 1,400 (of 3,500) federal police officers had been fired for corruption, and that 357 federal officers had been prosecuted (BINLEA 2000). Part of Zedillo's efforts to reduce corruption involved strengthening the role of the military; but instead, bringing the military into the drug war exposed them to even greater corruption (see Rocha 2005, 216). In addition to Gutiérrez Rebollo, at least fifteen high-ranking military officers were prosecuted in 1998, though only four were arrested in 2000 (Velasco 2005, 107). Indeed, analysis suggests that the substantial reforms under Zedillo's 1996–2000 national public safety program were not effective at reducing corruption (Magaloni and Zepeda 2004, 178).

52. In testimony before the Chamber of Deputies, Arturo González Aragón, the head of the ASF, offered a similarly pessimistic assessment, giving Mexico a failing grade in terms of fighting corruption under Fox's leadership. He claimed, for instance, that since 2001, the SHCP had not sanctioned officials or agencies for misuse of funds, and that the SFP had not fired anyone involved in illegal acts (data obtained from SFP seem to suggest otherwise). The nation's top accountant posited that Hacienda and the SFP tolerated corrupt officials, and argued that the ASF should have greater powers, noting that the ASF could not examine spending that took place through *fideicomisos,* or trusts (the fiscal reform of 2007 included clauses allowing the oversight of funds in *fideicomisos*). He further highlighted that, despite the recovery of billions of pesos in the Pemexgate case, it was unclear where the money went or who had been responsible for diverting the funds (cited in Garduño and Ballinas 2005).

Members of key congressional committees offered similar assessments during Secretary Romero's testimony before Congress. Many assailed the auditing role of the SFP. Emilio Martínez Álvarez (of the party Convergencia), for example, criticized the fact that the administration audited itself, suggesting that this should be the sole responsibility of the ASF. Guillermo Huisa Carranza (PRD) noted that the ASF produced far more irregularities than did the SFP, despite the fact that it conducted far fewer audits. While praising advances in transparency, the legislator nonetheless lashed out against government oversight: "There have been advances in transparency, however, it is also necessary to advance in terms of oversight, governmental audits and evaluations of dependencies and entities, to determine whether these are accomplishing their primary objectives, programs, and goals, and to make this known to the citizens." Others questioned the lack of progress in implementing the civil service reforms. Ruiz del Rincon (PAN), for example, stated that the program itself provided too much discretion. Others were perhaps more general in questioning the administration's assessment of the situation. According to Guillermo Velasco Rodríguez (PVEM), while there had been slow advances in the fight against corruption, much remained to be done, "because we are still one of the most corrupt countries on the planet, especially if we compare ourselves to our principal trading partners." Victor Hugo Islas Hernández (PRI), the chair of the Public Function Committee, offered perhaps the strongest criticism of the initiatives, adding: "And they have not been able to succeed for the simple reason that they offered much and have achieved nothing" (Cámara de Diputados 2005).

He went on to accuse the administration of simply going after former officials, but not those within the current administration.

53. Such dangers similarly haunt public officials. One former federal agent, for instance, stressed: "In this country, you talk about corruption and people kill you"

(Cámara de Diputados 2005). Though the agent lived to tell the tale, he was subsequently arrested in Tijuana for resisting arrest and bribery. Similar cases abound. General José Francisco Fallardo, for instance, was jailed in 1993 for calling for the creation of a military ombudsman to oversee cases of abuse of authority, human rights violations, and corruption in the military. Such pressures even occur within the Chamber of Deputies. Santiago Creel, the head of the congressional subcommittee in charge of investigating charges against Governors Roberto Madrazo of Tabasco and Victor Cervera Pacheco of Yucatán, for instance, reportedly received threats and pressures by government and PRI officials. In September 2001, Mexico City councilwoman Maria de los Angeles Tames (PAN) was killed, allegedly because of her efforts to expose corruption in Atizapan de Zaragosa, where she had been investigating the selling of zoning permits and city contracts to companies in exchange for bribes. She subsequently become a symbol of the fight against corruption ("A Year Later" 2002).

54. Starting in 2002 when the federal law was passed, state governments began adopting similar legislation. An evaluation of the eighteen access to information laws (state and federal) in existence as of June 2004, produced by Libertad de Información México A.C. and Innovación México–Proyecto Atlatl, noted a lack of uniformity in these laws, which were not always in compliance with the norms and principles of human rights and other organizations (*Atlatl* no. 20, 2004). Since 2002, all states have adopted access to information laws, and in 2007 they harmonized the particulars of these laws in accordance with a constitutional mandate.

55. Between December 2006 and April 2007, the new government of Calderon reportedly appointed 1,098 positions based on an emergency clause that should have been filled through the merit-based system (*Milenio* June 17, 2007).

56. The test is a simulation used to gauge the tendency of an individual to engage in corruption, as presented in Frank and Schulze 1998.

57. The charges in the forty-six cases included five for illicit enrichment, eleven for improper use of authority, nine for embezzlement, three for improper exercise of public authority, three for abuse of power, one for bribery, and fourteen classified as "other" (fraud, falsification of documents, etc.).

58. In 1998, SECODAM conducted 512 audits and 374 external audits; in 2000, 275 and 637 respectively; in 2001, 81 and 348; in 2002, 54 and 348; in 2003, 92 and 329 (SFP 2005a, 37).

59. Melanie Manion (2004, 35) uses data on corruption reported by citizens as indirect evidence of a sudden shift in mass public beliefs about anticorruption enforcement in Hong Kong, noting a doubling of reports within one year.

60. Insecurity, drug-related violence, and organized crime became priority issues of the Calderon administration during this time. This reached a crescendo in mid-2008 when a meeting of the three levels of government, NGOs, religious organizations, and business produced the *Acuerdo Nacional por la Seguridad, la Justicia, y la Legalidad*: a series of seventy-four compromises for change. This summit meeting was spearheaded by the organization Mexico Unido contra la Delincuencia and sparked in large part by the public outcry following the murder of the son of noted entrepreneur Alberto Marti during a bungled kidnapping in August 2008 (*Milenio* November 28, 2008).

61. Drug-related corruption ties into the lure of money and threat of death (*plomo o plata*). Recent revelations point not only to the nature of the payoffs, but the level of violence unleashed against local officials who have either refused to accept the payoffs, failed to comply with corrupt agreements, or are targeted by rival organizations.

62. In November 2008, the government released information showing that 50.2 percent of the 3,971 officials, prosecutorial agents, and justice secretaries of the Mexico City government failed the exam on judiciary knowledge a year earlier. Those that failed were forced to take training classes and were retested in 2008. Of the 1,943 that

originally failed, 1,253 passed this time. The PGJDF also conducted exams of 3,826 agents of the judicial police and reported that 99.29 percent of these passed the exam on knowledge about the application of force, human rights, and rights of police (*Milenio* November 25, 2008).

63. While the Calderon program acknowledges important advances under Fox and even the early reforms under Calderon in battling corruption, it recognizes the perception inside the country that corruption has not changed. It attributes this "lack of correlation between the policies enacted and public opinion" to the particular path of democratic change in the country and the unequal progress between structural and institutional changes and social and human development. It also notes that the government is facing a new form of corruption tied to regional and global organized crime.

5

Exploring Perceptions of Corruption

One way of assessing levels of corruption is to ask those who regularly deal with the system. Despite the challenges of measuring and tracking corruption, subjective-based yardsticks have gained substantial scholarly and political use in recent years. Essentially, there are two ways to use surveys to gauge corruption: one focuses on perception, the other on actual experience. Perception-based measures calculate the level of corruption based on the opinions held by country experts, members of the business community, aid workers, other specialized groups (as in Transparency International's Corruption Perception Index or the World Bank's Control of Corruption Index), or the public (as in Transparency International's Global Corruption Barometer or the Latinobarómetro polls). Presumably, these impressions depict individuals' intimate knowledge of the system. Experience-based indexes, in contrast, calculate corruption based on a respondent's actual contact with corruption. These polls may ask about the payment of bribes (or extraofficial payments), the witnessing of bribes being paid, or other firsthand knowledge of bribes either generally or as part of a process of acquiring a specific public service, within a particular institution (e.g., police) and over a specified period of time. Despite the differences, both approaches rest on the rather facile assumption that those within a society are aware of the level of corruption that takes place and, for that matter, whether things have changed. Methodologically, of course, neither approach escapes rather grueling criticism.[1]

This study disaggregates corruption into three dimensions—perception, participation, and pattern—examining each separately, here and in the next two chapters. Beginning with the more popularly employed perception-based measures of corruption, this chapter explores the nature of popular perceptions

133

of corruption and change in Mexico in recent years, and the underlying determinants and consequences of these views. The chapter begins by providing a descriptive profile of perceptions of corruption and change, and then broadens this profile to look at the public's views on the relative importance of corruption as a political problem, its tolerance toward corruption and illegal activity, views regarding the underlying causes and likely solutions to the corruption problem, and finally, popular assessments of the likelihood of change and how to bring it about. Attention then turns to a more detailed analysis of the determinants and consequences of individual perceptions of corruption and change using data from the Encuesta Nacional de Corrupción y Buen Gobierno (ENCBG) surveys conducted by Transparencia Mexicana in 2001, 2003, 2005, and 2007,[2] the Latin American Public Opinion Project (LAPOP) Mexico poll in 2004 carried out by Vanderbilt University,[3] and the Corruptómetro polls in 2001, 2002, and 2004 conducted by the newspaper *La Reforma*. Accepting *a priori* that the two classes of subjective indicators of corruption—perception and participation—are not identical but in fact tap into unique dimensions of corruption (see Morris 2008), the potential relationship linking these two, while incorporated briefly into the regression model here, is explored more fully in the next chapter.

Profiling Perceptions of Corruption and Change

Various polls have asked Mexicans and practitioners about the state of corruption. Despite different populations, sample sizes, question wording, response categories, and years, these polls consistently and collectively confirm that corruption—or at least the perception of corruption—is widespread throughout Mexico. In the 1998 Hewlett/MORI survey on popular conceptions of democracy, for instance, 76 percent of respondents claimed that "almost everyone" or "many" in government were corrupt. In the ENCBG polls, when asked to agree or disagree with the statement "all politicians are corrupt," 79 percent of respondents in 2001 and 78 percent in 2003 agreed, while only 11 percent and 10 percent respectively disagreed. Discriminating between total and partial agreement or disagreement in the 2005 ENCBG, 66 percent of respondents totally agreed, while another 24 percent partially agreed. Using a slightly different yardstick, the 2005 ENCBG also asked respondents to rate the level of corruption in the government on a scale of 1 (low) to 10 (high). Amazingly, a slight majority, 50.2 percent, selected the highest possible rating, while 29 percent offered ratings of 8 or 9. Asking respondents to gauge the level of corruption, taking into account their own experiences with paying bribes, witnessing bribes being paid, or being asked for a bribe, Vanderbilt's LAPOP poll in 2004 found 39 percent expressing the view that corruption is *"muy generalizada"* (very common) with another 44 percent considered it *"algo generalizada"* (somewhat common). The annual Latinobarómetro polls offer further evidence. In the 2002 poll, 77 percent of Mexicans considered civil servants corrupt, while in the 2004 poll, 65 percent of respondents felt that the probabilities of bribing a police were very high. In the latter poll, Mexico was ranked as being the most corrupt among Latin American countries (see Appendix A for data comparing Mexico to other countries).[4]

How accurate are these impressions? After all, how much knowledge does the public really have regarding corruption? Yet polls focused on smaller and more refined populations rather than on the general public offer similar results. Data from Transparency International's annual Corruption Perception Index and the World Bank's Control of Corruption Index, both based on a series of polls of experts outside the country, as shown in Table 5.1, consistently reveal that Mexico suffers relatively high levels of corruption. Polls of the private sector in Mexico provide further indications of the extent of corruption. One 2001 poll, for instance, found 62 percent of businesses stating that businesses like theirs routinely made extraofficial payments to lower-level officials, while 39 percent said that businesses like theirs made extraofficial payments to influence the content of laws, policies, and regulations (CEE 2002). In the 2001 Diagnostico Institucional del Sistema Federal de Control (DSFC) poll, even among internal auditors within the federal government, 60 percent recognized as "frequent" the acts of corruption within the areas they supervised.[5]

Because the polls do not span very many years, it is somewhat difficult to assess long-term historical trends and processes.[6] Even so, data do not seem to point to much change, despite (or because of?) the intense political focus on corruption during the period. Whether using the annual Corruption Perception Index, the various measures from the World Bank, the limited Corruptómetro polls or even the ENCBG polls, the degree of change is in fact rather small. Both the Corruption Perception Index and World Bank measures, for instance, show only a slight decline in the level of perceived corruption (an increase in clean government or corruption control) somewhere around the 2001–2004 period, followed by a return to earlier levels. The Transparency International measure for cleanliness peaked in 2001, while the World Bank measure peaked in 2003; but by 2006, the Transparency International index returned to the level of 1996, 1998, and 2000, improving slightly to 3.6 by 2008, while the World Bank measure pointed to further deterioration. By contrast, the ENCBG polls seem rather consistent over the years despite different response categories. If we collapse the total and partial agreement categories from 2005, the percentage of respondents who agreed in 2005 that politicians were corrupt was actually significantly higher than in 2001 or 2003. The Corruptómetro index of corruption also shows consistency over the period, with a slight increase well within the range of error.

A more direct approach to calculating change comes from questions asking respondents directly about their assessments of change over a certain time. Response categories include, quite simply, an increase, a decrease, or no change. Responses here tend to show rather consistently the perception that corruption

Table 5.1 Perceptions of Corruption

	1995	1996	1997	1998	1999	2000	2001	2002	2003	2004	2005	2006	2007	2008
Corruption Perception Index[a]	3.18	3.30	2.66	3.3	3.4	3.3	3.7	3.6	3.6	3.6	3.5	3.3	3.5	3.6
Control of Corruption Index[b]	—	−0.39	—	−0.53	—	−0.37	—	−0.26	−0.19	−0.35	−0.39	−0.34	−0.35	—

Sources: Transparency International; Kaufmann et al. 2008.
Notes: a. Scale 0–10: 0 = corrupt to 10 = clean.
b. Scale −2.5 (corrupt) to +2.5 (clean).

has either increased or, at best, remained the same. Few sense much in the way of a decline, despite the political changes taking place or the high-profile anticorruption efforts of the government during this time. In one of the earliest polls incorporating the topic, the 1994 Belden Russonello poll, 49 percent of respondents felt that corruption had increased over the preceding three years, compared to only 7 percent who believed that it had declined. Another poll, taken in December 1995, found more specifically that 57 percent felt there were more narcotraffickers in the government than in the past. The same poll also showed an increase since 1992 in the percentage of respondents viewing measures against corruption as insufficient. In Mexico City alone, a stunning 81 percent of respondents in 1998 felt that corruption had increased in the preceding few years, as opposed to just 18 percent who argued that it had merely remained the same or declined (Gutiérrez Vivó 1998, 189–197).[7] More specifically, 54 percent thought the government was achieving no success in stopping corruption, and only 5 percent said the government was acting significantly to control it (cited in Ferriss 1998).

More surprisingly, after the historic defeat of the Partido Revolucionario Institucional (PRI), when expectations of political change spiked, this perception that things had grown worse persisted. As shown in Table 5.2, the proportion of people who sensed a decline in corruption in these years was always far less than the proportion who sensed an increase. Similar to the Transparency International and World Bank pattern, these figures suggest some mild and immediate success in lowering the levels of corruption around the 2001–2003 period (the first half of the Vicente Fox government), but a return to the prior levels in the latter years. Nonetheless, despite the low numbers who saw positive changes over the prior year, a 58 percent majority in the 2002 Corruptómetro poll believed that there was less corruption than during past administrations, though 39 percent of respondents disagreed with that assessment.

Table 5.2 Perceptions of Change in Corruption

Year (Poll)	Perceived Change in Corruption (% response)			Time Frame
	Increase	Same	Decrease	
1994 (Belden Russonello)	49	7	7	since 1991
2001 (ENCBG)	35	43	21	past year
2001 (Reforma)	45	23	31	past year
2002 (Reforma)	48	29	22	past year
2003 (ENCBG)	34	47	19	past year
2004 (Reforma)	70	15	14	past year
2005 (ENCBG)	40	44	16	past year
2005 (Global Corruption Barometer)	59	29	11	past three years
2007 (ENCBG)	41	42	14	past year

Expanding the Perception-Based Profile

Before exploring determinants and consequences of the perceptions of corruption and change, it is useful to broaden the profile somewhat to offer a better panorama of Mexicans' views about corruption. Attention centers briefly on the public's position of the importance of corruption as a political problem, its tolerance toward corrupt acts, general views on the nature of corruption and approaches needed to address it, and finally, the public's expectations of change.

Seriousness

The prevalence of corruption (perceived or otherwise) says little about its importance as a national problem. In the case of Mexico, however, both general and targeted polls consistently show that Mexicans tend to view corruption as a serious matter, though rarely do they deem it the most important issue facing the country. In the 1998 Hewlett/MORI poll, for instance, 42 percent identified corruption (the most cited response) as the major obstacle to democracy. Respondents to the 2004 LAPOP poll ranked corruption's importance a bit lower, casting it as the third most cited problem facing the country (cited by 16 percent of respondents), behind unemployment (cited by 25 percent) and poverty (cited by 17 percent). In the nonrepresentative Corruptómetro polls, almost a third of respondents picked corruption as the most serious problem facing the nation in both 2001 and 2002, with corruption surpassed only by the issue of insecurity in the 2004 poll.

Targeted polls show a similar pattern: corruption is an important matter, but not the most important issue facing the nation. Businesses, for instance, ranked corruption high as a matter of concern in the 2001 Encuesta de Gobernabilidad y Desarrollo Empresarial (EGDE) survey, though insecurity and contraband/pirating were ranked as the greatest obstacle facing business.[8] Still, 87 percent of businesses considered bureaucratic corruption a serious problem, and more important than such issues as the informal economy, unions, and obtaining licenses. In perhaps a further indication of the "seriousness" of the issue, 57 percent of businesses generally and 62 percent of big businesses stated a willingness to provide resources to help battle corruption (Centro de Estudios Estratégicos 2002).

Tolerance

Some analysts contend that the presence of corruption in Mexico reflects an underlying cultural tolerance (Moreno 2002; Catterberg and Moreno 2006, 2007). Though I explore this factor at the micro level in the subsequent regression model, measures of tolerance toward corruption at the macro level offer at best a mixed picture. First, the mere fact that the public considers corruption a serious national problem suggests that tolerance is not extremely high. Second, data measuring the level of tolerance or permissiveness toward the rule of law point to a public that has seemingly high normative expectations, is quick to reject corruption and violations of the law, and is quick to condemn those engaged in such activities, at least in theory. In the 2001 ENCBG poll, for instance, 87 percent felt that politicians should be held accountable, and 80 percent believed that citizens should obey the law without exception. In 2001 and 2005, 73 percent and 74 percent, respectively, totally disapproved of giving gifts or money simply to speed up bureaucratic procedure (a decidedly petty form of corruption), while 84 percent and 62 percent disagreed with the popular Mexican saying *"el que no tranza, no avanza"* (he who does not cheat, does not get ahead). When presented with a list of twenty-one corrupt acts, including paying a bribe under various circumstances, providing false information on documents, running a red light, petty theft, and providing political favors to friends or family, the public consistently offered high levels of disapproval of such actions. In fact, the proportion of those who expressed a total, blanket disapproval of such examples of corruption rarely fell below 75 percent (the response options were total approval, partial approval, partial disapproval, or total disapproval). If we sum the twenty-one corrupt acts to create a composite measure of tolerance, 31–35 percent expressed total disapproval of all the acts, depending on the year of the survey, and 50–55 percent expressed high intolerance, with slight approval for fewer then three of the acts, leaving just a small number of people who even remotely might be considered tolerant of corruption.

Such views, in short, tend to depict a strong normative system among the population. Mexicans, in other words, easily distinguish right from wrong, the legal from the illegal, and more importantly, the way the system should work from the way it really works. Yet other questions and other polls eliciting views not based completely on a normative, hypothetical system—which may prompt respondents simply to offer the "proper" or socially expected response—hint at a certain willingness to accept a degree of corruption under certain circumstances. When asked whether public officials should be allowed to take advantage of their positions as long as they do good things in office—perhaps a more appropriate measure of tolerance or a trade-off—54 percent, 52 percent, and 59 percent of respondents in 2001, 2003, and 2005, respectively, agreed with the statement, while 39 percent, 37 percent, and 33 percent disagreed. This indicator of tolerance nestles neatly with the aforementioned views that corruption is perhaps of lesser significance than economic and security concerns. Another indictor of what could be interpreted as a sign of the public's tolerance toward corruption is their low inclination to denounce it. Though many believe that citizens play an important role in combating corruption, huge majorities—79 percent in 2001, 78 percent in 2003, and 77 percent in 2005—claim not to know the procedure for denouncing an act of corruption.[9]

Arguably, on the one hand, if corruption were of such importance and intolerance reigned, then one would expect the public, who have a key role to play in fighting corruption, to at least learn the procedures for denouncing it. Of course, on the other hand, the reasons given for not denouncing corruption could hardly be seen as a sign of tolerance. In the 2001 ENCBG survey, for instance, of those who admitted to having knowledge of a corrupt act and not denouncing it, the most cited reason for not doing so was to avoid problems or reprisals (23 percent), followed by a lack of efficacy (it would not make a difference, a view cited by 17 percent). Both of these are certainly rational responses based on a combination of self-interest and an understanding (or perception) of the nature of the political system, and do not indicate a lack of importance of the corrupt act itself nor any notion of tolerance. Even government auditors tend to agree with the public on this point. In the 2001 DSFC poll, 43 percent of auditors cited fear of reprisal as the most important reason why people do not denounce corruption. Lack of knowledge of how to report corruption came in second, cited by 25 percent of auditors.

Whereas linking corruption to tolerance certainly seems plausible, at the macro level the evidence seems to suggest a combination of widespread corruption alongside strong views condemning it. This curious combination echoes the findings from William Miller's study (2006, 378) of the Czech Republic, Slovakia, Bulgaria, and Ukraine: "The real problem of petty corruption is that so many citizens and officials who genuinely condemn it are pressured or tempted into practicing it." Formal models by Jens Andvig and Karl Moene (1990), Ajit Mishra (2006), and Jean Tirole (1996) show how the pervasiveness of corruption contributes to its persistence despite normative views to the contrary. In such settings, according to Tirole (1996, 350), "those who comply with the law or social standards often become victims of harassment, extortion, and alleged corrupt behavior." The cultural dimension of this aspect is explored in Chapter 8.

Various analysts allude to changes in the public's tolerance toward corruption (growing intolerance) or altering expectations (raising the bar) as growing from the underlying political dynamics. Given the increasing attention to corruption brought about by democratization, growing societal pluralism, the international context, and Fox's high profile anticorruption campaign, one might expect a reduction in the level of the public's tolerance toward corruption, and a concomitant strengthening of expectations and standards. Indeed, Adrián Acosta Silva (2004, 17) contends that "a more demanding and less docile public opinion in the face of the behavior of political actors has begun to take shape." Yet it is hard to confirm this trend based on the available data. The level of intolerance, already quite high in 2001, was only slightly higher in 2005, while the seriousness of corruption remained relatively unchanged over the period. If anything, as indicated by questions related to assessments of expected changes in corruption, expectation was high during the initial transition to democracy, setting the stage for disappointment and disillusionment as the

Fox term wore on. Expectations may have peaked following the election of Fox, falling thereafter.

Perceived Causes

Various questions profile Mexicans' understanding of the causal nature of corruption generally and in Mexico specifically. Because of different question wording, the precise pattern is somewhat mixed, but key factors still stand out. At one level, there is a strong sense that corruption exists because of the nature of the political system, the nature of politicians, and more specifically the weak enforcement of the rule of law. In one of the Mexico City polls, for instance, 77 percent of respondents in 1998 agreed that corruption prevailed because the guilty went unpunished (Gutiérrez Vivó 1998, 189–197). Another poll, in 2001, found a 54 percent majority expressing the view that the legislation that was applied was inadequate, while 37 percent felt that the laws were insufficient (Consultores Internacionales 2001). The internal auditors share this popular view; they too blame the system. In the 2001 DSFC poll, 79 percent of auditors agreed that the laws, regulations, and legal norms were not adequate to prevent and combat corruption, while 51 percent felt that their investigative authority needed to be strengthened. The ENCBG polls provide further support of these views condemning the system. In the 2001 ENCBG poll, for instance, 72 percent of respondents agreed that Mexicans were honest but that the system imposed corruption, while 74 percent agreed with the statement "corruption is due to politicians." And despite the popular argument that corruption stems from low pay, 78 percent claimed that officials engaged in corruption because of ambition, not poor pay. In 2005, 60 percent similarly cited ambition as the major cause of corruption, again the top choice among respondents, while in a separate question over a third of respondents, 36 percent, chose the response "because politicians are corrupt," more than double the number of respondents, 15 percent, who selected the response "because all Mexicans are corrupt." Meanwhile, the second most cited response, given by 23 percent, was "because the laws are not enforced." This differentiation is also evident in the distinct levels of corruption associated with the government versus society recorded in the Corruptómetro polls. While the average index of corruption in the government, on the 0–10 scale, stood at 8.05 in 2005, the average for social corruption (among citizens, businesses, teachers, etc.) was just 6.25.

Yet despite these views, another prominent factor shown by various polls centers on the underlying culture. Though again results vary in part because of different question wording and response categories, there is a clear sense among the public that corruption is part of Mexican culture. In the 2002 Corruptómetro poll, for instance, 44 percent of respondents identified "the culture and education of Mexicans" as the principal cause of corruption, clearly the top choice compared to just 14 percent (second-place response) who said "the lack of application of the law." Responses to a question regarding who initiates corruption (the government official or the citizen) also reveal this tendency. In 2001, respondents split, with a third citing the public official, another third the citizen, and the remaining third attributing it to both. Questions asking about the measures needed to fight corruption also illustrate this view about the culture. The most cited approach to fighting corruption fingers the general culture. Even so, despite this view that attributed at least part of the blame to culture, there is the clear perception that the individual respondent is not overly corrupt. When asked to rank themselves on a scale of 1 (very corrupt) to 10 (very clean), the average rating were 8.17, 8.05, and 7.64 in 2001, 2003, and 2005, respectively.

Some evidence suggests that public officials may have a slightly different take on the underlying causal factors. While a large segment of the public seems to blame politicians or both politicians and the public for corruption, public officials often blame the citizens. Niels Uildriks's (forthcoming) specialized poll of preventive and judicial police, for example, unearthed the general view that society makes the police corrupt: a view shared by 47 percent of preventive police and 57 percent of judicial police surveyed in 2005. According to one official, "I am not corrupt, but corrupted, and it is society that keeps corruption proliferating." Similarly, while the public is less likely to attribute corruption to necessity and poor pay, blaming ambition instead, the police are more likely to cite poor pay. In the poll, 42 percent of preventive police and 33 percent of judicial police attributed corruption to low pay. In fact, 55 percent of preventive police and 36 percent of judicial police considered police corruption inevitable given poor salaries. By contrast, only 8 percent of each group saw the need to pay off their superiors as the main reason feeding corruption. Considering the Secretaría de la Función Pública (SFP) to be highly corrupt, one justification given by the judicial police for taking bribes was that otherwise the prosecutor would get the money and this would cost the citizens even more. As a further sign of the corruption within these agencies, 30 percent of preventive police and 20 percent of judicial police considered internal affairs divisions (the Consejo de Honor y Justicia) corrupt.

Approaches to Combating Corruption

The Mexican public has been asked a host of questions about what they believe is needed to fight corruption, providing further insights into their perceptions of the underlying nature of corruption. Among the instruments or tools that might help fight corruption, one factor identified by the public is alternation in political power. In 2001, for instance, 49 percent of respondents believed that alternation in power would help reduce the level of corruption. Given the country's initial experience with such alternation, the percentage who agreed with the statement fell somewhat by 2003, to 42 percent. As noted, the public is somewhat split between seeing the combating of corruption as the responsibility of both the government and the people or simply the government. In 2001, 44 percent said it was the responsibility of both, 38 percent said it was the responsibility of the government, and 13 percent claimed it was the responsibility of the people. By 2005, a slightly larger portion of respondents, 41 percent, said it was the sole responsibility of the government, while 36 percent now said it was the responsibility of both, and 13 percent again said the people had the responsibility of combating corruption.

Other questions have dealt with the role of specific institutions and strategies. In the 2001 and 2003 ENCBG polls, the most important institution to fighting corruption was the family (indicative of corruption as a cultural problem) (see Table 5.3), while the top-rated strategy was improved education in the home (91 percent in 2001 and 88 percent in 2003 agreed that this would help). Punishing officials (89 percent in 2001 and 87 percent in 2003), improved education in the schools (85 percent in 2001 and 82 percent in 2003), simplifying *trámites* (77 percent in 2003), and modifying the laws (69 percent in 2001 and 67 percent in 2003) followed. This same pattern prevailed in 2005 when respondents picked the three most important measures to combat corruption: 32 percent opted for improving instruction in schools, 27 percent picked improving education at home, and 20 percent chose punishing officials. Though punishing officials is clearly important to the public, their pointing to the importance of family and teachers rather than the government seems to suggest the importance of attacking the values and morals associated with corruption.

Table 5.3 Role of Institutions in Fighting Corruption (ENCBG)

Institution	Helpfulness in Fighting Corruption[a]	
	2001	2003
Family	8.31	8.15
Military	7.08	6.85
Teachers	7.04	7.04
Church	6.82	6.45
Media	6.69	6.50
Government	5.51	5.23
International organs	—	5.48
Business	5.02	4.86
Police	4.88	4.51
United States	—	4.42
Unions	4.75	4.56
Political parties	4.57	4.39

Notes: The results for the two periods are almost identical, with a 0.997 correlation. As shown in Chapter 7, these are almost perfectly inversely correlated with perceptions of corruption within the institutions as expressed in the 2005 ENCBG poll and the Global Corruption Barometer.
a. Scale 1–10: 1 = least helpful, to 10 = most helpful.

In the 2001 ENCBG poll, even the church ranked higher than the government in terms of helping to combat corruption, perhaps again pointing to the cultural dimension of corruption as well as to the public's greater trust and confidence in religion compared to politics.

Expectations

One area where an individual's sense about the nature of corruption, particularly its depth, colludes with perceptions of political reality involves expectations of change. Many have noted the high hopes that accompanied the Fox victory and the PRI's defeat, including expectations that corruption would be dealt a severe blow. According to Acosta (2004, 18), "The PAN electoral victory . . . with reason strengthened the expectations that the legendary corrupt networks that had spread throughout the post-Revolutionary regime during the long period of PRI dominance, would finally come to an end." While the polls do confirm high expectations and optimism—62 percent in 2003 said the political will to combat corruption existed—it is surprising just how cautious this optimism really is. In the 2001 ENCBG poll (conducted about seven months after Fox took office), whereas 49 percent of respondents believed that alternation in power would help reduce corruption, almost 40 percent felt it would have little effect.[10] This is surprising given the long pent-up expectations tied to democratization. Similarly, in the 2002 Corruptómetro poll whereas 60 percent of respondents predicted that Fox would be able to reduce corruption "a little," just 13 percent believed he would be able to reduce it "a lot," and 25 percent said he would not be able to diminish it at all. As shown in Table 5.4, the expectation of a decline in corruption peaked in 2001, and fell significantly by 2005. As expectations ebbed—and disillusionment flowed—the proportion of respondents predicting an increase in corruption grew. Strikingly, five years into democracy, more than a third of respondents foresaw an increase in corruption in the coming year, more than double the percentage predicting a decline.

Perhaps the more telling question regarding expectations asks respondents simply whether they believe it is possible to end corruption. In 2001, 2003, and 2005 ENCBG polls, the public split almost evenly on this question,

Table 5.4 Expected Change in Corruption in the Coming Year (ENCBG, in percentage)

	Increase	Decrease
2001	29.6	33.4
2003	34.9	22.8
2005	41.0	17.9

with about a third believing that it was possible, another third expressing the view that it was *"poco possible"* (unlikely), and the remaining third deeming the task simply impossible: a telling indicator of the underlying political culture. In 2005, for instance, whereas 28 percent expressed the view that it was impossible, 35 percent believed it to be unlikely. Such a view—perhaps the product of years of corruption and disillusionment—has the potential to undermine social capital and cripple the efforts of the government to involve the public in its anticorruption efforts. Indicative, perhaps, of the perceived depth or embeddedness of corruption, 57 percent in 2001 believed, in fact, that "an honest person who was given a public post was more likely to become corrupt than to stay honest." Chapter 8 analyzes such views in the context of the cultural dimension to corruption.

Determinants of Perceptions of Corruption and Change

Despite relying on polling data from individual respondents, much of the empirical literature on corruption uses a cross-national research design, taking the country rather than the individual as the unit of analysis. Works along these lines have provided rich and robust insights into both the causes and the consequences of corruption at the national level. Such studies, for instance, find higher levels of corruption in countries that have lower levels of development, that suffer political instability, that have less open economies, that have non-Protestant and non-English cultures, that enjoy lower levels of interpersonal trust and social capital (La Porta et al. 1997; Serra 2006), and that have a greater level of permissiveness toward corruption (Moreno 2002), as outlined in Chapter 1. Of course, results from macro-level studies do not automatically translate into explanations of individual opinion (the ecological fallacy).

Studies analyzing individual views on corruption are less prevalent than cross-national studies, and for obvious reasons tend to focus on one country or a small set of countries. Though too few in number to offer definitive findings, there are studies that nonetheless highlight some of the key underlying determinants and effects of corruption. Damarys Canache and Michael Allison's study (2005) of a small set of Latin American countries, for instance, finds that women, older respondents, and those lacking interpersonal trust tend to perceive higher levels of corruption than do males, younger respondents, and those exhibiting trust. They also find that respondents with greater levels of political interest and information are more likely to perceive a level of corruption comparable to that expressed by country experts. Michael Smith (2008) finds that the social status of respondents is inversely linked to corruption perceptions, but that the strength of the association varies across countries, being less pronounced in those with high levels of corruption. Mitchell Seligson (1999), Roderic Camp, Kenneth Coleman, and Charles Davis (Camp, Coleman, and Davis 2000; Davis, Camp, and Coleman 2004), and Smith (2008) detect support linking a person's perception of corruption and their sense of interpersonal or social trust. Individuals with low levels of trust in others are more likely to perceive higher levels of corruption in the society, just as societies exhibiting low levels of trust tend to suffer higher levels of corruption. Davis, Camp, and Coleman (2004), in their study on Chile and Mexico, also discover that an individual's support for the party in power and a positive economic assessment tend to lower the level of perceived corruption. Gabriela Catterberg and Alejandro Moreno (2007), in turn, using Corruptómetro, data link an individual's perception of corruption to what they refer to as the individual's "detachment from the law." Defined as belief in, respect for, and compliance with the law, individuals who are attached to the law, they show, are slightly more likely to perceive higher levels of corruption than those who are detached from the law. They also find that individuals who are attached to the law are more likely to believe that corruption has increased over the prior year and more likely to attribute corruption to culture and education (and less likely to attribute it to weak law enforcement). Analysts link detachment not only to corruption, but also to distrust and dissatisfaction with democracy. Looking beyond respect for the law itself, Naci Mocan (2004) finds a close link between an individual's perception of corruption and their perception of the quality of public institutions. This sort of finding raises important questions regarding the issue of causal direction.

Using individual perceptions of corruption as the independent variable—that is, looking at the effects of perceived corruption—a handful of studies suggest that the perception of corruption undermines citizens' attitudes toward government officials and institutions, reduces feelings of regime legitimacy and satisfaction with democracy, and may alter the nature of political participation. Canache and Allison (2005), for instance, find that an individual's perception of corruption lowers their opinion of incumbent officials and political institutions, though they find no evidence that perceived corruption actually weakens support for democracy as a form of government. In a series of studies on select Latin American countries, Seligson (2001, 2002a, 2002b, 2006) finds conclusively that the perception of corruption reduces feelings of regime legitimacy and satisfaction with democracy. Looking at eleven countries, Eric Kite and Margaret Sarles (2006, 350) provide further support for this view, concluding that "corruption, along with citizen security concerns, has the most detrimental impact on citizens' confidence in democracy and democratic institutions." Christopher Anderson and Yuliya Tverdova's analysis (2003) of individual opinion in sixteen countries also uncovers this negative effect of corruption on citizens' attitudes toward government, but finds that the relationship largely disappears after controlling for vote for the party in power. In a similar way, Luigi Manzetti and Carole Wilson's study (2006) on Argentina shows that an individual's evaluation of the economy mediates the impact of corruption on their confidence in the government. Looking at political participation, analyses on Mexico by Davis, Camp, and Coleman (2004) as well as James McCann and Jorge Domínguez (1998) find perceived corruption to have no effect on voting for the opposition, but rather on the act of voting itself.[11] Individuals perceiving the electoral system or the political system in general as corrupt, they discovered, were more likely to abstain, though such a finding clearly refers to the period of PRI hegemony. A study on voting in Canada by André Blais and colleagues (2005), by contrast, shows that political scandal, independent of partisan loyalties, had a major impact on the 2004 vote. It also shows that prior views about politicians strongly affect how an individual perceives the scandal.[12] Finally, data show that in terms of the impact of corruption on assessments of corruption as a national problem, there is little connection. Galtung (2001b, 226) cites a report on Latin America that shows the lack of correlation linking perception of corruption as a very serious problem to actual or verifiable levels of corruption. He notes that in 2000, for example, more Chileans viewed corruption as a serious problem than did Mexicans, despite the higher perceived incidence of corruption in Mexico than in Chile. Frances Hagopian (2005) also notes this paradox: that the countries with the most reports of corruption (Mexico and Brazil) are not the countries where the public considers corruption the greatest problem or where there is political instability.

To date, almost no studies have focused on the issue of change, whether as a dependent or an independent variable. One study by Leticia Juárez González (2004), however, shows a direct link in Mexico between the ebbs and flows in public opinion on corruption and high-profile scandals. Tracking polling data over a period of time, Juárez shows how the video scandals of February and March 2004 (a series of revelations of politicians taking bribes in Mexico City—see Appendix B) greatly boosted the perception that corruption and impunity had increased and that corruption had become a more serious political problem. Accordingly, the proportion of citizens who saw corruption as the principal problem facing the country climbed from 2 percent in 1997 and 8 percent in August 2002 to 18 percent in March 2004 and to 23 percent in April 2004 following the scandals. Juárez (2004, 24) concludes: "The attitude of citizens toward corruption and impunity depends on the type of events and how they are reported more than the fact that some crime is committed" (see also Aguilar Camín 2000). Indeed, the video scandals provide a simple explanation for the jump in the percentage who sensed an increase in corruption in the 2004 Corruptómetro poll cited earlier (Table 5.2).

Analysis begins by briefly exploring the impact of primary demographic variables of age, sex, income, education, and region on perceptions of corruption, perceptions of change (past and future), corruption's importance, and one measure of tolerance using data from the 2001, 2003, and 2005 ENCBG polls, and the 2004 LAPOP poll. This largely descriptive approach helps provide a better panorama of the public's views on corruption. A brief look at the impact of political party in power at the state level and partisanship on these variables follows. Finally, I produce a series of regression models focusing on the causes of corruption (perception) and their impact on satisfaction with democracy, voting, regime legitimacy, and corruption's importance.

Demographic and Political Factors

Simple cross-tabulations reveal few significant patterns based on demographic differences or political differences, a finding corroborated in the regression models.

Sex. By a very slim margin, males tended to perceive higher levels of corruption than females in two of the ENCBG polls and the LAPOP poll. This contrasts with the findings by Canache and Allison (2005). Nonetheless, females were somewhat more likely to see an increase in corruption over the prior year than males and were slightly more pessimistic regarding change in the future. Based on the LAPOP data, males were slightly more likely to consider corruption a national problem than females. In terms of whether it is okay for politicians to take advantage of their positions as long as they do good things, females were slightly more likely to disagree with that statement than males.

Age. Age was broken down into three categories: 18–29, 30–49, and 50 and older. There were no significant differences with regard to perceptions of corruption. Older respondents (those over 50), however, were somewhat more likely to believe corruption had increased over the prior year than younger respondents, while younger respondents were somewhat more likely to consider corruption a national problem. There was no consistent pattern regarding predictions of the future or in allowing politicians to take advantage of their positions.

Income and education. Generally, there were no differences with regard to the overall perception of corruption across socioeconomic lines. Differences did surface with regard to perceptions and expectations of change, however. Respondents with higher incomes were slightly more likely to assess and predict a reduction in corruption than those with lower incomes, while the higher-educated group was slightly less likely to opine that corruption had increased or would increase in the near future. These differences, however, were rather small and barely significant. The LAPOP poll showed a much stronger tendency for the more affluent and better-educated to consider corruption a national problem. And, as might be expected, those from lower socioeconomic categories were much more likely to agree that it is okay for politicians to take advantage of their positions as long as they do good things. Whereas majorities of high-income and university-educated respondents disagreed with that view, majorities of those from the ranks of the lower- and middle-income groups and those having less than a university education agreed with the statement.

Region. To gauge potential regional differences, Mexico's thirty-two federal entities (thirty-one states plus the federal district) were categorized into five regions: border, north-central, south-central, Mexico City area, and south.[13] Regional differences, however, were minimal and inconsistent across the polls. The ENCBG polls showed slightly higher perception of corruption in the Mexico City area and the lowest level in the south, whereas the LAPOP poll showed border residents more likely to consider corruption *"muy generalizada"* and south-central respondents more likely to claim *"poco generalizada"* or *"nada generalizada."* No clear pattern emerged across the ENCBG polls regarding change in corruption, though border residents exhibited the greatest growth in belief that corruption had increased over the prior year. Concomitantly, expectations of corruption in the coming year among border residents, along with north-central residents, tended to suffer the greatest decline. Expectations that corruption would decrease fell more sharply in the border and north-central regions. Respondents from the Mexico City area were most likely to see corruption as a political problem, while those from the south were least likely. As would be expected, residents of the south were much more likely compared to those of other regions to envision poverty as the major problem facing the country, though surprisingly, residents of the south were not the most likely region to approve of politicians taking advantage of their positions in return for doing good. Respondents from the north-central region were much more likely to agree with that view, while residents from Mexico City were least likely to agree.

Political party in power. The ENCBG polls provide limited data on the political or partisan views of respondents. The 2001 and 2005 polls, however, do differentiate based on the party ruling at the state level (as determined by the party of the state governor). The LAPOP poll, by contrast, provides information on an individual's party identification based on retrospective voting in the 2000 presidential election and the 2003 mid-term election, and based on approval ratings of the Fox administration. Here, we see that the overall perceptions of corruption vary little across party lines. Respondents in states ruled by the Partido Revolucionario Institucional (PRI) were no more likely to consider corruption widespread than those in areas held by the Partido Acción Nacional (PAN) or the PRD. According to the 2004 LAPOP poll, by contrast, those who voted for Cuauhtémoc Cárdenas Solórzano in 2000 were much more likely to consider corruption widespread than those who voted for Fox or Francisco Labastida Ochoa. And yet, PAN supporters in 2003 were more likely to consider corruption *"muy generalizada"* and PRD supporters were more likely to consider it *"algo generalizada."* Appraisal of the Fox government seemed to have virtually no effect on general perceptions of corruption, with those who provided a negative assessment of the Fox government only slightly more likely to consider corruption *"muy generalizada."* Regarding assessments of change in the preceding year and expectations of change in the coming year, respondents in PRD-held areas were slightly more likely to believe that corruption had increased or would increase, while those from PAN-held entities were more likely to believe that corruption had decreased or would decrease, at least until 2005. There were limited differences between perceptions of change at the national level versus the state level. Data on state-level changes were included given the distinction based on the party controlling the state. With regard to considering corruption a national problem, as might be expected, respondents who voted for the PRI candidate in 2000 or the party in 2003 were significantly less likely to deem corruption as the nation's major problem compared to PAN and PRD supporters. This is understandable given the tendency at the time to see the PAN and the PRD as the opposition and parties of change. Finally, respondents from PRI-held areas proved to be somewhat more likely to agree that it is okay for politicians to take advantage of their positions, a finding that may reflect the higher poverty rates in PRI-controlled states.

Regression Models

This section statistically explores the determinants of individual perceptions of corruption, change, and expectations of change, and then analyzes their impact on democratic satisfaction, voting, regime legitimacy, and identification of corruption as a serious national problem. Analysis begins by focusing on the determinants of individual perceptions of the level of corruption among public officials using data from the 2001, 2003, and 2005 ENCBG polls. For each, the dependent variable—perception of corruption—is coded as –1 for disagreement with the statement "all politicians are corrupt," 0 for neither agreement nor disagreement, and 1 for agreement. The following independent variables are then entered into the regression equation:

> *Interpersonal trust.* Measured by response to the question: "Generally, would you say you can or cannot trust the majority of people?" (dummy variable).
>
> *Political trust.* Measured by agreement, disagreement, or neither with the statement: "Upon making laws, the opinions of people like me are taken into account."
>
> *Tolerance.* Two indicators are used. The measure "Tolerance1" is based on the sum of all the approval/disapproval responses to the twenty-one types of illegal or unethical acts, broken down into four categories (from 1 = intolerant, to 4 = tolerant). The indicator "Tolerance2" records the respondent's agreement, disagreement, or neither with the statement: "Public officials can take advantage of their position as long as they do good things in office."
>
> *Knowledge of the process to denounce corruption.* Measured by whether or not the respondent knows of the process to denounce corruption (dummy variable).

Participation in corruption. Though the argument is developed and elaborated on more fully in the next chapter, this measure reflects actual participation in corruption and is derived from responses to questions regarding the actual payment of a bribe in the use of thirty-eight services in 2001 and 2003 and thirty-five services in 2005. Responses are summed and recorded into three groups reflecting low, medium, and high participation rates.

State party. The party in control at the state level, coded as a dummy variable as "PRI" or "non-PRI."

Control variables. The customary control variables of sex (dummy variable for male), income, education, and age are used.

Though explaining very little of the overall variation (given the huge sample size), the results in Table 5.5 seem not only consistent across the ENCBG

Table 5.5 Determinants of Perceptions of Corruption (ENCBG) (ordered probit regression)

Independent Variable	2001	2003	2005
Constant	.675***	.737***	1.632***
	(.035)	(.027)	(.052)
Interpersonal trust	−.049***	−.071***	−.102***
	(.015)	(.015)	(.025)
Political trust	−.021**	−.016*	−.032***
	(.007)	(.007)	(.005)
Tolerance1	−.014	−.021*	−.052***
	(.008)	(.009)	(.013)
Tolerance2	.027***	.029***	.017**
	(.007)	(.007)	(.005)
Knowledge to denounce (dummy)	−.017	−.002	−.036
	(.016)	(.016)	(.021)
Participation	.044***	.042***	.079***
	(.010)	(.011)	(.015)
State party (PRI)	.023	—	.029
	(.013)	—	(.017)
Sex (dummy) (male)	.033*	.038*	.002
	(.013)	(.016)	(.022)
Age	−.015	.000	−.031*
	(.009)	(.001)	(.013)
Income	.006	−.019	.005
	(.012)	(.013)	(.012)
Education	.014	−.003	−.016
	(.009)	(.007)	(.009)
N	10,649	9,051	11,070
Adjusted R^2	.006	.006	.009
F score	6.825***	6.891***	9.969***

Notes: Coefficients are unstandardized. Robust standard errors in parentheses.
*** = < .001, ** = < .01, * = < .05.

surveys, but also consistent with previous findings. Individuals with low levels of trust (in others and the political system), those who were more tolerant of corruption if politicians do good things, those who had paid bribes recently, and males were generally more likely to see higher levels of corruption than their counterparts. At the same time, tolerance of illegalities, knowledge of how to denounce corruption, whether the PRI controls the state government, age, and socioeconomic position had no significant impact on one's assessment of the level of corruption.

Because of the different questions used, the 2004 LAPOP poll allows us to examine the impact of a rather different set of variables. The regression model presented in Table 5.6 examines the impact of political interest (as measured by newspaper readership), social capital (measured by extent of community involvement and interpersonal trust), and participation in corruption. Based on prior studies, I hypothesize that those with greater political interest and lower levels of social capital (less social involvement and lower sense of interpersonal trust) and greater participation in corruption will perceive more corruption. The model also incorporates individuals' assessments of the nation's economic situation and of their own personal economic situations, as well as a retrospective vote for Fox, as possible intervening variables, and includes the standard demographic variables as controls.

As the results show, despite previous findings of an inverse relationship, here interpersonal trust had a mild positive influence on perceptions of corruption. Those with low levels of trust were less rather than more likely to envision high levels of corruption. Trust in the police had a much more significant effect on perceptions of corruption than did notions of trust or faith in the general political system. As predicted, those who judged the nation's economic situation as positive were more likely to see less corruption, though assessments of their own personal situations had no impact. Although in the expected direction, the impact of participation—controlling for all other variables—had no direct effect on perception. Similarly, political interest, community involvement, retrospective vote for Fox, and the demographic variables had no direct effect on one's perception of corruption.

I now turn to an analysis of the determinants of perceptions of change and expectations of change using data from the ENCBG polls. The two dependent variables are taken from the questions regarding change in the prior year and expectation of change in corruption in the coming year, coded as –1 for less, 0 for same, and 1 for more. The following independent variables are examined:

> *Perception of corruption.* Arguably, individuals sensing that all politicians are corrupt may be less likely to see any changes or a worsening of corruption, and certainly are less likely to foresee future changes.
> *Interpersonal trust and political trust.* As previously noted.
> *Alternation in power.* Agreement with the statement that alternation in power reduces the level of corruption (coded 1 for agree, 0 for neither

Table 5.6 Determinants of Perceptions of Corruption (LAPOP 2004)
(ordered probit regression)

Independent Variable	Model 1	Model 2	Model 3
Constant	.884***	.915***	.932***
	(.181)	(.184)	(.187)
Political Interest – Read Paper	.022	.025	.020
	(.027)	(.028)	(.028)
Community involvement	.062	.069	.041
	(.058)	(.067)	(.069)
Interpersonal trust	.078***	.082***	.086***
	(.024)	(.024)	(.024)
Political trust	.038*	.036	.038
	(.019)	(.019)	(.020)
Police trust	−.108***	−.110***	−.109***
	(.018)	(.018)	(.018)
Economic situation of country	−.124**	−.138**	−.143***
	(.043)	(.044)	(.044)
Personal economic situation	.042	.054	.060
	(.047)	(.047)	(.048)
Corruption as problem	.073	.066	.075
	(.084)	(.085)	(.086)
Sex (male)	.121	.129*	.117
	(.062)	(.063)	(.064)
Age	.017	.030	.025
	(.046)	(.047)	(.048)
Education	.050	.045	.034
	(.036)	(.036)	(.037)
Income	.008	.001	−.023
	(.048)	(.048)	(.049)
Political			
PAN voter		−.018	−.020
		(.079)	(.080)
PRI voter		−.138	−.109
		(.078)	(.080)
Fox approval		.056	.065
		(.042)	(.043)
Participation			.080
			(.047)
N	1,185	1,168	1,138
Adjusted R^2	.047	.049	.048
F score	5.850	4.980	4.603

Notes: Coefficients are unstandardized. Robust standard errors in parentheses.
*** = < .001, ** = < .01, * = < .05.

agree nor disagree, −1 for disagree). I hypothesize that those who agree will be more likely both to see changes compared to the prior year (since alternation occurred) and to foresee changes in the future.

Anticorruption willingness. This refers to assessment of the willingness of the government to fight corruption (coded 1 for agree, 0 for neither agree nor disagree, −1 for disagree). Again, I hypothesize that those

who feel that there is a willingness to fight corruption will be more
likely to see or foresee a decline in corruption.

Eliminate corruption. This is based on the question of whether it is possible to eliminate corruption in the country (coded 1 for agree, 0 for
neither agree nor disagree, –1 for disagree). Those sensing that it is
possible to eliminate corruption may be more likely to see reductions
in corruption or predict such elimination.

Participation. As previously noted. I hypothesize that individuals having
limited recent experience in corruption will be more likely to sense a
reduction than those having more significant recent experience. Those
who have paid bribes, by contrast, may be more likely to sense an increase in corruption.

State party. The party in control at the state level, coded as a dummy variable as "PRI" or "non-PRI."

Control variables. The customary control variables of sex (dummy variable for male), income, education, and age are used.

Once again, as shown in Table 5.7, these variables account for very little
of the overall variation in the public's assessment regarding change in corruption over the prior year. Still, the results do confirm the impact of a series of
key variables. Individuals perceiving high levels of corruption and exhibiting
low levels of trust in others were more likely to believe that corruption had increased. Similarly, as expected, those expressing the view that alternation in
power helps reduce corruption, that there is a willingness to fight corruption,
and that it is possible to eliminate corruption were more likely to believe that
corruption had declined or remained the same. Females, older respondents,
those from lower socioeconomic groups, and those from non-PRI-held states
for 2005 were more likely to believe that corruption had increased.

Looking at expectations of change in the near future, in Table 5.8, the same
predictors are once again significant. Yet in this equation, the most significant
factor determining expectation of change was the individual's assessment of the
recent past. In short, those sensing an increase in corruption during the prior
year were much more likely to predict a further increase in the next year. Overall, the model still only accounts for about 20 percent of the variation.

The Impact of Corruption and Perceptions of Change

Turning to the consequences of the perception of corruption and perceptions
of change, I begin with simple cross-tabulations based on the 2005 ENCBG
data, which include a question on satisfaction with democracy. As presented in
Table 5.9, and consistent with previous studies, individuals seeing politicians
as corrupt were more likely to express limited satisfaction with democracy.
Similarly, those sensing less corruption than in the prior year were more likely

**Table 5.7 Determinants of Perceptions of Change (ENCBG)
(ordered probit regression)**

Independent Variable	2001	2003	2005
Constant	2.171***	.291***	.219***
	(.046)	(.025)	(.038)
Perception of corruption	.039***	.036***	.036***
	(.011)	(.011)	(.007)
Interpersonal trust	−.063***	−.114***	−.041*
	(.016)	(.016)	(.020)
Political trust	−.019*	−.015	−.008
	(.008)	(.008)	(.004)
Alternation in power	−.051***	−.030***	−.016***
	(.008)	(.008)	(.005)
Willingness	−.052***	−.031***	−.021***
	(.009)	(.009)	(.005)
Eliminate corruption	−.056***	−.055***	−.060***
	(.005)	(.006)	(.005)
Participation	−.019	−.009	−.008
	(.011)	(.012)	(.011)
State party	−.014	—	−.074***
	(.014)	—	(.013)
Sex	−.144***	−.051**	−.058***
	(.014)	(.017)	(.017)
Age	.058***	.000	.047***
	(.010)	(.002)	(.010)
Income	−.033*	−.034*	−.011
	(.013)	(.014)	(.009)
Education	−.032***	−.036***	−.016*
	(.008)	(.008)	(.007)
N	11,036	9,679	1,1332
Adjusted R^2	.047	.033	.028
F score	46.379	31.167	28.650***

Notes: Coefficients are unstandardized. Robust standard errors in parentheses.
*** = < .001, ** = < .01, * = < .05.

to register satisfaction with democracy. This suggests that tackling corruption—or at least the perception of corruption—may be an important ingredient in positive assessments of democracy. This fits the more general view identifying corruption as a potential threat to democratic survival.

Analysis turns now to a regression using the LAPOP data, focusing on four dependent variables identified in the literature: satisfaction with democracy, (retrospective) voting, legitimacy, and ranking of corruption as the nation's biggest political problem. The question gauging satisfaction with democracy asked respondents how satisfied they were of democracy as it actually functions in the country. Responses included very dissatisfied, dissatisfied, satisfied, and very satisfied. To avoid temporal ordering problems in the manipulation of data, voting

**Table 5.8 Determinants of Expectations of Change (ENCBG)
(ordered probit regression)**

Independent Variable	2001	2003	2005
Constant	1.330***	−.009	.123***
	(.049)	(.025)	(.036)
Perception of corruption	.024*	.050***	.040***
	(.010)	(.011)	(.007)
Change in prior year	.401***	.405***	.413***
	(.009)	(.010)	(.009)
Interpersonal trust	−.082***	−.080***	−.025
	(.015)	(.016)	(.019)
Political trust	−.013	.006	−.007
	(.007)	(.008)	(.004)
Alternation in power	−.074***	−.040***	−.012**
	(.007)	(.008)	(.004)
Willingness	−.054***	−.038***	−.025***
	(.009)	(.008)	(.005)
Eliminate corruption	−.089***	−.089***	−.073***
	(.005)	(.005)	(.005)
Participation	.020	−.029**	.004
	(.010)	(.011)	(.011)
State party	−.058***	—	−.074***
	(.014)	(.013)	—
Sex	−.017	.002	−.034*
	(.014)	(.017)	(.016)
Age	−.034***	.001	.009
	(.010)	(.001)	(.010)
Income	−.054***	.023	−.011
	(.013)	(.013)	(.009)
Education	−.038***	−.005	.001
	(.008)	(.007)	(.007)
N	10,748	9,679	10,984
Adjusted R^2	.225	.211	.209
F score	241.386	211.969	224.768

Notes: Coefficients are unstandardized. Robust standard errors in parentheses.
*** = < .001, ** = < .01, * = < .05.

ideally should occur after the measures for the independent variables, but that is impossible using a single poll. Despite this problem, I constructed a simple binary variable for voting in 2000. This relies, obviously, on the respondent's recollection of whether they voted or not four years prior. Governmental legitimacy is measured following the profile created by Mitchell Seligson (2006). This incorporates the sum of responses for five questions and then transforms the data into a 0–100 scale. The five questions used to create the legitimacy index include ratings on (1) extent that courts guarantee free trial, (2) respect for political institutions, (3) pride in the political system, (4) support for the political system, and (5) trust in the police. The extent that corruption is considered a problem in the country is measured as before. Like voting, this variable is recorded in binary form, with those identifying corruption as the nation's

Table 5.9 Impact of Corruption and Change on Satisfaction with Democracy (ENCBG 2005)

Satisfaction with Democracy	Agreement/Disagreement with Statement "All politicians are corrupt" (% response)				
	Total Agreement	Some Agreement	Neither Agree nor Disagree	Some Disagreement	Total Disagreement
Very satisfied	3.7	3.6	5.9	4.0	10.7
Somewhat satisfied	30.7	38.0	38.5	40.3	30.2
Little satisfied	40.2	41.7	34.9	37.7	39.3
Not satisfied	25.4	16.7	20.7	18.0	19.8

Note: Kendall tau-b = −.085***, Kendall tau-c = −.066***.

Satisfaction with Democracy	Change in Corruption over Prior Year (% response)		
	More	Same	Less
Very satisfied	3.7	3.2	6.6
Somewhat satisfied	29.4	33.1	41.7
Little satisfied	39.1	42.6	36.9
Not satisfied	27.9	21.1	14.8

Note: Kendall tau-b = −.107***, Kendall tau-c = −.104***.

major problem versus those that identified any other issue. Many of the same variables tested earlier and the customary demographic variables are used as controls.

As shown in Table 5.10, the perception of corruption played no statistically significant role in determining satisfaction with democracy, retrospective voting, or corruption as a political problem, though the impact was in the expected direction. Perception of corruption did, however, significantly influence regime legitimacy, independent of the impact of assessments of the economic situation and Fox's approval rating. Once again, the amount of the overall variation explained by this model remains quite low. The results, nonetheless, confirm the pernicious effects of perceived corruption on regime legitimacy.

Conclusion

It is clear that many consider corruption widespread and deeply ingrained in Mexico. Not only do large majorities feel that politicians and civil servants are corrupt, but relatively few sense any positive changes in recent years—despite the view that alternation in political power should reduce corruption and the sense that there is a willingness on the part of the government to fight corruption. For

Table 5.10 Consequences of Perceptions of Corruption
(logit and probit regression)

	Dependent Variable			
Independent Variable	Satisfaction with Democracy	Voted[a]	Legitimacy	Problem[a]
Constant	.490**	−1.072*	64.212***	−2.874***
	(.175)	(.160)	(3.336)	(.388)
Perception	−.053	−.119	−1.751**	.086
	(.029)	(.069)	(.550)	(.077)
Corruption as problem	.013	−.057	−.626	—
	(.085)	(.193)	(1.594)	—
Economic situation	.174***	−.039	1.970*	.202
	(.044)	(.100)	(.826)	(.110)
Personal economic situation	.133**	.006	.633	.014
	(.048)	(.112)	(.891)	(.122)
Interpersonal trust	−.012	.047	1.859**	.099
	(.036)	(.054)	(.685)	(.062)
Community involvement	−.022	.318*	1.158	.214
	(.067)	(.160)	(1.271)	(.168)
Fox approval	.300***	.098	5.528***	−.007
	(.040)	(.092)	(.761)	(.103)
Sex	.005	−.161	−.389	.223
	(.063)	(.144)	(1.196)	(.161)
Age	−.026	1.041***	−.017	.034
	(.047)	(.116)	(.888)	(.120)
Education	−.104**	.128	−.955	.301***
	(.036)	(.083)	(.680)	(.087)
Income	−.005	.117	−.185	.163
	(.049)	(.110)	(.923)	(.122)
N	1,197	1,201	1,085	1,206
Adjusted/Pseudo R^2	.099	.088	.080	.032
F score	12.714		9.568	

Notes: Coefficients are unstandardized. Robust standard errors in parentheses.
*** = < .001, ** = < .01, * = < .05.
a. Logit regression for binary dependent variables.

many, the prospects of change are equally dim, with a significant segment deeming it impossible to reform the system. While the widespread corruption in Mexico does not seem to reflect a tolerant culture, many feel that the solution rests with better education within the family and the schools.

Looking more closely at individual perceptions of corruption and change in the past and the future, analysis shows first that the perception of corruption is partially shaped by low levels of interpersonal trust (though results were mixed), a willingness to allow corruption in return for politicians doing good things, real participation in corruption, a lack of trust in the police, poor assessments of the economic situation facing the country, and sex (male). The perception of an increase in corruption, in turn, relates to perceived corruption itself as well as limited interpersonal trust. Individuals believing that alternation in power helps reduce corruption, that a willingness exists to fight corruption, and that it is in fact possible to reduce corruption are more likely to believe that corruption has declined in recent times or at least remained the same. Meanwhile, assessments of the recent past strongly influence predictions about the future of corruption. At the same time, analysis shows that tolerance of illegalities, knowledge of how to denounce corruption, age, socioeconomic position, party in control at the state level, political interest, community involvement, and retrospective voting for Fox have no significant impact on an individual's perception of corruption or change.

Turning to an exploration of the impact of perceived corruption, analysis confirms that corruption—at least perceived corruption—takes its toll. Individuals perceiving widespread corruption and those sensing an increase in recent years are more likely to express dissatisfaction with the workings of democracy or, based on a distinct data set, regime legitimacy, independent of the impact of assessments of the economy or the president. Perceived corruption, however, seems to have no impact on voting or the ranking of corruption as a national problem. Even so, the results clearly highlight the tendency for corruption to weaken support for the government—though not necessarily the appeal of democracy as a political system—and suggest that tackling the perception of corruption is paramount to strengthening democracy.

Yet perceptions of corruption and of change constitute just one side of the equation and one of the approaches used to measure corruption. We must also analyze participation-based measures of corruption, including the level of real corruption in Mexico, the degree of real change, the relationship linking perception and participation, and the underlying determinants and impacts.

Notes

1. On the methodological problems with these measures of corruption, see, for instance, Del Castillo 2003; Knack 2006; Lambsdorff 2005; Sampford et al. 2006; Treisman 2007; Soreide 2006. Problems range from the normal methodological challenges in the social sciences, to the difficulties of agreeing on a definition of corruption itself.

2. The 2001 ENCBG survey of households was conducted in June and July, approximately seven months after Vicente Fox was sworn in as the nation's first non-PRI president in more than seventy years. The survey thus came on the heels of the unveiling of the president's high-profile anticorruption program. It was based on a probabilistic sample and included 13,790 interviews nationwide, with between 388 and 506 interviews per national entity. The 2003 ENCBG survey was also based on a probabilistic sample, this time 14,019 households, with 388 to 514 interviews per national entity. It was conducted in June and July, midway through the Fox *sexenio* and following the implementation of the Fox anticorruption campaign in early 2001 and the passage of critical legislation like the access to information law in 2002. The 2005 ENCBG survey, conducted from November 2005 to February 2006, included a sample of 15,123

households, with between 397 and 569 interviews per national entity. It measured just thirty-five services, eliminating seven from the earlier studies and adding four. With that exception, these three surveys contained essentially the same questions. The 2007 survey, for which I had access only to the results and not the raw data, included a probabilistic sample of 14,836 households.

3. The 2004 LAPOP survey, titled "The Political Culture of Democracy in Mexico," was conducted in March by Vanderbilt University and Instituto Tecnológico Autónomo de México. It was based on a national probabilistic sample of 1,556 individuals stratified by region and urban versus rural. The interviews were conducted in 130 sites distributed in 29 of the 32 federal entities, and in 89 of the 2,445 municipalities. The estimated margin of error was +2.8 (see http://sitemason.vanderbilt.edu/lapop/home).

4. In a 1998 poll focused just on Mexico City, over 85 percent of respondents expressed the view that corruption was widespread; 62 percent admitted that at times it was necessary to bribe in order to resolve a problem with the government; and 53 percent agreed with the view that it was so difficult to comply with laws and regulations that, at times, corruption was the only way to get things done (Gutiérrez Vivó 1998, 189–197). In another poll of Mexico City, in 2004, 90 percent of respondents asserted that corruption by the police occurred on a daily basis (Parametria 2004).

5. The 2001 DSFC survey, comprising approximately 200 federal auditors *(contralorías internas)* of the federal public administration, was conducted by Transparencia Mexicana in January and March 2001.

6. Axel Dreher, Christos Kotsogiannis, and Steve McCorriston (2004), through a "multiple indicators, multiple causes" model, show an increase in corruption in Mexico from 1980 to 1997.

7. See McCann and Domínguez 1998; "Encuesta Omnibus III" 1995; Gutiérrez Vivó 1998, 189–197.

8. The 2001 EGDE survey was conducted by the Tec de Monterrey and included interviews with 3,985 representatives of private companies.

9. R. R. Soares (2004) shows that the perception of corruption discourages victims from reporting crimes, reflecting the lack of confidence in officials. Presumably, this would include the reporting of corruption as well.

10. The failure of alternation in power to substantially curtail corruption is illustrated by a handful of cross-state studies described in Chapter 2. For example, in a poll of residents of the state of Jalisco in 2002, after the PAN had held power for eight years, 68 percent felt that corruption had remained the same, while a larger proportion felt that it had increased (20 percent) compared to the proportion who felt that it had decreased (13 percent) ("Percepciones de la población de la Zona Metropolitana de Guadalajara" 2002).

11. Charles Davis, Roderic Camp, and Kenneth Coleman (2004) link perception of corruption to nonvoting in Chile and Costa Rica as well.

12. General (nonempirical) studies on Venezuela by Walter Little and Antonio Herrera (1996) and Carlos Subero (2004, 371) also blame corruption for voters' rejection of the traditional parties and their concomitant support for the outsider candidate, Hugo Chávez. Kathryn Hochstetler (2005) finds that corruption scandals tend to precede the falls of presidents in Latin America.

13. The fivefold regional classification comprises: border (Baja California, Coahuila, Chihuahua, Nuevo León, Sonora, Tamaulipas); north-central (Aguascalientes, Baja California Sur, Durango, Nayarit, San Luis Potosí, Sinaloa, Zacatecas); south-central (Colima, Guanajuato, Hidalgo, Jalisco, Michoacán, Morelos, Puebla Querétaro, Tabasco, Tlaxcala, Veracruz); Mexico City (federal district); and south (Campeche, Chiapas, Guerrero, Oaxaca, Quintana Roo, Yucatán).

6

Participation in Corruption

The prior chapter has shown that perceptions of corruption remained quite high throughout the Vicente Fox *sexenio* and into the initial year under Calderon, declining slightly during the initial years under Fox only to rebound afterward. Despite the substantial structural and institutional changes, the view largely persisted that corruption was high and on the increase or at least stagnant rather than falling as democratic theory predicted and President Fox promised. Perception of corruption, however, is not the same as the existence of real acts of corruption, and therefore may say little about the true level of corruption, the true impact of the structural or institutional changes, or the types of corruption present. As a second empirical take on the primary research question, this chapter explores actual experiences with corruption. Like the preceding chapter, I begin by profiling participation rates and change based on recent polling data. Discussion then turns to a more detailed analysis of the differences separating perception and participation and an examination of the theoretical and empirical relationships linking the two.[1] The chapter then provides a more detailed analysis of the underlying causes and consequences of corruption based on participation measures. In the concluding section, I try to differentiate these findings from those related to perception.

Profiling Participation in Corruption and Change

Participation-based measures of corruption derive from questions asking respondents about their direct experience with corruption. Direct experience encompasses the payment of a bribe, the witnessing of a bribe, or being asked to pay a bribe. Questions and approaches vary. They may refer to the overall percentage of respondents with such experiences, just those within a specific institutional setting, or the percentage of respondents using a particular service who had to pay a bribe (noting that not everyone has sought services during a specified time period), and thus the percentage of times bribery was used to obtain a particular service within a given time frame.

Data on participation rates show, first, that the level of actual experience of corrupt acts is substantially lower than the levels suggested by perceptions of corruption. This pattern is evident everywhere and points to one of the key differences between perception and participation-based measures of corruption. Even so, participation-based measures in Mexico still point to relatively high rates of corruption (Appendix A provides comparative data). According to Transparency International's Global Corruption Barometer, for instance, the proportion of Mexican households who paid bribes in the previous twelve months ranged from 19 percent in 2004 to 31 percent in 2005. In the 2002 Corruptómetro survey, 24 percent of respondents admitted having paid a bribe during the prior six months, while in the 2004 Corruptómetro survey, 83 percent admitted to having paid a bribe to transit police, 39 percent to officials to obtain a license, 31 percent to judges or public ministers, and 27 percent to officials to obtain a permit. The 2004 Latin American Public Opinion Project (LAPOP) poll posed a series of questions that distinguished the payment of a bribe, being requested to pay a bribe, and witnessing a bribe. As shown in Table 6.1, a greater proportion claimed to have witnessed a bribe than to have paid one.

It is important to emphasize what these indexes are measuring, and two limitations imposed by the nature of the survey questions. First, as presented, for instance, in the LAPOP data shown in Table 6.1, it is impossible to know

Table 6.1 Participation in Corruption (LAPOP 2004) (selected questions)

Bribe Requested
- Has a police requested a bribe from you within the last year? (n = 1,545)
      Yes   18.0%   No   82.0%
- Has a public employee requested a bribe from you within the last year? (n = 1,527)
      Yes   12.9%   No   87.1%

Bribe Paid
- To process something at city hall/city delegation (such as a permit, for example) during the last year, have you had to pay an amount besides that demanded by law? (n = 571)
      Yes   20.7%   No   79.3%
- Have you had to pay a bribe in the courts during the last year? (n = 422)
      Yes   13.5%   No   86.5%

Bribe Witnessed
- Have you seen anyone bribe a police within the last year? (n = 1,542)
      Yes   39.1%   No   60.9%
- Have you seen anyone pay a bribe to a public official for any type of favor within the last year? (n = 1,530)
      Yes   22.6%   No   77.4%

how many respondents were stopped by police or who solicited a service from the municipal government during the prior year and therefore actually had the opportunity to pay a bribe or to be asked for one. This makes it impossible to calculate the extent of corruption as a proportion of overall interactions with the government. Data from the Encuesta Nacional de Corrupción y Buen Gobierno (ENCBG) polls address this problem and thus provide a different sort of measure. Second, data fail to show overall experiences with corruption because they specify experience within a specified period. Since any past involvement in corruption might influence a person's overall views on the government, restricting the response to just a year's worth of experience or less seems quite limiting. After all, it is not every year that the average person gets stopped by police or has to engage the bureaucracy for some sort of service. Though such restrictions facilitate measuring corruption during that precise period, experiences from two years, five years, or even twenty years prior, particularly in the absence of more recent experience, may well continue to shape one's perceptions regarding corruption, expectations of the behavior of others, and other factors.

The ENCBG polls, like LAPOP, also compile participation-based measures of corruption, but the ENCBG measures reflect a much more extensive and elaborate series of questions gauging corruption. These polls ask respondents about their experiences in the acquisition of thirty-eight different types of public services (thirty-five for 2005 and 2007),[2] ranging from acquiring utility services or paying their property tax to getting out of traffic citation or acquiring a routine license. The time limitation is still included, but varies. Some questions (e.g., registering for school) specify the previous twelve months; some (e.g., vehicular inspection) refer to the prior six months; some (e.g., garbage collection) refer to the prior week; and some (e.g., acquiring a construction license) refer to any prior instance. More important, the ENCBG polls incorporate whether the respondent actually utilized the particular service, and then ask whether a bribe was paid to acquire it. Based on these questions, the ENCBG polls calculate a corruption and good government index, computed on a 0–100 scale, based on the ratio of the number of times a service was obtained by the payment of a bribe to the total number of times the service was actually sought during the period. For instance, in 2001, the score of 10.5 presented in Table 6.2 suggests that in just over 10 of 100 cases, a bribe was paid to acquire all the services combined. In sum, the ENCBG polls in 2001 registered 214 million acts of corruption in the use of public services during the preceding twelve months, 101 million in 2003, 115 million in 2005, and 197 million in 2007. They also calculated the overall amount paid in bribes (e.g., 10.7 billion pesos [US$1 billion] in 2003) and the average amount paid (e.g., 107 pesos [US$10] per bribe in 2003).

More refined and targeted surveys offer similar findings regarding actual rates of corruption. Within the business community, for example, the 2009 Encuesta de Gobernabilidad y Desarrollo Empresarial (EGDE) survey found that

Table 6.2 Participation in Corruption (selected measures and polls)

A
Percentage of households who paid bribes in past twelve months:

2004	2005	2006
19	31	28

Source: Global Corruption Barometer (Transparency International).

Percentage of respondents who paid bribes:

2001	2002	2003	2004	2005	2006
65	59	53	53	50	26

Source: Latinobarómetro.

Percentage of respondents who paid one or more bribes for public services:

2001	2003	2005
23.7	14.4	18.3

Source: ENCBG.

B
Corruption as a proportion of services rendered:

2001	2003	2005	2007
10.5	8.5	10.1	10.0

Source: ENCBG.

Percentage of respondents who paid bribes (or whose family members paid bribes) for selected purposes:

Purpose of Bribe	2001	2003	2005	2007
Prevent car from being impounded by transit police or get car out of impound	57.2	53.3	60.2	50.1
Avoid a ticket or being detained by transit police	54.5	50.3	50.0	56.2
Avoid detention, file a complaint or charges, or push for a case to be investigated	28.3	21.3	23.6	—
Present a case before the courts	15.4	10.8	15.0	—
Obtain a drivers license	14.5	11.9	10.9	—
Obtain a government job	—	—	6.2	—
Request a permit to open a business or establishment	—	—	6.7	—
Obtain a passport	6.4	5.1	5.4	—

Source: ENCBG.

39 percent of businesses acknowledged that businesses like their own made extraofficial payments to influence laws or policies, and that 62 percent recognized that businesses like their own made such payments to administrative officials (CEE 2002). In acquiring permits and licenses, for instance, 57 percent of the businesses that solicited such services reported using extraofficial payments to help secure them. A 2008 survey on fraud and corruption by the international accounting firm KPMG found that 44 percent of businesses interviewed provided extraofficial payments to public officials. From a much closer angle, the 2001 Diagnostico Institucional del Sistema Federal de Control (DSFC) survey found that 60 percent of internal auditors recognized "frequent" acts of corruption within the areas they supervised.

Though no survey asks specifically about change based solely on participation rates, various polls allow for the tracking of such rates over the years. Part A of Table 6.2 shows periodic measures calculating the percentage of respondents paying bribes based on data from the Global Corruption Barometer, Latinobarómetro, and the ENCBG polls. Results vary. The Global Corruption Barometer shows an increase in participation rates from 2004 to 2006. Spanning more years, the Latinobarómetro data show a significant reduction from 2001 to 2005, followed by a rather dramatic drop in 2006. The ENCBG polls, in turn, show a rather substantial reduction from 2001 to 2003, followed by an increase in 2005—a pattern similar to the one seen with respect to perceptions—but overall a clear reduction from 2001 to 2005. Part B in Table 6.2 focuses on the ENCBG corruption and good government index, which measures the percentage of times respondents paid a bribe when acquiring specific services. It too shows a reduction from 2001 to 2003, followed by an increase in 2005 and almost no change in 2007. Overall, these index data show an overall reduction of 6 percent in the level of corruption from 2001 to 2007. (Chapter 7 looks at patterns of corruption to explore changes in participation rates in specific service areas.)

What could be considered one dimension of "participation" entails participation in the other direction: fighting rather than engaging in corruption. Data on the public's involvement in denouncing corruption could point to a key dimension of the underlying political changes and even the effectiveness of recent anticorruption efforts. Official governmental statistics, which refer to the actual number of complaints (as opposed to the number of individuals filing complaints), cited in Chapter 4, show a peak in the overall number of complaints in the early part of the Vicente Fox term and in the Felipe Calderon term. The ENCBG polls, by contrast, measure the proportion of respondents denouncing corrupt acts rather than the total number of overall complaints. However, when respondents were asked if they denounced corruption the last time they encountered it, the rate of denunciation remained virtually unchanged from 2001 to 2005 (in 2001, of those affected by a case of corruption [31 percent overall], 36 percent said they had denounced it; in 2003, of those affected by a case

[31 percent], 35 percent said they had denounced it; and in 2005, of those affected by a case [29 percent], 37 percent said they had denounced it). If, building on Melanie Manion's analysis (2004), we consider this an indicator of the public's confidence in the government's efforts to fight corruption, it suggests little change over the period, despite the rhetoric, the political changes, and the reforms.

Participation and (or?) Perception

Up to this point, we have examined two measures of corruption and change in Mexico: one looking at perception, the other at participation rates or personal experience. To what extent are these different? To what extent are they connected? Which is a better measure of corruption?

Though both perception and participation have been used to measure corruption in recent studies, conceptually, of course, the two are not the same: one refers to actual behavior or at least direct observation, the other to general beliefs about the nature of the political system and the behavior of others. Owing in part to this difference, the two metrics seem to draw on or tap different dimensions of corruption and reflect distinct levels of specificity. Whereas questions relating to participation are quite specific, referring to very concrete acts and times, questions regarding perception are more broadly gauged and ambiguous, drawing therefore on a wide range of experiences, periods, and like factors. It is relatively clear whether one has paid a bribe or not when obtaining say a driver's license; but criteria used to determine an individual's perception of whether corruption is widespread or generalized is far from clear. Moreover, the two measures seem to relate to different levels of the political system, though again the levels of specificity differ. Questions regarding participation relate clearly to areas where the citizen interacts with state officials: the points of contact involving lower levels of the bureaucracy. For general questions used to assess perception, however, it is difficult to know what the citizen might have in mind when responding, whether interactions with bureaucrats or the police, or politics in a much more amorphous and abstract sense reaching beyond the scope of normal everyday interactions. In fact, the citizen may simply be responding based on reputation or press reports. Certainly, few citizens participate in drug-related corruption, for example (hence it is not gauged by participation questions), but drug-related corruption may go a long way in shaping an individual's overall perceptions of corruption in the political system or among politicians. Some perception-based questions do specify particular institutions (e.g., police, bureaucracy, Congress), but again, what the expressed opinion is based on remains unclear. Such distinctions, of course, raise questions regarding the potential relationship linking the two (perception and participation) and also raise the underlying question of which measure is a better one to gauge corruption. These points also present some interesting empirical questions that can be subjected to testing.

Though analysts—most of whom use perception-based measures in their studies—routinely acknowledge the fact that perception of corruption is not the same thing as the existence of actual corruption, few have seriously addressed questions about how these two concepts may be related.[3] Generally, three non–mutually exclusive possibilities present themselves. The first possible relationship is inductive. It suggests that participation and first- or even second-hand experience with corruption—real-life experience with paying bribes or knowing about bribes through actual events—influences a person's perceptions about the nature of corruption in the broader system. Individuals, in other words, generalize based on their own experience and the experience of those around them. According to this view, polls tapping perceptions of corruption represent a proxy measure, providing a second-best approach to gauging the level of corruption that exists within society. Indeed, the methodological utility of perception-based measures rests fundamentally on this inductive perspective. Using perception as a proxy of actual corruption rests largely on two assumptions: that it is difficult to get those involved in corruption to admit to any wrongdoing, and second, that those who deal with a system on a regular basis know what is happening in that system.

A second theoretical possibility, however, is deductive and reverses the causal arrow. It suggests that perceptions about how the political system operates shape individual behavior under specific conditions. The simple, guiding assumptions of institutional theory and rational choice apply here: that an individual's perceptions of risks and opportunities within a given institutional setting determine behavior. In other words, if one believes that corruption is widespread, normal, routine, and expected, then such views influence one's conduct. This deductive perspective, however, also taps the endogenous component inherent in looking at perceptions of corruption and even raises the possibility that the diffusion of perception-based measures of corruption in recent years may actually influence the sort of behavior they seek to measure, or, to use a famous Mexican saying, *"crea fama y echate a dormir"* ("create fame, and go to sleep"; that is, reputations are hard to overcome). Using focus groups in Mexico City, for instance, Arturo Del Castillo and Manuel Guerrero (2004) find some support for this proposition. They show how a person's perception of whether a specific institution in Mexico is considered corrupt (e.g., the police) actually influences that person's decisions about whether to offer a bribe or to expect the official to request one.[4] This perspective also suggests that individuals may take their cues from key dimensions of the political culture.

A third theoretical possibility is that these two dimensions of corruption—participation and perception—are largely unrelated, stem from distinct sets of factors, and behave independently of the other. Or, as Philip Oldenburg (1987, 532–533, cited in Manion 2004, 20) suggests, "the folklore of corruption can flourish independently of the practice." This view builds particularly on the supposition that the two measures reflect different types and patterns of corruption, respond to different sets of determinants, and face distinct validity problems. As noted, participation in or experience with corruption refers almost exclusively to petty levels of bureaucratic corruption, since it is only here where the average citizen even has the opportunity to engage in a corrupt act, while perceptions capture a much broader range of experiences and sentiments, stretching beyond the bureaucratic level and encompassing the broader political realm. Whereas a political scandal involving the president, a high-level administrative official, a member of Congress, or elections might significantly influence popular perceptions of corruption, these would seem to play only a minor role, if any, in influencing whether one pays or is asked to pay a bribe to obtain a permit at a local government office. It can still be argued, of course, that even though the two measures focus on different levels or types of corruption (low- versus high-level corruption, petty versus grand corruption), the two are still closely aligned: that if there is extensive corruption at the top, there will be widespread corruption at the bottom, and vice versa. This, however, becomes a testable hypothesis linking different levels of corruption rather than perception and participation per se.

The regression models presented in Chapter 5 provide some evidence of a rather limited yet weak positive relationship linking perception and participation. Evidence shows that individuals who have more recent experience with paying bribes are just slightly more likely to perceive higher levels of corruption compared to those without recent experience, even when controlling for the effects of other variables. In terms of perceptions of change and expectations of change in the near future, the ENCBG polls also hint slightly that those who have greater experience with paying bribes are somewhat more likely to anticipate more corruption in the future, but in most cases this relationship falls short of statistical significance. Exploring this relationship further, Table 6.3 presents simple cross-tabulations of the impact of direct experience on perceptions of the level of corruption. It shows that for both the ENCBG data and the LAPOP data, respondents with recent experience of corruption were more likely to agree that politicians were corrupt or that corruption was *"muy generalizada."* According to data from the LAPOP poll, in four of the six cases, those who were involved in corruption (by either being asked to pay a bribe, paying a bribe, or witnessing a bribe) were more likely to feel that corruption among public officials was *"muy generalizada"* compared to those who did not experience corruption within the past year. Interestingly enough, however, the two cases in which those participating were slightly less likely to assess high levels of corruption among officials correspond precisely to actually paying the bribe (as opposed to being asked to pay a bribe or witnessing a bribe being paid), suggesting that actual participation itself may have no or a very limited impact on perception.

At a fundamental level, the weak positive correlation linking perception and participation demonstrates that the two are not identical and may be tapping unique dimensions of corruption. As seen in Chapter 5, participation in

Table 6.3 Cross-Tabulations of Perception and Participation

ENCBG

Perception	2001 Number of Bribes			2003 Number of Bribes			2005 Number of Bribes		
	None	1	2+	None	1	2+	None	1	2+
Agree	77.8	81.4	83.5	76.6	81.3	83.2	64.4 / 24.7	68.6 / 23.3	74.9 / 17.7
Neither	10.6	9.2	7.3	13.2	10.0	8.6	4.8	3.3	2.4
Disagree	11.6	9.4	9.2	10.1	8.7	8.2	2.4 / 3.8	2.1 / 2.6	1.9 / 3.1

Note: For 2005, slashes indicate agreement / partial agreement, and disagreement / partial disagreement, with the statement "All politicians are corrupt."

LAPOP (2004)

Participation		Percentage Considering Corruption *"muy generalizada"*
Has a police requested a bribe from you within the last year?	Yes	40.3
	No	38.4
Has a public employee requested a bribe from you within the last year?	Yes	45.6
	No	37.8
To process something at city hall/city delegation (such as a permit, for example) during the last year, have you had to pay an amount besides that demanded by law?	Yes	38.5
	No	40.2
Have you had to pay a bribe in the courts during the last year?	Yes	34.7
	No	40.6
Have you seen anyone bribe a police within the last year?	Yes	46.1
	No	33.7
Have you seen anyone pay a bribe to a public official for any type of favor within the last year?	Yes	49.4
	No	35.6

corruption explains very little of the variation in perception, and—as we will see—perception explains little of the variation in participation rates. This means that both perception and participation have, in a sense, a life of their own, and hence that addressing one may not address the other, that changes in one may not register in the other, and that their determinants and consequences may vary.[5] Exploring the causes and consequences of participation provides an opportunity to compare and contrast the results with the causes and consequences of perception-based measures of corruption.

Determinants of Participation in Corruption and Its Impact

Who participates or experiences corruption in Mexico? In contrast to the number of studies using perception-based measures of corruption, there are very few studies detailing participation rates. Mitchell Seligson (2006) (one of the leaders in the use of such measures, which he refers to as "victimization" rates) finds that males, higher-income earners, and those with higher levels of education are more likely to participate in corrupt acts than females and those from the lower socioeconomic ranks. He accounts for this finding in a straightforward manner: "those who use the public sector more frequently are more likely to be victimized by it" (2006, 398). Naci Mocan (2004) similarly finds higher-income and higher-educated males, as well as aged twenty to thirty-nine and living in large cities, to be more likely to be asked to pay a bribe. Exploring participation in Mexico using data from the 2001 ENCBG, Manuel Guerrero and Eduardo Rodríguez-Oreggia (2008) also find a positive relationship linking participation (bribery) to income, education, and maleness, and inversely to an individual's perception of the state's institutional strength. They find no relationship, however, to the variables of fear (measured by those who claim to abide by the law out of fear of punishment), interpersonal trust, or region.

Even fewer works seek to assess the consequences of participation, but the results from the few studies that exist are rather parsimonious. In a series of studies, Seligson (2001, 2002a, 2002b, 2006) reveals conclusively that participation in corruption reduces individual feelings of regime legitimacy and satisfaction with democracy. Daniel Gingerich (2007), taking it a step further, links participation in corruption to protest behavior in Bolivia and the demise of traditional parties. As alluded to earlier, participation also affects, in some small way, one's overall perception of corruption.

Demographic and Political Factors

Analysis begins, as in the prior chapter, by briefly exploring the impact of the demographic variables of age, sex, income, education, and region on participation in corruption using data from 2001, 2003, and 2005 ENCBG polls and the 2004 LAPOP poll. As before, I take this largely descriptive approach to help provide a better profile of those who experience corruption in Mexico. A brief look at the impact of the political party in power at the state level and partisanship follows.

Sex. In all four polls analyzed, males were shown to be more likely to participate in or have had experience with corruption than females, a finding consistent with those of Mocan (2004), Seligson (2006), and Guerrero and Rodríguez-Oreggia (2008). In the LAPOP poll, for instance, the difference in participation rates surpassed 10 percentage points (48 percent of males versus 60 percent of females answered no on all six questions regarding personal experience with corruption).

Age. The ENCBG polls showed the mid-level age cohort (30–49 years) to be slightly more likely than the younger group (18–29 years) and much more likely than the older group (over 50) to pay bribes, at least in 2003 and 2005. In the LAPOP poll, the older group was again much less likely to experience corruption than younger respondents, with the youngest group slightly more likely to experience corruption, consistent with the findings of Mocan (2004).

Income and education. Rather consistently, the higher the socioeconomic group (income and education), the greater the likelihood of paying bribes or experiencing bribery. This is consistent with the findings of Mocan (2004), Seligson (2006), and Guerrero and Rodríguez-Oreggia (2008). This was true in all the ENCBG polls, with both the upper-income and university-educated groups more likely to have been involved in paying bribes. In the LAPOP poll, while the upper-income group was more likely compared to other income groups to have experienced bribery, the university-educated group was slightly less likely to have experienced bribery than the preparatory-educated group, though more likely compared to the group with less than high school education. The differences here were rather large and significant. In the LAPOP poll, for instance, 67 percent from the lower-income group, compared to 39 percent from the upper-income group, reported no involvement in bribery. In the ENCBG polls, roughly a third of respondents with a university education paid at least one bribe, compared to less than 20 percent among those with primary education and less than 25 percent among those with secondary education.

Region. Regional differences revealed quite clearly, in all the polls, a higher rate of corruption in the Mexico City area. Indeed, the proportion of respondents in Mexico City who paid bribes was, on average for the three years of the ENCBG, 13 percentage points higher than in the region that reported the second-highest participation rate (south-central), and over 17 percentage points higher than in the region with the lowest participation rate (south). In the LAPOP poll, whereas the north-central region reported the lowest level of experience with bribery, respondents from the Mexico City region were still twice as likely to have experienced some form of corruption than those from the north-central region.[6]

Political party in power. Participation in bribery differed very little according to the political party in control at the state level or according to respondents'
retrospective votes in the 2003 federal election. Respondents from states controlled by the Partido de la Revolución Democrática (PRD), as well as those
who voted for the PRD, were slightly more likely to have participated in the
payment of bribes compared to those from states controlled by the Partido Revolucionario Institucional (PRI) and the Partido Acción Nacional (PAN), and compared to partisans, though the difference was minimal and not statistically
significant. The exceedingly high levels registered in the PRD-controlled Mexico City area may account for much of this tendency.

Regression Models

Similar to the prior chapter, this section explores the determinants of participation as well as the impact of participation on satisfaction with democracy, voting, regime legitimacy, and viewing corruption as a political problem. Analysis
begins examining the likely determinants of participation rates. In addition to
perception of corruption, I test the same set of independent variables used in the
prior chapter: interpersonal trust, political trust, tolerance, knowledge of the
process to denounce corruption, party in control at the state level, and the customary control variables. I hypothesize that those with lower levels of trust in
others and in the political system, tolerance toward corruption, a lack of knowledge of the procedure to denounce corruption, living in states still controlled by
the PRI, and perceiving high levels of corruption will be more likely to engage
in bribery.

Though accounting for very little of the overall variation, the ENCBG data
presented in Table 6.4 nonetheless confirm the impact of living in the Mexico
City region, maleness, and socioeconomic position on participation rates. The
model also shows the positive impact on bribery of perceptions of corruption
and tolerance toward corruption, confirming my hypothesis. By contrast, those
who know the process to denounce corruption appear slightly more likely to engage in bribery than those who are unfamiliar with the process.

As before, the LAPOP data facilitate the exploration of a series of variables not calculated in the ENCBG data. The regression model presented in
Table 6.5, based on the LAPOP poll, thus examines the impact of political interest (as measured by those expressing the view that they read the newspaper),
social capital (measured by extent of community involvement and interpersonal trust), trust in the political system and the police, and perceptions of corruption. Similar to my previous hypothesis, I hypothesize here that those with
greater political interest, lower levels of social capital (less social involvement
and lower sense of interpersonal trust) and political trust, and greater perceptions of corruption will be more likely to engage in or witness bribery. To introduce a political component, I include the approval rating for President Fox.
The model also includes the standard demographic variables as controls.

**Table 6.4 Determinants of Participation in Corruption (ENCBG)
(ordered probit regression)**

Independent Variable	2001	2003	2005
Constant	−.245***	−.238***	−.375***
	(.044)	(.027)	(.035)
Interpersonal trust	−.006	−.013	−.005
	(.014)	(.014)	(.016)
Political trust	−.001	.009	−.017***
	(.007)	(.007)	(.003)
Tolerance1	.008*	.108***	.144***
	(.004)	(.008)	(.008)
Tolerance2	.103***	.009	−.003
	(.010)	(.007)	(.003)
Knowledge to denounce (dummy)	.102***	.075***	.091***
	(.015)	(.015)	(.013)
Perception	.037***	.036***	.032***
	(.009)	(.010)	(.006)
State party (PRI)	.025*	—	.050***
	(.013)	—	(.011)
Sex (dummy) (male)	.078***	.046**	.083***
	(.013)	(.016)	(.014)
Age	−.025**	.000	−.002
	(.009)	(.001)	(.009)
Income	.088***	.089***	.072***
	(.012)	(.012)	(.008)
Education	.060***	.064***	.044***
	(.007)	(.007)	(.006)
Mexico City region (dummy)	.292***	.322***	.171***
	(.026)	(.027)	(.024)
N	10,479	9,051	11,070
Adjusted R^2	.073	.071	.072
F score	69.988	64.131	72.436

Notes: Coefficients are unstandardized. Robust standard errors in parentheses.
*** = < .001, ** = < .01, * = < .05.

As before, regression based on the LAPOP data shows the impact of the Mexico City region, sex, socioeconomic status, and in this case age. Consistent with the general hypothesis that individuals who are more active in the public arena are more likely to be involved in bribery, here individuals with greater political interest and community involvement are more likely to be involved in bribery or witness bribery. A lack of trust in the police plays a minor role in shaping participation, as expected, but not general trust in the political system. Though the relationship to perception of corruption is in the expected direction, it falls short of statistical significance in this model.

Unfortunately, the data on participation do not permit regression analysis of change. Turning then to focus on the consequences of participation in corruption, I utilize the LAPOP data, using the same model as before. Presented

Table 6.5 Determinants of Participation in Corruption (LAPOP 2004)

Independent Variable	Ordered Probit Regression
Constant	.279*
Political interest/read papers	.069***
	(.017)
Community involvement	.154***
	(.041)
Interpersonal trust	.035
	(.022)
Political trust	−.004
	(.012)
Trust police	−.023*
	(.011)
Fox approval (dummy variable)	−.010
	(.025)
Perception	.032
	(.018)
Sex (male)	.124***
	(.039)
Age	−.090**
	(.029)
Education	.057*
	(.022)
Income	.106***
	(.029)
Mexico City region	.378***
	(.047)
N	1,162
Adjusted R^2	.162
F score	19.732

Notes: Coefficients are unstandardized. Robust standard errors in parentheses.
*** = < .001, ** = < .01, * = < .05.

in Table 6.6, the results show that participation in corruption plays a significant role in undermining regime legitimacy, consistent with the findings of Seligson (2006), and independent of the effects of perceptions of corruption on regime legitimacy. Participation, however, has no statistically significant impact on satisfaction with democracy, retrospective voting, or viewing corruption as the nation's top political problem. In short, firsthand experience with corruption partially shapes feelings of regime legitimacy, but plays no role in influencing an individual's assessment of democracy, their vote, or the importance of corruption as an issue.

Comparing the Results for Perception and Participation

Looking at cross-national studies on corruption, Daniel Treisman (2007, 212) refers to the "puzzling dichotomy" in which perceived corruption is highly correlated with a variety of factors, but in which measures of actual experience

Table 6.6 Consequences of Participation in Corruption
(logit and probit regression)

	Dependent Variable			
Independent Variable	Satisfaction with Democracy	Voted[a]	Legitimacy	Problem[a]
Constant	.497**	−1.143***	64.017***	−2.942***
	(.177)	(.342)	(3.339)	(.394)
Participation	−.076	.068	−3.282***	.138
	(.047)	(.107)	(.880)	(.115)
Perception	−.056	−.104	−1.546**	.090
	(.030)	(.069)	(.551)	(.078)
Corruption as problem	.020	−.108	.122	—
	(.086)	(.195)	(1.600)	—
Economic situation	.175***	−.029	2.139**	.194
	(.044)	(.101)	(.828)	(.111)
Personal economic situation	.141**	−.009	.760	.008
	(.048)	(.113)	(.890)	(.123)
Community involvement	−.025	.274	1.259	.235
	(.068)	(.162)	(1.281)	(.170)
Interpersonal trust	−.007	.053	−1.780**	.094
	(.036)	(.055)	(.687)	(.078)
Fox approval	.321***	.128	5.522***	.020
	(.041)	(.094)	(.773)	(.106)
Sex (male)	.012	−.192	−.052	.173
	(.064)	(.147)	(1.204)	(.163)
Age	−.035	1.069***	−.097	.051
	(.048)	(.118)	(.891)	(.121)
Education	−.094**	.129	−.365	.280**
	(.037)	(.084)	(.684)	(.088)
Income	.001	.109	−.031	.161
	(.049)	(.112)	(.926)	(.124)
N	1,147	1,170	1,055	1,175
Adjusted/Pseudo R^2	.108	.092	.095	.033
F score	12.517		10.170	

Notes: Coefficients are unstandardized. Robust standard errors in parentheses.
*** = < .001, ** = < .01, * = < .05.
a. Logit regression for binary dependent variables.

hardly correlate. Indeed, analysis here of the determinants of perception and participation at the micro level shows contrasts and similarities. As presented in Table 6.7, interpersonal trust and political trust are inversely linked to perception of corruption (those with little trust perceive a lot of corruption), but largely unrelated to actual participation (the LAPOP model shows a weak relationship linking participation to confidence in the police). More income and education translates into a greater likelihood of engaging in corruption, but has no impact on an individual's perception of corruption. By contrast, those who are tolerant of corruption among politicians and males are more likely to perceive higher levels of corruption and more likely to participate in corruption.

Table 6.7 Determinants of Perceptions of and Participation in Corruption and Their Impact

Determinants

| | Dependent Variable | | | |
| | Perception | | Participation | |
Independent Variable	ENCBG	LAPOP	ENCBG	LAPOP
Political interest / Read papers		none		+
Community involvement		none		+
Interpersonal trust	–	+	none	none
Political trust	–	none	none	none
Trust in police		–		–
Tolerance toward corruption	+		+	
Economic situation of country		–		
Personal economic situation		none		
Corruption as problem		none		
Knowledge to denounce	none		+	
Participation in corruption	+	none	n.a.	n.a.
Perception of corruption	n.a.	n.a.	+	none
PRI in power at state level	none		+	
Party vote		none		
Sex (male)	+	none	+	+
Age	none	none	+	
Education	none	none	+	+
Income	none	none	+	+
Mexico City resident	+		+	+

Note: Blank cells indicate untested variables. "None" indicates no relationship; "+" refers to positive relationship; "–" refers to negative relationship.

Impact

| | Dependent Variable | | | |
Independent Variable	Satisfaction with Democracy	Voting	Regime Legitimacy	Corruption as Problem
Perception	none	none	–	none
Participation	none	none	–	none

Similarly, residents of the Mexico City region (state of Mexico and the federal district) are more likely to participate in corruption and more likely to perceive corruption. Participation in corruption, in turn, plays a role in influencing perception, just as perception influences participation, though this factor falls slightly short of statistical significance in the LAPOP model.

Looking at the consequences of perception and participation shows that both dimensions of corruption exert an independent influence over individual feelings of regime legitimacy. This suggests that both the perception and the experience of corruption cost the regime in terms of legitimacy. The effects of these on one's satisfaction with democracy are not statistically significant, however, particularly when controlling for the effects of Fox's approval ratings and assessments of the economic situation, though in both cases the influence is in the expected direction: individuals who register higher levels of corruption express less satisfaction with the state of democracy. Although the perception of corruption and actual participation in corrupt exchanges influence perceptions of the regime, neither has a dramatic effect on perceptions of corruption's importance as a national issue. Similarly, neither voting nor partisanship seems to play a particularly strong role in influencing perceptions or participation.

Conclusion

Based on far more specific and targeted survey questions, real participation in corruption is not nearly as prevalent as the perception of corruption. Still, cross-national data suggest that participation is nonetheless relatively high in Mexico. Given the specific nature of questions regarding participation in corruption, it is precisely here where one might expect the greatest sensitivity to changes in corruption arising from the structural and institutional reforms described in earlier chapters. Yet as the current chapter has shown, while there have been some reductions in the overall rates of participation, progress has been exceedingly slow. This finding raises a wide range of questions about the implementation of reforms and their effectiveness as well as the cultural underpinnings or setting of the corruption and the reforms. This chapter has also shown that participation in corruption and perception of corruption are not the same. The two stem from different factors, and are only weakly and mutually related. This leaves open the question as to whether solutions targeting one really have much effect on the other. Though stemming from different forces, both participation and perception nonetheless have pernicious effects on feelings of regime legitimacy.

Such conclusions, however, are tendered at a very broad level of abstraction, as if corruption—whether perception or participation—were a concise, unidimensional phenomenon. To disaggregate corruption even further, we must turn our attention toward the patterns of corruption in Mexico. What specific types of corruption or what specific areas within the government exhibit the highest and lowest levels of corruption (based on both perception and participation)? Is it possible to differentiate patterns of change within specific areas? Has the broad mix of corruption altered in recent years because of the structural and institutional changes taking place in the country?

Notes

1. This analysis draws extensively on Morris 2008.
2. The 2005 survey eliminated seven of the least-used services from the prior surveys and added four. The 2007 survey duplicated the areas from the 2005 survey.

3. Studies by Claudio Weber Abramo (2008) and myself (Morris 2008) examine the empirical relationship linking perception and participation. Both reveal a very weak to nonexistent correlation. In a study on Russia, Richard Rose and William Mishler (2007) focus on the gap between perception and participation. They contend that while contact with officials determines the experience of bribery, perceptions relate more to beliefs in government fairness and exposure to media sources. At the cross-national level, Daniel Treisman (2007, 217) notes that the correlation between the two types of measures is quite high, but that there is much greater variance in reported bribery particularly where perceived corruption is high. Finally, the 2007 Global Corruption Barometer reported a strong correlation between "people's perception of corruption in key services and their experience with bribery when coming in contact with the same services." It also revealed "a strong correlation between citizens' experiences with bribery and experts' perceptions of corruption." This suggests that in institutions with which citizens interact regularly, involvement in corruption shapes perception, but that perception stems from something else in institutions with little citizen interaction.

4. Pranab Bardhan (1997) refers to "frequency-dependent equilibrium," wherein one's participation in corruption is a function of their expectation of the corrupt behavior of others. Micro-level studies by Roberta Gatti (2003), William Miller (2006), and Naci Mocan (2004), and formal mathematical models by Jens Andvig and Karl Moene (1990), Ajit Mishra (2006), and Jean Tirole (1996), assess, test, and demonstrate this deductive formula.

5. Though a person's participation in paying a bribe is only weakly related to their perception of corruption in government or among politicians, an interesting question is whether those who participate in corruption see themselves as more corrupt. Analysis here shows a negligible impact ($r = -0.098$ for 2001; $r = -0.127$ for 2003), with those who have recently participated in corruption being only slightly more likely to consider themselves as corrupt.

6. The 2001 EGDE business survey similarly showed the Mexico City region as suffering the highest levels of corruption.

7

Shifting Patterns
of Corruption

Unfortunately, mainstream measures of corruption are one-dimensional, simplifying a complex phenomenon and ignoring corruption's myriad forms or institutional settings (Johnston 2005; see also Soreide 2006). In seeking to move beyond these measures, attention now shifts to the patterns of corruption. Disaggregating corruption and analyzing patterns allows us to assess the predominant types or locations of corruption and explore change in specific areas. More important, differentiating patterns facilitates a more nuanced assessment of change whereby some types of corruption may be falling while other forms may be increasing.

This chapter explores the patterns of corruption in Mexico using a range of data and approaches. It begins by focusing on patterns based on perceptions of corruption, using two approaches. One approach uses polling data to disaggregate perceptions. Here, analysis highlights the institutions and actors perceived to be the most and the least corrupt, the forms and location of corruption that determine an individual's overall perception of corruption in government and among politicians, and changes in particular institutional settings. Still operating at this broad level of perception, attention then turns to a brief analysis of press reports of corruption. Recognizing the fundamental role media play in shaping the public discourse on corruption and hence in molding perceptions about the types and locations of corruption, I briefly examine data from newspapers to determine the forms of corruption most often reported in the media, the broad narrative employed, and possible changes during the period. Bribing the police to avoid a traffic citation may be an everyday event and constitute the most common form of corrupt activity in Mexico, but rarely does it make the headlines.

The analysis next shifts attention to participation and actual experience with corruption and anticorruption. Again, I employ multiple approaches and data sets to tease out underlying patterns. One approach looks at polling data to focus on the specific areas in which bribes are paid or solicited. A second approach breaks down official data on administrative sanctions and citizen complaints. Like media reports, these data do not necessarily provide a clean, objective measure of the underlying patterns of corruption; nonetheless, they do provide insights into the areas exhibiting irregularities as well as the nature of the government's anticorruption measures. Both thus offer complementary means of exploring change.

Disaggregating Perceptions of Corruption

Chapter 5 assesses general or aggregate perceptions of corruption. These polls differentiate such perceptions by institutions, actors, and types of corrupt transaction, providing a better sense of the underlying patterns of corruption in Mexico and allowing for a more careful examination of how distinct forms of corruption shape overall views on corruption, politicians, and institutions, and where change, if any, may be occurring. Analysis differentiates corruption by different levels, institutions, and political parties.

State vs. Society
Mexicans clearly consider corruption more pronounced in the public than in the private arena.[1] Rankings of the level of corruption in the 2005 Encuesta Nacional de Corrupción y Buen Gobierno (ENCBG) poll, in the 2004–2006 Global Corruption Barometer, and in the 2001–2004 Corruptómetro surveys show that private sector institutions (including citizens, journalists, nongovernmental organizations [NGOs], religious institutions, teachers, priests, etc.), on the whole, are considered less corrupt than public institutions.[2] Similarly, citizens consider themselves less corrupt than politicians. Internal auditors within the government express a similar view: that corruption is more likely to involve federal funds than private sector funds. In the 2001 Diagnostico Institucional del Sistema Federal de Control (DSFC) survey, when asked the source of illegal resources—the federal budget or the private sector—49 percent of auditors said federal money, 29 percent said both, and 22 percent said the private sector.

State Institutions, Political Parties
Focusing solely on the public sector itself, the public feels that corruption is greatest at the "highest levels" of government. As indicated in Table 7.1, over 40 percent of respondents in each of the ENCBG polls cited the "upper level" as the area with the highest levels of corruption, while a third felt it was most pronounced at all three levels. Of course, what respondents meant by "high," "middle," and "lower" levels is not entirely clear from the question wording,

Table 7.1 Perceived Frequency of Corruption by Level (% response)

ENCBG

	2001	2003	2005
Highest levels	44.4	42.5	42.1
Middle levels	9.2	10.0	10.0
Lower levels	8.6	9.0	8.3
All levels	37.9	38.5	39.6

Corruptómetro

	2001	2002
Federal	38.0	35.0
State	19.8	22.5
Municipal	16.6	12.9
All equal	21.3	25.5
Don't know	4.3	4.1

nor is there any expectation that the meanings of those terms might be consistent. Using a somewhat different approach, the 2001 and 2002 Corruptómetro polls asked respondents to differentiate corruption among the three layers of government (federal, state, and municipal): a clearer yardstick. Although by a somewhat smaller margin, respondents again concurred that corruption was higher at the federal level.[3]

Ratings of the level of corruption by institution and actors, presented in Table 7.2, provide a somewhat clearer profile of the pattern of popular perceptions of corruption. The most corrupt institutions, according to perception, are prisons, "the government," the justice system, political parties, the legislature, and, among the *diputados,* politicians generally, as well as police and union officials. This perception of high levels of corruption in the criminal justice system (prisons, justice system itself, and police) is further confirmed in the telephone-based Corruptómetro polls. In the 2002 poll, 80 percent of respondents believed that the greatest level of corruption occurred in prisons. Below these institutions that encompass upper-level politics and the criminal justice system, we find the more bureaucratic, intermediate-level types of services, with bribes to obtain permits ranking relatively high. The medical and educational systems—though both largely public sector institutions—rank lower. In fact, the public envisions teachers as the least corrupt of public employees, and the military as least corrupt of public institutions.[4]

Different samples focusing on specific institutions provide further insight. The Encuesta de Gobernabilidad y Desarrollo Empresarial (EGDE) survey of business opinion ranked the federal police, the Procuraduría General de la República (PGR) (attorney general), the Instituto para la Protección al Ahorro

182

Table 7.2 Perceived Level of Corruption by Actor

ENCBG (scale 1–10: 1 = clean, to 10 = corrupt)

Actor	2005
Politicians	8.93
Prisons	8.79
Deputies	8.69
Police	8.68
Government	8.62
Judges	8.43
Justice system	8.08
Union leaders	8.02
Unions	7.97
Bureaucrats	7.67
Big business	7.57
Citizens	6.81
Commerce	6.80
Media	6.55
Journalists	6.32
Teachers	5.58
Religious institutions	5.02
Priests	4.64

Global Corruption Barometer (Transparency International)
(scale 1–5: 1 = not corrupt, to 5 = corrupt)

Actor	2004	2005	2006	Change 2004–2006
Police	4.5	4.7	4.5	0
Parties	4.5	4.7	4.4	−0.1
Legal system/judiciary	4.3	4.5	4.2	−0.1
Legislature	4.2	4.4	4.3	+0.1
Tax services	4.0	3.9	3.8	−0.2
Registry and permit services	3.8	4.0	3.9	+0.1
Business/private sector	3.7	3.5	3.7	0
Utilities	3.7	3.6	3.5	−0.2
Media	3.6	3.3	3.5	−0.1
Medical services	3.5	3.2	3.0	−0.5
Education system	3.4	3.1	3.2	−0.2
Nongovernmental organizations	3.3	3.3	3.2	−0.1
Military	3.2	3.1	3.2	0
Religious bodies	3.1	2.9	3.2	+0.1
Military	3.2	3.1	3.2	0
Average	3.77	3.73	3.69	−0.08

Corruptómetro (scale 1–10: 1 = clean, to 10 = corrupt)

Actor	2001	2002	2004
Prisons	8.51	8.49	8.54
Politicians	8.33	8.39	8.64
Deputies	8.05	8.38	—
Senators	8.20	—	—

(continues)

Table 7.2 continued

Actor	2001	2002	2004
Police	8.10	8.18	8.31
Electoral campaigns	8.04	—	—
Unions	7.75	8.01	8.00
Union leaders	7.73	7.77	7.97
Justice system	7.65	7.69	8.09
Judges	7.54	7.52	7.77
Charity donation campaigns	7.21	—	—
Bureaucrats	7.19	7.23	7.30
Citizens	6.90	6.94	7.09
Big business	6.69	6.87	7.19
Businesspeople	6.63	6.72	7.00
Media	6.27	6.15	—
Religious institutions	5.39	5.96	—
Commerce	5.89	6.31	6.43
Journalists	5.32	5.45	5.59
Priests	4.76	5.50	—
Teachers	4.77	5.16	5.31

Bancario (IPAB, bank bailout institution), Customs, Petroleos Mexicanos (PEMEX), Congress, and the Instituto Mexicano de Seguro Social (IMSS) as the most dishonest institutions, and, by contrast, Bancomext, the Banco de México, and the Presidencia as the most honest. Similar to the public's views, the list features law enforcement, Congress, and two of the largest decentralized bureaucratic agencies as suffering the highest levels of corruption, and the more professionalized financial-related bureaucracies and the presidency as the least corrupt. This survey also asked businesses about the capacity of social groups to influence government decisionmaking through bribes. The groups they identified as having the greatest corrupt influence included narcotraffickers and organized crime, followed by multinational corporations, national businesses, and labor unions (CEE 2002).

Providing a bit more specificity, the 2004 Corruptómetro poll ranked the perception of corruption by political party. Here, as shown in Table 7.3, we see a rather clear tendency to view the Partido Revolucionario Institucional (PRI) as more corrupt than the other two major parties, but the difference lies primarily with respect to the distinction between "a lot" and "some" corruption. It is worth noting here that the PAN is not seen uniquely as a reform party, despite Fox's emphasis on anticorruption. By contrast, the PAN and PRD are viewed in roughly similar terms reflecting perhaps their historic opposition to the PRI. Even so, all parties are held in rather low regard by the public as the data suggests.

Determinants of Perceptions of Corruption

What specific areas of corruption shape an individual's overall perception of corruption? In an effort to address this question, Table 7.4 presents simple

Table 7.3 Perceived Level of Corruption by Political Party (Corruptómetro 2004) (% response)

	PAN	PRI	PRD
A lot	45.7	67.8	47.0
Some	31.8	19.9	30.0
A little	16.7	7.8	15.5
None	0.7	1.1	2.1
Don't know	4.6	3.8	5.5

correlation coefficients linking the ratings of corruption by institution and actor with the more general perceptions of corruption in government and among politicians. Generic views on corruption in government are most closely associated with individual perceptions of corruption within the judiciary, among politicians, and among *diputados* (r > 0.50), followed by individual perceptions of corruption among the police, unions, bureaucrats, or citizens. Perceived corruption among politicians is most closely aligned to perceptions of corruption among *diputados,* judges (rather than the judiciary), the government, and the police (r > 0.50). Since perceptions of corruption are only partially determined by actual experience with corruption, as reported earlier, this suggests that general perceptions of corruption in Mexico are built more on overall perceptions of corruption among politicians, the political parties, members of Congress, judges, and the judiciary than on perceptions of corruption among the police and bureaucrats (administrative level; those whom citizens regularly come into contact with) or of corruption within society (business, media, teachers, religious institutions, and priests).[5] Moreover, this suggests that the perception of corruption fits within a larger narrative regarding the nature of politics, politicians, and authority in Mexico rather than actual experience: a line developed more fully in Chapter 8, which ponders the role of culture.

Type of Government Activity

A somewhat different but related approach to disaggregating perception focuses on the specific forms of corruption or purposes of corrupt transactions rather than on institutions and actors. Though overall assessments of corruption seem to relate to perceptions of corruption among politicians, the judiciary, and the police, the public clearly recognizes the *mordida*—the petty bribe designed to avoid a traffic citation or facilitate a bureaucratic service—as the most common form of corruption in Mexico. In one of the few polls that asked about the different forms of corruption, including bribes, unexplained wealth, favoritism, and influence peddling, respondents to a local survey in the Guadalajara metropolitan area provided a clear and detailed ranking. Shown in Table 7.5, the *mordida* was clearly considered the most frequent corrupt act, with influence peddling considered the least common. Ratings of the perceived

Table 7.4 Corruption in Government and Among Politicians (ENCBG 2005) (bivariate correlations of public ratings, two-tailed significance)

Corruption in Government	
Judiciary	.605**
Politicians	.546**
Deputies	.510**
Big business	.477**
Judges	.477**
Union	.443**
Police	.431**
Prisons	.409**
Businesspeople	.380**
Union leaders	.364**
Bureaucrats	.362**
Media	.322**
Citizens	.298**
Commerce	.298**
Journalists	.270**
Teachers	.227**
Religious institutions	.198**
Priests	.173**
Participation	.020*
Political trust	−.045**
Belief in justice system	−.063**

Corruption Among Politicians	
Deputies	.681**
Judges	.657**
Government	.546**
Police	.533**
Judiciary	.441**
Businesspeople	.427**
Union leaders	.422**
Bureaucrats	.406**
Big business	.367**
Union	.372**
Prisons	.355**
Commerce	.302**
Media	.252**
Citizens	.298**
Journalists	.252**
Teachers	.220**
Religious institutions	.198**
Priests	.143**
Participation	.038**
Political trust	−.177**
Belief in justice system	−.038**

frequency of various forms of corruption in the 2002 Corruptómetro poll echoed this finding, with bribery of transit police topping the list as the most frequent form of corruption, followed by bribery of inspectors and other bureaucrats.

Table 7.5 Perceived Frequency of Corruption by Type

Type of Corruption	Percentage of Respondents[a]
Bribery (mordida)	62.7
Diversion of funds	43.5
Unexplained enrichment	37.6
Providing jobs and benefits to friends and family	37.6
Influence peddling	25.4

Source: "Percepciones de la población" 2002.
Notes: a. Respondents who chose 10 (corrupt) on a ten-point scale where 1 = clean, 10 = corrupt.

Businesses hold a similar view relating to the forms of corruption perceived as most common. Such views on the perceived frequency of certain types of acts occupy the realm somewhere between perception and participation.

The perceptions of those actually responsible for investigating corruption provide a somewhat more refined view of the types of corruption plaguing Mexico. In the 2001 DSFC survey of government auditors, 39 percent said that the most frequent form of corruption involved individuals operating with the knowledge of other workers at various levels in the organization (systemic corruption); 31 percent indicated corruption involving a group, with the collaboration of workers at various levels (syndicated corruption); 12 percent indicated corruption by individuals working in secret; and 6 percent indicated corruption by individuals with the knowledge of others at the same level. Such findings suggest that corruption tends to be systemic rather than individualized.

Change

Whereas Chapter 5 tracks change based on overall perceptions of corruption, the task here is to examine change based on the different types or locations of corruption. Unfortunately, the lack of good longitudinal data limits the potential insights. Data presented in Tables 7.1 and 7.2, for instance, reveal virtually no significant changes in any of the areas. The Global Corruption Barometer, however, only looks at a two-year period (2004–2006), while the Corruptómetro polls show a rather consistent increase in the corruption ratings in every single area. Though the ENCBG polls do not provide data on specific institutions for the earlier years, they do differentiate change at different levels; but as shown in Table 7.1 and in Table 7.6, evidence of change in perception seems inconclusive. Table 7.1 suggests a reduction at the highest level and a slight increase at the middle level (though again, what these levels mean is not entirely clear). By contrast, Table 7.6 points to the perception of corruption falling more at the state level than at the federal level, and actually growing more at the federal level. While in both cases the initial optimism regarding recent and future change fell at roughly equal rates, individual assessments of change and expectations of change were always slightly better at the state level. This is

Table 7.6 Expected Change in Corruption by Level (prior year and coming year) (ENCBG) (% response)

	2001	2003	2005
Change in Corruption over Prior Year			
National corruption			
More	35.5	34.0	40.0
Less	21.5	19.0	15.7
State corruption			
More	29.6	29.8	33.8
Less	33.4	20.4	17.9
Expected Change in Corruption in Coming Year			
National corruption			
More	29.6	34.9	41.0
Less	33.4	22.8	17.9
State corruption			
More	25.0	30.5	35.4
Less	34.0	24.1	19.7

interesting given democratization at the federal level and the high-profile anti-corruption campaign by President Vicente Fox. Yet this pattern nestles nicely within the context of viewing corruption as much more pronounced at the upper levels and within the federal government to begin with. It also suggests that the impact of democratization may occur more at the local level, though the degree of change at the state level remains limited (Morris 2009).

The 2001 ENCBG poll also included a series of questions regarding expectations of change in specific institutional arenas. The results suggest a somewhat different pattern. As indicated in Table 7.7, respondents were especially pessimistic about changes in the judiciary, state government, and city government, and were more optimistic about changes in the presidency, the ministries, and the federal government generally. This suggests, of course, that much of the optimism in 2001 centered on the federal government and the Fox administration. This is logical, since the anticorruption initiatives under Fox focused primarily on the federal executive.

Business opinion presents a somewhat similar pattern. Expectations of a decrease in corruption centered more on the presidency and the executive, and less on the legislative and judicial branches; and on the federal level as opposed to the state and municipal levels, for which a larger proportion of businesses predicted an increase as opposed to a decline in corruption. At the more precise bureaucratic level, however, businesses pointed to some real changes.

Media Reports of Corruption

Press reports of corruption provide a crude gauge of its extent and nature. Though earlier regression analysis showed that newspaper readership did not

Table 7.7 **Expected Change in Corruption over Next Two Years Among Businesses (ENCBG 2001) (% response)**

	Increase	Decrease
By federal branch		
Presidency	14	38
Ministries	16	30
Legislature	19	22
Judiciary	24	19
By administrative level		
Federal	19	24
State	22	19
Municipal	23	21

influence individual perceptions of corruption, the press nonetheless reflects and molds the public discourse. News stories—as a medium—inform the public about what public officials are doing and thinking with respect to corruption. They offer a vehicle to publicly accuse someone of wrongdoing, and to report on investigations of alleged corruption and on the nature and outcome of official investigations and court cases. The press also presents the political context surrounding charges and countercharges of corruption. As such, news stories and scandals frame the issue. I am not suggesting that the press offers a truly objective measure of corruption—far from it. News stories reflect the normal biases: information from primary sources and issues that the press or the government deems important, newsworthy, or of interest to readers. They stress information provided by politicians, the government, and their own investigations, and scandals, personalities (rather than institutions), and high-level corruption. In short, media dramatizes and personalizes politics (Acosta Silva 2004). As Erhard Blankenburg (2002, 914) points out, "The opportunity of triggering corruption scandals does not correlate with any measurable degree of corruption but rather with media competition, institutional competence, and power constellations."

So how prevalent then are news stories on corruption in Mexico? What types of corruption dominate press coverage of corruption and what changes, if any, are present? Figure 7.1 charts simply the number of corruption-related articles by month in the family of newspapers *Milenio*.[6] It shows that the average number of articles on corruption during the period fluctuated slightly, averaging around forty per month. Spikes occurred in conjunction with particular scandals. The biggest jump centered around the 2004 video scandals (see Appendix B for details). Research by Leticia Juárez González (2004), cited earlier, shows how the numerous reports nurtured the public's perceptions of corruption. As noted in Chapter 5, the public's perceptions of the extent of corruption and its importance as a national problem increased dramatically during this time.

Figure 7.1 Number of Corruption-Related Articles in *Milenio*

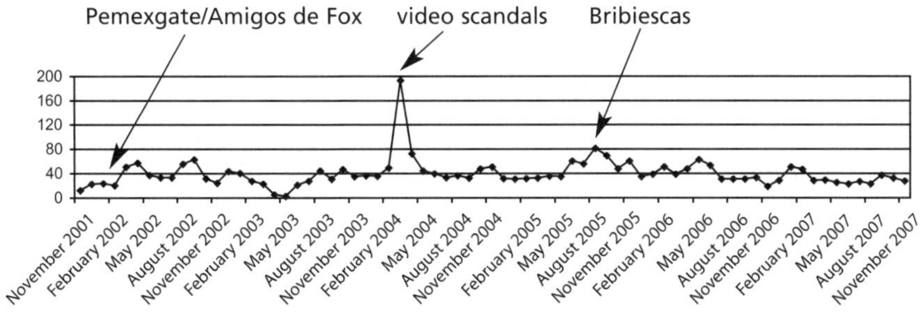

Beyond these spikes, questions arise as to what specifically the roughly forty articles on corruption per month say—the picture they paint. Taken as a whole, what sort of narrative on corruption do they construct? And what, if any, changes can be discerned? Though a systematic content analysis of the 2,697 articles on corruption during the period reported in the *Milenio* family of newspapers is beyond the scope here, a general review based on a rather close reading of most of those articles over the years highlights some rather clear patterns:

First, many of the news stories center on efforts by government to curtail corruption, including local, state, national, and even international initiatives. Coverage of the Secretaría de la Contraloría y Desarrollo Administrativo (SEC-ODAM) and Secretary Francisco Barrio was particularly high in the early years of the *sexenio*. These stories not only focused on the Fox anticorruption efforts, but also the launching of official investigations of alleged corruption at PEMEX, Customs, and in the PGR. Such stories fueled the expectations of change during the period. The movement had a sort of demonstration effect as agencies within the government publicized their anticorruption efforts and state and local governments embraced their own. For instance, on February 19, 2001, the Instituto de Seguridad y Servicios Sociales de los Trabajadores del Estado (ISSSTE) was the first to publicize its anticorruption plan, including promises to make budgetary matters public. On the same day, Rigoberto Garza Faz (PRI), former interim mayor of Reynosa and then city council member, announced a contest for the best videos, audios, and photographs revealing acts of corruption and promised a monthly prize of 5,000 pesos (US$515) to the five best works (*La Reforma* February 19, 2001). On July 12, 2002, as reported in *La Reforma,* Hacienda (SHCP) stated that it would conduct audits of the hundred most important companies in the country.

Second, many if not a majority of the news stories on corruption present allegations—specific or general—of wrongdoing, often in conjunction with a broader discussion of efforts to battle corruption. As indicated, the spikes in coverage in Figure 7.1 refer to the high-profile cases of Amigos de Fox, Pemexgate, the video scandals, and the allegations against the Bribiesca brothers. Because of their extremely high profile, the types of corruption involved are important to understanding broader perceptions of corruption in the country. These cases involved illegal campaign financing, as discussed in Chapter 2, the bribery of local officials by a wealthy businessman, and allegations of influence peddling and the awarding of government contracts to members of the president's family.[7] Among the other major cases that received substantial press coverage were Towelgate, beginning in June 2001, which raised questions about President Fox's personal expenditures; the continuing case against Raul Salinas, which eventually ended with the exoneration of the former president's brother; allegations of conflict of interest against Senator Diego Fernández de Cevallos; the Fondo Bancario de Protección al Ahorro (FOBAPROA) banking scandal, "considered by many as the biggest corruption scandal in Mexico's history" (Reyes 2004a); accusations against the first lady, Marta Sahagún, and her NGO Vamos México, for channeling public funds; and numerous cases of corruption involving drug trafficking, the police, and at times the military.

Third, many of the articles on corruption deal extensively with the underlying political context, giving coverage to the political allegations and to the responses offered by partisans, who usually contend that the accusations are politically motivated. Partisan allies of those accused of corruption often frame the issue in terms of witch-hunts and conspiracies. Both the video scandals against Partido de la Revolución Democrática (PRD) officials and the allegations of corruption against the first lady and her sons—among the highest-profile cases of the period—brought extensive coverage of accusations of political maneuvering. The video scandals, in particular, raised questions about the sources of the videos themselves and fed a sort of widely held conspiracy theory that Fox was going after the popular PRD mayor Andrés Manuel López Obrador. Subsequent efforts by the Fox government to remove the mayor for failing to carry out a judicial order regarding a construction project in Mexico City seemed to confirm this theory. In almost poetic fashion, the allegations and investigations against the first lady, her sons, and President Fox himself after his term ended, for illicit enrichment, influence peddling, and fraud, were similarly cast by the president and his supporters as unfounded and politically motivated.

Fourth, there is a pronounced tendency in the press to routinely attribute problems and policy failures to corruption. Following a series of prison killings in 2004, for example, capped by the December 31 killing of drug trafficker Arturo Guzmán Loera (El Pollo) at La Palma prison, the press highlighted the role of corruption inside prisons. Accusations surfaced that drug-trafficking organizations controlled not only La Palma and Puente Grande federal prisons, but also scores of state prisons. The attorney general was clear in his indictment: "What is happening is that a breakdown is occurring because of corruption" (*SourceMex* January 12, 2005). This tendency to blame corruption also accompanies most national tragedies. Following the explosions at the Pasta de Conchos mine in the state of Coahuila in February 2006, which killed sixty-five miners, for instance, accusations swirled of corruption involving the company, inspectors from the Ministry of Labor, the president, and the governor. The case prompted an official investigation in the Chamber of Deputies and generated over 600 articles in *Milenio* newspapers between 2006 and May 2008. A similar pattern emerged following the accident on PEMEX's oil platform Usumacinta in the Sonda de Campeche in October 2006 that killed twenty-two workers. The incident triggered not only investigations by the PGR and Congress, but also widespread speculation of the involvement of the Bribiescas (see Cervantes and Santana 2007). The deadly floods in the state of Tabasco in 2007 gave rise to similar reports: "As always, the cause of the disaster in Tabasco—which as of last Friday the second had left more than a million people homeless and hundreds of thousands stranded in the waters—is not the torrential rains and rivers overflowing their banks, but rather the lack of foresight, the negligence, the diverting of funds and the corruption of the authorities" (Guzmán 2007, 37). Indeed, Miguel Ángel Granados Chapa (2007) refers to the interior minister's certainty that, despite funds for public works in the area, because of corruption the actual work was never done.[8]

The dominant narrative crafted in part by the media also entails what is conspicuously absent from the stories. Few stories praise the government's efforts—except with regard to transparency. Few stories describe or celebrate the punishment of those charged with being corrupt, making impunity a prominent theme. Though the Instituto Federal Electoral (IFE) imposed substantial fines on both the PRI and the Partido Acción Nacional (PAN) for violating campaign finance and reporting laws, the main actors in the Pemexgate and Amigos de Fox scandals, among them Senator Deschamps (PRI) and Lino Karrodi, were never indicted or prosecuted. Despite multiple accusations and assumptions of wrongdoing, no one was ever convicted in the FOBAPROA, Vamos México, and Bribiescas scandals, to mention just a few. In some instances, of course, a political cost was paid, and officials resigned, such as Fox's personal secretary following the Towelgate scandal. Only in a few cases, such as Mario Villanueva, the governor of Quintana Roo, and René Bejarano of the PRD, were formal charges brought.

Another theme largely absent in the press is petty forms of corruption or bureaucratic efforts to fight low-level corruption. Lofty rhetoric and general policy pronouncements regarding the fight against corruption receive substantial coverage, but details of specific efforts within the bureaucracy gain little press attention. This reflects a point noted earlier by one of the participants I surveyed in the 2007 accountability seminar: the public is unaware of the changes taking place within the bureaucracy. Indeed, the slight reduction in actual participation rates does not match the increase in the perception of corruption.

Finally, though the tracking of articles on corruption itself shows almost no change over the period, press attention to related areas does reveal some important shifts. First, as shown in Figure 7.2, the number of articles featuring the issue of transparency climbed dramatically during the period to reach a level comparable to the number of stories on corruption. Though closely related to the issue of corruption, stories on transparency tend to stress a narrative rooted more in democratic demands for accountability and the efforts of the government to guarantee access to information. Reflecting this shift in the public discourse, stories on the Instituto Federal de Acceso a la Información (IFAI), the agency charged with guaranteeing freedom of information, also climbed sharply during the period. At the same time, however, articles focusing on the agency responsible for preventing corruption, SECODAM (now the Secretaría de la Función Pública [SFP]), fell. Reflecting the fanfare associated with Fox's anticorruption campaign—the establishment of the Comisión Intersecretarial para la Transparencia y el Combate a la Corrupción en la Administración Pública Federal (CITCC), the announcement of the Programa Nacional, public pronouncements of allegations and investigations by officials, and so

Figure 7.2 Number of News Reports on Selected Accountability Topics

Reports on Transparency

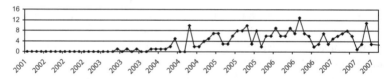

Reports on SECODAM/SFP

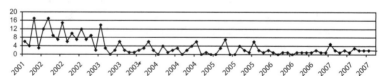

Reports on the IFAI

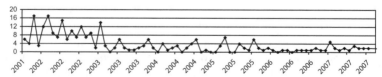

forth, in the early years—by 2003, SECODAM was rarely in the news, suggesting that official investigations were either less glamorous or less noteworthy or had in fact declined. In some ways, this suggests that the narrative on anticorruption shifted away from the preventive and enforcement measures that characterized the early years, to center more simply on transparency.[9]

In summary, four key dimensions of the press's narrative on corruption stand out. First, the broad coverage of corruption cases tends to confirm or reaffirm the popular notion not only that corruption is widespread in Mexico, but also that it is particularly widespread among high-level officials. Given the media's emphasis on personalities, this comes across as owing to personal rather than institutional factors. Moreover, the stories tend to highlight the private use of public resources, bribery, and more recently, conflict of interest and influence peddling. These new forms of corruption seem to complement the more traditional stories on police- and drug-related corruption, and fraud within such large agencies as PEMEX. Second, the fact that so few cases ever result in the sentencing or imprisonment of prominent public officials (few "big fish" are fried), the stories tend to (1) confirm the popular view that high-level officials enjoy impunity, (2) undermine the credibility of the government's promises to fight corruption, and (3) characterize the criminal justice system as weak, perhaps even the weakest link in the chain. Third, in that so many of the cases include a strong partisan or political undertone, the revelations tend to lend support to notions regarding the widespread abuse of authority and the law by public officials rather than casting anticorruption moves as part of a sincere effort to assert the rule of law. In other words, the press portrays even efforts to fight specific cases of corruption as politically motivated, arising from the same forces that give rise to the corruption itself. Finally, as seen with respect to the increase in attention to transparency, it appears that the dominant narrative on anticorruption shifted away from preventive and enforcement measures that marked the early years, particularly within the SECODAM, to center more simply on transparency and the work of the IFAI. In some ways, "transparency" became almost synonymous for "anticorruption" at some point in the Fox *sexenio,* as if opening access to information would by itself effectively battle corruption.

Participation in Corruption

Turning attention now to actual participation and experiences with corruption and anticorruption, analysis begins by discerning particular patterns of corruption using participation-based data. I follow this approach by looking briefly at the specific patterns behind citizen complaints of irregularities and sanctions by the government for corruption and abuse of authority.

Data on participation confirms that, like perception, corruption is more common within the public sector as opposed to the private sector. Among the thirty-eight services examined in the 2001 and 2003 ENCBG polls and the thirty-five services in the 2005 and 2007 polls, the services exhibiting the highest proportion of bribery clearly involve the public sector. With the exception of paying someone to park in a public area (a private sector area of bribery)—which enjoyed the second-highest ranking overall—bribes involving private sector services (e.g., admittance to a hospital, soliciting a loan from a private bank, connection of private-owned utilities, etc.) were all paid in less than 10 percent of cases (see Table 7.8). The payment of a bribe to acquire a vehicular inspection, which involves a public concession to a private company, was slightly higher. Moreover, as with perception of corruption, the most frequent forms of participation in corruption involved the criminal justice system. In fact, five of the top six services for which bribing occurred involved the police or the public justice ministry: preventing the impoundment of a car, avoiding a ticket, recovering a stolen auto, avoiding detention, and filing a complaint or pursuing a case. The other government service in the top six—Customs—is also an enforcement agency, though one having less direct contact with the public. At a second tier are certain municipal services such as working or selling in a public area, the hauling of garbage, and obtaining construction permits. Other municipal services as well as an assortment of federal services appear further down the table, indicating much lower levels of bribery. Indeed, despite the perception that more corruption exists at the upper levels and within the federal government, the greatest level of participation clearly occurs at the lower levels.

Data from the 2004 Latin American Public Opinion Project (LAPOP) poll and from the Corruptómetro polls also offer some insights into the different types of corruption that take place based on participation rates. According to the LAPOP data, presented in the prior chapter, it was somewhat more common for police to solicit a bribe than a public employee (18 percent versus 13 percent) and it was more common for a citizen to pay a bribe to process something at city hall than to pay a bribe in the courts (21 percent versus 13 percent). Since these data are based on the actual number of bribes paid or witnessed, this of course may be due to the fact that there are more opportunities (given more interactions) to bribe the police than bureaucrats, and to pay bribes in city hall than in the courts. According to the 2004 Corruptómetro poll, whereas 83 percent claimed to have paid a bribe to transit police, only 39 percent claimed to have paid a bribe to an official to obtain a license, 31 percent to a judge or public minister, and 27 percent to an official to obtain a permit. These data again, however, confirm the notion that the area of greater corruption in terms of actual experience involves the police.

Participation Rates Among Businesses

Business surveys also provide a look at specific patterns of participation. Like the public, businesses are more likely to engage in lower-level corruption with the bureaucracy than higher-level corruption. According to the 2001 EGDE

Table 7.8 Level of Corruption by Service (ENCBG)

Service	ENCBG (% response)				Percentage Change, 2001–2007
	2001	2003	2005	2007	
Prevent car from being impounded by transit police or get car out of impound (police)	57.2	53.3	60.2	50.1	–.12
Park car in public place controlled by someone who claims to own that place (private concession)	56.0	45.9	53.1	58.2	+.04
Avoid a ticket or being detained by transit police (police)	54.5	50.3	50.0	56.2	+.03
Pass items through customs, pass a checkpoint, or cross border (customs)	28.5	25.8	31.3	28.8	+.01
Recover stolen automobile (public ministry)	30.3	26.0	28.9	24.0	–.21
Avoid being detained, file a complaint or charges, or push for a case to be investigated (public ministry)	28.3	21.3	23.6	24.1	–.15
Obtain approval for working or selling in a public area (local officials)	18.7	16.0	23.4	17.5	–.06
Obtain garbage removal (municipal service)	27.0	24.4	22.8	27.1	.00
Present a case before the courts (judiciary)	15.4	10.8	15.0	14.7	–.05
Obtain license or permit for construction, destruction, or additions (municipal service)	16.8	13.2	13.9	15.1	–.10
Pass vehicular inspection (private concession)	14.5	11.5	13.3	17.1	+.18
Update paperwork for vehicle (e.g., change of ownership) (municipal service)	12.0	9.3	11.6	10.9	–.09
Obtain a drivers license (municipal service)	14.5	11.9	10.9	10.6	–.27
Obtain water service (municipal service)	12.9	11.3	10.7	14.9	+.16
Obtain license or permit for land use (municipal service)	10.1	9.2	9.8	10.0	–.01
Connect or reconnect electricity in the home (private concession)	10.7	8.3	9.4	9.9	–.07
Obtain credit or loan for home, business, or auto from a public institution (federal service)	9.4	8.1	8.1	7.0	–.26
Solicit proof of land use or other service from public registry (municipal service)	a	a	7.1	3.8	–.46[b]

(continues)

Table 7.8 continued

Service	2001	2003	2005	2007	Percentage Change, 2001–2007
Obtain or accelerate provision of birth certificate, death certificate, marriage license, or divorce papers from civil registry (municipal service)	10.0	7.9	6.7	6.6	–.34
Apply for permission to install a business or open an establishment (public service, all levels)	a	a	6.7	9.7	+.45[b]
Enter a job with the government (public service, all levels)	a	a	6.2	6.1	–.02[b]
Obtain or regularize service: water, sewage, lighting, paving, park and garden maintenance, etc. (municipal service)	8.5	6.3	6.1	6.1	–.28
Obtain urgent medical care for a patient or admittance to a clinic or hospital prior to appointment time (private concession)	4.3	2.5	5.7	3.2	–.26
Obtain or accelerate issuance of passport (federal service)	6.4	5.1	5.4	3.0	–.53
Obtain proof of studies (transcripts) or exams from public schools (public service)	4.7	3.4	4.9	3.1	–.34
Obtain approval to visit a patient in a hospital outside visiting hours (private concession)	3.7	3.3	4.8	6.9	+.86
Obtain credit or loan for house, business, or auto from a private institution (private concession)	5.0	3.2	3.6	3.5	–.30
Receive assistance from or subscribe to a government program (federal service)	5.9	2.8	3.0	2.8	–.53
Obtain military service card or exemption (federal service)	3.9	3.0	3.0	2.0	–.49
Obtain entry into an official school (public service)	3.8	3.3	2.7	2.9	–.24
Connect telephone (private service)	3.0	3.9	2.6	2.1	–.30
Receive mail (federal service)	3.8	3.2	2.2	1.5	–.61
Apply for scholarship at a private or public school	a	a	1.5	0.7	–.53[b]
Pay property tax (private concession)	1.6	1.4	0.3	0.3	–.81
Total average	10.6	8.5	10.1	10.0	–.06

Notes: a. Question not asked.
 b. Change reflects different years.

poll, 62 percent of members of the business community acknowledged making extraofficial payments to lower-level officials, while only 39 percent made such payments to higher-level officials. As shown in Table 7.9, while businesses tended to pay bribes to bureaucrats at all levels, the chief purpose was to speed up bureaucratic processes.[10] Indeed, when asked about the consequences of not paying a bribe, 47 percent said that it would simply slow the process, though 27 percent said it would result in unjustified fines and 21 percent said it would result in loss of contracts. Nonetheless, while "speed money" constitutes the most common form of corruption engaged in by businesses, when gauged by the proportion of bribes by service rendered, the most corrupt institutions again feature those tied to the criminal justice system, including state police, state courts, and the federal police.

Table 7.9 Business Participation in Corruption (EGDE 2001)

By Prevalence

Service	Percentage of Respondents Who Paid Bribe to Obtain Service
Accelerate issuance of federal permits and licenses	57
Accelerate issuance of state permits and licenses	56
Accelerate connection of federal public services	56
Accelerate issuance of municipal permits and licenses	56
Accelerate connection of municipal public services	53
Avoid problems with federal IMSS inspectors	51
Avoid problems with federal SHCP	49
Avoid being bothered by municipal inspectors	48
Obtain state government contracts	43
Avoid being bothered by state police	41

Note: In areas registering more than 40% participation.

By Frequency

Service	Percentage of Occasions When Bribe Was Paid to Obtain Service
State police	36
State courts	32
Federal police	30
Federal judges and public ministry	29
Municipal police	25
Municipal permits and licenses	25
Municipal land use permits	24
Federal permits for use of natural resources	24
Municipal construction permits	23

Note: In areas registering more than 20% participation.

Participation and Perception
The prior chapter showed a weak correlation linking participation in corruption and general perceptions of corruption. This finding begs the question as to precisely what types of perceptions are fostered by participation in corruption. The 2007 Global Corruption Barometer, for instance, reported a strong correlation between "people's perception of corruption in key services and their experience with bribery when coming in contact with the same services." This suggests that in institutions with which the people interact regularly, involvement in corruption plays a much greater role in determining perceptions, but that general perceptions of corruption within institutions with which citizens have limited interaction stem from something else. Table 7.10 seeks to explore this question. It presents the simple correlations linking experiences with and perceptions of corruption within specific institutions. Somewhat consistent with the cross-national finding, paying bribes is somewhat more closely associated with perceptions of corruption among such institutions as the police and bureaucracy compared to perceptions of corruption among politicians, the government, or the justice system more generally. Again, this supports the notion—relevant in the subsequent chapter, on culture—that while perceptions of corruption among certain institutions like the police and the bureaucracy may partially stem from actual experiences, views regarding corruption in other institutions reflect something other than actual experience with corruption.

Change
Chapter 6 documented some changes in the rates of corruption. The ENCBG corruption and good government index—a measure of the percentage of times a bribe was paid to obtain a service—fell by over 2 percentage points from 2001 to 2003, though by 2005 it regained some of that ground. Overall, from 2001 to 2005, participation in bribery fell only 5 percent (despite the anticorruption initiatives of the period and the bureaucratic overhauls), and just another 1 percent by 2007. Looking at change within the specific areas reveals a more nuanced picture, as shown earlier in Table 7.8. At one level, simple correlations of the level of corruption in the thirty-plus areas over the four periods

Table 7.10 Participation in Corruption and Perceptions of Specific Institutions (ENCBG 2005) (correlation coefficients)

Unions	.050**
Police	.041**
Bureaucrats	.039**
Politicians	.038**
Government	.020*
Justice system	.008
Business	−.004

Note: *** = < .001, ** = < .01, * = < .05.

reveal minimal change. In fact, the coefficients linking the four measures never fell below 0.98. Even so, the range of change did vary. Over the entire 2001–2007 period, the greatest declines in corruption took place in the areas of "pay property tax" (from 1.6 to 0.3), "receive mail" (from 3.8 to 1.5) and "obtain or accelerate obtaining a passport" (from 6.4 to 3.0). By contrast, the greatest increases in corruption were recorded in "visit a patient at a hospital" (from 3.7 to 6.9), "approve vehicle inspection" (from 14.5 to 17.1), and "obtain water from the delegation or municipal pipes" (from 12.9 to 14.9).[11] Interestingly, simple correlation reveals that the greatest reductions in corruption tended to occur in services already relatively free of corruption, and vice versa. Though only limited change seems to be present even in these cases, this pattern points to the difficulties of reforming areas in which corruption is more entrenched.

Complaints and Sanctions

A final look into the patterns of corruption focuses on administrative sanctions and citizen complaints: data presented at the aggregate level in Chapter 5. Data on administrative sanctions cover 1995 to 2006. During this period, the administrative units that received the most sanctions for abuse of authority and bribery or extortion—the two categories most relevant—were the Office of the Attorney General (1,590 sanctions for abuse of authority and 291 for bribery or extortion), the Mexico City government (1,527 and 385 sanctions, respectively), the Ministry of Public Security (548 and 94), the Ministry of Education (579 and 17), and the Federal Preventive Police (201 and 74) (the appendix to this chapter presents the data in summary form). Three of the top five units that received the most sanctions for these violations involve law enforcement. Looking at just the 2001–2006 period, the greatest number of sanctions for abuse of authority and bribery or extortion were leveled against officials in the Office of the Attorney General (411 and 107 sanctions, respectively), the Federal Preventive Police (201 and 74), the Immigration and Naturalization Service (47 and 99), the Tax Department (79 and 36), and PEMEX (58 and 23). Once again, the top three are law enforcement–related. Whereas, overall, the number of sanctions generally and specifically for abuse of authority and bribery or extortion fell from the Ernesto Zedillo years to the Vicente Fox years, the greatest declines actually took place in the Office of the Attorney General, where the number of sanctions for abuse of authority fell from 1,179 in the period 1995–2000 to 411 in the period 2001–2006, and for bribery or extortion from 184 to 107. Increases in the number of sanctions were most noteworthy in the recently created Federal Preventive Police (established in 2001; sanctions for abuse of authority reached 87 in 2005), and in the Immigration and Naturalization Service. Also notable, in terms of decreases in number of sanctions, was PEMEX, where the number of sanctions for abuse of authority, after peaking at an average of 30 per year from 1998 to 2000, fell rather dramatically during the Fox years to fewer than

10 annually. Again, it is difficult to interpret such trends. A decline could signify a decline in corruption or simply a relaxation of controls, detection, and
punishment.

Data on citizen complaints of irregularities in the government cover only
2000 to 2007, with serious doubts regarding the validity of the data for the year
2000.[12] Even so, the agencies most often targeted by citizen complaints for the
period 2001–2006 were the Social Security and Services Institute for State
Workers, the Tax Department, the Mexican Social Security Institute, the Ministry of Education, and PEMEX. These five entities alone accounted for 42
percent of all complaints filed with the government. These results are not that
surprising given that all of these entities have immediate and frequent contact
with citizens (save perhaps PEMEX), enjoy large budgets and personnel rolls,
and provide key governmental services. With regard to change, complaints
against the Federal Preventive Police grew the most during the period (an increase of 106.6 percent), followed by complaints against the Ministry of Education (34.2 percent). During the same period, complaints against the Office
of the Attorney General fell (a decline of 41.2 percent), as did those against the
Mexican Social Security Institute (40.2 percent). And yet, in 2007, complaints
grew across the board, particularly against the Ministry of Education (an increase of 74 percent compared to 2006).

Comparing the entities that received complaints with the number of sanctions for the same period is instructive. The Tax Department and PEMEX appear
on both lists. The Tax Department received the highest number of citizen complaints and the fourth highest number of sanctions for abuse of authority and
bribery or extortion. PEMEX ranked fifth in both complaints and sanctions.
Interestingly, law enforcement agencies that dominated the list of sanctioned
entities were not among the top entities against which complaints were filed.
Complaints against the Office of the Attorney General and the Federal Preventive Police—among the most sanctioned agencies—were nonetheless high, ranking sixth and seventh, respectively. On the flip side, sanctions against officials in
the Social Security and Services Institute for State Workers, the Mexican Social
Security Institute, and the Ministry of Education—agencies that receive numerous complaints of administrative wrongdoing—for abuse of authority and bribery
or extortion, were not particularly high, though these agencies did receive numerous sanctions for minor administrative offenses such as negligence.

Interestingly, despite indications of widespread corruption within the judiciary, this entity received virtually no administrative sanctions over the period
(complaints against judges or the courts accrue to a separate entity rather than
the SFP). This contrasts the number of complaints and sanctions associated
with other areas of law enforcement. Even so, in 2006 a report pointing to dramatic crackdowns in the judiciary surfaced, highlighting a dramatic 300 percent
increase over four years in the number of cases against judges and magistrates
for corruption and the misapplication of justice. According to the report, in

2005 alone, the government opened investigations against seventy-six judicial officials. Noting the pattern of impunity in the past, the report highlighted exceptions to that rule, including the 2002 case against Judge Juan Carlos Rayo Mares, who was detained for extortion and for soliciting sexual favors in exchange for helping a convict transfer (he was caught on video), and the 2003 case against Judge Ricardo Ojeda Gándara, who was charged with crimes against the administration of justice for allegedly preventing the processing of two persons involved in fraud.

Conclusion

Corruption is a broad, amorphous concept. Throughout the course of this study, I have sought to disaggregate perception or perceived corruption from actual participation in corruption. Evidence based on polls suggests that perceived corruption has increased in recent years, while participation in corruption has fallen somewhat. Disaggregating corruption to focus on the underlying patterns and types, this chapter has explored the types or locations of corruption associated with both perception and participation as well as with specific areas of change. Evidence suggests that in terms of perception, corruption is more pronounced in government than in society; more pronounced among politicians than among citizens; and more pronounced (though less so, comparatively) in the political sector (parties, politicians, legislature, union officials) and the criminal justice sector (police, courts, prisons) than in the bureaucracy (permits, tax services). In terms of perception, corruption is less common within the more decentralized services, like medical and educational sectors and the military. And, although the military has been linked to considerable drug-related corruption scandals, it maintains a relatively clean public image.

This pattern of perceptions differs from direct experience with corruption. Based on actual experience, the most common form of corruption involves bribes *(mordida)* paid to police and bureaucrats for a range of services, but not equally. Some services, like obtaining a scholarship or a passport, are largely free of corruption, while others, like avoiding a ticket or getting through customs, entail much higher rates of corruption. Participation does seem to influence perceptions of corruption within the institutions with which citizens have frequent contact, but plays less of a role in shaping perceptions about other institutions. This suggests that general perceptions of corruption reflect a broader narrative on politics and politicians in Mexico: a narrative echoed and reinforced in part by the press and, arguably, by politicians themselves. In terms of change, much of the data reviewed here suggest that few dramatic changes have taken place, despite democratization and Fox's high-profile anticorruption program. Public opinion data, in particular, reveal a strong degree of continuity. The press—as demonstrated by certain scandals—seems to exhibit a growing emphasis on issues of influence peddling and bribery, particularly concerning members of Congress.

At the same time, the press has been rather consistent in terms of its overall coverage of corruption, though it has placed much greater emphasis in recent years on transparency. If anything, the press perpetuates a rather paradoxical image of widespread corruption and impunity amid countercharges that the accusations of corruption are politically motivated and unfounded. The fact that the system rarely finds officials guilty, furthermore, tends to confirm the sense that impunity reigns, rather than the possibility that there is no proof of wrongdoing or that the allegations and charges are without merit.

The next chapter begins the process of taking stock of these findings by exploring the extent to which corruption—including its resilience, despite underlying structural and institutional changes—might reflect key aspects of the Mexican culture.

Appendix:
Administrative Sanctions and Citizen Complaint Tables

Sanctions Applied by Federal Government, 1995–2006

Government Entity	Percentage of Total Sanctions Applied	Percentage of Sanctions for Bribery or Extortion
Internal control organs	87.7	77.5
State comptroller	7.4	7.5
Public ministry	2.9	1.6
District judges	1.3	10.7

Type of Sanction Applied	Percentage of Total Sanctions Applied	Percentage of Sanctions for Bribery or Extortion
Admonishment (private or public)	24.7	4.9
Banned from future government employment	24.0	38.0
Suspension	21.5	23.2
Fine	15.5	6.7
Destitution (fired)	11.1	26.7
Warning (private or public)	3.3	0.3

Origin of Case	Percentage of Total Cases	Percentage of Cases for Bribery or Extortion
Citizen complaint or charge	51.2	83.0
Audit	34.1	6.0
Internal investigation	13.5	10.7

Sanctions Against Public Officials by Year

	1995	1996	1997	1998	1999	2000	Total	Average, 1995–2000
Number of all sanctions	6,061	6,223	8,055	7,054	7,427	8,473	43,293	
Abuse of authority	986	1,218	797	575	596	614	4,786	
Bribery or extortion	314	234	198	161	140	101	1,148	
Number of officials	269	195	168	128	99	75	934	191

	2001	2002	2003	2004	2005	2006	2007	Total	Average, 2001–2006
Number of all sanctions	6,472	7,740	5,940	6,465	7,254	6,079	5,043	39,950	
Abuse of authority	323	440	314	397	412	512	303	2,398	
Bribery or extortion	119	193	105	90	152	101	97	760	
Number of officials	82	125	82	70	91	69	52	519	127

Bribery/Extortion Sanctions Against Federal Government

	1995	1996	1997	1998	1999	2000
Office of the Attorney General	122/34	126/23	98/14	208/31	293/46	332/36
Mexico City government	619/178	598/99	202/51	49/20	6/6	12/11
PEMEX	0/2	1/0	4/0	21/3	25/2	43/3
Tax Department	0/0	0/0	1/0	14/18	9/20	14/6
Federal Preventive Police	—	—	0/0	—	—	0/0
Ministry of Public Security	73/17	188/33	188/34	32/3	0/0	—
Immigration and Naturalization Service	10/2	15/5	6/7	4/2	6/4	0/0
Presidency	0/0	0/0	0/0	0/0	2/0	0/0
Judiciary	0/0	0/0	0/0	0/0	1/0	0/0

	2001	2002	2003	2004	2005	2006
Office of the Attorney General	90/37	102/38	39/8	18/8	51/20	111/4
Mexico City government	6/5	17/6	7/0	0/0	4/4	7/5
PEMEX	14/0	7/13	13/0	13/0	5/10	6/0
Tax Department	9/1	16/15	7/6	38/4	6/9	3/1
Federal Preventive Police	0/0	5/0	4/0	28/18	87/26	77/30
Ministry of Public Security	5/0	16/0	18/5	8/0	13/2	7/0
Immigration and Naturalization Service	0/4	14/30	9/16	7/13	5/14	12/26
Presidency	0/0	0/0	2/0	0/0	1/0	0/0
Judiciary	0/0	0/0	0/0	0/0	0/0	1/0

Citizen Complaints for Irregularities, by Government Entity and Year

	2000	2001	2002	2003	2004	2005	2006	2007	Total, 2000–2007
Total	2,500	13,801	17,175 (+24.4%)	14,743 (−14.2%)	11,596 (−21.3%)	12,450 (+7.4%)	12,292 (−1.3%)	15,458 (+25.8%)	97,515

Dependencies with Greatest Volume

	2000	2001	2002	2003	2004	2005	2006	2007	Total, 2000–2007
ISSSTE		1,368	1,686	1,799	1,341	1,044	1,420	1,811	10,469 (10.7%)
SAT		1,952	1,776	1,297	797	1,714	1,260	1,065	9,861 (10.1%)
IMSS		1,454	1,391	863	686	845	869	1,051	7,159 (7.3%)
SEP		590	893	1,093	955	922	792	1,379	6,624 (6.8%)
PEMEX (combined)		617	1,097	1,140	861	727	708	1,074	6,224 (6.4%)
PGR		979	1,007	926	824	736	576	910	5,958 (6.1%)
PFP		274	702	823	717	703	566	747	4,532 (4.6%)
INM		399	324	216	160	283	480	379	2,241 (2.3%)
CFE		388	226	146	263	338	403	536	2,300 (2.4%)
INEGI		174	750	164	99	180	132	165	1,664 (1.7%)
SEGARPA		293	219	121	84	85	84	129	1,015 (1.0%)

Change in Number of Citizen Complaints, by Government Entity (percentages)

Entity	2001–2006	2006–2007
ISSSTE	+3.8	+27.5
SAT	−35.4	−15.5
IMSS	−40.2	+20.9
SEP	+34.2	+74.1
PEMEX (combined)	+14.7	+51.7
PGR	−41.2	+58.0
PFP	+106.6	+32.0

Note: Entities that received fewer complaints are excluded here.
Source: SFP data obtained through SISI by official requests in 2007.

Notes

1. Data on fraud come from a 2008 survey conducted by KPMG of 235 directors of business in Mexico. It found that 77 percent of businesses suffered at least one case of fraud during the previous year (46 percent of those cases were committed by personnel within the businesses). Most cases involved the robbing of inventory.

2. This does not rule out the notion, held by many, that Mexican society and culture lies at the heart of the corruption problem, as reported in Chapter 6, or that the perceived solution rests with cultural change and education.

3. Simple bivariate correlation shows that participation in corruption may play a slight role in perception of the level of corruption where corruption is most pronounced. In the 2001, 2003, and 2005 ENCBG surveys, those who reported no recent experience with bribery were slightly more likely to say that there was more corruption at all levels, while those with more experience were more likely to say that corruption was more common at the highest levels. This is particularly interesting because paying bribes—participation—clearly takes place predominantly at the lower level.

4. The three indexes on perceptions of corruption within institutions are similar, exhibiting an r = 0.925 (sig. > 0.01 two-tailed). It is also clear that these views on the perceived level of corruption within institutions are proportional to opinions on the role of specific institutions in combating corruption, as presented in Chapter 6. Simple regression with the 2005 corruption-rating data within institutions exceeded r = –0.90 (sig. > 0.01 two-tailed) and the average grading of institutions in the Global Corruption Barometer surpassed r = 0.88 (sig. > 0.01 two-tailed). In other words, confidence in a particular institution to fight corruption is inversely related to the level of perceived corruption in the institution.

5. These measures also correlate strongly with general rankings of confidence in specific institutions. In other words, perceived corruption, as would be expected, undermines general confidence in the institution.

6. The simple electronic keyword search conducted from the Milenio.com website identified articles with corruption in the subject heading.

7. This pattern continued beyond the Fox term with the revelation that payments for 281,000 campaign spots that ran during the 2006 presidential campaign were not acknowledged by the parties. The parties acknowledged having paid 2.2 billion pesos (US$203 million) for radio and television spots, yet the unclaimed spots represented another 710 million pesos (US$66 million) (*Milenio* October 17, 2007).

8. This tendency to attribute tragedies in part to corruption often has an element of truth. Following the tragic airplane crash in November 2008 that killed Secretary of Government Juan Camilo Mouriño and other officials in the Calderon government, reports suggested that the flight crew had acquired their licenses improperly and that SEGOB officials had failed to check the crew's licenses. Noting the tragic connection, both Salvador Vega Casillas, the secretary of FP, and Gustavo Madero, the head of the Mexican Senate, stated on separate occasions that the case demonstrates how corruption was responsible for the officials' deaths: that corruption, in short, kills (*Milenio* November 27, and December 4, 2008).

9. I agree with Jonathan Fox (2007, 351), who is critical of the tendency in Mexico to conflate transparency and accountability: "The empirical evidence from Mexico and internationally indicates that transparency is necessary but far from sufficient to produce accountability."

10. The 2008 KPMG poll similarly showed more bribes among businesses paid at the municipal level (33 percent) compared to the state level (26 percent), the federal level (24 percent), and public agencies (17 percent) (e.g., notaries, customs, water, sanitation). It also indicated that the major reason that businesses engaged in bribery was

to speed up processes (43 percent), followed by obtaining licenses and permits (32 percent), impeding the abuse of authority (21 percent), winning government contracts (16 percent), and participating in public bidding (11 percent).

11. From 2001 to 2003, the level of corruption increased in 30 areas and fell in 1; from 2003 to 2005, corruption increased in 10 and fell in 19; and from 2005 to 2007 the level climbed in 20 areas and declined in 12.

12. As shown in the appendix to this chapter, the government only showed 2,500 total complaints for 2000, dramatically below the numbers for other years.

8

The Role of Culture?

Scholars disagree over the role and significance of culture in corruption. The current mainstream approach championed by Transparency International, the World Bank, and others stresses institutional and structural determinants and downplays cultural causes. Yet a rather rich and interesting literature ties corruption to culture. Previous chapters have also highlighted important cultural factors related to corruption, from the anticorruption programs orchestrated by state and social agents seeking to transform social norms, to perception about the nature of corruption.

This chapter addresses the role of culture, and attempts to fold culture into a broader narrative. Discussion begins with an overview of the theoretical controversy pitting the prevailing institutionalist perspective against the cultural perspective. A brief review of the treatment of culture from prior chapters leads to an effort to describe a broader perspective that incorporates culture into a mutual causal model and its application to the Mexican case. The chapter concludes by addressing the central issue of change.

Corruption, Culture, and Theoretical Controversies

The Cultural Approach

Despite recent developments in the subfield, attributing corruption to something cultural enjoys a rather distinguished scholarly pedigree. Most early thinkers on corruption—whom Robert Klitgaard (1988, 9) refers to as "moralists"—portrayed corruption as an ethical issue arising from the moral fabric or ethos of a society. The modernization perspective that dominated Western comparative politics during the post–World War II period moved beyond such moralistic views, but only slightly. It still tended to tie corruption to cultural values and the challenges posed by modernization, depicting corruption as arising from the clash between traditional customs and particularistic norms and the more modern values of universalism and legal rationalism.[1] Even today, it remains somewhat common to link corruption to virtue. As John Noonan (1984, 702–703) notes, the fact that bribery is universally condemned suggests its "moral nature." As such, "a solid morality constitutes the antidote that allows for the maintenance of honesty . . . a low morality facilitates corruption."

Cultural explanations of corruption have been particularly prevalent in Latin America. Historians contend that corruption during colonialism reflected a dualistic structure featuring a formal, legal order set alongside an informal political reality characterized by clientelism, personal loyalty, and favors (see, for instance, Burkholder and Johnson 1994; Ewell 1977; Gibson 1966; Hopkins 1969, 1974; McFarlane 1996; Miller 1996; Nef 2001; Phelan 1960, 1967; Posada-Carbó 2000; Smallman 1997; Whitehead 2000, 2002; Yarrington 2003). Claudio Lomnitz (1995, 32) describes this dualism as a unique style of politics involving "pragmatic accommodation while formally adhering to discursive orthodoxy." Many trace the pattern back to Hernán Cortés's famous dictum to King Charles: *"obedezco pero no cumplo"* (I obey but I do not comply). Glen Dealy's cultural model of Latin America (1992) features a similar framework. Bypassed by the Reformation, Latin America inherited a Catholic, two-morality philosophy that separated the values of the private from those of a Machiavellian public life. Family and personal relationships consequently became all-important values, eclipsing, in the process, the role of impersonal institutions and abstract universal principles. Friends, in short, became the currency to ascendant power: "Friends make the impossible probable, from renewing a suspended driver's license to obtaining an import license for the prohibited car" (Dealy 1992, 69). Hence, rather than governments based on law, the region produced governments based on friendships, a pattern facilitated in large measure by corruption.

Contemporary explanations of corruption echo these historical arguments by pointing either to the region's long history of corruption to explain its ongoing prevalence, or to the persistence of these cultural traits. In fact, analysts cite a wide array of cultural attributes to explain corruption. Among these are the people's weak collectivist identity, strong sense of hierarchy, views on the nature of authority, low levels of interpersonal trust, social capital, and political trust, and even the intense desire to get ahead within a society offering few opportunities (González-Fabre 1996; Hooper 1995; Husted 1999, 2002; Lipset and Lenz 2000; Zaniartu 1996). Seymour Lipset and Gabriel Lenz (2000), for instance, emphasize how feelings of solidarity with the extended family, coupled with hostility toward outsiders, foster a self-interested culture that sustains corruption. Jorge Nef (2001) points, in turn, to the region's strong sense of particularism (within the inner circle), formalism (the double standard), expectations of dispensing favors, corporatism, authoritarianism, and even centralism to explain corruption. These attitudes, Nef contends, feed indifference and create a tolerance toward elite corruption and higher dissemination of "informal practices" for daily survival. Some see this tolerance, however, as growing from a lack of civic consciousness or virtue, which in turn prevents society from demanding accountability and limiting the power of public officials (Guerrero 2004). Argentine psychologist Roberto Lerner, for example, associates corruption with cultural patterns in which people feel responsible for themselves and those close to them, but not for the community at large. "There's no concept of a common good—our country is made up of 'me' and 'you,'" he said. "Until there's an 'us,' a true sense of common welfare, the *coima* [bribe] will continue to be accepted" (*NotiSur* April 4, 2003).

Empirical studies—which can ascertain correlation but not settle the thorny issue of causality—lend some support to these theoretical propositions. Cross-national studies show that countries with low levels of interpersonal trust (La Porta et al. 1999; Seligson 2001, 2002a), no British legal or colonial tradition (Blake and Martin 2006; La Porta et al. 1999; Lederman, Loayza, and Soares 2005; Sandholtz and Koetzle 2000; Swamy et al. 2001; Treisman 2000), low proportions of Protestants (Blake and Martin 2006; Sandholtz and Koetzle 2000; Treisman 2000), severe ethnolinguistic factionalism (Mauro 1995), and a generalized tolerance toward corruption (Catterberg and Moreno 2002, 2007) tend to suffer higher levels of corruption. Cross-national studies by Hector Correa (1985) and Seymour Lipset and Gabriel Lenz (2000) show corruption to be higher in societies where amoral familism is strong, as in Latin America. Bryan Husted (1999, 2002) finds higher levels of corruption in countries that have a strong collectivist orientation, higher levels of "power distance" (defined as "the extent to which the less powerful members of institutions and organizations within a country expect and accept that power is distributed unequally"), and more pronounced feelings of masculinity, as in Latin America. In one study focusing on individual opinion, Matthew Cleary and Susan Stokes (2006) link clientelism and vote-buying in Argentina and Mexico to a political culture strong on personal trust in politicians, but weak on trust in institutions. Micro-level studies by Roberta Gatti (2003), William Miller (2006), and Naci Mocan (2004), and formal mathematical models by Jens Andvig and Karl Moene (1990), Ajit Mishra (2006), and Jean Tirole (1996), further highlight the role that societal and cultural factors play in influencing citizens' perceptions of corruption and hence their participation in corrupt acts. These models build on Pranab Bardhan's notion (1997) of a "frequency-dependent equilibrium" wherein one's participation in corruption is a function of their expectation of the corrupt behavior of others. But it is not just the perception or expectation of corruption that feeds such participation. According to Xiaohui Xin and Thomas Rudel (2004, 298), merely a culture of mistrust elevates the amount of perceived corruption in society, which in turn provides a justification for such behavior.

In sum, those adopting a cultural position tend to depict culture as providing a broader and more encompassing framework or the parameters within which institutions, laws, and structures operate and influence behavior, including corruption. One implication of this approach relates to the issue of change. Envisioning culture as deeply ingrained, and hence sticky, most consider it slow to change, thereby providing, in a sense, a deeper explanation, beyond those centered on more immediate and even ephemeral structural, institutional, or personal factors, to the persistence of corruption and the slow impact of reforms.

The Institutional Approach

Despite the underlying logic of the cultural argument, its pedigree, or even the size of the choir, the institutional approach that dominates the contemporary boom in the study of corruption tends to discount the role of culture. It does this essentially by denying it agency. As illustrated by the approach taken in this study, the institutional approach attributes corruption to the structure of the state and society, the mechanics of checks and balances, and the institutional nature of discretionary power and accountability, as in Klitgaard's famous formula (1988): $C = M + D - A$ (Corruption = Monopoly power + Discretionary authority – Accountability). As such, the institutional approach recasts many of the cultural traits highlighted by cultural analysts to be a consequence of corruption rather than a root cause. As with the broader critique of the political culture school, the institutional approach does not deny the existence of these cultural phenomena, nor does it ignore them. Instead, it contends that the lack of interpersonal trust or political trust, weak political capital, disrespect for the rule of law, social tolerance, limited confidence in public institutions, lack of a sense of national solidarity, weak sense of regime legitimacy, and the like, are all part and parcel of the pernicious effects of corruption, but not its causes.[2] In short, corruption fosters distrust, not the other way around. As Gerald Caiden (2001, 230) notes: "Every incident of corruption that comes to light and the seeming inability or indifference of public leaders and institutions to correct it disillusions people and serves to undermine their leaders' credibility." Such lack of trust in institutional effectiveness and institutional fairness, in turn, influences support for the overall political system (Miller and Listhaug 1999) and "one's own choices as to participation or nonparticipation in politics" (Johnston 2002, 174). Coupled with impunity, corruption thus fosters a skeptical public: "Official versions are dismissed beforehand and the promises to follow an investigation to its ultimate consequences are received with general skepticism" (Aguilar Zinser 2000). In addition, corruption affects and undermines the public's "commitment to collective projects [and] civic behavior" (Doig and Theobald 2000, 6, cited in Seligson 2002a, 412). In such a setting where corruption and impunity represent the norm, corruption and breaking the law simply become strategies of everyday survival (Uslaner 2004, cited in Catterberg and Moreno 2007, 6). From this perspective, even social tolerance toward corruption becomes a consequence of widespread corruption and not a cause.

As with the cultural approach, empirical studies bolster these claims— again demonstrating correlation, but not necessarily causality. Christopher Anderson and Yuliya Tverdova (2003), for example, using a dual macro-micro empirical approach, find that the higher the perception of corruption among individuals, the lower their support for democratic political institutions, just as societies with higher levels of corruption tend to exhibit more negative attitudes toward civil servants. Mitchell Seligson (2002a, 2006), as noted earlier, similarly confirms corruption's corrosive impact on political trust and regime legitimacy. Shaun Bowler and Jeffrey Karp (2004), Susan Pharr (2000), and John Peters and Susan Welch (1980) all show how corruption helps mold the public's attitudes about government, political institutions, and incumbent politicians, influencing voting patterns. In fact, in Japan, Pharr (2000) finds misconduct in office a better predictor than policy performance of low levels of political confidence. The theoretical thrust of these studies is that corruption produces these pernicious cultural effects on society, not the other way around.

Implicit in discounting the agency of culture, the institutional perspective envisions the mechanics of change differently. Rather than change taking place in a very slow and gradual manner as culturalists contend, the institutional approach suggests that changing key institutional and structural conditions can have an immediate effect on behavior, overcoming what may first appear as deeply rooted cultural constraints. Analysts are quick, for example, to point to the success of Hong Kong's Independent Commission Against Corruption in reining in widespread corruption in Hong Kong in the 1970s (see Klitgaard 1988; Manion 2004). Though Hong Kong's anticorruption program included an important public education component focusing on the culture, its primary focus was on the institutional variables shaping enforcement and prevention (Manion 2004, 36–52).

In simple methodological terms, then, the cultural perspective casts culture as an independent variable; the institutional perspective treats it as a dependent variable. Of course, it is rather easy to juxtapose the two and dismiss them as mutually exclusive. Some may see corruption arising from a culture of tolerance (Nef 2001, 171), while others blame corruption for fostering tolerance (Nieto 2004).[3] Consistent with this notion of theoretical incompatibility, most analysts seem to merely embrace one or the other approach, dismiss (sometimes even mock) the opposing viewpoint, and ignore the dilemma.[4]

The Role of Culture in Prior Chapters

Of course, despite the institutionalist bent, culture has not been absent from the discussion thus far. Chapters 3 and 4 describe an array of anticorruption initiatives, led by both the state and civil society organizations, targeting popular

attitudes and the general culture. These programs seek to fundamentally transform Mexican attitudes and culture and instill a sense of ethics among families, businesses, and individuals. The Secretaría de la Contraloría y Desarrollo
Administrativo (SECODAM), in its *Primer Informe,* for instance, points out
how the administration "seeks to construct a new culture where values of transparency and honesty predominate" (SECODAM 2001b). Underlying these initiatives is the view that culture indeed matters. Fighting corruption from the
ground up, these anticorruption efforts also aim to mobilize the population to
fight corruption, thereby strengthening the mechanisms of vertical and social
accountability. Even the government pursues a policy to encourage citizens to
file complaints against public officials. Beyond these programs, Chapter 5 also
highlights the public's perceptions regarding corruption that envision culture—education in the school and families—as the key ingredient in fighting
corruption, despite the fact that they do not see themselves or the society generally as particularly corrupt.[5] These views also echo those informing the initiatives of the state and social organizations. Finally, by pointing to how the
perception of corruption is more widespread than direct experience with or firsthand knowledge of corruption, and largely independent of participation—or, as
Roderic Camp, Kenneth Coleman, and Charles Davis (2000, 4) contend, that the
perception of corruption "reflects more than actual conditions"—Chapters 6 and
7 suggest that the perception of corruption actually taps broader aspects of the
political culture.

Incorporating Culture into a Broader Narrative

Bridging the theoretical dilemma and incorporating culture into a broader narrative means recognizing culture as consequence, facilitator, and cause of corruption, and as a critical factor conditioning reformist efforts. First, culture
constitutes the product of mediated experiences, including corruption. One article in SECODAM's *Para Leer Sobre Transparencia* (no. 6, 2002), titled "Co-
responsibility in the Fight Against Corruption: Recovering the Confidence,"
for example, illustrates this point. It stresses how corruption has created the
perception in Mexico that "breaking the rules is okay." It has undermined confidence in the law, government, and society, and has distanced citizens from
their government. In fact, the government contends that there exists what it calls
"anti-values," which "are taught and learned as if they were values, for example:
'he who takes advantage of others lives better,' 'those who are good are bored,'
'laws are made to be broken,' among others" (Loria 2001, 5).

Second, despite being a product of the past, culture still influences the
present and future by fashioning the broader context through which one interprets institutions, events, and the behavior and intentions of self and other. Culture shapes expectations and understandings; it determines which is the rule,
and which is the exception; and it contextualizes state and social institutions

and behavior, defining risks and opportunities. At this level, culture can be seen as facilitating corruption. Formal models, as noted, illustrate how the existence of corruption forges expectations about the behavior of others, thereby making corruption essentially a self-fulfilling prophecy. Regardless then of how we got here (the causality issue), a prisoner's dilemma exists, trapping society in an equilibrium position featuring widespread corruption. Similarly, culture plays a critical role in shaping key institutional variables, particularly citizen involvement in the mechanisms of social accountability, which many see as a critical determinant of corruption. As Gerald Caiden, O. P. Dwivedi, and Joseph Jabbra (2001, 3) point out, "There seems to be a direct correlation with the extent to which people as citizens are empowered in their societies. Where they fully participate in governance and where a lively civic culture thrives, those in authority have greater difficulty hiding corruption." Indeed, "an organized public constitutes the backbone of political will" (Caiden 2004: 286). As a result, many consider the types of programs that target society and culture as critical in the fight against corruption, even though these may not address a primary causal component of corruption.[6]

Third, culture plays a somewhat more independent causal role given the fact that perceptions of corruption represent broader and more encompassing views than the actual existence of corruption. Perception of corruption, in short, relates more to the public's narrative on authority, politicians, institutions, political trust, interpersonal trust, and the rule of law than it does to bribery or other empirical factors. In some ways, of course, these two interact. As described in Chapter 5, general views regarding politics and specific views regarding corruption play off one another so that the political culture deductively shapes individual conduct as it relates to corruption, while one's experiences with corruption inductively shape the broader political views. This distinction between perception of corruption and real corruption—and conflating the perception of corruption to the level of political culture—also means that addressing corruption per se may be insufficient to tackle the broader perception of corruption, which itself, by conditioning expectations, may contribute to real corruption (the endogeneity issue). Stated differently, if the other, broader factors that influence generalized perceptions of corruption are not addressed—or have not been addressed through traditional anticorruption efforts—then the public may be unable to even perceive any real changes in corruption or respond in ways that help fight corruption.

Finally, culture influences the present most decisively by providing the broader context or narrative used to interpret institutions, behavior, change, and the like. Interpretations of current experiences, of risks and opportunities, for instance, take place within a cultural context shaped by the past. Normally it is easier to interpret current events in ways that conform to and confirm our existing thinking about politicians, politics, self, and others, than it is to interpret events in ways that challenge this mode of thinking. Interpretations of the present thus tend to reinforce past narratives that have long served as a guide to behavior and provide coherent meaning. For this reason, culture will always tend to be stickier, more difficult, and slower to change than institutions and, as such, will condition and perhaps even limit the impact of institutional changes. Of course, cultural change is not impossible. Although culture may limit and condition them, institutional and structural changes nonetheless seek to alter behavior, experience, and, in the final analysis, the culture itself. Institutional and structural changes seek to challenge old views, render them inoperable, and force the adoption of new interpretations and new meanings. In a context of widespread corruption then, as Melanie Manion (2004, 1) points out, anticorruption involves changing shared expectations.

A mutual causal view linking culture and corruption thus holds that corruption (both actual participation and perception) arises from a combination of attitudes and expectations (culture) that are the product of past experience (including but not solely forged from experiences related to corruption) and from institutions that are designed and interpreted within a given cultural context. In interactive fashion, akin to Michael Johnston's notion (2005) of a corruption syndrome, culture informs the nature of institutions and behavior, while it absorbs and interprets experiences based on repeated interactions with others, authority figures, and institutions. Corruption, in short, fosters a culture that sustains corruption partly by conditioning options, rewarding certain types of behavior (personalistic), and discouraging others (community-based), creating a setting in which corruption becomes expected but not accepted.

Mexican Political Culture and Corruption

The broader, prevailing political narrative in Mexico envisions politicians, government institutions, and the law as part of a system designed and operated by the few for the pursuit of their own self-interest. People tend to consider politicians corrupt, believe that institutions operate according to the whims and interests of the powerful rather than to the rule of law or to the benefit of the whole, and see the law itself as serving the interests of the powerful rather than those of the weak. Instead of being rigid, the law is seen as flexible; rather than applying equally to all, it is thought to be selectively applied in accordance to wealth, privilege, and position ("guilty until proven rich"); and in lieu of restraining those in power, it protects them, facilitating the abuse of power. The perception and reality of corruption, of course, are central within this political narrative.

Data from the 2001, 2003, and 2005 Encuesta Nacional de Cultural Política (ENCUP) surveys corroborate key aspects of this narrative.[7] In 2001, for instance, majorities expressed little confidence, no confidence, or almost no confidence in mayors (51 percent), the Supreme Court (63 percent), Congress (64 percent), political parties (75 percent), and the police (77 percent). The only institutions in which less than half of respondents expressed a lack of confidence in 2001—the Instituto Federal Electoral (IFE) (39 percent), governors (47 percent), and the presidency (46 percent)—hardly enjoyed strong levels of confidence. Behind this lack of confidence lies a sense that the government does not operate according to the interests of the people or the pursuit of justice. When asked in 2005 what interests congressional deputies take into account upon making laws, 43 percent (the top response) said the parties' interests (and parties are held in particularly low esteem), while 25 percent said personal interests. By contrast, only 16 percent believed that deputies take the public's interests into account when making laws. When asked more generally about the purpose of the law, 33 percent said it was to defend the interests of the powerful, while 26 percent said it was to commit *arbitrariedades* (arbitrary acts). Only 19 percent and 16 percent, respectively, said the purpose of the law is to pursue justice and to defend the interests of society. Focusing more closely on this notion of justice, among the 40 percent of respondents in 2001 who assessed the work of the courts and judges as poor or very poor, one-third claimed outright that there was "no justice" in Mexico, while another third blamed the courts' poor performance on "corruption and impunity." Given these views, it is not surprising then that in the word-association exercise in the 2001 ENCUP survey, the top response to the word "politics," given by 21 percent of respondents as their first choice and by 13 percent as a second choice, was in fact "corruption."

This broad narrative stems from a historical experience that includes but is not limited to a long history of corruption. It seems likely, though data are lacking to confirm or compare this conclusion, that the public has long considered authority in Mexico suspect: they have never really trusted politicians as a class (though they have trusted some leaders), they have always seen the law as flexible, and they have always seen institutions as operating in accordance to informal rules and personalism. Corruption has been widespread, the prosecution of officials has been rare, the law has been selectively applied and abused, and real change has come not from within the system, but too often from without, through nonsystemic means. According to José Crespo (2007, 11), "In Mexico, the historical experience produces a negative result in terms of democratic culture. . . . [I]t is natural that the majority of citizens maintain a skeptical vision and lack of confidence in power and political institutions."[8] In fact, according to the 1981 and 2000 World Values Surveys, public confidence in key institutions in Mexico hardly budged over the twenty-year period, though it did deteriorate slightly, despite the political changes overhead (Martínez Puón 2002, 7).[9]

Within this political narrative, the lack of trust in politicians, institutions, and rule of law fashions expectations and a generalized framework from which the public interprets political events (past and future). Among the effects, it fosters a tendency to assume corrupt behavior or corrupt motives and to reject prosystemic, normative-based interpretations of events in favor of those rooted in avarice, and nurtures pessimism regarding the potential for change. This narrative, hence, shapes or shades political and democratic developments, particularly the contours of public efforts to fight corruption. This means that speculations, accusations, and rumors of corruption are usually accepted as truth (unless targeted at partisans), regardless of the outcomes of investigations or resolutions, simply because it harmonizes within the narrative. The public then sees the subsequent failure to prosecute officials who have already been tried in the court of public opinion as further proof of the underlying impunity—rather than an indication of the effective pursuit of justice. Even when the system successfully prosecutes "corrupt" officials, it is often seen not as a conquest in the battle against corruption, but as a manipulation of the law orchestrated by those in authority to eliminate opponents, to consolidate power, or simply for show or to hide what they are really doing. Meanwhile, the public dismisses accusations against partisans and allies as politically motivated, as part of this narrative rather than an affront to it.

One impact of the lack of trust in institutions is a sort of epistemological dilemma in which it becomes hard to agree on what constitutes truth, or to determine if and when the exercise of authority is in fact legitimate (consistent with the rule of law) or an abuse of authority motivated by political (particularistic) reasons. Since there is little trust in politicians or public institutions, few accept their conclusions regarding what is legal or not, or what is true or not. This includes, particularly, promises to pursue corrupt officials generally, or reports, investigations, and legal proceedings in specific cases. This makes sense given that the law historically has served as "a resource at the disposal of the politician to combat enemies and to cover for his friends" (Elizondo Mayer-Serra 2006, 45). This means that some will dismiss what may seem to be completely credible revelations of wrongdoing, as simply trumped-up charges motivated by and for political reasons. Certainly, as the disbelievers will readily note, such things have happened before. In a similar way, what may seem like credible proof one day, can seemingly evaporate the next. The institutions providing the information—whether the accusations and proof, or the determination of the lack of proof—are, after all, tainted, so their actions are seen as confirming rather than disconfirming the broader narrative.[10]

Viewing the law as a tool of the powerful and hence a form of oppression has other effects as well. At one level, it nurtures a certain degree of alienation and social atomization. As Philip Mauceri (2003, 35) argues with reference to the Andean region, such increased alienation and atomization makes it difficult to convince people "that their interests are tied to others, inhibiting sustained collective action." Viewing the law as oppressive also makes abiding by the law or following legally sanctioned institutional paths—despite acknowledging their normative virtue—difficult, because it becomes a form of submitting to that oppression. This means, on the one hand, obeying the law and the authorities when necessary for practical reasons—due to the structure of political exploitation—and yet, on the other hand, taking advantage of the system whenever possible, just like everyone else presumably does whenever possible. In this sense, avoiding the law, manipulating it, or getting around it constitute a form of protest—of political contestation, of resistance: of being the exploiter rather than the exploitee—and even a form of *machismo.* Not only does corruption thus become a part of everyday survival, as Eric Uslaner (2004, cited in Catterberg and Moreno 2007, 6) contends, but it also becomes a mechanism used to get ahead and exploit the system's weaknesses for personal gain. The perception of the law as exploitative and flexible thus helps justify the breaking of the law and participation in illegalities such as bribery. In the 2001 ENCUP survey, when asked whether one should always abide by a law even if it is unjust, 72 percent said no. In a separate question, 56 percent agreed that people should disobey unjust laws. The notion that the law is flexible, in short, seems widespread both in thought and particularly in deed.

Of course, paying a bribe (or extortion) often reflects the abuse of power by public officials rather than a mechanism of choice for citizens to get ahead. In this context, paying a bribe is seen as either being forced on the citizen by public officials—and there is a tendency to attribute corruption more to the public official than to the citizen—or being forced on the citizen by the circumstances of the system itself: a form of power exploitation. This interpretation, moreover, helps the citizen assign blame to greedy politicians and thereby guard their sense of personal integrity.

Abiding by an unjust law and even acceding to an extortion payment touch on the complex notion of trade-offs. The idea of trade-offs complicates our interpretation of public opinion and cultural values, since an opinion supporting something may indicate an absolute preference or may simply signify a relative preference given the available alternatives. Incumbent within the political narrative is a relatively clear distinction between the "reality" of the rule of law in the society, and a normative sense of justice (particularly the idea of social justice, which corrects past wrongs). As profiled in Chapter 5, large majorities in Mexico feel that politicians should be held accountable, that the law should be obeyed, and that giving gifts or money simply to speed up bureaucratic procedures is wrong. Though quick to distinguish right from wrong and the ultimate legitimacy of the rule of law and democracy, the public also understands how the system actually works, understands its unwritten rules and informal operations, and knows how to function accordingly. This is where trade-offs come into play. One may ideally prefer the written law—hence generalized support for the prevailing normative order—but given the reality of politics in a country where the rule of law rarely operates, bribery becomes a second-best alternative. Such trade-offs also include the tendency to look to politicians—via personalism and clientelism—rather than to the law or institutions, to get things done. Matthew Cleary and Susan Stokes (2006) note in their study of Argentina and Mexico how trust in institutions and trust in individual politicians are mutually exclusive; where institutions are distrusted, citizens exhibit trust in individual politicians (see also Manzetti and Wilson 2009). Generally, the willingness to accept such trade-offs serves merely as practical acknowledgment of the constraints rooted in the system rather than as any sort of absolute moral permissiveness. Hence, what Gabriela Catterberg and Alejandro Moreno (2007) interpret as a central paradox of corruption in Latin America—where corruption is seen as a central problem, but this awareness rarely translates into vigilant attitudes or actions on the part of the public—can be seen, rather than as a sign of cultural tolerance, instead as an acknowledgment of the lack of efficacy in denouncing corruption because of the corrupt nature of the system itself.[11]

Certainly, these views on power, authority, and corruption combine to form part of a broader assessment of the nation's performance and its future. Throughout the period under analysis, more people have been dissatisfied than satisfied with the way democracy has been operating. The 2005 ENCUP survey sums up the situation in the following way: "The democratizing process in Mexico has rendered fruits in the area of institutional transformations; however, the bulk of the changes promoted until now have not been able to affirm themselves, categorically, to the total judgments that the population holds regarding public life, which, to an important degree, manifests a weak interjection of the values and practices that are fundamental to any democratic order." Even so, José Crespo (2007) argues that a certain level of optimism is still apparent and that democratic disillusionment has not become too widespread. In 2001, 51 percent said the nation's democracy would be better in the future, compared to 47 percent in both 2003 and 2005, though by 2005 almost a third of respondents felt that things would grow worse. Unfortunately, the public does not share this level of optimism regarding corruption.

The Issue of Change

While this static view of the political narrative helps contextualize corruption, the big issue, of course, centers on change. If corruption fosters a culture that sustains itself by conditioning options, rewarding certain types of behavior (personalistic), and discouraging others (community-based), then the dilemma centers on how to break free of this low-level equilibrium and achieve some sort of tipping point. What, then, are some of the implications of this broader narrative regarding corruption and the issue of change? What might be the mechanisms by which corruption changes? As noted, the cultural approach envisions change as a slow, even generational process. This prompts one to ask whether there are any indications that such long-term changes are occurring at this deeper cultural level that might eventually affect corruption.

One question centers on the mechanics of change. Here, it is important to draw a distinction between participation and lower-level corruption, on the one hand, and perception and upper-level corruption, on the other. It would seem that it would be easier to detect changes in corruption at the lower level, since it is here that the most interactions between state and citizen occur. Since there is no direct interaction, changing the public's broader perceptions of politicians might take longer. This, then, would privilege measures focusing on actual participation, making it the lead indicator of change in corruption. But even if such lower-level changes are occurring, do such changes really challenge the underlying assumptions about the nature of the state, authority, and citizens, thereby forcing the narrative to be revised and altering expectations? As argued by Uslaner (2004, cited in Catterberg and Moreno 2007, 6) and demonstrated somewhat by the present analysis, big corruption (scandals) tends to play a much greater role in shaping people's attitudes toward government and each other than does lower-level corruption. One potential pattern of change, then, would be for bureaucratic, lower-level forms of corruption to diminish without having an impact on the broader perceptions of corruption among politicians and the decisionmaking system. And yet, in circular fashion, if such practical changes are not perceived to be taking place at the higher level, then the behavior of both bureaucrats and citizens may lack a certain reinforcement or validation, prompting a tendency for backsliding, particularly once vigilance is relaxed.

As documented in Chapter 6, lower-level participation in corrupt acts in Mexico did decline somewhat from 2001 to 2007, but this decline clearly failed to nurture the broader perception that corruption had decreased. By contrast, news reports and scandals throughout this period reinforced the perception that high-level corruption continued relatively unabated, with a spike in cases related to elections and campaigns (Pemexgate, Amigos de Fox, the video scandals), drug trafficking, and conflicts of interest (see Appendix B). Some of these cases even touched on the supposed architect of the national anticorruption campaign, President Vicente Fox himself (Towelgate and the injunction against Andrés Manuel López Obrador), or on Fox's immediate family (Marta Sahagún and the Bribiescas).

As noted, perceptions of corruption are rooted in broader forces rather than direct participation in bribery: indirect knowledge regarding the operation of institutions and the behavior of politicians as filtered through the media, the rhetoric of politicians, the views of experts, and so forth. This raises a question with respect to change: Have politics, broadly conceived, changed in Mexico to such an extent as to challenge the basic tenets of the prevailing narrative? At one level at least, Mexican politics during the Fox era seem almost to have deteriorated, not improved, reinforcing rather than challenging the political narrative. The intense partisan splits, the bickering among politicians, the lack of transparency in decisionmaking, the inability of the government to institute much-needed structural reforms, the lack of progress on a range of policy issues, and particularly the lack of punishment of presumably corrupt officials, all seem to have contributed to the view that things remained largely unchanged and that corruption persisted. Partisan battles prompt politicians to denounce others as corrupt, nourishing the view that all politicians are corrupt instead of the view that the government is effectively addressing corruption. Pundits, politicians, and experts frequently and summarily blame corruption, almost reflexively, for any policy failures (an easy approach in that it blames the failure on implementation of policies rather than blaming the policies themselves, and calls for perfecting the system rather than changing it), again reinforcing the prevailing perceptions of politics, politicians, and governmental institutions as corrupt.

A large part of this owes to the fact that Fox—the first democratically elected president who championed his campaign and his administration on change—seemed unsuccessful at truly convincing the public that the basic nature of government in Mexico had changed or, more specifically, that his promises to fight corruption were serious or producing real results. Over the course of the *sexenio,* expectations of change diminished, together with views on Fox himself. José Crespo (2007, 21, 37) cites Mitofsky polling data showing that from 2000 to 2006, the perception that Fox was honest fell from 61 percent to 36 percent, while the perception that he was truly in charge of the reins of the country dropped from 59 percent to 24 percent. Part of this decline reflects the fact that many saw the removal of immunity of López Obrador as a decidedly political move, motivated more by politics than the rule of law or a concern for justice (Crespo 2007, 28). Either way, in the end, evaluations of Fox's anticorruption efforts mirror general interpretations of his overall performance. So for many, rather than prompting an erosion of the tenets of the underlying political narrative, Fox and the Partido Acción Nacional (PAN) came to be viewed through the same lens, as either unable to battle the entrenched corruption of the system (a strong reinforcement of the narrative) or as partisan and corrupt themselves (again, reinforcing the narrative). Rather than change, for many it simply became more of the same.

Of course, it is important to ask how difficult is it at this level to challenge the assumptions of a political narrative crafted and reified by years of experience. What ingredients might help convince citizens that their politicians and the government now, truly and finally, represent their interests, or that the law now pursues justice, protects the powerless, constrains the powerful, and applies to all equally. At both symbolic and real levels, broad changes in the operation of the political system, such as increased cross-partisan cooperation, effective policy changes, and real progress in promoting security, prosperity, employment, and the like, can all help chip away and challenge the broad perceptions of corruption within the political system, increasing the sense that the law mirrors popular rather than particular interests. In overly simplistic terms, if policy failures magnify the issue of corruption, then policy successes can contribute to a view that the government is effectively addressing corruption.

Another dimension of change, however, centers on possible changes taking place at the level of the underlying political culture itself. Does the deeper political culture in Mexico show any signs of change that might eventually alter popular views related to corruption or feed demands for accountability? Has the bar, in a sense, been raised, strengthening the exigencies for change (and hence the frustration and deception), thereby setting the stage for greater accountability and a curtailment of corruption at some point in the future? Gauging cultural change, of course, is no easy task. At one level at least, the few polls from earlier, predemocratic periods tend to show a strikingly similar pattern to those of the democratic period or even a worsening of the situation. Even during the democratic period, it is hard to point to substantial changes in the political culture of mistrust of government institutions and politicians.

Other evidence, however, does suggest an underlying change in Mexican political culture that might potentially alter the nature of corruption. Chapter 2 describes the development of new accountability institutions and mechanisms that are arguably forging a new sort of bureaucratic subculture within certain areas of the nonmonolithic state, what John Ackerman (2003) refers to as embedded professionalism. Chapter 3 describes a growing demand within society for a culture of accountability that, often in concert with the substratum of the state, promotes ethics and exposes wrongdoing. One central ingredient in this state-society trend that builds on the ideological and cultural foundations of democracy involves the grafting of the language of transparency and accountability onto the Mexican political narrative. Indeed, the 2003 transparency law not only goes a long way in providing a real, institutional mechanism to uncover and expose information once considered the exclusive domain of an authoritarian government—thereby strengthening access to and use of such information by the press and civil society—but also, perhaps more importantly, symbolically reifies the fundamental rights of citizens, the subordinate role of the government, and the principle of accountability. In fact, Crespo (2007, 18) contends that the passage of the transparency law and the creation of the Instituto Federal de Acceso a la Información (IFAI) are fashioning a new culture of transparency in Mexico and the beginnings, perhaps, of a culture of legality. Arguably, then, such institutional moves are slowly grafting a new layer onto the political culture that considers transparency a given, thereby challenging key tenets of the broader political narrative.

Illustrations of the pivotal role of transparency in the Mexican political narrative abound. In one survey of experts, legislators, journalists, academics, and internal comptrollers, Jorge Romer León (2005), for example, highlights the increase in transparency within the government; he finds that, in 2005, 69 percent of respondents agreed that the transparency law represented an important step. At the same time, however, he found a decline in positive assessments of budgetary oversight, from 41 percent in 2003 to 32 percent in 2005, suggesting that the translation of transparency into effective policy or a reduction in corruption remains a work in progress. The press's treatment of the issue offers a further example of the centrality of transparency to the political discourse. As shown in Chapter 7, the number of news reports highlighting the issue of transparency and the IFAI by the news group *Milenio* increased markedly after 2003, averaging over twenty-five articles per month. Meanwhile reports on corruption remained relatively constant during the time. In short, transparency and accountability have become fundamental to the Mexican political lexicon, challenging the old ways and old interpretations. Whether (and how) these underlying cultural changes will translate into a strengthening of the institutional mechanisms of accountability or, in the end, become overwhelmed by political realities, remains uncertain. The change at this level, however, is clear.

Conclusion

Despite the debate in the literature over the role of culture in shaping corruption, this chapter has cast culture as the product of years of corruption and impunity—the learning process—and as a major factor that feeds the conditions conducive to corruption and conditions the fight against it. Locked in a state of low-level equilibrium, corruption becomes a rational response to the opportunities and risks presented by the institutions, fully consistent with and reifying the dominant political narrative. Where the public sees the law (its content, implementation, or both) as oppressive and serving the interests of the powerful, corruption becomes both a form of exploitation and a form of resistance. Where corruption prevails within a setting of weak institutions, the public will even see efforts to battle it as corrupt and politically motivated.

From this perspective, the analysis from earlier chapters seems to suggest, on the one hand, that the many structural and institutional changes in Mexico have hardly challenged key components of the dominant political narrative that springs from and nurtures corruption. Instead, the operation of the system and the conduct of officials and citizens since democratization have tended to reinforce the narrative, thereby feeding this vicious cycle. These institutional changes, in short, face an uphill battle against long-standing attitudes regarding the nature of power and authority. Yet, on the other hand, the structural and institutional changes do show some signs of having altered certain aspects of the underlying political culture itself. Institutional changes have grafted onto the state and the culture such novel concepts as accountability and transparency, thereby challenging certain long-held tenets of a political narrative that originated in authoritarianism and exploitation. Such changes feed further pressures for more effective changes in the future. Understanding the interactions of these two—developing a framework that encompasses both cultural changes as well as structural and institutional changes—may be the key to understanding the nature of changes in corruption in Mexico as it struggles to deepen and consolidate democracy.

Notes

1. For years, the moral overtones of this approach (the sense that the developed countries were morally condemning the developing countries), coupled with assumptions regarding the impact of social modernization (that traditional values would eventually disappear, so corruption was ephemeral), combined to make research on corruption largely taboo (Klitgaard 1988, 9).

2. For a critique of the political culture approach, including the civic culture theory, postmaterialism, and theories of political capital, see Muller and Seligson 1994; Knight 2001; Seligson 2002b, 2002c.

3. Such contrasting views, when stated by the same author, can seem rather baffling. José López Presa (1998, 113, 115), for example, first stresses the underlying ethical problem behind corruption, pointing clearly to the causal role of culture: "We believe that ethics, understood as the totality of moral principles that permits every person to control their own behavior, moderating their desires to make them compatible with those of society, is an indispensable variable that must be taken into consideration for the study of the phenomenon of corruption. A solid morality constitutes the antidote that permits one to stay honest . . . a low morality leads to corruption."

And yet just two pages later, he casts this same problem as a consequence of corruption: "Corruption does not just have economic costs; its damaging character derives principally from the fact that it weakens moral principles, affects the rule of law, damages the principles of authority."

4. This theoretical standoff between institutionalists and culturalists is not inevitable, of course. Various forms of reconciliation exist. In what I consider merely a partial reconciliation, some seem to envision culture as a residual variable, attributing to culture all that cannot be explained by institutional or structural factors. This sets up a type of stepwise methodological formula whereby one examines the immediate behavioral, institutional, and structural variables before looking at culture to deal with the residual. Charles Call (2003, 861) exemplifies this approach in his detailed analysis of the restructuring of the police in El Salvador following that nation's civil war. He finds that despite the deep transformational institutional reforms, political culture and informal clientelism "made it difficult to define new relations between police and society and that favoured in persistent corruption." In the case of Mexico, this approach then might attribute the failure of democratization to curb corruption in recent years to underlying and more deeply rooted cultural factors within society.

Another approach sees the culture-corruption link as spurious and the product of a third factor. This requires analysts to identity a third factor that is conceptually independent from both corruption and culture and yet determinant of both. One likely candidate explored by some centers on economic variables and economic ideology, including the extreme levels of inequality and the unique structure of economic dependency found in Latin America. General approaches that associate corruption with characteristics of capitalism, for instance, would also seem to exemplify this sort of reconciliation (see Brown and Cloke 2004, 2005). Indeed, Pinar Bedirhanoglu (2007) argues—rather convincingly—that the prevailing views of corruption dominating the debate are ahistoric, biased, contradictory, and politicized, fulfilling an ideological and political function within the post–Washington Consensus.

A final approach entails mutual causality. Many analysts, for example, link trust—both interpersonal and political trust—to corruption in a vicious cycle (Della Porta and Vannucci 1997, 1999; Hetherington 1998; Johnston 2005; Rothstein and Stolle 2002; Wesberry 2004). Donatella Della Porta and Alberto Vannucci (1999, 261), for example, plot the circularity in the following sequence of events: misadministration, mistrust in the implementation of citizens rights, search for protection, propensity for paying bribes, demand for corruption, selective inclusion, and increased perception of misadministration.

Mitchell Seligson (2002a, 414), as well, points to the methodological problem of mutual causality when he notes that, since the perception that bribes are needed may be a function of a low evaluation of government, we cannot be sure whether corruption is responsible for the decline in trust in government, or is the result.

5. The public's views on this point, however, are somewhat perplexing. While evidence shows that Mexicans are quick to condemn corruption, believe in obeying the law and in accountability, and blame their politicians for corruption, they nonetheless see education (culture), particularly within the family and schools, as the best approach to fighting corruption. It is unclear, though, what aspects of the culture Mexicans might want the family and schools to alter in order to address corruption if they already consider corruption wrong, demand accountability, and individually do not see themselves as corrupt.

6. The World Bank and other institutions engaged in the global anticorruption movement clearly also embrace this strategy. Whereas the World Bank (1999) acknowledges that "corruption is a symptom of fundamental economic, political and institutional causes" and that "the major emphasis must be put on prevention, that is, on reforming economic policies, institutions, and incentives," it nonetheless emphasizes a key role for civil society: "Civil society and an independent media are, arguably, the two most important factors in controlling systemic corruption in public institutions. Corruption is controlled only when citizens are no longer prepared to tolerate it" (see also World Bank 2001).

7. The ENCUP polls were designed by the Dirección General de Desarrollo Político del Secretaría de Gobernación and administered by the Instituto Nacional de Estadística y Geografía (INEGI). The polls were based on probabilistic and stratified national samples of 4,183 (2001), 4,580 (2003), and 4,700 (2005) respondents. The Secretaría de Gobernación's website (http://www.encup.gob.mx/encup/) presents results.

8. José Crespo (2007, 10) cites Francisco Zarco, who referred to the situation in Mexico in 1850 in the following terms: "great apathy and civic deception, where the citizenry, without wanting to take part in public negotiations . . . simply lacks confidence in everything that the factions promise."

9. Micro-level empirical analyses point to the linkages among the various views on corruption, the views on the law and interpersonal and political trust, and highlight key determinants. My analysis in Chapter 5 and elsewhere (Morris and Klesner forthcoming), for instance, indicates that low levels of political trust and interpersonal trust increase the level of perceived corruption, bolster the belief that it is impossible to fight corruption, and contribute to the perception that corruption has increased (or remained the same) in the near past and will follow that pattern in the near future. Completing the circle of mutual causality, my analysis also shows both perception of corruption and views on the possibility of eliminating corruption to be statistically significant determinants of interpersonal trust and political trust.

10. Examples of this dizzying dilemma abound. One of particular note involves Raul Salinas, the brother of former president Carlos Salinas de Gortari. Despite the "evidence" that led to Salinas's conviction on murder charges and substantial revelations of illicit wealth, the courts in the end exonerated Salinas for lack of evidence. Was it, then, his prosecution that was politically motivated, as the Salinas family contends, or was it his release that was political? Another example centers on the case against Carlos Ahumada, the major figure in the video scandals of 2004. In 2006, 61 percent of respondents considered Ahumada a political prisoner, part of a plot by the federal government to discredit Andrés Manuel López Obrador and undermine his quest for the presidency. Yet following Ahumada's release from prison in 2007, 69 percent opined that he was guilty and that he had been released because the authorities were incompetent (*Milenio* September 26, 2006 and May 14, 2007) (see Appendix B).

11. Limited confidence in institutions and the rule of law also translates into a degree of politicization stemming from the inevitable clash pitting the law against justice. The absence of the belief that the law (in either substance or implementation) adequately pursues justice or the common good—this disjuncture—nurtures conduct designed to fill the void, such as vigilante justice or taking justice into one's own hands. Where state and society respect the rule of law, parties to a dispute no longer have to negotiate a solution every time a certain situation arises; instead, they appeal to laws and institutions to resolve the conflict. In the absence of such credible laws and institutions, however, everything becomes subject to negotiation from mobilized positions of strength.

9

Conclusion

Despite democratization, corruption clearly remains a prominent feature of Mexican politics. At the level of perception, embedded within the political culture, much of the public still considers politicians, members of Congress, the political parties, the judiciary, labor union officials and the police as corrupt. Large segments of the population believe that politicians cast their own personal and political interests above those of society, manipulating the law to commit arbitrary acts and to forge a shield of impunity. Moreover, rather than protecting the weak from the powerful, many tend to see the law itself as a device used, abused, and manipulated by the powerful to achieve their own ends. These perceptions, however, do not encompass all institutions within government or society. The public clearly sees some institutions as less corrupt, even looking to these as critical in the fight against corruption. This includes certain institutions within the government like the accountability institutions and even the military, key institutions within society like the church and the schools, and even individual citizens who do not consider themselves corrupt. In terms of actual experiences or participation, corruption continues to be an everyday mode by which citizens interact with state officials. Most Mexicans have experienced corruption at some point in their lives as victims, having been abused or extorted by authority figures, or engaged in it as beneficiaries, taking advantage of the flexibility that corruption, such as bribery, offers. Even so, the frequency of bribery within institutions and service areas varies widely, led clearly by the police. Still, many service areas are relatively free of corruption, and in any given year, perhaps despite the misperception, most public and private services in Mexico are rendered without the payment of a bribe. Of course, in some ways these two dimensions of corruption play off one another. Direct, quotidian experience in paying bribes shapes in some small way popular perceptions of corruption, while perceptions of corruption related to the nature of politics, authority, and the rule of law condition the behavior of citizens and officials alike.[1]

Rather than offer a simple snapshot perspective based on the available evidence, this study has sought to explore the dynamics of corruption amid the spectacular political changes of recent years. Though the evidence shows that corruption remains prominent, the temporal framework itself complicates the drawing of conclusions about the impact of these changes. The fact that democratization and the Vicente Fox presidency failed to curb or fundamentally alter corruption in Mexico lends itself to three different interpretations. First, one can see the evidence as an indication of the failures of recent changes and recent reforms. These failures may be due to the inability of the anticorruption measures to match the magnitude of the problem, the continuation of authoritarian enclaves and the "old corruption" that undermines the superficial reforms, the emergence of "new corruption" arising from the institutional and structural changes themselves, or the adaptive power of corruption to overcome newly erected and weak barriers. A second perspective, however, suggests that recent changes are, in a sense, working, albeit slowly, and will take much more time to produce clear and unequivocal results. Though we know relatively little about the dynamics of corruption—despite the significant evidence suggesting that democracy reduces corruption with time—it is quite feasible that it takes more time for real structural and institutional changes brought on by democratization to register in the public's perception and influence actual behavior.

A third explanation nestles somewhere between these two. It sees some progress in battling certain areas of corruption, such as lower-level, bureaucratic corruption and even grand corruption, incipient ideological and cultural change in support of transparency and accountability, and the possibilities of much greater change in the near future as the institutions of accountability mature and as a new generation of state and social leaders emerges. At the same time, however, this view recognizes the lack of change in other areas such as in the criminal justice system, the rise of new forms of corruption accompanying the fragmentation of power, the resilience of corruption, and even its deep cultural roots. Officials accused of wrongdoing are much more likely today than in the past to be questioned publicly about their activity by other officials in the government, by the press, and by the public, and are more likely to suffer at least some sort of political consequence, though the likelihood of criminal prosecution remains limited. Even here, changes following the Fox era, particularly the judicial reforms of 2007–2008, hold out the potential and hope of further strengthening accountability and curbing deep-seated corruption. Yet at the same time, bribery and even state capturing by social actors has grown, and the capacity of the state to assert and establish its will vis-à-vis particularistic interests has seemingly diminished. This is particularly true and pernicious with respect to the penetration of organized crime into law enforcement agencies. This mixed perspective, moreover, sees the political opening and even the anticorruption efforts of recent years as embellishing the public's perceptions of corruption rather than challenging those views.

Elaborating further on these points, this concluding chapter returns to the three topics that have guided this research: the impact of democratization on the perceptions of, participation in, and patterns of corruption; the conditions under which anticorruption reforms are possible; and the role of culture in accounting for corruption and change.

The Impact of Democratization

At the broadest level, despite theoretical expectation, democratization ended neither the widespread perceptions of corruption in Mexico, nor its quotidian occurrence. In fact, the perception of corruption has actually increased during the initial period of democratization, while lower-level corruption may have declined slightly.

Democratization's impact on corruption takes place through a combination of mechanisms, both structural and institutional, as well as ideological and cultural. At the structural and institutional level, early democratization in Mexico has had a mixed effect on corruption. By redistributing and fragmenting power, it has opened up some new opportunities for corruption (state capturing, conflict of interest, new clientelism, campaign finance) and even facilitated the continuation of certain authoritarian enclaves (by removing the informal controls that once existed on state and local governments, and leaving unions virtually unaccountable). At the same time, by strengthening competition and official mechanisms of accountability, democratization has heightened the exposure (and accusations) of corruption, greatly "politicized" the issue, and triggered real institutional reforms that seem to be playing a role in limiting the ability of officials to hide grand corruption, that guarantee transparency, and that seem to be slowly depoliticizing the administration, thereby limiting older forms of petty, bureaucratic corruption. Evidence suggests that red tape is down somewhat and that bureaucratic efficiency is nudging upward. The political changes have also empowered new actors within society and the state to conduct oversight of government operations in a freer and more transparent setting, effectively pitting ambition against ambition.

Three factors, however, have severely limited the ability of these structural and institutional changes in the early stages of democratization from working to rein in corruption effectively, particularly the perception of corruption. First, the intense polarization accompanying democratization and growing pluralism have greatly limited the scope and pace of the reforms. Polarization made it difficult for Fox to put together reformist coalitions, and crippled his early intentions of prosecuting former officials from the Partido Revolucionario Institucional

(PRI) *gobierno* or even touching areas of entrenched corruption. So rather than developing and strengthening accountability, polarization and pluralism complicated governance, resulting in competing institutions exercising oversight in ways that were widely interpreted as partisan and ineffective rather than as spawning and leading an anticorruption movement. In a setting of weak institutions, muddled and incomplete accountability reaffirms the public's perception that the rule of law is weak and that politicians are corrupt. By feeding wild accusations of abuse of authority across partisan lines, polarization further adds to the popular notion that politicians continue to enjoy impunity and that "politics as usual" prevails despite the defeat of the PRI.

A second factor limiting the ability of the structural and institutional changes of democratization from functioning in a way necessary to rein in corruption has been the absence of reforms that would strengthen the government's ability to investigate and prosecute officials for wrongdoing. The failure of this essential feature of the accountability chain severely undermines or weakens the initial reformist steps and neutralizes the rhetoric of change, again reinforcing the popular notion that impunity exists and that nothing has changed for the better. Though certain institutions—products of democratization—have emerged and been empowered to promote greater oversight in such areas as elections, transparency, and the bureaucracy, in the absence of a judiciary capable of strengthening the enforcement component, these continue to be rather weak and somewhat marginalized. Administrative sanctions, for instance, though numerous, do little to convince the public that their officials are being held accountable.

A third factor centers on the social setting itself. The power of certain segments of society (near-monopolies in business, entrenched unions, organized crime) in the face of a weakening state (due to the fragmentation of power and dismantling of old informal institutions) has contributed to both the blocking of needed reforms and continued corruption. According to the World Bank (2007, viii), "the capacity of special interests to mobilize resistance outside of formal electoral and legislative arenas mitigates the accountability effects of elections." In a sense, Mexico has gone from having a relatively strong state built on informal rules to one unable to assert state interests and the rule of law. In many ways, this facilitates a change in the pattern of corruption: the rise of bribery over extortion as the predominant mode whereby agents of society use extralegal means to capture and influence state officials. This form of corruption is particularly damaging in that it further divides the state and prevents the pursuit of collective interests.[2]

At the ideological and cultural level, democratization has altered expectations and the political discourse, strengthening demands for accountability from both within the government and within society. In many ways, it is at this level that the bar has ratcheted upward. And it is arguably here where the greatest changes in Mexico have occurred. Demands for "accountability" and "transparency"—words not previously found within the Mexican political lexicon—have grown exponentially with democratization. Echoed within society (via nongovernmental organizations, citizens, and the press) and operationalized within newly empowered oversight institutions within the government (the Instituto Federal Electoral [IFE], the Instituto Federal de Acceso a la Información [IFAI], public administration), this new anticorruption force tends to battle the entrenched interests and the "politics of usual" of the past.

In many ways, the disappointment and disillusionment are great. The actual performance of the Fox government—despite some real changes in terms of transparency—seemed to do little to challenge the traditional narrative about the nature of Mexican politics. Reminiscent of the days of the PRI, his departure from the scene took place amid (largely partisan) accusations of electoral fraud and speculations of his own abuse of power, corruption, and ill-gotten gain. Despite the democratic pedigree of the post-2000 government, by the end of the *sexenio,* politicians were still considered corrupt and the rule of law was still considered a device used by the powerful to exploit the weak. The failure of the first democratically elected government to take advantage of the opportunity to effectively challenge the perceptions of corruption at the highest levels, especially the corruption plaguing the criminal justice sector, weakened regime legitimacy and the public's satisfaction with democracy. At the same time, the failure to alter perceptions about how politics operates at the highest levels tempers the ability of the various bureaucratic reforms to make much headway in battling lower-level forms of corruption. Though bureaucrats may feel the pressures of real reforms, citizens still cast their own behavior in the same broader context through which they view politicians.

The rising forces of anticorruption in Mexico—though far short of a social movement—nonetheless clearly complicate the continuation of "politics as usual." Using newly empowered institutional stages to voice demands and access information to expose previously unknown operations, new actors with new ideas—a new generation of public servants even—have added a new dimension or layer to Mexican politics. Accountability, to be sure, feeds on itself: what Jonathan Fox (2007, 342) refers to as "accountabilities of scale" whereby "the more accountability one has, the more one can get."

In continuing the struggle, effective change requires due diligence in keeping the pressure on initial reforms, since neglect facilitates the return of corrupt practices. Vigilance is needed to ensure the full implementation of the civil service reform and to prevent the administration from being used politically in clientelistic fashion, as still occurs at the local level. Vigilance is needed in effectively implementing the judicial reforms that will potentially transform this key sector over the long haul. Similar vigilance is needed to maintain and broaden the levels of transparency and to prevent the distortion of government practices to evade transparency requirements (Ackerman 2007; Arellano 2007).

Care is needed to ensure that the new accountability institutions do not become overly politicized and fall into the trap of becoming arenas for partisan disputes, as many see occurring within the IFE. At the same time, new laws are needed to keep pace with the new political realities. This includes measures to protect whistleblowers, to control lobbyists, to better define conflict of interest, and to limit the development of a revolving door between big business and politicians. Reforms are also needed to ensure more effective use of oversight materials like declarations of wealth and official audits. Electoral reforms—maybe regarding reelection of members of Congress—and a weakening of congressional party leadership operating behind closed doors, may also be necessary to strengthen vertical accountability and thus enable Congress to conduct effective oversight of the executive. At the same time, the congressional accounting arm, the Auditoria Superior de la Federación (ASF), must be empowered to sanction abuses. Measures are needed to strengthen the role of civil society in conducting oversight (Ackerman 2007) while simultaneously fighting corruption within civil society itself. Similarly, measures are needed to strengthen the level and scope of cooperation bridging state and society. As noted, societal support is critical in fighting crime, establishing the rule of law, battling corruption, and building accountability (Ackerman 2003; Reames 2007, 128; Shirk and Ríos Cázares 2007, 5). And just as the state cannot handle the struggle alone without the support of civil society, neither can civil society develop the tools of accountability alone without the support and cooperation of the state. Measures must also be taken to strengthen the investigation and prosecution of corrupt officials. As Adolfo Aguilar Zinser (2000) contends, the objective is not so much to eliminate corruption, but to eliminate impunity. Finally, and perhaps above all, the fight against corruption must be seen as credible, above both reproach and the political fray. Institutional designs housed in and dependent on the executive tend to either get bogged down in the political priorities of the administration or face severe deficits of credibility (see "Indice Latinoamericano de Transparencia Presupuestaria" 2005).

Clearly, Mexican democratization remains incomplete: seemingly effective and advanced in terms of the competition for power among the elite, but not in the exercise of that power (Guerrero 2004). In exercising power, politicians have yet to be forced to relinquish the privileges and discretion they enjoy, though they are now being forced to open up the operations of the government to public scrutiny: a critical first step on the road to accountability. As similarly found in other studies on the impact of electoral competition in Mexico (e.g., Beer 2003; Cleary and Stokes 2006; Fox 2007; Moreno-Jaimes 2007), the heightening of such competition amid a setting of weak rule of law, while it may enhance efforts to provide effective services, does little to strengthen the rule of law or the public's faith in the legal system. In many ways, the findings here match those offered by Jonathan Fox's study (2007, 333, 334) of politics in the countryside. Though he praises the spread of the "right to have rights" obtained through decades of mobilization, he concludes that "the transition to competitive electoral politics" has not led to accountability politics and enforced rights.

To be sure, Mexico faces many problems and, as polls indicate, corruption is generally not considered the most pressing of these. Politics, after all, revolves around priorities, and corruption, in confronting more important economic and security issues, often gets relegated to the margins, becoming merely a tangential issue. Given the reality of Mexican politics and these more pressing matters, this means that much of the public is willing to allow politicians to take advantage of their positions if they can address these other issues of importance. If politicians who accomplish good things—owing perhaps to skirting institutional and legal constraints—remain unaccountable, however, then the factors contributing to corruption remain intact, as does "politics as usual." In this scenario, only unpopular officials are held accountable to the rule of law. Politicians, of course, make similar deals and entertain similar trade-offs. In that corruption represents the unintended consequences of public policies—the side effects of their efforts to do good—fighting corruption often becomes merely secondary. To address such major issues as security, for instance, the strengthening of already-corrupt institutions and allowing them free rein to fight crime may help address the issues of insecurity, but at the same time may actually facilitate rather than address the deep-seated corruption found in these areas, ultimately limiting their ability to achieve their primary objectives. Just as the strengthening of the military in certain Latin American countries undermines efforts to enhance human rights, the increasing reliance on law enforcement to battle organized crime and drugs may do little to address the corruption in the ranks of the police.[3] If anything, it exposes them to greater corruption and more abuses. In certain respects, this is largely what happened to Fox. Despite good intentions, corruption—both the emergence of new corruption and the persistence of old corruption—eventually became secondary to his other political initiatives and interests (some would even say, his personal interests in using state power to help his immediate family and his own fortune). He did not go after former officials because this would have jeopardized negotiations with members of the PRI and the bureaucracy for needed reforms, and he did not go after his own officials because this would have undermined his base of support and image of running a clean government.

In some ways, the forces of anticorruption, rooted in the structural and institutional as well as ideological and cultural underpinnings of democracy, are not simply the negation of the causes of corruption. The causes of corruption in Mexico lie instead, in part at least, in the political system's authoritarian past, which both structurally and institutionally and through the political culture continues to influence the behavior of politicians and citizens, their perceptions of one another, and their expectations. The causes of corruption rest in the nature of Mexico's unique transition to democracy itself; in the evaporation of old informal institutions and the underdevelopment of new ones; and in the economic changes of neoliberalism, along with the economic distortions and the intense poverty and inequality that make everyday survival such a struggle as to trump concerns about individual integrity or about holding others to strong ethical standards. The causes of corruption stem from a low-level equilibrium in which society engages in a form of behavior that it simultaneously condemns; but at the same time, society understands that, as in a prisoner's dilemma, probity in the face of its opposite is both foolish and counterproductive. In the end, while corruption remains prominent in politics, the desire to address it—and the acknowledgment that it needs to be addressed, through a truly accountable government that itself abides by the rule of law and expects society to do the same—has grown.

Conditions for Reforms

Closely related to this overarching question regarding the impact of democratization on corruption, the study has also sought to shed some light on reform and the conditions that make effective anticorruption reform possible. Above all, the case of Mexico shows how democratization, coupled with polarization and the strength of key segments of society, has severely complicated the task of reform (Lehoucq 2007; World Bank 2007). Despite the expectation of change, Fox actually made fewer constitutional changes than his predecessors, largely owing to the lack of political opportunity and political skill. Paradoxically, as noted earlier, despite being the president of change, the president lacked the space to make change (Elizondo Mayer-Serra 2006, 77). In contrast to the government's failure to transform such key areas as energy, taxes, or labor, it was able to pass some of its major anticorruption initiatives: transparency and civil service reform—arguably the most important reforms of the period. It also set the stage for the judicial reform that came after. Passed in response to demands made during the presidential campaign and championed by key interest groups such as Grupo Oaxaca, the transparency law in particular generated rapid change in the way the government operated and in the way the public (and the press) viewed government operations. The government also faced limited opposition in Congress to the civil service reform, though implementation has been slow. Here, resistance comes not from Congress, but from the bureaucracies facing implementation. Reforms of the criminal justice system have faced more formidable obstacles and proved largely ineffective under Fox, though again he did help set the stage for future judicial change. Despite efforts to restructure and retrain the police, corruption within law enforcement continues to plague the country.

Leadership is crucial to reform-mongering. Leaders need to demonstrate that it is possible to curb corruption without committing political suicide. In many ways, however, Fox made some rather cautious choices and the intensity of the anticorruption effort dwindled as time wore on, replaced largely by a singular focus on transparency and bureaucratic simplification. Instead of translating anticorruption gains into a broadening of his bases of political support and building on this to further challenge the entrenched interests of the past, Fox relied on many of the old pillars of the PRI regime for support, leaving these bases largely untouched and unchallenged. Part of the problem relates to the dilemma of reform: while losers are known beforehand and poised to resist, the beneficiaries are unknown and hence unorganized. Electoral changes in the 1990s occurred because the political parties were intent on pushing them. Even the PRI supported electoral reforms to protect power. Yet, according to Carlos Elizondo Mayer-Serra (2006), no organized group has a great interest in strengthening government institutions and the rule of law. In fact, he contends, the winners of illegality are large, entrenched groups, from street vendors to taxi drivers.

The Role of Culture

The final research query centers on the limits of the institutional approach and the role of culture in understanding corruption and change. The mainstream approach to corruption—embraced here—focuses almost exclusively on structural balances and institutional designs. From this perspective, curbing corruption entails the creation of effective institutional mechanisms that control discretion, circumscribe authority, make officials accountable for their actions, and detect wrongdoing and punish it. Even so, questions arise as to the effectiveness of the institutional approach to explain change or, more precisely, the lack of change. The failure of democratization by itself to fundamentally alter the presence of corruption—in Mexico and many other countries—not only crystallizes the question regarding the limits of an exclusively institutional approach, but also raises the question of whether culture might be a factor in contributing to the stubborn persistence of corruption amid institutional change.

On the one hand, the present analysis does not point to the exhaustion of the institutional approach. It shows, instead, that the structural and institutional changes associated with democratization have not operated in a cohesive, coherent, or linear way to lower the probability of corruption—as perhaps expected. Some changes have opened new opportunities for corruption; others have proved insufficient to battle deeply entrenched corruption from the past. The structural and institutional changes in Mexico remain a work in progress and much remains to be done.

Even so, there still may be a role for culture in understanding the nature of corruption and change in Mexico. Culture, as described in Chapter 8, represents the lessons gained from the past. It provides the lens or filter used to interpret events, the nature of the political system, and the motives of others. It provides cues to calculate risks and opportunities and to develop strategies of individual behavior. In certain ways, the political culture—the wisdom of the past—stands as a sort of obstacle that the institutional and structural changes must surmount. If changes in the operation of the political system and the behavior of others arising from the structural and institutional transformations do not make sense within the given cultural narrative, creating a sort of dissonance, the situation prompts some form of cultural adaptation and change. This forces individuals to revise and adjust their assumptions about the nature of power and authority. But if the political changes fail to overcome this difficult hurdle and instead are simply perceived as confirming rather than challenging the cultural assumptions, then the culture itself becomes a factor perpetuating the behavior and thereby limiting or conditioning the reforms themselves.

In Mexico, unfortunately, the experience of Fox's administration—despite the legitimacy associated with his dramatic rise to power—failed to change the modes of exercising political power to the degree necessary to challenge basic assumptions about how politicians, government, and authority operate. To be sure, democratically induced demands for accountability, rule of law, and justice, including demands that corrupt officials from the past be punished, nurtured expectations for change; but in the face of reality, these expectations dissolved into disillusionment and dissatisfaction with the course of democracy.

It is not just past experience with corruption, favoritism, impunity, and the weak rule of law that have formatted this political culture and shaped views of politicians and authority. Economic inequality, monopolistic control of resources, poverty, racism and classism, and repression have all played a role in shaping a political culture in Mexico that distrusts politicians, the government and its institutions, and the rule of law and justice system, and dismisses their lofty promises of change. In such a setting, informal mechanisms and solutions outside the law, centering on personal relationships, become keys to survival. Here again, addressing these peripheral issues may contribute further to building a more accountable political system, not only by controlling the influence of particular interests through institutional mechanisms, but also by crafting a new political culture that sees politics, government, and authority in a distinct way. Citizens are far more likely to abide by the law if they feel that it applies to all equally, particularly to those in positions of power, and that it represents their interests.

The rule of law bridges the institutional and the cultural. Clearly, a weak state and a weak culture of legality undermine state-led efforts at reform, providing reforms with limited traction: a statement bordering perhaps on tautology. As Fernando Escalante Gonzalbo (2006, 23) points out, "The Mexican State has never been capable of imposing compliance with the law, not even among public officials." If in the past governance occurred in the absence of real rule of law owing to a sort of elite pact and strong informal institutional arrangements centering on one-party hegemony and presidentialism, today the absence of rule of law amid the breakdown of these informal institutions severely complicates governance and reform. In fact, in a setting of weak rule of law, democratization has arguably weakened the state's capacity to govern

(Elizondo 2006). Stated differently, if the state is weak, then reforms from the state to curb the abuse of power mean little. As Adrián Acosta Silva (2004, 20) notes, without a culture of legality, reforming the system becomes difficult: "Neither codes of ethics, an oath to principles, or acts of repentance are sufficient to create confidence in politics."

* * *

In the end, change, as they say, is inevitable; but so too, as they rarely say, is continuity. Much has changed in Mexican politics in recent years, including the patterns of corruption and the struggle to impose the rule of law. In stunning contrast to just a decade ago, the effort against corruption and abuse of power has taken on new adherents and, ideologically at least, has become the norm rather than the exception. Still, as Mexico struggles to address a range of pressing issues in its transformation from an authoritarian into a truly democratic state, corruption continues to shape the nature and course of Mexican politics.

Notes

1. The Mexican case presents some similarities with the Chinese case. As in Mexico, leaders in China neglected enforcement strategy in favor of institutional design; yet partisan control undermined their efforts. The legal system also remained weak in China (see Manion 2004).

2. By contrast, I have argued (Morris 1991, 1999) that the impact of corruption characterized by extortion—the power of state officials over society—functions largely to solidify the elite and strengthen the pursuit of state interests. Of course, in the authoritarian, presidentialist system of the twentieth century, this meant the interests of the PRI-controlled state.

3. Complaints against the military filed before the Comisión Nacional de Derechos Humanos increased in line with the military's broadened role in fighting organized crime under Felipe Calderon. During his first year in office, Calderon deployed 27,000 troops to engage in joint efforts with police in regions hard-hit by drug-related violence. From the start of the Calderon term until May 2008, a total of 634 complaints were filed, representing a fifth of all complaints against the military in the commission's eighteen-year history (*Milenio* May 25, 2008; see also "Early Concerns About Aid to Mexico" 2007).

Appendix A

Mexican Corruption in Comparative Perspective

With a focus on change, this study seeks to compare corruption in Mexico to itself at different points in time. A cross-national comparison, however, provides additional insight into the nature and the extent of corruption in the country. This appendix briefly compares corruption in Mexico to that in other countries, particularly those of Latin America. While data generally show that Mexico suffers relatively high levels of corruption compared to other countries, the national pattern tends to fit rather than deviate from the global pattern.

Perceptions of Corruption

Transparency International offers the most widely used cross-national measures of corruption. In its 2008 Corruption Perception Index, based on the views of experts and country analysts, Mexico ranked 72nd among 180 countries, with a score of 3.6 on the 0 (corrupt) to 10 (no corrupt) scale. This score positioned Mexico near average for the 20 Latin American countries in the study (see Figure A.1), with higher levels of corruption than such regional leaders as Chile and Uruguay, but less corruption than Ecuador or Argentina.

Transparency International's Global Corruption Barometer disaggregates public views of corruption. Table A.1 compares the perceived level of corruption by institution in 2006.[1] As shown, Mexicans consider almost all the institutions included in the study as slightly more corrupt than the worldwide and the Latin American averages. Vis-à-vis the world, this is particularly noteworthy with respect to political parties, the legislature, the police, and the legal system. Whereas worldwide the public considered political parties the most

241

Figure A.1 Corruption Perception Index for Latin America (2007)

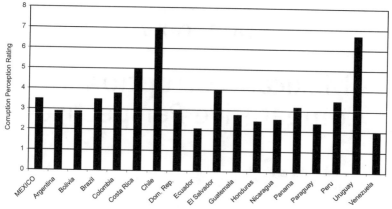

Source: Transparency International.

Table A.1 Perceived Level of Corruption by Institution (2006)

	Mexico	Latin America (n = 9)	World (n = 61)
Parties	4.4	4.2	4.0
Legislature	4.3	4.1	3.7
Business	3.7	3.5	3.6
Police	4.5	4.2	3.5
Legal system / judiciary	4.2	4.1	3.5
Media	3.5	3.3	3.3
Tax revenue	3.8	3.5	3.3
Medical services	3.0	3.1	3.1
Education services	3.2	3.0	3.0
Military	3.2	3.5	3.0
Utilities	3.5	3.3	3.0
Registry and permit services	3.9	3.5	2.9
Nongovernmental organizations	3.2	3.1	2.9
Religious institutions	3.2	2.8	2.8

Source: Global Corruption Barometer 2006. Data for Mexico based on a sample of 700 interviews.

Note: Scale 1–5: 1 = not corrupt at all, to 5 = extremely corrupt.

corrupt institution, Mexicans view the police as slightly more corrupt than parties. The Mexican pattern of perception aligns more closely with the regional averages, but again Mexicans perceive the parties, the legislature, the police, and other areas as more corrupt than do their Latin American brethren. The only two areas in which Mexicans rank their institutions as less corrupt than the norm are medical services and the military.

Table A.2 compares Mexicans' perceptions of the impact of corruption and their assessment of the government's efforts to fight corruption using data from the 2006 Global Corruption Barometer, and their expectations of future corruption based on data from the 2007 Latinobarómetro poll. Mexicans gauge the impact of corruption on political life as slightly less pronounced, and its impact on personal and family life somewhat more pronounced, compared to citizen assessments in most other countries. Consistent with the finding in this study, however, Mexicans' assessment of the government's willingness to fight corruption is much more negative in comparison to citizen assessments in other countries, with a majority of Mexicans feeling that the government either does not fight corruption at all or, worse, actually encourages it. Nevertheless, according to data from the 2007 Latinobarómetro poll, they are not nearly as pessimistic regarding the future of corruption as their Latin American counterparts, with their assessment falling well below the regional average.

Participation Rates

Cross-national measures of corruption based on participation rates, rather than perception, show Mexico to have a relatively high rate of corruption. In the 2006 Global Corruption Barometer, for example, 28 percent of Mexicans admitted to having paid a bribe within the preceding twelve months, compared to an average of just 17 percent for Latin American countries and an average of only 9 percent worldwide. Data from Latinobarómetro polls, as shown in Table A.3, which compares participation rates from 2001 to 2007, similarly point to consistently high levels of corruption in Mexico compared to other nations throughout the period. Interestingly, these data point to a rather substantial reduction in the level of bribery in Mexico from 2001 to 2007.

Related Measures: Governance Indicators

In 1996, the World Bank began tabulating measures of governance for most countries based on a combination of the views of many enterprises, citizens, and experts. The governance indicators include distinct measures for voice and accountability, political stability (including absence of violence), government effectiveness, regulatory quality, rule of law, and control of corruption. Table A.4, which presents the 2006 data, shows Mexico to be above the middle ranking in the areas of voice and accountability, government effectiveness, and regulatory quality, but below the middle ranking in the areas of control of corruption, rule of law, and political stability. Mexico's 2006 ranking for corruption compares closely to the rankings of Ethiopia, Macedonia, Peru, Serbia, and Sri Lanka, while its ranking for rule of law places it in the company of such nations as Brazil, Burkina Faso, the Dominican Republic, and Lebanon.

Table A.2 Assessments of the Impact of Corruption and the Government's Fight Against It, and Expectations for the Future

Assessment of the Impact of Corruption (2006)

	Mexico	Latin America (n = 9)	World (n = 61)
Political life	3.0	3.3	3.4
Business life	2.9	2.9	3.1
Personal and family life	2.8	2.5	2.3

Source: Global Corruption Barometer. Data for Mexico based on a sample of 700 interviews.
Note: Scale 1–4: 1 = low, to 4 = high.

Assessment of the Government's Fight Against Corruption (2006) (% response)

	Very or Somewhat Effective	Not Effective	Does Not Fight Corruption At All	Actually Encourages Corruption
Mexico	9	27	20	43
Latin America	25	29	19	23
World	22	38	16	15

Source: Global Corruption Barometer.
Note: Data for Mexico based on a sample of 700 interviews.

Expectations for Corruption in the Next Generation (2007)

Survey Population	Percentage of Residents Who Predict Increased Corruption in Their Country
Nicaragua	59
Peru	58
Uruguay	57
Brazil	56
Colombia	54
Guatemala	50
Ecuador	48
El Salvador	47
Argentina	43
Venezuela	43
(average)	(43)
Costa Rica	41
Chile	41
Panama	34
Dominican Republic	33
Paraguay	29
Mexico	28
Bolivia	28
Honduras	21

Source: Latinobarómetro.

Table A.3 Participation in Bribery in Latin America

Percentage of Respondents Who Paid a Bribe

	2001	2002	2003	2004	2005	2006	2007
Argentina	24	25	19	18	14	14	23
Bolivia	32	20	20	17	19	12	16
Brazil	69	61	56	54	74	68	66
Chile	13	13	6	10	8	9	9
Colombia	11	19	11	10	14	12	13
Costa Rica	18	24	17	28	21	16	23
Dominican Republic	28	17	17	12	—	—	—
Ecuador	27	21	15	13	16	8	12
El Salvador	19	16	20	14	9	12	12
Guatemala	16	31	10	23	12	19	10
Honduras	24	23	16	16	8	10	9
Mexico	65	59	53	53	50	26	33
Nicaragua	17	41	18	21	16	13	10
Panama	21	23	18	15	8	6	6
Paraguay	24	22	20	15	19	14	21
Peru	22	25	12	16	14	12	23
Uruguay	18	13	12	9	10	12	17
Venezuela	27	27	24	15	16	13	22

Source: Latinobarómetro 2007.

Table A.4 World Bank Governance Indicators for Mexico (2006) (percentile ranks)

Voice and Accountability	Political Stability	Government Effectiveness	Regulatory Quality	Rule of Law	Control of Corruption
52.4	32.7	60.7	63.4	40.5	46.6

Source: World Bank, http://siteresources.worldbank.org/intwbigovantcor/resources/1740479-11504025 82357/2661829-1158008871017/gov_matters_5_tables.pdf.

Note: Percentile ranks indicate the percentage of countries worldwide that Mexico scored above. Higher values indicate better governance ratings.

Note

1. The more recent 2007 Global Corruption Barometer does not include the case of Mexico.

Appendix B

Cases and Scandals

Analysis of corruption normally takes place at a high level of abstraction. Yet corruption is always a micro-level phenomenon involving individual acts, actors, and decisions that are shrouded in mystery and that, when revealed, unleash an avalanche of allegations, investigations, cover-ups, and intrigue. Of course, the sheer quantity of cases makes it impossible to pay much attention to individual acts of corruption. Nonetheless, the major cases and scandals highlight key patterns regarding the type and location of corruption in society; they display what the government is and is not doing; and they play a role in shaping political perceptions and feeding national debates. While almost any given case could be the subject of extensive analysis, this appendix seeks to provide simple briefs on key cases and scandals that dominated the news in Mexico during the Vicente Fox period and the initial years under Felipe Calderon.

Spillover Cases from the Prior Sexenio

Raul Salinas

Raul Salinas, the brother of former president Carlos Salinas de Gortari (1988–1994), was arrested on February 28, 1995, in a dramatic showdown at his home in Mexico City for his involvement in the September 1994 murder of Chamber of Deputies leader (and Raul's former brother-in-law) José Francisco Ruiz Massieu. Following his arrest, authorities uncovered over US$300 million under false names and in hidden accounts around the world, prompting multiyear investigations in Mexico, France, Switzerland, and the United States for suspected embezzlement, illegal enrichment, and the laundering of proceeds from drug sales. In 1995, Swiss authorities arrested Salinas's spouse while she was attempting to withdraw funds from a Swiss account. Swiss officials seized over 980 million pesos (US$90 million) from the accounts of Salinas. In January 1999, Salinas was convicted and sentenced to fifty years in prison for masterminding the murder of Ruiz Massieu. On appeal, because of the weakness of the prosecution's case, the sentence was reduced to twenty-seven and a half years. In 2002, Swiss officials, having failed to obtain sufficient evidence to prosecute, decided to hand the case over to the Mexican authorities (*Source-Mex* August 7, 2002); in 2005 they discontinued their investigation. In Mexico, Salinas was convicted in 2002 for embezzling 207 million pesos (US$23 million) from a secret presidential account (*SourceMex* August 7, 2002), but the charges were suspended soon afterward and then overturned in December 2004, leaving only the government's investigation into illicit enrichment still standing. In June 2005, Salinas won an appeal overturning the murder conviction. The three-member appellate court ruled that he had been jailed based on insufficient evidence. He was subsequently released on bond pending the ongoing investigation into the charges of illicit enrichment in the amount of 161 million pesos (US$18 million) (*Milenio* June 14, 2005). In May 2006, Salinas was acquitted in a French court for laundering US$3.8 million in drug money. The case was not appealed or turned over to the Mexican authorities (*Milenio* May 15, 2006). Throughout the lengthy affair, Salinas maintained his innocence, claiming that the multimillion-dollar funds—far beyond his salary as a mid-level bureaucrat—had originated from business deals, and insisting that the charges had all been politically motivated (he presents part of his story in the book *Diálogos de un día,* coauthored with Alejandra Zorrilla Martínez). From October 2001 to October 2007, there were 154 news stories in *Milenio* dealing with Raul Salinas.

Carlos Cabal Peniche

Carlos Cabal Peniche, the former president of Banca Cremi-Union, faced formal charges of defrauding the bank of 670 million pesos (US$200 million) in 1994. After fleeing the country, Cabal was captured in Australia, where he insisted that officials had used his bank to channel funds illegally into PRI election campaigns, including US$5 million for the 1994 presidential campaign of Ernesto Zedillo (*SourceMex* August 16, 2000). After fighting extradition for almost three years from inside an Australian prison, Cabal returned to Mexico in August 2001 to face fifteen separate charges (*SourceMex* August 15, 2001). In January 2004, however, Cabal was absolved of the generic charges of fraud, though a few months later he faced new charges for defrauding the company Cerfa of 167 million pesos (US$14.7 million). In 2006, while released on an injunction, he was arrested and charged for tax fraud in the amount of 371 million pesos (US$33 million), for which he was found guilty a year later (*Milenio* April 16, 2007).

Oscar Espinosa Villareal

Oscar Espinosa Villareal, the former head of the Mexico City government (Departamento del Distrito Federal, 1994–1997) and secretary of tourism (1997–2000) under Ernesto Zedillo, fled the country in 2000 after it was revealed that he was under investigation by the internal comptroller and the attorney general of the new PRD-held Mexico City government for embezzling 428 million pesos (US$86 million) during his term and for mismanaging millions of pesos in city funds. The city's attorney general obtained arrest warrants for seventy-five former members of the Espinosa administration on charges ranging from embezzlement to abuse of authority (*SourceMex* August 16, 2000). Authorities captured Espinosa in Nicaragua in December 2000 and extradited him to Mexico in August 2001 (*SourceMex* December 6, 2000). It was at this time that the federal government also indicated that it was investigating Espinosa for misuse of 9.8 million pesos (US$1.1 million) during his tenure as secretary of tourism (*SourceMex* August 15, 2001). Though convicted and sentenced to seven years in prison for embezzlement, he subsequently won an injunction that overturned his conviction based on a jurisdictional question (*Milenio* August 9, 2006). At the time that the allegations and charges against Espinosa surfaced, PRI officials accused the PRD government in Mexico City of conducting a witch-hunt. According to one official "The prosecutor [was] acting in a partisan fashion and [was] obsessed with getting Espinosa, guilty or not" (*SourceMex* August 16, 2000).

Mario Villanueva Madrid

Mario Villanueva Madrid, the former governor of Quintana Roo, is to date the highest-ranking official formally accused of drug trafficking and racketeering in Mexico. He disappeared in April 1999 just days before the end of his term (and immunity) amid allegations by both US and Mexican officials that he had accepted bribes in return for protecting cocaine shipments through his state. In an interview with *Milenio* from hiding, Villanueva acknowledged that he had accepted millions of dollars in kickbacks and bribes during his term, but insisted that he was not involved in drug trafficking. He claimed that high officials within the government had betrayed him (*SourceMex* March 1, 2000). In what at the time was widely seen as an important victory for the Vicente Fox anticorruption campaign, authorities arrested Villanueva in May 2001 on charges of providing assistance to drug traffickers (protecting the Juarez cartel), laundering drug profits, and misusing public funds (*SourceMex* May 30, 2001). He was convicted that same year to six years in prison for money laundering, but absolved of the charges of drug trafficking and organized crime. He won release in June 2007 after serving the sentence, but was promptly rearrested to face extradition to the United States to face charges from a New York court on drug trafficking (*Milenio* June 21, 2007).

Jorge Carillo Olea

In 1998, Jorge Carillo Olea, the governor of the state of Morelos, faced multiple accusations of kidnapping, condoning prisoner torture, protecting drug traffickers, and violating state and federal constitutions in nominating candidates to high posts. After taking a leave of absence (and protecting his immunity), Carillo refused to return to the state to face impeachment charges. The opposition-controlled state legislature asked for a court order to place the former governor under house arrest. Even a special subcommittee of the Chamber of Deputies in 1998 voted to support impeachment proceedings against Carillo (*SourceMex* March 1, 2000). The governor was never formally impeached, however, and in February 2003 was exonerated of wrongdoing and released (*Milenio* February 18, 2003).

"Dirty War"

In accordance to a campaign promise and indicative of a desire to clarify crimes of the past, Vicente Fox appointed a special prosecutor to address past social and political movements (the FEMOSPP) shortly after taking office. High-profile efforts to bring charges against former officials, including former president Luis Echeverría, who had been accused of ordering the 1968 repression at Tlatelolco and the Jueves de Corpus incident in 1971 dramatically passed through a series of legal obstacles, dominating the news at each hurdle. This included the testimony of the former president himself, who was forced into the limelight. From 2003 to 2006, the courts issued a series of rulings and reversals of previous rulings regarding questions about the statute of limitations, immunity, and genocide. In late November 2006, an appellate court reinstated an arrest warrant against Echeverría on charges of genocide related to 1968, overturning an earlier decision in July that the charges could not be pursued because of the statute of limitations. This new ruling rested on the position that the clock for the statute of limitations had not really started until Echeverría left office. That same month, Echeverría was placed under house arrest, becoming the first Mexican president in history to be tried for a crime committed while in office. It was considered unlikely, however, that the former president would ever be sent to prison, because of his ill health.

In February 2004, following a 2003 Supreme Court decision upholding the government's right to prosecute former officials, the government arrested Miguel Nazar Haro, the former chief of the DSF, as well as Luis de la Barreda and Juventino Romero Cisneros both also of the DSF, for coordinating the campaign against leftists during the 1970s and early 1980s (all cited in *SourceMex* April 26, 2006). After years of investigations, in the end, these were the only officials ever prosecuted for past crimes by the special prosecutor. In an amazing turn of events, Nazar Haro and others were released in May 2006 after the law itself was overturned. Through an injunction, their lawyers were able to change the initial charges from illegal custody to violation of *garantias* in the case of the disappearance of Ignacio Salas Obregón in 1974 (*Milenio* June 22, 2006).

In April 2006, the PGR announced its decision to phase out the FEMO-SPP and transfer its duties to other units. Accordingly, in November 2006, the government unceremoniously released an 800-page report on the "dirty war" (the report was initially withheld and then leaked to the press) titled "Informe Histórico a la Sociedad Mexicana 2006." Based on data found in recently released government archives—made available through the new freedom of information act—the report asserted that presidents Gustavo Díaz Ordaz, Luis Echeverría, and José López Portillo had all developed a policy to suppress leftist dissent. The report documented 1,650 cases of torture, massacres, disappearances, and other crimes. The government's efforts, however, met with sharp criticism. Human rights activists considered the final report disappointing and fraudulent, saying that it only "skate[d] over the surface of what happened in the Dirty War" (Latin American Regional Report, Mexico and NAFTA, December 2006, 7–8). In fact, the lack of results prompted many human rights activists to question whether Vicente Fox had ever intended to prosecute (*SourceMex* December 13, 2006). Denise Dresser even accused Fox of complicity with the former PRI, contending that Ignacio Carrillo, the special prosecutor, had been set up to fail (*SourceMex* March 2, 2005).

FOBAPROA

FOBAPROA, the agency created to handle the banking crisis in 1995, is "considered by many as the biggest corruption scandal in Mexico's history" (Reyes 2004a). Numerous irregularities were committed in the process of buying up billions of dollars in unpaid loans to recapitalize the banking system. Audits in 1998 revealed that some of the biggest loans went to bank shareholder companies and to already-bankrupt companies. In 1999, an independent Canadian audit found US$7 billion in "unusual transactions." Three subsequent audits found more than US$4 billion in irregular loans. In 1999, the Mexican Congress actually released the list of beneficiaries, detailing over 2,500 operations. The list contained the names of major bankers and friends and family of wealthy and powerful individuals. Yet in September 2003, a judge ruled in favor of the banks to stop new audits, and in November the Supreme Court ruled in favor of Vicente Fox's effort to block the ASF and Congress from reducing the debt. Despite accusations and strong indications of irregularities, nobody has been investigated or prosecuted for defrauding the government (*SourceMex* August 15, 2001).

Campaign-Related Cases

The Lottery Scandal

In June 2002, the government launched an investigation of former officials in the Secretaría de Gobernación who had been involved in the Milenio Millonario lottery, organized in 2000 by the national committee of the PRI to obtain campaign resources (*Proceso* June 28, 2002). The government alleged that the winner of the lottery had to withdraw the money and turn it over to party officials. Considered to be a possible laundering operation involving the PEMEX money (see discussion of Pemexgate below), one report claimed that the lottery had laundered 125 million pesos (US$13 million) (*El Universal* June 5, 2002; *SourceMex* August 7, 2002).

CAPUFE Scandal

CAPUFE, the agency charged with administering federal roads and bridges, under the leadership of PRI deputy Gustavo Carvajal, provided 111,000 liters of paint for advertisements and slogans for Francisco Labastida Ochoa's presidential campaign in 2002 (60 percent of the campaign's paint production that year), according to an internal audit by SECODAM (*El Mural* July 8, 2002; *Reforma* August 13, 2002; *SourceMex* August 7, 2002). The audit also revealed other acts of wrongdoing, including contracting of ghost firms, the purchase of unnecessary materials, and various networks of corruption involving over 12 million pesos (US$1.2 million) (*El Norte* June 10, 2002). In an interesting twist, Gustavo Carvajal reported that an official from SECODAM had tried to extort 1 million pesos (US$100,000) from him in exchange for dropping the investigation. According to his contact inside, SECODAM had been ordered to find anything it could against Carvajal (*El Universal* June 10, 2002).

Pemexgate

In January 2002, SECODAM officials alleged that several high-ranking officials within PEMEX and its labor union, including the head of PEMEX, Rogelio Montemayor, and labor leader Senator Carlos Romero Deschamps (PRI), had illegally laundered more than 120 million pesos (US$13 million) in PEMEX operating funds via the STPRM's account to fund the presidential campaign of Francisco Labastida in 2000. Congress, the attorney general, and the IFE all launched investigations. In September 2002, the ASF oversight secretary stated that the former director of PEMEX and the leader of the union had used unauthorized administrative agreements, including an unauthorized transfer of 250 million pesos (US$26 million). In testimony before Congress, the ASF confirmed that PEMEX "gave resources to the petroleum workers union in a way that was illegal, illegitimate, and improper" (*El Universal* September 10, 2002).

The PGR conducted two investigations. The first, conducted by a special unit on organized crime, focused on whether public funds had been stolen and whether the agreement between PEMEX and the union was legal; the other investigation, by the electoral institute, explored whether electoral crimes had been violated. In the legal case, the government issued arrest warrants in September 2002 against Romero Deschamps, federal deputy Ricardo Aldana Prieto (union treasurer), and Rogelio Montemayor, and asked Congress to strip the two union leaders of their legislative immunity. The SECODAM investigation revealed that more than 1.6 billion pesos (US$172 million) had been trans-ferred illegally from PEMEX to the STPRM in 2000, and that some of that money had gone to the Labastida campaign (*SourceMex* September 18, 2002). Montemayor fled to the United States, where he fought extradition for two years. He returned to Mexico in September 2004 (see *SourceMex* January 30, 2002, September 18, 2002, November 3, 2004). Initial charges of money laun-dering and racketeering against officials of the STPRM were eventually with-drawn. By July 2003, the PGR special unit said there was insufficient evidence that funds used for the campaign had originated from an illegal source (*SourceMex* March 19, 2003). Indeed, a federal judge approved a pardon against three other officials, including a former finance secretary and a former PRI em-ployee originally charged with mishandling half of the 1.1 billion pesos (US$118 million) allegedly diverted from PEMEX to the campaign (*SourceMex* October 15, 2003). Administratively, the former director of PEMEX, Raúl Muñoz Leos, was prohibited from holding any public post for ten years and fined 862 mil-lion pesos (US$82,000) by the SFP. As of 2008, the PGR investigation was still ongoing (*Milenio* April 15, 2008).

The IFE absolved the union of wrongdoing early on (*SourceMex* January 30, 2002), and given the numerous obstacles it faced in obtaining detailed bank-ing information, it was eventually only able to prove that the PRI had failed to report 500 million pesos (US$53,000) and, consequently, had surpassed the legal spending limit (Córdova and Murayama 2006, 61). In March 2003, the IFE fined the PRI 1 billion pesos (more than US$90 million), representing the amount of federal financing the PRI would have received in 2003 and half its allocation for 2004, according to the IFE (*SourceMex* March 19, 2003).

During the initial phase of the scandal, PRI legislators accused Vicente Fox of conducting a witch-hunt and issued clear political threats: "It is not possible for us to heed [Fox's] call to unity while also facing a series of false accusa-tions" (*SourceMex* September 18, 2002). In the end, given the lack of prosecu-tions, some accused the government of having made a deal with the PRI. Rumors included the notion that the government had dropped the charges in ex-change for leniency in the Amigos de Fox case (*SourceMex* July 30, 2003).

"Amigos de Fox"

The original complaints that the Vicente Fox campaign was receiving foreign funds (prohibited by law) surfaced even before the election from PRD and PRI officials. Initial IFE investigations into the origins of funds, however, were suspended because of a lack of evidence. In a major decision, the electoral tri-bunal ruled in May 2002 that the bank secrecy law did not apply and ordered the CNBV to release the bank records related to the Fox campaign and instructed the IFE to reopen the investigation. Still, it was not until April 2003 that the IFE was able to obtain access to bank information. The investigation revealed a num-ber of irregularities and a complex network to channel campaign funds. Among the many irregularities, the electoral alliance of the PAN and the PVEM failed to report 99 million pesos (US$10 million), failed to identify the sources of 77 million pesos (US$8 million) in funding, spent beyond the campaign limit, surpassed the individual donation limit, received funds from public agencies, businesses, and foreign sources, provided payments to third parties for media that went unreported, and failed to respond to IFE inquiries for clarification. The investigation, in addition, revealed a parallel network of campaign funding, with most of the funds channeled into the Asociación Civil Amigos de Fox, the Fideicomiso para el Desarrollo y la Democracia en México and the Fox campaign (Córdova and Murayama 2006, 111, 166). The IFE fined the two parties of the coalition more than 500 million pesos (US$48 million). Despite the investigation, the legal case never prospered and in October 2003 the PGR exonerated Amigos de Fox of any wrongdoing (*SourceMex* October 15, 2003).

Drug-Related Cases

Puente Grande

In January 2001, the leader of the Sinaloa drug cartel, Joaquín "el Chapo" Guzmán escaped from the federal prison, Puente Grande, in the state of Jalisco. Subsequent investigations revealed that much of the prison staff had been receiving regular payments from the drug trafficker while in prison. In June 2006, the former director of the prison received a sentence of eighteen years and four months for his responsibility in the escape and for bribery. The former assistant director of internal security at the prison received a sentence of eight years. All together, fifty-seven people were convicted and sentenced to between six and eight years in prison; two officials were released (*Milenio* June 30, 2006).

The Military and Drug Trafficking

In August 2000, following a number of high-profile cases in the 1990s—the 1991 resignation of navy secretary Mauricio Schleske Sánchez after authorities discovered that he had used bribes from drug traffickers to purchase two homes in Houston worth about US$700,000, and the 1997 arrest of the head of the drug enforcement agency, General Jesús Gutiérrez Rebollo, and two other officers for protecting drug kingpin Amado Carillo Fuentes (Gutiérrez Rebollo was sentenced to seventy-one years in federal prison; *SourceMex* August 9, 2000)—military prosecutors arrested two generals for aiding the Carillo Fuentes drug cartel and attempted bribery: retired general Francisco Quiros Hermosillo and brigadier-general Mario Arturo Acosta Chaparro. At the time, the defense ministry (SEDENA) reported that it had opened investigations against forty-five other members of the military for their connections to drug traffickers. Acosta is said to have directed operations that resulted in the disappearance, torture, and assassination of at least 500 individuals suspected of having links to the EPR, a guerrilla organization (*SourceMex* September 20, 2000). In April 2001, the government arrested three more military officers for collaborating with drug traffickers, this time for aiding members of the Gulf cartel: Brigadier-General Ricardo Martínez Perea, Captain Pedro Maya Díaz, and Lieutenant Ricardo Antonio Quevedo (*SourceMex* April 18, 2001). In October 2002, SEDENA confined to base for more than ten days an entire battalion responsible for destroying poppy and marijuana plantations in Sinaloa so that military authorities could investigate drug-trafficking charges against the soldiers and officers (*SourceMex* October 16, 2002).

FEADS

In 2003, the Fox government dissolved FEADS, the federal agency in charge of conducting investigations into drug trafficking, after six agents were arrested in Tijuana on charges of trying to extort US$2 million from a drug cartel in exchange for the release of two alleged traffickers and nearly five tons of marijuana. The military seized control of the FEADS offices in eleven states, and federal authorities reported an investigation of 700 antidrug agents. This was the second time the government had made such a move. In 1997, it shut down the Instituto Nacional para el Combate a las Drogas (INCD) following the arrest of General Jesús Gutiérrez Rebollo (*SourceMex* January 29, 2003).

Ma Baker

The arrest of drug trafficker Ma Baker in August 2002 prompted a series of revelations profiling the extensive involvement of police in drug trafficking and other crimes. Through protected informants, details emerged of how a network of public officials at the federal, state, and municipal levels had been protecting the criminal organization led by Delia Patricia Buendia Gutiérrez (also known as Ma Baker). Reports surfaced that federal police agents had picked up cocaine from airplanes and delivered it, and that Ma Baker had frequently sent presents to officials inside the PGR (*Proceso* September 2, 2002; *El Universal* August 27, 2002). The allegations prompted the attorney general and the Supreme Court to publicly promise to conduct a thorough investigation of official involvement of judicial officials in drug trafficking.

October 2002 Crackdown

In October 2002, the government arrested more than twenty-four government employees alleged to have been working on behalf of drug traffickers as the result of an undercover operation. Suspects included retired military personnel, law enforcement officials, and mid-level bureaucrats in the PGR, SEDENA, and the SSP on accusations of providing information to drug traffickers in exchange for bribes (*SourceMex* October 30, 2002).

Local Officials

A number of reports spanning the country tied local officials to drug traffickers. A report by journalist Jesús Blancornelas in *Seminario Zeta* said that at least twenty-four mid-level officials of the state of Baja California were on the payroll of the Tijuana cartel, mainly in the area of security. A story in *La Reforma* accused former governor Ruben Figueroa Figueroa (1975–1981) and his son Ruben Figueroa Alcocer in Guerrero of receiving expensive gifts from traffickers in exchange for protection. Reports also linked drug trafficking to other governors, including Mario Villanueva of Quintana Roo, Flávio Romero de Velazques of Jalisco (1977–1983), Agustín Acosta Lagunes of Veracruz (1980–1986), and Sergio Estrada Cajigal of Morelos.

Sergio Estrada Cajigal (PAN)

In 2004, allegations surfaced that Sergio Estrada Cajigal, governor of the state of Morelos, had colluded to allow the powerful Juarez cartel to use the state as a collection and distribution site. SIEDO had already filed charges against a Morelos judicial police officer, that officer's top aide, and five other state police officers. According to SIEDO, top state officials had accepted bribes in exchange for protecting airfields, warehouses, and other locations. Investigations also implicated members of the PFP who had alerted the traffickers about federal surveillance operations. Governor Estrada reacted to the scandal by dismissing 552 members of the judicial police and announcing a restructuring of the entire force. The ensuing scandal forced the resignation of two key members of the Estrada administration: the state attorney general and the state secretary. Demands for Estrada to step down grew. Congress even threatened to call for a political trial against the governor if he refused to resign. Nonetheless, the PGR exonerated Estrada of all charges, triggering more political controversy, as "opposition parties immediately criticized Macedo [the attorney general] for being too quick in exonerating Estrada." In mid-April, legislators from all parties except the PAN approved a resolution calling on the attorney general to offer a clear and convincing explanation as to why Estrada was exonerated in secret. The PRD accused the PGR of playing politics by favoring the PAN governor (*SourceMex* April 21, 2004).

Judiciary-Related Cases

Juan Carlos Rayo Mares

In October 2002, in one of the few reported actions against an official within the judiciary, authorities detained a penal judge, Juan Carlos Rayo Mares, for soliciting sexual favors from the wife of a former prisoner in exchange for eliminating criminal charges against her husband. Though the case received only limited public attention, it reached the level of scandal because the victim had recorded the conversation and the PGR had used marked bills in the payoff ("100 jueces bajo investigación" *Milenio Semanal* January 20, 2006; see also *Milenio* October 10, 2002). The final outcome of the case, however, seems to have gone unreported. Nonetheless, an extensive report in 2006 noted a series of pending cases against judicial officials.

Hugo Muñoz Arreola
In 2003, Federal judge Hugo Muñoz Arreola was removed by Tribunal Superior de Justicia del DF to allow for prosecution. The judge stood accused of taking money to issue rulings that made it easier for the transportation company TMM to suspend payments to creditors (*SourceMex* July 16, 2003).

Other Scandals

PEMEX
In November 2002, the director of PEMEX, Raul Muñoz Leos, resigned under pressure in the midst of widespread allegations of corruption and mismanagement. Among other irregularities, several news outlets reported that the director had negotiated an ill-advised contract agreement with union workers without consulting the PEMEX board of directors. During this time, the Vicente Fox government also made an effort to prosecute the former director of PEMEX, Rogelio Montemayor Seguy, for allegedly laundering funds through the union, the STPRM, to help finance Francisco Labastida Ochoa's campaign (see separate discussion of Pemexgate earlier in this appendix). In a separate case, in May 2005, a total of 2.8 billion pesos (US$255 million) in fines were levied by the SFP against six former PEMEX officials, including Montemayor, for misuse of company funds. The government accused all the officials of illegally diverting PEMEX funds to the union (*SourceMex* May 18, 2005). One report in June 2007 noted that Muñoz Leos was under investigation for the illegal transfer of 1.7 billion pesos (US$158 million) to the union and the use of PEMEX funds to finance personal trips. The report noted that the SFP investigation was also targeting other PEMEX officials, including former PEMEX attorney Juan Carlos Soriano and former administrative director Octavio Aguilar Valenzuela. The ASF, in the meantime, was also reportedly investigating Muños Leos for use of PEMEX funds for personal expenses. Muños stood accused of making six unapproved trips to London and Madrid at a cost of almost 300,000 pesos (US$27,000) (*SourceMex* June 20, 2007).

Towelgate
In June 2001, *Milenio* reported that President Vicente Fox had spent US$600,000 on remodeling and US$1 million on household items for the presidential residency, Los Pinos, including embroidered towels costing US$500 each and

sheet sets costing US$1,500, all from a supplier that did not officially exist. *Milenio* reportedly obtained this information from state-run Internet sites. The obscurity surrounding the vendor and what seemed exorbitant prices for everything from bath towels to sets of electronically operated curtains led many to suspect corruption. The news triggered a firestorm of criticism. Facing intense questions and pressures, Francisco Barrio, the head of SECODAM, promised a complete audit of presidential expenses, while Carlos Rojas, the president's personal secretary and friend, was forced to resign. Congress agreed to keep a close watch, but to delay its own investigation until the completion of SECODAM's. Roughly nine months after the initial revelation, SECODAM concluded that irregularities existed and that Rojas and five other officials in the administrative office of the presidency had violated regulations regarding public procurement. Though they levied no fines, the minor officials were suspended for periods ranging from three to six months. Rojas was suspended from working for the government for a period of two years (*Milenio* March 18, 2002). During the scandal, various opposition figures pointed out that it was not right that an arm of the executive (SECODAM) was in charge of investigating the executive for corruption. Noting Fox's anticorruption mandate, *The Times* (United Kingdom), on June 26, 2001, referred to the so-called Towelgate scandal as "one of the stiffest tests yet for president Fox's stated commitment for greater accountability in government."

Video Scandals of 2004

Though the initial salvo in the 2004 video scandals involved a leader of Mexico's green party, the PVEM, they later came to focus on key former and current city officials within the PRD and close associates of Manuel Andrés López Obrador, who was the mayor of Mexico City at the time and a likely presidential candidate for the 2006 election. The scandals featured the dramatic exposure of politicians stuffing money into briefcases, investigations at various levels of the government, official expulsions from the PRD, and wild accusations of a conspiracy at the highest levels designed to tarnish the image of López Obrador. The scandals involved four distinct but related cases and various strands.

First, on February 23, 2004, a cable news program showed a video of Senator Jorge Emilio González Martínez (senator and president of the PVEM) negotiating a US$2 million deal with businessman Francisco de Paula León in exchange for his help in promoting two tourist projects in Cancún, Quintana Roo, a municipality governed at the time by the PVEM. The newspaper *El País* had reported the existence of the video that day (*Milenio* February 24, 2004). Santiago León Aveleira, one of the leaders of the PVEM's dissident group Democracia Verde, filmed the meeting clandestinely. He also made other allegations against González, including the charge that PVEM representatives on the local assembly in Mexico City had issued 750,000 pesos (US$66,000) in checks in one month to the party leader. In his defense, González insisted that he was merely trying to see how far the businessman, Francisco de Paula León, would go before he denounced him for attempted bribery. González also contended that the local assembly official, Santiago León, had attempted extortion to keep him quiet. Officially, González and the PVEM called the accusations and the video an attack on the party by President Vicente Fox, because of the party's recent withdrawal from the political coalition that was supporting the president (on the exact conversation, see *El Universal* February 24, 2004; see also *SourceMex* March 10, 2004).

Second, about a week later, on March 2, 2004, Televisa's *El Noticiero,* directed by Joaquín López Dóriga, reported that Gustavo Ponce Meléndez, the finance minister of the Mexico City government, had made frequent trips to Las Vegas, where he spent and gambled lavishly, even enjoying VIP standing in Bellagio Casino. Supported with photographs, documents, and videos, the report held that between 2002 and 2004, Ponce made at least seventeen trips to Vegas and that on his last trip, in February 2004, he spent over 30,000 pesos (US$2,600). In response, the Mexico City attorney general announced that he had filed an official complaint against Ponce back on January 28 (*Milenio* March 2, 2004; *SourceMex* March 10, 2004). After initially demonstrating his public support for Ponce, López Obrador later removed him from his post. Ponce subsequently fled the country. A few days later, the Mexico City attorney general reported that he was opening an investigation into illicit enrichment (*Milenio* March 4, 2004). PAN federal deputy Federico Doring, who was responsible for making the videotapes available to the press, accused López Obrador of allowing Ponce to flee (*SourceMex* April 21, 2004).

Third, one day after the report on Ponce, on March 3, 2004, a morning news program exhibited yet another video, this one showing René Bejarano, the former personal secretary of López Obrador and the PRD's leader in the Mexico City assembly, receiving thousands of dollars (allegedly US$45,000) from businessman Carlos Ahumada Kurtz (*Milenio* March 4, 2004). Many concluded that the money was a bribe to restore city contracts to Ahumada's various companies that had been canceled by the new city government. Bejarano admitted to taking the money, but said it was a legal campaign contribution (*SourceMex* March 10, 2004). In response to the video, the PGR's organized crime unit (SIEDO) opened an investigation into whether drug-trafficking organizations may have played a role in the case, since there was some evidence linking Ahumada to money-laundering operations. The IFE, for its part, also opened an investigation into whether any of the bribes were being used for election campaigns (*SourceMex* April 21, 2004). The Chamber of Deputies, too, opened an investigation, stripping Bejarano of his legislative immunity: just the second time in history that the chamber had exercised such a power (*SourceMex* November 10, 2004). After spending eight months in prison, however, Bejarano was released in 2005, exonerated of all charges filed by the Mexico City government as well as the federal government's charge of money laundering (*SourceMex* February 22, 2006).

Fourth, in yet another video released on March 3, 2004, Ahumada was shown giving large sums of money (allegedly US$53,000) to Carlos Imaz from the PRD, one of Mexico City's delegational mayors. Imaz testified that the funds had been a donation to assist the former head of the Mexico City government, Rosario Robles, in her bid to become head of the PRD (*SourceMex* March 10, 2004). Imaz was found guilty and fined, while the allegations against Robles and her personal relationship with Ahumada crippled her political career.

Three threads to the video scandals captured significant press and public attention. One thread involved Carlos Ahumada himself. Following the initial video, the Argentine businessman fled to Cuba. Mexican government officials subsequently found a total of twelve videos in his office. In a letter published in the press, Ahumada claimed that the payment to Bejarano had been not a bribe, but rather an extortion. Now a national figure with almost celebrity status, Ahumada became a highlight of the press, including his multiple business dealings and his close ties to Rosario Robles of the PRD, the former head of the Mexico City government. In April 2004, Ahumada was arrested in Cuba and deported to Mexico (*SourceMex* April 21, 2004). In April 2005, when the possibility peaked that Ahumada would be found innocent of charges and released, the Mexico City government charged him for low-quality work on a city contract. Ahumada was released from prison in May 2007, presumably with the aid of Senator Fernández de Cevallos (*Milenio* May 14, 2007).

A second thread of the video scandals centered on revelations directly implicating Rosario Robles, the former mayor of Mexico City, and her close associate, Ramon Sosamontes, the subsecretary of security for the federal district, former secretary of political relations for the PRD, and former delegational mayor. Facing certain expulsion from the executive committee of the PRD, Robles and Sosamontes both resigned from the party in disgrace soon after the video scandals erupted. Both faced investigation by the Mexico City attorney general for questionable contracts with Ahumada's firm Grupo Quartz (*Milenio* July 22, 2004). In one of the videos found by authorities in Ahumada's office, Sosamontes was discussing city contracts with Ahumada (*Milenio* March 21, 2004). Another video showed that Sosamontes knew of Ahumada's plan to release the video showing the Bejarano exchange. It showed Ahumada explaining to Sosamontes his plan to release the video if he did not obtain certain political favors (*Milenio* July 23, 2004). In November 2005, yet another video surfaced, this one showing Sosamontes handing over a suitcase full of dollar bills to Ahumada. On that same November day, another video broadcast showed the PRD's former candidate for the Oaxaca governorship, Gabino Cué, asking Ahumada for a campaign contribution (Global Integrity Timeline 2006).

The third thread in this mega-scandal involved the notion of a high-level conspiracy by President Fox against center-left leader López Obrador. Many raised questions as to how the television station had obtained the videos of Ponce from the Vegas hotel, and how PAN senator Diego Fernández de Cevallos had seemed to know about the tapes even before they were publicly released (*SourceMex* March 10, 2004). As part of this drama, López Obrador presented confidential documents from the US Treasury Department detailing an ongoing investigation of Ponce for possible financial crimes. Obtained from the Mexican government by the federal district's attorney general, Bernardo Bátiz Vázquez, under the pretext that they were needed for the probe, the documents, in López Obrador's eyes at least, demonstrated that the federal government was conspiring against him, since it knew before the scandal broke that Ponce was corrupt. Both the Mexican government and the US government reacted harshly to this violation of the cooperation agreement among police from the two countries. Adding further support to López Obrador's claims, a video testimony of Ahumada in 2006 revealed the businessman suggesting that the videos were indeed part of an effort to attack López Obrador; Ahumada also accused Fernández de Cevallos, former president Carlos Salinas, and Santiago Creel and Rafael Macedo of Fox's cabinet of having prior knowledge of the videos (*Milenio* August 21, 2006). Subsequent efforts by the Fox administration to press charges against López Obrador for violating a court order gave credence to these speculations and conspiracy theories.

Individual Cases

Nahum Acosta Lugo

Nahum Acosta Lugo, the travel coordinator under Vicente Fox's private secretary, Emilio Goicochea Luna, was arrested in February 2005 for allegedly passing confidential information to members of the Sinaloa drug cartel. The investigation focused on a gift of US$5,000 that Acosta received from the cousin of the leader of the drug cartel and, reportedly, uncovered numerous documents and objects that demonstrated his ties to Arturo Beltrán Leyva of the Sinaloa cartel (*SourceMex* February 23, 2005). Two months later, however, a court in Toluca exonerated the official because of a lack of evidence (*La Jornada* March 26, 2007).

Porfirio Barbosa and ISSSTE

In October 2006, Porfirio Barbosa, the former chief of staff of the Mexico City mayor and former head of the transportation commission in the state of Michoacán, was arrested for committing fraud against the Mexico City government and the ISSSTE. His arrest was part of a three-year investigation by the PGR, the ASF, and the SFP into irregular sales of *vales* (coupons) from the

ISSSTE to the Mexico City government. The original investigation centered on eight former officials of the Mexico City government, eighteen from the ISSSTE, and a few from the Sistema Transporte Colectivo. At the time of Barbosa's arrest, the PGR issued seven additional arrest warrants, most against officials from the ISSSTE. The PGR found that Barbosa had made at least ten deposits into the accounts of ghost companies. Barbosa was released after paying 129 million pesos (US$11.8 million) for reparations, 18,120 pesos (US$1,700) in fines, and a 50,000 peso bond (US$4,600) (*Milenio* October 25, 2006, October 26, 2006).

The Bribiescas

Following allegations in a book by Olga Warmut on the first lady and her family, Congress formed a series of special committees stretching from 2005 until 2007 to look into the accusations of influence trafficking by Manuel, Jorge Alberto, and Fernando Bribiesca Sahagún, the sons of the first lady, Marta Sahagún. Among the various allegations was that the Bribiescas had used their connections to obtain 2.5 billion pesos (US$229 million) in government construction contracts. The SFP initially declined to investigate the case, because the Bribiescas were not public officials, but did decide to take up the case later. Even so, the SFP eventually discontinued its investigations of the public contracts, owing to a lack of evidence of wrongdoing. Congress took a different approach. The ASF had already raised questions about the spending of the first lady and the size of her staff (*SourceMex* May 18, 2005). The congressional commissions, the focus of the scandal, highlighted the rapid enrichment of the family's businesses, which was widely publicized in the press. The capital of just one company owned by the children, for example, went from 50,000 to more than 7 million pesos (US$4,600 to US$670,000) in a period of ninety days (*Milenio* January 26, 2006). The congressional committees also raised serious questions about a number of government contracts with various companies with ties to the family (see *Proceso* February 19, 2006). According to the head of one of the congressional committees, Jesús González Schmall (of the party Convergencia), the sons used the presidential jet, entertained guests at the president's farm, closed off national monuments, and brought in Brazilian girls on cruise ships. The most substantive accusation, however, was that the president's stepsons were given privileged information from the bank rescue agency that enabled them to make money by buying property (Latin American Regional Report, Mexico and NAFTA, August 2006). New files obtained in March 2007 from IPAB pointed to Manuel and Jorge Alberto obtaining illegal benefits during the purchase of bad loans during the rescue. According to one official, the two benefited from the valuation of houses and properties rescued by state funds, and later in an obscure bidding process, IPAB granted the two the bid (*La Jornada* March 17, 2007).

The Bribiesca case became highly charged and extensively politicized. PAN-istas stressed the lack of evidence showing any wrongdoing and denounced the opposition for using the allegations to attack the president. According to PAN senator Diego Fernández de Cevallos, the opposition "created a perverted political flurry" (*Milenio* February 2, 2006). The accusations also prompted an angry Marta to publicly defend her children and to question the integrity of the head of the committee, González Schmall, calling him a coward. She even threatened him by saying that his *fuero* (immunity) had limits (*Milenio* July 30, 2006). González Schmall, of course, defended the work of his committee, seeing it as part of "a frontal attack against corruption in the highest spheres of political power in Mexico" (*La Jornada* March 17, 2007). He often characterized the president as an obstacle in the investigation.

CONALITEG
In 2002, the ASF announced that it had uncovered a series of irregularities in the 2000 budget of the National Textbook Commission, CONALITEG. According to the report, CONALITEG was provided funds to publish books on ecology that were never published (*El Universal* July 18, 2002). The secretary of education promised to file charges against CONALITEG for committing fraud in the amount of 3 billion pesos (US$306 million) over a two-year period. The case also implicated the former private secretary of President Ernesto Zedillo (*El Universal* July 12, 2002).

Diego Fernández de Cevallos
During 2002 and 2003, a series of reports raised questions about possible influence trafficking by PAN senator and former presidential candidate Diego Fernández de Cevallos. In July 2002, PRD deputies promised to file legal charges with the attorney general against Fernández for influence trafficking, fraud, and illicit enrichment (*Milenio* July 23, 2002). The charges stemmed mainly from Fernández's provision of legal representation in cases against the government, including one against the secretary of agrarian reform that resulted in the government paying an indemnity of over 1 billion pesos (US$102 million). The complaint also included charges against officials within the Ministry of Agrarian Reform and the company involved. Subsequent reports surfaced accusing the senator of operating essentially as a "coyote," facilitating various deals for companies with the government (*Milenio* July 23, 2002, August 14, 2003, August 24, 2003). In March 2003, members of Congress presented a constitutional revision designed to prevent themselves from providing professional services (as lawyers, consultants, etc.) that would give the appearance of influence trafficking or abuse of power (*Milenio* August 14, 2003).

Fondengate
During a 2005 Senate hearing, PRI senator Noemí Guzmán Lagunes accused the coordinator of *Protección Civil,* María del Cármen Segura Rangel, of diverting federal disaster relief funds to help PAN candidates (*Milenio* March 14, 2005; *SourceMex* October 12, 2005). An ASF audit revealed irregularities

of more than 1.2 billion pesos (US$122 million) between 2001 and 2004 in the Fonden budget. The ASF called on the Secretaría de Gobernación to apply sanctions against the officials involved within seventy-five days, noting that if the Gobernación failed to act, the ASF could promote the removal of its head (*Milenio* December 5, 2005). The head of the SFP was specifically asked about progress on the case during a congressional hearing in January 2006 (Cámara de Diputados 2005). While an official investigation by the PGR was considered to be ongoing, the internal comptroller of the Secretaría de Gobernación reported that it had uncovered no evidence of administrative wrongdoing by Carmen Segura Rangel or the other officials involved in the case (*Milenio* November 28, 2005, March 2, 2006). The investigation resulted in no indictments.

Napoleón Gómez Urrutia

Napoleón Gómez Urrutia, the leader of the mining union, was removed from office in March 2006 by the labor secretary after it was revealed that Gómez was under investigation by the PGR for multiple charges of corruption brought by the union. The PGR issued a warrant for his arrest for defrauding more than 3,000 workers out of US$55 million received from the company Grupo México for the union (*Milenio* May 13, 2006). Allegedly tipped off by someone inside the government, Gómez fled to Canada. A presidential spokesperson said there was evidence of corruption *"en grado extremo"* by the labor leader. In August and September, a number of officials close to Gómez were arrested. The former leader, however, insisted that the government was pursuing him because he had denounced acts of corruption by the president's stepchildren, the Bribiescas (see separate discussion of the Bribiesca case earlier in this Appendix) (*Milenio* March 7, 2006). His forced removal, however, sparked a labor strike and protests. The labor union held a meeting and refused to recognize the new leader, but instead confirmed Gómez as their leader despite the pending arrest order. The union also promised to go after Vicente Fox and Felipe Calderon (*Milenio* May 13, 2006). In December 2006, the government requested Gómez's extradition from Canada (*Milenio* December 31, 2006). By April 2007, there was talk of reinstating Gómez as the union's leader if the accusations proved to be unfounded (*Milenio* April 13, 2007). In September 2007, an independent audit commissioned by the steelworker and industrial metalworker unions found no foundation for the criminal charges against Gómez. The audit showed the proper use of the funds in question (*Milenio* September 5, 2007).

Mario Marin Torres

Revelations of a phone conversation in February 2006 between Mario Marin Torres, who was the governor of the state of Puebla, and Kamel Nacif Borge, a textile manufacturer, in which the governor discussed having reporter and author Lydia Cacho imprisoned and arranging to have her raped by a prison guard, unleashed a wave of activity and intense public debate. Caho's book *Los demonios de Eden* indirectly linked Nacif to a pedophile from Cancún who at the time was in prison in Arizona and awaiting extradition. Cacho had been arrested in Quintana Roo and was being transported to Puebla to face charges of defamation and libel when the conversation occurred. Cacho filed formal charges against the governor, Nacif, the Puebla attorney general, and the judge who had presided over her hearing for abuse of power, influence peddling, torture, and attempted rape. During the ensuing months, there were countless calls for the governor to resign, yet the PRI rallied behind him. At the federal level, a congressional investigation revealed serious violations of the Constitution and federal laws and in April the Supreme Court agreed to appoint two jurists to investigate whether Marin had violated Cacho's civil rights. The case was also under investigation by the special office of crimes against journalists (Fiscalia Especial para la Atención de Delitos Cometidos contra Periodistas) (FEADP) (*SourceMex* April 26, February 22, 2006). In addition to defending Mario, the PRI focused attention on the illegal way the wiretap had been conducted, with some accusing the Vicente Fox government of orchestrating the scandal.

Arturo Montiel

In October 2005, Arturo Montiel, the former governor of the state of Mexico and at the time the leading contender against Roberto Madrazo for the PRI's nomination for president, was accused by a city official in Tlanepantla, Mexico, of inexplicable wealth. The attorney general revealed that the former governor was already under investigation for fiscal crimes, money laundering, and possible federal fraud (*Milenio* November 30, 2005, December 1, 2005). After twelve months of investigation, the state comptroller found no evidence of wrongdoing, though the federal investigation by the PGR and Hacienda continued. A PAN spokesperson claimed the exoneration by state-level officials was "more oriented toward covering-up" than revealing the unexplained fortune of the former governor (*Milenio* December 18, 2005). In that the allegations and investigation forced Montiel to drop out of the presidential race, many shared the view of the governor that Roberto Madrazo, the eventual nominee, was behind the charges (*SourceMex* October 26, 2005).

Provida and Jorge Serrano Limón

In June 2004, six Mexican civil society organizations conducted a "citizens' audit" of a Ministry of Health program run by the private company Provida (*La Jornada* April 5, 2006). The audit uncovered numerous examples of corruption, prompting a public outcry and triggering investigations by the ASF and the SFP. In April 2005, the SFP suspended the director of Provida, Jorge Serrano Limón, for a period of fifteen years, from working in the public sector, and fined him over 13 million pesos (US$1.2 million) for irregular handling of 34 million pesos from the Secretary of Health, including unauthorized purchases. Three officials from the health ministry were also removed from office (*Milenio* April 18, 2005; Global Integrity Timeline 2006). An audit by the ASF also confirmed the irregularities and resulted in the filing of formal charges with the PGR. The attorney general's investigation, however, failed to uncover sufficient evidence to prosecute (*Milenio* December 31, 2005). Members of the opposition accused the government of covering up the corruption at Provida and diverting over 30 million pesos (US$2.7 million) due to the influence of the far right on the Vicente Fox government (*Milenio* April 10, 2006). In October 2006, the Supreme Court denied Serrano Limón's request for an injunction. In an important ruling, the Court held that private actors charged with administering public funds were subject to the federal anticorruption law (Ley de Responsabilidades), as applicable to public officials.

Tobacco Bribery Scandal

In October 2005, PAN deputy Miguel Ángel Toscano accused various members of Congress of accepting bribes in the form of paid excursions to Europe and Central and South America, as well as cash, from transnational tobacco companies in exchange for their votes against a tax increase on cigarettes and against a series of tobacco-related recommendations by the World Health Organization. Toscano also accused the tobacco companies of financing political campaigns. Congress and the political parties refused to pursue the case, though, even after Toscano began to release the names of those involved, including the secretaries of committees in charge of health and treasury. The congressional debate, however, did bring up some questions regarding the nature of lobbying and the need for more extensive regulations (*Milenio* October 27, 2005, November 4, 2005, November 8, 2005, November 30, 2005). Soon afterward, the press reported that the International Framework Convention on Tobacco Control had cataloged Mexico as one of the easiest counties for tobacco companies to manipulate, earning it the appellation *"cenicero sucio"* (dirty ashtray) (*Milenio* February 10, 2006).

Vamos México

Vamos México, the charitable foundation created and operated by Mexico's first lady, Marta Sahagún, faced numerous allegations of wrongdoing throughout the Vicente Fox *sexenio*, centering on charges of influence trafficking, mismanagement of funds, and fraud. In 2001, for instance, soon after the establishment of the foundation, opposition senators attacked the use of public funds to support private organizations like Vamos México (*Milenio* November 11, 2001). More high-profile allegations against the first lady for mismanaging the charity's funds first appeared in the Britain-based *Financial Times,* which claimed that Vamos México had inadequately stated its finances and accused the first lady of using her position to promote the foundation. Noting the large amount of donations received by the foundation, many speculated that it was being used to garner political influence with the Fox government. Even the Mexican Conference of Bishops called for an investigation of the foundation (*Milenio* July 1, 2004). Congress, through its Comisión de Vigilancia de Contaduria Mayor de Hacienda—operating through the ASF—conducted numerous audits to investigate influence trafficking, embezzlement, and misuse of public funds, but failed to provide any conclusive evidence of wrongdoing. An official investigation by the attorney general in 2004, carried out at the request of Vamos México and focusing on misuse of funds and fraud in the handling of a lottery, also failed to show any wrongdoing (*Milenio* November 26, 2004). Accusations continued, however, despite official exoneration. Many accused the Fox government of blocking inquiries into the foundation and using it to triangulate funds (*Milenio* January 16, 2006).

Allegations and Investigations of President Fox

Formal allegations and investigations against President Vicente Fox (2000–2006) emerged soon after he left office. The president first attracted attention in an interview with the magazine *Quien,* which documented the extensive improvements to his ranch in Guanajuato and resulted in questions about the source of the funds and the former president's new lavish lifestyle. "The San Cristobal ranch, where paint once peeled from the walls, now boasts expensive furniture, remodeled rooms, a swimming pool and immaculately kept grounds with peacocks and deer" (Garibian 2007). The issue prompted the weekly *Proceso* to devote the cover story of its September 30, 2007, edition to the homes of former presidents. In addition questions about the source of Fox's wealth, concerns were also raised about his involvement in the 2006 election in violation of the electoral law, compounded by statements in which he took credit for the presidential victory of his successor, Felipe Calderon. In response to the intense speculation about corruption, in October 2007 the Chamber of Deputies established a special committee to investigate the allegations against Fox, specifically whether Fox had enriched himself with public money. Allegations included charges that Miguel Moreno Vélez, a businessman who had supplied Fox with a red Jeep free of charge, had been rewarded with a contract from the Vamos México foundation (see Espinosa and Vera 2007; Espinosa 2007a, 2007b; Jáquez 2007; Maza 2007). "Never before has congress investigated a former president so soon after he left office" (Latin American Regional Report, Mexico and NAFTA, December 2007). The congressional investigation, however, was limited to the president only and did not include his family, despite lingering accusations against the first lady and her sons. Fox also faced an investigation by the PGR stemming from formal charges filed by Ricardo Monreal (PRD senator, former governor, and manager of Andrés Manuel López Obrador's presidential campaign) for illicit enrichment

(Latin American Regional Report, Mexico and NAFTA December 2007, 6–7; on corruption involving President Fox, see also Díaz 2007; Zamora Briseño 2007; and Espinosa 2007a, 2007b).

Operación Limpieza

In October 2008, the government arrested over thirty officials from SIEDO, the justice department's special investigations into organized crime, for providing information to the cartel led by Arturo and Alfredo Beltran Leyva in exchange for monthly payments between US$150,000 and US$450,000. The PGR learned about the scheme after an informant who participated in the operation turned himself in at the Mexican Embassy in Washington. The informant, who was quickly entered into the US Witness Protection Program, identified two high-level SIEDO officials as the coordinators of the scheme inside the agency. Those officials—Fernando Rivera Hernandez, senior director of intelligence, and Miguel Colorado Gonzales, general technical director—had been in custody since August. More than a dozen other employees of SIEDO, other agencies of the PGR, the PFP, and Defense were also taken into custody over the course of a month, including Mexico's main liaison officer with Interpol, Ricardo Gutierrez Vargas (*SourceMex* November 5, 2008). Information from the ongoing investigation revealed that drug trafficking organizations had infiltrated law enforcement agencies at the highest levels, seriously compromising government efforts to battle organized crime (Ravelo 2009).

Acronyms

AFA	Agencia Federal Antisecuestros (Federal Antikidnapping Agency)
AFI	Agencia Federal de Investigaciones (Federal Investigation Agency)
AMAID	Academia Mexicana de Auditoria Integral y al Desempeño (Mexican Academy of Integral and Performance Auditing)
ANUIES	Asociación Nacional de Universidades e Instituciones de Educación Superior (National Association of Universities and Institutions of Higher Education)
ASA	Aeropuertos y Servicios Auxiliares (Airport Authority)
ASF	Auditoria Superior de la Federación (Superior Auditing Agency)
BANCOMEXT	Banco Nacional de Comercio Exterior (National Export Bank)
BINLEA	Bureau of International Narcotics and Law Enforcement Affairs (US Department of State)
CANACINTRA	Cámara Nacional de Industria de la Transformación (National Chamber of Manufacturing)
CAPUFE	Caminos y Puentes Federales (Federal Roads and Bridges Agency)
CCE	Consejo Cordinador Empresarial (Coordinating Business Council)
CEE	Centro de Estudios Estratégicos (Center of Strategic Studies, Monterrey Tech)

CEESP	Centro de Estudios Económicos del Sector Privado (Center of Economic Studies of the Private Sector)
CFE	Comisión Federal de Electricidad (Federal Electricity Commission)
CIDE	Centro de Investigación y Docencia Económica (Center for Economic Research and Teaching)
CIRT	Cámara de la Industria de la Radio y la Televisión (National Association of Broadcasters)
CITCC	Comisión Intersecretarial para la Transparencia y el Combate a la Corrupción en la Administración Pública Federal (Intersecretarial Commission for Transparency and the Combating of Corruption)
CNA	Comisión Nacional de Agua (National Water Commission)
CNBV	Comisión Nacional Bancaria y de Valores (National Banking and Securities Commission)
CNC	Confederación Nacional de Campesinos (National Peasant Confederation)
CNDH	Comisión Nacional de Derechos Humanos (National Human Rights Commission)
CONACULTRA	Consejo Nacional para la Cultura y las Artes (National Council of Culture and the Arts)
CONALITEG	Comisión Nacional de Libros de Textos Gratuitos (National Free Textbook Commission)
CONCAMIN	Confederación de Cámaras Industriales (National Confederation of Industrial Chambers)
CONCANACO	Confederación de Cámaras Nacionales de Comercio (National Confederation of Commerce Chambers)
COPARMEX	Confederación Patronal de la República Mexicana (Mexican Employers Confederation)
CROC	Confederación Revolucionaria de Obreros y Campesinos (Revolutionary Confederation of Workers and Peasants)
CTM	Confederación de Trabajadores de Mexico (Confederation of Mexican Workers)
DSF	Dirección Federal de Seguridad (Federal Security Agency)
DSFC	Diagnostico Institucional del Sistema Federal de Control (Institutional Diagnostic Survey of the Federal Control System)
ENCBG	Encuesta Nacional de Corrupción y Buen Gobierno (National Survey of Corruption and Good Government) (Transparencia Mexicana)
ENCUP	Encuesta Nacional de la Cultura Política (National Survey of Political Culture) (SEGOB)

EGDE	Encuesta de Gobernabilidad y Desarrollo Empresarial (Survey of Governability and Business Development)
FEADS	Fiscalía Especializada para la Atención de Delitos Contra la Salud (Special Prosecutor for Drug Crimes)
FEMOSPP	Fiscalía Especializada para Movimientos Sociales y Políticos del Pasado (Special Prosecutor for Social and Political Movements of the Past)
FOBAPROA	Fondo Bancario de Protección al Ahorro (Banking Fund for the Protection of Savings)
IFAI	Instituto Federal de Acceso a la Información (Federal Access to Information Institute)
IFE	Instituto Federal Electoral (Federal Electoral Institute)
IMAI	Instituto Mexicano de Auditores Internos (Mexican Institute of Internal Auditors)
IMEF	Instituto Mexicano de Ejecutivos de Finanzas (Mexican Institute of Finance Executives)
IMSS	Instituto Mexicano de Seguro Social (Mexican Social Security Institute)
INCD	Instituto Nacional para el Combate a las Drogas (National Drug Control Institute)
INEGI	Instituto Nacional de Estadística y Geografía (National Statistical and Geographic Institute)
INM	Instituto Nacional de Migración (National Immigration Institute)
IPAB	Instituto para la Protección al Ahorro Bancario (Institute for the Protection of Bank Savings)
IPADE	Instituto Panamericano de Alta Dirección de Empresa (Panamerican Institute for High Business Direction, Universidad Panamericana)
ISSSTE	Instituto de Seguridad y Servicios Sociales de los Trabajadores del Estado (Social Security and Services Institute for State Workers)
IST	Indicador de Seguimiento para la Transparencia (Indicator of Transparency Compliance)
ITESM	Instituto Tecnológica de Estudios Superiores de Monterrey (Technological Institute of Monterrey; also known as Tec de Monterrey)
ITESO	Instituto Tecnológico y de Estudios Superiores de Occidente (Institute of Technology and Higher Studies of the West)
LAPOP	Latin American Public Opinion Project (Vanderbilt University)
LOTENAL	Lotería Nacional (National Lottery Office)
LyFC	Luz y Fuerza del Centro (state-owned electric company)

NAFTA	North American Free Trade Agreement
MECRI	Mexican Corporate Reputation Index
MIDO	Modelo Integral de Desempeño de Órganos de Vigilancia y Control (Integrated Model of the Work of Oversight and Control Organs)
NGO	nongovernmental organization
OAS	Organization of American States
OECD	Organization for Economic Cooperation and Development
OICs	*órganos internos de control* (internal control organs)
PAN	Partido Acción Nacional (National Action Party)
PEMEX	Petroleos Mexicanos (Mexican petroleum company)
PFP	Policía Federal Preventiva (Federal Preventive Police)
PGR	Procuraduría General de la República (Office of the Attorney General)
PJF	Policía Judicial Federal (Federal Judicial Police)
PRD	Partido de la Revolución Democrática (Party of the Democratic Revolution)
PRI	Partido Revolucionario Institucional (Institutional Revolutionary Party)
PVEM	Partido Verde Ecologista de México (Mexican green party)
SACTEL	Sistema de Atención Telefónica a la Ciudadana (citizen telephone hotline system)
SAT	Servicio de Administración Tributaria (Tax Department)
SEAC	Sistema Electrónico de Atención Ciudadana (citizen electronic hotline system)
SECODAM	Secretaría de la Contraloría y Desarrollo Administrativo (Office of the Comptroller General)
SEDENA	Secretaría de Defensa Nacional (Ministry of Defense)
SEGARPA	Secretaría de Agricultura, Ganadería, Desarrollo Rural, Pesca y Alimentación (Ministry of Agriculture, Cattle, Rural Development, Fishing and Food)
SEGOB	Secretaría de Gobernación (Ministry of Government)
SEMARP	Secretaría de Medio Ambiente, Recursos Naturales y Pesca (Ministry of Environment, Natural Resources, and Fishing)
SEP	Secretaría de Educación Pública (Ministry of Education)
SFP	Secretaría de la Función Pública (Ministry of Public Function)
SHCP	Secretaría de Hacienda y Crédito Público (Ministry of Treasury)
SICS	Sistema Integral de Contraloría Social (Integrated Social Comptroller System)

SISI	Sistema de Solicitudes de Información (IFAI's electronic system for requesting information)
SSP	Secretaría de Seguridad Pública (Ministry of Public Security)
SIEDF	Subprocuraduría de Investigación Especializada en Delitos Federales (Assistant Attorney General for Special Investigations into Federal Crimes)
SIEDO	Subprocuraduría de Investigación Especializada de Delincuencia Organizada (Assistant Attorney General for Special Investigations into Organized Crime)
STPRM	Sindicato de Trabajadores Petroleros de la Republica Mexicana (Mexican Petroleum Workers Union)
TEPJF	Tribunal Electoral del Poder Judicial de la Federación (Federal Electoral Tribunal)
UN	United Nations
UNAM	Universidad Nacional Autonoma de México (National Autonomous University of Mexico)
USAID	US Agency for International Development

References

Ackerman, John M. 2003. "Engaged Autonomy: The Struggle for Accountability in Mexico." Paper presented at the annual meeting of the Latin American Studies Association, Dallas, March 27–29.

———. 2004. "Co-governance for Accountability: Beyond 'Exit' and 'Voice.'" *World Development* 32 (3): 447–463.

———. 2007. Presentation at the seminar "Transparencia, Confianza Ciudadana e Instituciones." Mexico City: Instituto de Acceso a la Información Pública del Distrito Federal (INFODF), October 25–26.

———. 2008. "Conflictos de interés." *Proceso* 1629 (January 20): 53.

Acosta Córdova, C. 1998. "Quebranto por 34,000 millones en Nafin . . ." *Proceso* 1107 (January 18): 36–40.

Acosta Silva, Adrián. 2004. "La corrupción política y sus hogueras." *Nexos: Sociedad, Ciencia, Literatura* 26 (318): 15–21.

Ades, Alberto, and Rafael Di Tella. 1997a. "The Causes and Consequences of Corruption: A Review of Recent Empirical Contributions." *Institute of Development Studies Bulletin* 27: 6–12.

———. 1997b. "The New Economics of Corruption: A Survey and Some New Results." *Political Studies* 45 (3): 465–515.

Adserá, Alicia, Charles Boix, and Mark Payne. 2003. "Are You Being Served? Political Accountability and Quality of Government." *Journal of Law, Economics, and Organization* 19 (2): 445–490.

Aguilar Camín, Héctor. 1990. *Después del Milagro.* Mexico City: Cal y Arena.

———. 2000. "Procuradores de injusticia." *Proceso* 1216 (February 20): 49.

———. 2006. "Introducción el dilema: ¿a dónde vamos?" In *Pensar en México,* José Antonio Aguilar Rivera et al. Mexico City: Fondo de Cultura Económica, 13–18.

Aguilar Rivera, José Antonio. 2006. "El capital social y el estado: algunas aproximaciones al problema." In *Pensar en México,* José Antonio Aguilar Rivera et al. Mexico City: Fondo de Cultura Económica, 91–128.

Aguilar Zinser, Adolfo. 2000. "El combate a la corrupción." *La Reforma,* September 8.

Alcalde, Arturo. 2006. "Transparencia sindical, primeros pasos." *La Jornada,* June 10.

Alducín, Enrique, Agustín Basave, Ulises Beltrán, Santiago Creel, and Fernando Escalante. 1996. "La corrupción: entre la legalidad y las reglas no escritas." *Este País* 66.

Ali, Abdiweli M., and Hodan Said Isse. 2003. "Determinants of Economic Corruption: A Cross-National Comparison." *Cato Journal* 22 (3): 449–466.

Anderson, Christopher J., and Yuliya V. Tverdova. 2003. "Corruption, Political Allegiances, and Attitudes Toward Government in Contemporary Democracies." *American Journal of Political Science* 47 (1): 91–109.

Andvig, Jens C. 2006. "Corruption and Fast Change." *World Development* 34 (2): 328–340.

Andvig, Jens C., and Karl Ove Moene. 1990. "How Corruption May Corrupt." *Journal of Economic Behavior and Organization* 13: 63–76.

Ard, Michael J. 2003. *An Eternal Struggle: How the National Action Party Transformed Mexican Politics.* Westport: Praeger.

Arellano Gault, David. 2007. "Fallas de transparencia: hacia una incorporación efectiva de políticas de transparencia en las organizaciones públicas." DTAP, No. 191. Centro de Investigación y Docencia Económicas (CIDE).

Arellano Gault, David, and Juan Pablo Guerrero Amparán. 2003. "Stalled Administrative Reforms of the Mexican State." In *Reinventing Leviatán: The Politics of Administrative Reform in Developing Countries,* eds. Ben Ross Schneider and Blanca Heredia. Miami, FL: North-South Center, 151–179.

Arellano Trejo, Efrén. 2005. "Impacto de la corrupción en la desconfianza política." Mexico City: Centro de Estudios Sociales y de Opinión Pública, Cámara de Diputados.

Avilés Fabila, René. 2008. "Conaliteg, corrupción de estado bajo la lupa de la prensa." http://casoconaliteg.com/index2.php?do_rtf=1&id=90.

Bailey, Catherine M. 1998. "NGOs Take to Politics: The Role of Non-Governmental Organizations in Mexico's Democratization Effort." Paper presented at the annual meeting of the Latin American Studies Association, Chicago, September 24–26.

Bailey, John. 1994. "Centralism and Political Change in Mexico: The Case of National Solidarity." In *Transforming State-Society Relations in Mexico: The National Solidarity Strategy,* eds. Wayne A. Cornelius, Ann L. Craig, and Jonathan Fox. San Diego: Center for US-Mexican Studies, University of California, 97–119.

———. 2009. "Corruption and Democratic Governability in Latin America: Toward a Map of Types, Arenas, Perceptions, and Linkages." In *Corruption and Democracy in Latin America,* eds. Charles H. Blake and Stephen D. Morris. Pittsburgh: University of Pittsburgh Press.

Bardhan, Pranab. 1997. "Corruption and Development: A Review of Issues." *Journal of Economic Literature* 35: 1320–1346.

———. 2006. "The Economist's Approach to the Problem of Corruption." *World Development* 34 (2): 341–348.

Bedirhanoglu, Pinar. 2007. "The Neoliberal Discourse on Corruption as a Means of Consent Building: Reflections from Post-Crisis Turkey." *Third World Quarterly* 28 (7): 1239–1254.

Beer, Caroline. 2003. *Electoral Competition and Institutional Change in Mexico.* South Bend, IN: University of Notre Dame Press.

———. 2006. "Judicial Performance and the Rule of Law in the Mexican States." *Latin American Politics and Society* 48 (3): 33–61.

Beltran del Rio, P. 1998. "Con una información de cuatro bandas 'The Washington Times' puso en predicamento a Labastida, al gobierno mexicano y a la Casa Blanca." *Proceso* 1110 (February 8): 99–100.

"Bienvenido a la narcopolítica." 2007. *Proceso* 1614 (October 7): 24–27.

BINLEA (Bureau of International Narcotics and Law Enforcement Affairs). 2000, 2002, 2003, 2004, 2005. *International Narcotics Control Strategy Report.* Washington, DC: US State Department.

Blais, André, Joanna Everitt, Patrick Fournier, and Elisabeth Gidengil. 2005. "The Political Psychology of Voters' Reactions to a Corruption Scandal." Paper presented at the annual meeting of American Political Science Association, Washington, DC, August 31–September 3.

Blake, Charles H., and Christopher Martin. 2006. "The Dynamics of Political Corruption: Reexamining the Influence of Democracy." *Democratization* 13 (1):1–13.

Blake, Charles H., and Stephen D. Morris, eds. 2009. *Corruption and Democracy in Latin America.* Pittsburgh: University of Pittsburgh Press.

Blankenburg, Erhard. 2002. "Judicial Anti-Corruption Initiatives: Latin Europe in Global Setting." In *Political Corruption: Concepts and Contexts,* eds. Arnold J. Heidenheimer and Michael Johnston. New Brunswick, NJ: Transaction, 911–924.

Bowler, Shaun, and Jeffrey A. Karp. 2004. "Politicians, Scandals, and Trust in Government." *Political Behavior* 26 (3): 271–287.

Brachet-Marques, Viviane. 1995. *The Dynamics of Domination: State, Class, and Social Reform in Mexico, 1910–1990.* Pittsburgh: University of Pittsburgh Press.

Brown, Ed, and Jonathan Cloke. 2004. "Neoliberal Reform, Governance, and Corruption in the South: Assessing the International Anti-Corruption Crusade." *Antipode* 36 (2): 272–294.

———. 2005. "Neoliberal Reform, Governance, and Corruption in Central America: Exploring the Nicaraguan Case." *Political Geography* 24: 601–630.

Bruhn, Kathleen. 1996. *Taking on Goliath: The Emergence of a New Left Party and the Struggle for Democracy in Mexico.* University Park: Pennsylvania State University Press.

Brunetti, Aymo, and Beatrice Weder. 2003. "A Free Press Is Bad News for Corruption." *Journal of Public Economics* 87 (7–8): 1801–1824.

Burkholder, Mark A., and Lyman L. Johnson. 1994. *Colonial Latin America.* 2nd ed. New York: Oxford University Press.

Caiden, Gerald E. 2001. "Corruption and Democracy." In *Where Corruption Lives,* eds. Gerald E. Caiden, O. P. Dwivedi, and Joseph G. Jabbra. Bloomfield, CT: Kumarian, 227–244.

———. 2004. "A Cautionary Tale: Ten Major Flaws in Combating Corruption." *Southwestern Journal of Law and Trade in the Americas* 10 (2): 101–124.

Caiden, Gerald E., O. P. Dwivedi, and Joseph G. Jabbra, eds. 2001. *Where Corruption Lives.* Bloomfield, CT: Kumarian.

Call, Charles T. 2003. "Democratisation, War, and State-Building: Constructing the Rule of Law in El Salvador." *Journal of Latin American Studies* 35: 827–862.

Cámara de Diputados. 2005. *Boletín* 2601 (September). Mexico City.

Camerer, Marianne, and Jonathan Werve. 2005. "The Public Integrity Index: Assessing Anti-Corruption Architecture." In Transparency International, *Global Corruption Report 2005.* London: Pluto, 252–254.

Camp, Roderic Ai. 2007. *Politics in Mexico: The Democratic Consolidation.* 5th ed. New York: Oxford University Press.

Camp, Roderic Ai, Kenneth Coleman, and Charles Davis. 2000. "Public Opinion About Corruption: An Exploratory Study in Chile, Costa Rica, and Mexico." Paper presented at the annual meeting of the World Association of Public Opinion Research, Portland, May 17–18.

Campbell, Tim. 2003. *The Quiet Revolution: Decentralization and the Rise of Political Participation in Latin American Cities.* Pittsburgh: University of Pittsburgh Press.

Canache, Damarys, and Michael Allison. 2005. "Perceptions of Political Corruption in Latin American Democracies." *Latin American Politics and Society* 47 (3): 91–111.

Carbonell, Miguel. 2004. "When Impunity Is the Rule: The Reform of Mexico's Criminal Justice System." *Voices of Mexico* 68: 7–10.

———. 2007. "Judicial Corruption and Impunity in Mexico." In Transparency International, *Global Corruption Report 2007: Corruption in Judicial Systems.* New York: Cambridge University Press, 225–228.

Carrasco Altamirano, Diódoro. 2008. "El informe de la Suprema Corte." *La Jornada,* December 18.

Casar, Mario Amparo. 2000. "Coaliciones y cohesión partidista en un congreso sin mayoría: La Cámara de Diputados de México, 1997–1999." *Política y Gobierno* 7 (1): 183–202.

Catterberg, Gabriela, and Alejandro Moreno. 2006. "The Individual Bases of Political Trust: Trends in New and Established Democracies." *International Journal of Public Opinion Research* 18: 31–48.

———. 2007. "Particularized Trust, Private Politics, and Corruption in New Democracies: The Experiences of Argentina and Mexico." Paper presented at the WAPOR Latin American Congress, Colonia, Uruguay.

CEE (Centro de Estudios Estratégicos). 2002. "La corrupción gobierno-empresas en México: perspectiva del sector privado." Mexico City.

CEESP (Centro de Estudios Económicos del Sector Privado). 2007. "Encuesta sobre el costo de la regulación par alas empresas en México." May.

Cejudo, Guillermo M., and Laura Sour. 2007. "¿Cuánto cuesta vigilar al gobierno federal?" Mexico City: Centro de Investigación y Docencia Económica (CIDE).

Cervantes, Desusa, and Rosa Santana. 2007. "'Accidentes' por corrupción." *Proceso* 1618 (November 4): 18–20.

Chand, Vikram K. 2001. *Mexico's Political Awakening.* La Jolla, CA: University of Notre Dame Press.

CITCC (Comisión Intersecretarial para la Transparencia y el Combate a la Corrupción). 2002. *Reporte de Avances a la Sociedad, 2001–2002.*

Cleary, Matthew R., and Susan C. Stokes. 2006. *Democracy and the Culture of Skepticism: Political Trust in Argentina and Mexico.* New York: Russell Sage.

Clifton, Judith. 2000a. "On the Political Consequences of Privatisation: The Case of Teléfonos de México." *Bulletin of Latin American Research* 19 (1): 63–79.

———. 2000b. *The Politics of Telecommunications in Mexico: Privatisation and State-Labour Relations, 1982–1995.* London: Macmillan.

Colazingari, Silvia, and Susan Rose-Ackerman. 1998. "Corruption in a Paternalistic Democracy: Lessons from Italy for Latin America." *Political Science Quarterly* 113 (3): 447–470.

Comité de Abogados para los Derechos Humanos. Centro de Derechos Humanos "Miguel Agustín Pro Juárez." 2001. *Injusticia legalizada: procedimiento penal mexicano y derechos humanos.* Mexico City.

Comunicado de Prensa. 2005. "Denuncian red de corrupcion a traves de la cual trabajadores en activo afiliados al ISSSTE estan cobrando el saldo del SAR 92, sin haber cumplido con los requisitos legales." Mexico City.

Consultores Internacionales. 2001. "Estudio sobre honestidad y corrupción" *Este País* 40 (May): 40–44.

Cook, Maria Lorena, Kevin J. Middlebrook, and Juan Molinar Horcasitas. 1994. *The Politics of Economic Restructuring: State-Society Relations and Regime Change in Mexico.* US-Mexico Contemporary Perspectives no. 7. San Diego: Center for US-Mexican Studies, University of California.

Córdova, Loreno, and Ciro Murayama. 2006. *Elecciones, dinero y corrupción: Pemexgate y Amigos de Fox.* Mexico City: Cal y Arena.

Corduneanu, Isabela, Manuel Alejandro Guerrero, and Eduardo Rodríguez-Oreggia. 2004. "Actitudes y percepciones sobre corrupción a través de los 'Cineminutos por la Tranparencia.'" Mexico City: CIE Consulting and Research.

Cornelius, Wayne A. 2002. "La eficacia de la compra y coacción del voto en las elecciones mexicanas de 2000." *Perfiles Latinoamericanos* 20: 11–32.

Cornelius, Wayne A., Todd A. Eisenstadt, and Jane Hindley, eds. 1999. *Subnational Politics and Democratization in Mexico.* San Diego: Center for US-Mexican Studies, University of California.

Cornelius, Wayne A., and David A. Shirk, eds. 2007. *Reforming the Administration of Justice in Mexico.* San Diego: Center for US-Mexican Studies, University of California.

Correa, Hector. 1985. "A Comparative Studies of Bureaucratic Corruption in Latin America and the USA." *Socio-Economic Planning Science* 19 (1): 63–79.

Cossio, José Ramón. 2005. "The Judicial Branch of the Mexican Federation." In *Mexican Governance: From Single-Party Rule to Divided Government,* eds. Armand B. Peschard-Sverdrup and Sara R. Rioff. Washington, DC: Center for Strategic and International Studies, 108–143.

Crespo, José Antonio. 2007. "Cultura política y consolidación democrática (1997–2006)." Mexico City: Centro de Investigación y Docencia Económica (CIDE).

Dahl, Robert A. 1998. *On Democracy.* New Haven: Yale University Press.

Davis, Charles L., Roderic Ai Camp, and Kenneth M. Coleman. 2004. "The Influence of Party-Systems on Citizen's Perceptions of Corruption and Electoral Responses in Latin America." *Comparative Political Studies* 37 (6): 677–703.

Davis, Diane E. 2006. "Undermining Rule of Law: Democratization and the Dark Side of Police Reform in Mexico." *Latin American Politics and Society* 48 (1): 55–86.

Dealy, Glen Caudill. 1992. *The Latin Americas: Spirit and Ethos.* Boulder: Westview.

"Decálogo del marco normativo del derecho de acceso a la información pública." 2004. Mexico City: Libertad de Información México A.C. (LIMAC) and Innovacioin Mexico–Proyecto Atlatl.

Dehesa, Germán. 2002. *"¿Cómo nos arreglamos?": prontuario de la corrupción en México.* Mexico City: Transparencia Mexicana and Editorial Diana.

de la Barreda Solórzano, Luis. 1995. *La lid contra la tortura.* Mexico City: Cal y Arena.

De Speville, B. 1997. *Hong Kong: Policy Initiatives Against Corruption.* Paris: OECD Development Center.

De Swan, M., and Juan Molinar Horcasitas. 2003. "Movimientos graduales y pendulares: transición democrática y dispersión del poder en México." In *Gobernabilidad: Nuevos Actors, Nuevos Desafios,* vol. 2, eds. Alberto Ortega Venzor et al. Mexico City: Editorial Porrúa.

Del Castillo, Arturo. 2003. *Medición de la corrupción: un indicador de la rendición de cuentas.* Mexico City: Auditoría Superior de la Federación.

———. 2004. "Integrity Assessment." In *Global Integrity Report 2004.* Center for Public Integrity. http://www.global integrity.org.

Del Castillo, Arturo, and Manuel Alejandro Guerrero. 2004. "Percepciones de la corrupción en la ciudad de México: ¿predisposición al acto corrupto?" Mexico City: CIE Consulting and Research.

Del Castillo, Arturo, Manuel Alejandro Guerrero, Eduardo Rodríguez-Oreggia, and Eduardo R. Ampudia. 2005. "Indice de Honestidad y Eficiencia en la Generación de Infraestructura Pública: análisis acumulado en la generación de infraestructura pública en los últimos 30 años." Mexico City: CEI Consulting and Research.

Della Porta, Donatella. 2000. "Social Capital, Beliefs in Government, and Political Corruption." In *Disaffected Democracies: What's Troubling the Trilateral Countries?* eds. Susan J. Pharr and Robert D. Putnam. Princeton: Princeton University Press, 202–230.

Della Porta, Donatella, and Alberto Vannucci. 1997. "The 'Perverse Effects' of Political Corruption." *Political Studies* 45: 516–538.

———. 1999. *Corrupt Exchanges: Actors, Resources, and Mechanisms of Political Corruption.* New York: de Gruyter.

DePalma, Anthony. 1996. "How a Tortilla Empire was Built on Favoritism." *New York Times,* February 15.

Di Tella, Raphael, and Ernesto Schargrodsky. 2003. "The Role of Wages and Auditing During a Crackdown on Corruption in the City of Buenos Aires." *Journal of Law and Economics* 46: 269–292.

Díaz, Gloria Leticia. 2007. "El Cancún de los Bribiesca." *Proceso* 1618 (November 4): 6–10.

Díaz-Cayeros, Alberto. 2004. "Decentralization, Democratization, and Federalism in Mexico." In *Dilemmas of Political Change in Mexico,* ed. Kevin J. Middlebrook. London: Institute of Latin American Studies, 198–234.

Doig, Alan, and Robin Theobald, eds. 2000. *Corruption and Democratization.* London: Cass.

Dollar, D., Raymond Fishman, and Roberta Gatti. 1999. "Are Women Really the 'Fairer' Sex? Corruption and Women in Government." Policy Research Working Paper no. 4. Washington, DC: World Bank.

Domingo, Pilar. 2000. "Judicial Independence: The Politics of the Supreme Court in Mexico." *Journal of Latin American Studies* 32: 705–735.

Domínguez, Jorge I., and Chappell Lawson, eds. 2004. *Mexico's Pivotal Democratic Election: Candidates, Voters, and the Presidential Campaign of 2000.* San Diego: Center for US-Mexican Studies.

Downs, Anthony. 1957. *An Economic Theory of Democracy.* New York: Harper.

Dreher, Axel, Christos Kotsogiannis, and Steve McCorriston. 2004. "Corruption Around the World: Evidence from a Structural Model." *Journal of Comparative Economics* 35 (3): 443–466.

Duncan, Nick. 2006. "The Non-Perception Based Measurement of Corruption: A Review of Issues and Methods from a Policy Perspective." In *Measuring Corruption,* ed. Charles Sampford. Burlington: Ashgate, 131–162.

"Early Concerns About Aid to Mexico." 2007. *The Advocate,* October.

Eisenstadt, Todd A. 1999. "Electoral Federalism or Abdication of Presidential Authority? Gubernatorial Elections in Tabasco." In *Subnational Politics and Democratization in Mexico,* eds. Wayne A. Cornelius, Todd A. Eisenstadt, and Jane Hindley. San Diego: Center for US-Mexican Studies, University of California, 269–293.

———. 2004. *Courting Democracy in Mexico: Party Strategies and Electoral Institutions.* New York: Cambridge University Press.

———. 2007. "The Origins and Rationality of the 'Legal Versus Legitimate' Dichotomy Invoked in Mexico's 2006 Post-Electoral Conflict." *PS: Political Science and Politics* 40 (1): 39–43.

Eisenstadt, S. N., and Rene Lemarchand 1981. *Political Clientelism, Patronage, and Development.* New York: Sage.

Eisenstadt, Todd A., and Alejandro Poire. 2005. "Campaign Finance and Playing Field 'Levelness' Issues in the Run-Up to Mexico's July 2006 Presidential Election." San Diego: Center for US-Mexican Studies, University of California, October 4.

Eker, V. 1981. "On the Origins of Corruption: Irregular Incentives in Nigeria." *Journal of Modern African Studies* 19 (1): 173–182.

"El crimen organizado, beneficiado del desmantelamineto de la PJF." 2000. *Proceso* 1261 (December 31): 22.

Elizondo Mayer-Serra, Carlos. 2006. "Democracia y gobernabilidad en México." In *Pensar en México,* José Antonio Aguilar Rivera et al. Mexico City: Fondo de Cultura Económica, 37–90.

"Encuesta Omnibus III." 1995. Bulletin no. 3. Mexico City: Mori de México.

Escalante Gonzalbo, Fernando. 2006. "México, fin de siglo." In *Pensar en México,* José Antonio Aguilar Rivera et al. Mexico City: Fondo de Cultura Económica, 19–36.

Espinosa, Verónica. 2007a. "El José, prosperidad dinástica." *Proceso* 1618 (November 4): 15–17.

———. 2007b. "San Cristóbal como Agualeguas." *Proceso* 1616 (October 21): 14–17.

Espinosa, Verónica, and Rodrigo Vera. 2007. "Horizonte sin límites . . . ," *Proceso* 1612 (September 23): 6–16.

Estévez, Federico, Beatriz Magaloni, and Alberto Díaz-Cayeros. 2002. "A Portfolio Diversification Model of Policy Choice." Paper presented at the conference "Clientelism in Latin America: Theoretical and Comparative Perspectives," Stanford University, May 21–22.

Etzioni-Halevy, Eva. 2002. "Exchanging Material Benefits for Political Support: A Comparative Analysis." In *Political Corruption: Concepts and Contexts,* 3rd ed., eds. Arnold J. Heidenheimer and Michael Johnston. New Brunswick, NJ: Transaction, 233–250.

Evans, Peter, and James E. Rauch. 1999. "Bureaucracy and Growth: A Cross-National Analysis of the Effects of 'Weberian' State Structures on Economic Growth." *American Sociological Review* 64 (5): 748–765.

Ewell, Judith. 1977. "The Extradition of Marcos Pérez Jiménez, 1959–63: Practical Precedent for Enforcement of Administrative Honesty?" *Journal of Latin American Studies* 9 (2): 291–313.

Fabbri, José Miguel. 2002. "Corruption in Bolivia: Reforming the Judiciary System." *CIPE.org Feature Service,* March 13.

Faundes, Juan Jorge. 2002. "Periodimso de investigación en Sudamérica: obstáculos y propuestas." Capitulo Chileno de Transparencia Internacional, Corporación FORJA. http://www.geocites.com/athens/forum/2829/cinep1/libroperinvestigativo.pdf.

Ferriss, Susan. 1998. "Citizens Developing New Intolerance for Corruption, Crime in Mexico." *Cox News Service,* September 13.

Fix-Fierro, Hector. 2003a. "Judicial Reform in Mexico: What Next?" In *Beyond Common Knowledge: Empirical Approaches to the Rule of Law,* eds. Erik G. Jensen and Thomas C. Heller. Palo Alto: Stanford University Press, 240–289.

———. 2003b. "Notes on the Impact of Lawyer Performance on the Administration of Justice in Mexico." San Diego: Center for US-Mexican Studies, University of California.

Fleischer, David. 2002. *Corruption in Brazil: Defining, Measuring, and Reducing.* Washington, DC: Center for Strategic and International Studies.

Fox, Jonathan. 2000. "Assessing Binational Civil Society Coalitions: Lessons from the Mexico-US Experience." Paper presented at the meeting of the Latin American Studies Association, Miami, Florida, March 16–18.

———. 2002. "La relación reciproca entre participación ciudadana y la rendición de cuentas: la experiencia de los Fondos Municipales en el México rural." *Política y Gobierno* 9 (1): 95–133.

———. 2007. *Accountability Politics: Power and Voice in Rural Mexico.* New York: Oxford University Press.

Franco-Barrios, Adrian. 2003. "Building a Transparent and Honest Government in Mexico: Institutional Reforms and Anticorrupcion Policy." http://www.programaanti corrupcion.gob.mx.

Frank, Björn, and Gunther G. Schulze. 1998. "How Tempting Is Corruption? More Bad News About Economists." Working Paper no. 164. http://ssrn.com/abstract=100968.

Galán, José. 2006. "Según un sondeo, en cuatro meses se desplomó la confianza en el IFE." *La Jornada,* November 11.

Galtung, Fredrik. 2001a. "Overview." In *Global Corruption Report 2001.* Berlin: Transparency International, 224–231.

———. 2001b. "Transparency International's Network to Curb Global Corruption." In *Where Corruption Lives,* eds. Gerald E. Caiden, O. P. Dwidedi, and Joseph Jabbra. Bloomfield, CT: Kumarian, 189–206.

García Rojas Castillo, Sandro. 2004. "La lucha contra la corrupción en México: la reforma integral en material de justicia en el marco juridico mexicano frente al reto de la lucha anticorrupción." IX Congreso Internacional del CLAD Sobre la Reforma del Estado y de la Administración Pública, Madrid, November 2–5.

Garduño, Roberto, and Victor Ballinas. 2005. "Hacienda y SFP toleran la impunidad de 'funccionarios corruptos': ASF." *La Jornada,* September 29.

Garibian, Pablo. 2007. "Mexico's Fox Falls from Grace amid Corruption Probe." *Reuters,* October 24.

Garrido, Luis Javier. 1993. *La ruptura: la corriente democratic del PRI.* Mexico City: Grijalbo.

Gatti, Roberta. 2003. "Individual Attitudes Toward Corruption: Do Social Effects Matter?" Policy Research Working Paper no. 3122. Washington, DC: World Bank.

Geddes, Barbara. 1994. *Politician's Dilemma: Building State Capacity in Latin America.* Berkeley: University of California Press.

Geddes, Barbara, and Artur Ribeiro Neto. 1992. "Institutional Sources of Corruption in Brazil." *Third World Quarterly* 13 (4): 641–661.

———. 1998. "Institutional Sources of Corruption in Brazil." In *Corruption and Political Reform in Brazil: The Impact of Collor's Impeachment,* eds. Keith S. Rosenn and Richard Downes. Boulder: Lynne Rienner, 21–48.

Gentleman, Judith, ed. 1987. *Mexican Politics in Transition.* Boulder: Westview Press.

Gerring, John, and Strom C. Thacker. 2004. "Political Institutions and Corruption: The Role of Unitarism and Parliamentarism." *British Journal of Political Science* 34: 295–330.

Gibson, Charles. 1966. *Spain in America.* New York: Harper and Row.

Gingerich, Daniel W. 2007. "Corruption and Political Decay: A Causal Analysis Based on the Bolivian Case." Unpublished manuscript.

Global Integrity. 2004. "Mexico: Corruption Timeline." In *Global Integrity Report 2004.* http://www.globalintegrity.org/reports/2004/2004/countryb937.html?cc=mx&act=timeline.

———. 2006. "Mexico: Corruption Timeline." In *Global Integrity Report 2006.* http://www.globalintegrity.org/reports/2006/Mexico/index.cfm.

Goldsmith, Arthur A. 1999. "Slapping the Grasping Hand: Correlates of Political Corruption in Emerging Markets." *American Journal of Economics and Sociology* 58 (4): 865–883.

Gómez Tagle, Silvia. 1987. "Democracy and Power in Mexico: The Meaning of Conflict in the 1979, 1982, and 1985 Federal Elections." In *Mexican Politics in Transition,* ed. Judith Gentleman. Boulder: Westview Press, 153–180.

———. 2004. "Public Institutions and Electoral Transparency in Mexico." In *Dilemmas of Political Change in Mexico,* ed. Kevin J. Middlebrook. London: Institute of Latin American Studies, 82–107.

González-Aréchiga, Bernardo. 2007. "Corrupción y Fallas de Estado: Respuestas Estratégicas para una Buena Gobernanza." Presentation at the seminar "Transparencia, Confianza Ciudadana e Instituciones." Mexico City: Instituto de Acceso a la Información Pública del Distrito Federal (INFODF), October 25–26.

González Compeán, Miguel. 2006. "Justicia o legalidad: el discurso revolucionario y la descomposición de las reglas escritas." In *Pensar en México,* José Antonio Aguilar Rivera et al. Mexico City: Fondo de Cultura Económica, 278–324.

González-Fabre, R. 1996. "Las estructuras culturales de la corrupción en Venezuela." In *Eficiencia, corrupción y crecimiento con equidad,* eds. Aula Abierta de Ética. Bilbao, Spain: Universidad de Deusto.

Graeff, P., and G. Mehlkop. 2003. "The Impact of Economic Freedom on Corruption: Different Patterns for Rich and Poor Countries." *European Journal of Political Economy* 19 (3): 605–621.

Granados Chapa, Miguel Ángel. 2007. "Tabasco: el capitalism salvaje en vivo." *Proceso* 1618 (November 4): 62–63.

Grayson, George. 1998. *Mexico: Corporatism to Pluralism.* Ft. Worth, TX: Harcourt Brace.

Greene, Kenneth. 2007. *Why Dominant Parties Lose: Mexico's Democratization in Comparative Perspective.* New York: Cambridge University Press.

Guerrero, Isabel, Luis Felipe López-Calva, and Michael Walton. 2006. "The Inequality Trap and Its Links to Low Growth in Mexico." Paper presented at World Bank–Harvard Rockefeller Center conference on equity and growth in Mexico, Mexico City, November 27–28.

Guerrero, Manuel Alejandro. 2004. *México: la paradoja de su democracia.* Mexico City: Universidad Iberoamericana and CEI Consulting and Research.

Guerrero, Manuel Alejandro, and Eduardo Rodríguez-Oreggia. 2008. "On the Individual Decisions to Commit Corruption: A Methodological Complement." *Journal of Economic Behavior and Organization* 65 (2): 357–372.

Guerrero Gutiérrez, Eduardo. 2002. "La reinvención del gobierno en la transición democrática: rendición de cuentas en la administración pública de México." VII Congreso Internacional del CLAD Sobre la Reforma del Estado y de la Administración Pública, Lisbon, October 8–11.

Gutiérrez, Alejandro. 2001. "La familia feliz del zar anticorrupción." *Proceso* 1266 (February 4): 16.

Gutiérrez Viggers, Leticia H., and Claudia B. Cano López de Nava. 2004. "Hacía una gestión gubernamental ética para combatir la corrupción." IX Congreso Internacional del CLAD Sobre la Reforma del Estado y de la Administración Pública, Madrid, November 2–5.

Gutiérrez Vivó, J. ed. 1998. *El otro yo del mexicano.* Mexico City: Oceano.

Guzmán, Armando, 2007. "Negligencia criminal." *Proceso* 1618 (November 4): 37–41.

Hágalo usted mismo: su caja de herramientas contra la corrupción. Mexico City. http://www.hagalouestedmismo.gob.mx.

Hagopian, Frances. 2005. "Conclusions: Government Performance, Political Participation, and Public Perceptions of Contemporary Democracy in Latin America." In *The Third Wave of Democratization in Latin America: Advances and Setbacks,* eds. Frances Hagopian and Scott P. Mainwaring. Cambridge: Cambridge University Press, 319–362.

Haro Bélchez, Guillermo. 1998. "La lucha contra la corrupción en México." Foro Iberoamericano Sobre el Combate a la Corrupción, Santa Cruz de la Sierra, June 15–16.

Heidenheimer, Arnold J. ed. 1970. *Political Corruption: Readings in Comparative Analysis.* New York: Holt, Rinehart, and Winston.

Hetherington, Marc. 1998. "The Political Relevance of Political Trust." *American Political Science Review* 92 (4): 791–808.

Hill, Kim Quaile. 2003. "Democratization and Corruption." *American Politics Research* 31 (6): 613–632.

Hill Mayoral, Benjamín G. 2005. "Génesis y retos del servicio profesional de carrera en México." *Bien Común* 125 (May): 31–34.

Hiskey, Jonathan T. 2003. "Political Entrepreneurs and Neoliberal Reform in Mexico: The Salinas Requisa of the Port of Veracruz." *Latin American Politics and Society* 45 (2): 105–132.

Hiskey, Jonathan T., and Shaun Bowler. 2005. "Local Context and Democratization in Mexico." *American Journal of Political Science* 49 (1): 57–71.

Hochstetler, Kathryn. 2005. "Rethinking Presidentialism: Challenges and Presidential Falls in South America." Paper presented at the annual meeting of the American Political Science Association, Washington, DC, August 31–September 3.

Hofbauer, Helena. 2005. "Latin American Index of Budget Transparency." In Transparency International, *Global Corruption Report 2005*. London: Pluto, 278–281.

———. 2006. "Citizens Audit in Mexico Reveals Paper Trail of Corruption." In *Global Corruption Report 2006*. Berlin: Transparency International, 43–45.

Hooper, John. 1995. *The New Spaniards*. London: Penguin.

Hopkins, Jack W. 1969. "Comparative Observations on Peruvian Bureaucracy." *Journal of Comparative Administration* 1: 301–320.

———. 1974. "Contemporary Research on Public Administration and Bureaucracies in Latin America." *Latin American Research Review* 9: 109–139.

Hughes, Sallie. 2006. *Newsrooms in Conflict: Journalism and the Democratization of Mexico*. Pittsburgh: University of Pittsburgh Press.

Human Rights Watch. 1999. *Abuso y desamparo: tortura, desaparición forzada y ejecución extrajudicial en México*. Mexico City.

Huntington, Samuel P. 1991. "How Countries Democratize." *Political Science Quarterly* 106 (4): 579–617.

Husted, Bryan W. 1999. "Wealth, Culture, and Corruption." *Journal of International Business Studies* 30 (2): 339–360.

———. 2002. "Culture and International Anti-Corruption Agreements in Latin America." *Journal of Business Ethics* 37: 413–422.

Idalia Gómez, María. 2001. "La corrupción en el gobierno de Albores." *Milenio,* August 13.

IFAI (Instituto Federal de Acceso a la Información). 2007. *Estudio comparativo de leyes de acceso a la información pública*. Mexico City. http://www.ifai.org.mx/test/eym/estudio_comparativo.pdf

Inclán Oseguera, Silvia. 2004. "Judicial Reform and Democratization: Mexico in the 1990s." PhD diss., Boston University.

"Indice Latinoamericano de Transparencia Presupuestaria." 2005. http://www.fundar.org.mx/indice2005.

Jáquez, Antonio. 2007. "El arte del embuste." *Proceso* 1613 (September 30): 12–15.

Johnston, Michael. 1986. "Right and Wrong in American Politics: Popular Conceptions of Corruption." *Polity* 18 (3): 367–391.

———. 1996. "The Search for Definitions: The Vitality of Politics and the Issue of Corruption." *International Social Science Journal* 149: 321–335.

———. 1998. "Corruption and Democracy: Threats to Development, Opportunities for Reform." Subsequently published as "Corruption et démocratie: menaces pour le développement, possibilités de réforme." *Revue Tiers Monde* 161 (January–March 2000): 117–142.

———. 2000. "It Is Possible to Measure Corruption, But Can We Measure Reform?" Subsequently published as "Es possible medir la corrupción: ¿pero podemos medir la reforma?" *Revista Mexicana de Sociología* 2 (2005): 229–269.

———. 2002. "Right and Wrong in American Politics: Popular Conceptions of Corruption." In *Political Corruption: Concepts and Contexts*, eds. A. J. Heidenheimer and M. Johnston. New Brunswick, NJ: Transaction Publishers, 173–194.

———. 2005. *Syndromes of Corruption: Wealth, Power and Democracy*. New York: Cambridge University Press.

Jordan, Mary. 2001. "Mexico Fights Broad Customs Corruption." *Washington Post Foreign Service,* April.

Juárez Aldan, César Vladímir. 2006. "Análisis de las percepciones sobre instituciones, corrupción y transparencia: una perspectiva de la Función Pública de México." Master's thesis, Instituto de Investigaciones Dr. José María Luis Mora, Univeridad Nacional Autónoma de México.

Juárez González, Leticia. 2004. "¿Tenemos remedio en asuntos de corrupción e impunidad?" *Nexos,* June.

Kaufmann, Daniel, Aart Kraay, and Pablo Zoido-Lobaton. 1999. "Governance Matters." Policy Research Working Paper no. 2196. Washington, DC: World Bank.

Kaufmann, Daniel, Aart Kraay, and Massimo Mastruzzi. 2002. "Governance matters II: Updated indicators for 2000/01." Policy Research Working Paper 2772. The World Bank Development Research Group and World Bank Institute Governance, Regulation and Finance Division.

———. 2003. "Governance Matters III: Governance Indicators for 1996–2003." Policy Research Working Paper no. 3106. Washington, DC: World Bank.

———. 2006. "Measuring Governance Using Cross-Country Perceptions Data." In *International Handbook on the Economics of Corruption,* ed. Susan Rose-Ackerman. Cheltenham: Elgar.

———. 2008. "Governance Matters VII: Governance Indicators for 1996–2007." Washington, DC: World Bank.

Kaufmann, Daniel, and Shang Jin Wei. 1999. "Does 'Grease Money' Speed Up the Wheels of Commerce?" Working Paper no. 7093. Washington, DC: National Bureau of Economic Research.

Keck, Margaret, and Kathryn Sikkink. 1998. *Activists Beyond Borders.* Itahaca: Cornell University Press.

Kite, Eric, and Margaret Sarles. 2006. "Survey Research Sheds Light on Latin Americans' Experience with Corruption." In Transparency International, *Global Corruption Report 2005.* London: Pluto, 350–353.

Kitschelt, Herbert, Zdenka Mansfeldova, and Radoslaw Markowski. 1999. *Post–Communist Party Systems: Competition, Representation, and Inter-Party Cooperation.* Cambridge: Cambridge University Press.

Klesner, Joseph L. 2001. "Legacies of Authoritarianism: Political Attitudes in Chile and Mexico." In *Citizen Views of Democracy in Latin America,* ed. Roderic Ai Camp. Pittsburgh: University of Pittsburgh Press, 118–138.

Klitgaard, Robert. 1988. *Controlling Corruption.* Berkeley: University of California Press.

Klitgaard, Robert E., Ronald Maclean-Abaroa, and H. Lindsey Parris. 2000. *Corrupt Cities: A Practical Guide to Cure and Prevention.* Richmond, CA: Institute for Contemporary Studies.

Knack, S. 2006. *Measuring Corruption in Eastern Europe and Central Asia: A Critique of the Cross-Country Indicators.* Washington, DC: World Bank.

Knight, Alan. 1996. "Corruption in Twentieth Century Mexico." In *Political Corruption in Europe and Latin America,* eds. Walter Little and Eduardo Posada-Carbó. London: Institute of Latin American Studies, 219–236.

———. 2001. "Polls, Political Culture, and Democracy: A Heretical Historical Look." In *Citizen Views of Democracy in Latin America,* ed. Roderic Ai Camp. Pittsburgh: University of Pittsburgh Press, 223–242.

Kossick, Robert. 2004. "The Rule of Law and Development in Mexico." *Arizona Journal of International and Comparative Law* 21 (3): 715–834.

Kossick, Robert M., Jr., and Rubén Minutti Z. 2007. "Citizen Access and Professional Responsibility in the Mexican Justice System." In *Reforming the Administration of Justice in Mexico,* eds. Wayne A. Cornelius and David A. Shirk. San Diego: Center for US-Mexican Studies, University of California, 299–322.

Kruckeberg, Katerina Tsetsura, and Frank Ovaitt. 2005. "Global Index of Bribery for News Coverage." In Transparency International, *Global Corruption Report 2005.* London: Pluto, 258–261.

Kunicová, J., and Susan Rose-Ackerman. 2005. "Electoral Rules and Constitutional Structure as Constraints on Corruption." *British Journal of Political Science* 35: 573–606.

Kurtzman, Joel, and Glenn Yago. 2008. *Opacity Index 2007–2008: Measuring Global Business Risks.* Santa Monica, CA: Milken Institute.

La Palombara, Joseph. 1994. "Structural and Institutional Aspects of Corruption." *Social Research* 61 (2): 325–350.

La Porta, Rafael, Florencio López-de-Silanes, Andrei Shleifer and Robert W. Vishny. 1997. "Trust in Large Organizations." *American Economic Review: Papers and Proceedings* 87 (2): 333–338.

———. 1999. "The Quality of Government." *Journal of Economics, Law, and Organization* 15 (1): 222–279.

Laffont, Jean-Jacques, and Tchetche N'Guessan. 1999. "Competition and Corruption in an Agency Relationship." *Journal of Development Economics* 60 (20): 271–296.

Lambsdorff, Johann Graf. 1999. "Corruption in Empirical Research: A Review." Berlin: Transparency International, November.

———. 2000. "The Precision and Regional Comparison of Perceived Levels of Corruption: Interpreting the Results." Background paper to the 2000 Corruption Perceptions Index. Berlin: Transparency International.

———. 2002. "Framework Document 2002." Berlin: Transparency International, July.

———. 2005. "Corruption Perceptions Index 2004." In Transparency International, *Global Corruption Report 2005.* London: Pluto, 233–238.

Lane, Jan-Erik. 2000. *New Public Management.* London: Routledge.

Langston, Joy. 2006. "The Birth and Transformation of the *Dedazo* in Mexico." In *Informal Institutions and Democracy: Lessons from Latin America,* eds. Gretchen Helmke and Steven Levitsky. Baltimore: Johns Hopkins University Press, 143–159.

LAPOP (Latin American Public Opinion Project). 2004. *The Political Culture of Democracy in Mexico: Mexico in Times of Electoral Competition.* Nashville, TN: Vanderbilt University Press.

Laufer, Peter. 2004. *Wetback Nation: The Case for Opening the Mexican-American Border.* Chicago: Ivan R. Dee.

Lawson, Chappell H. 2002. *Building the Fourth Estate: Democratization and the Rise of a Free Press in Mexico.* Berkeley: University of California Press.

Lederman, Daniel, Norman V. Loayza, and Rodrigo R. Soares. 2005. "Accountability and Corruption: Political Institutions Matter." *Economics and Politics* 17 (1): 1–35.

Lehoucq, Fabrice. 2003. "Electoral Fraud: Causes, Types, and Consequences." *Annual Review of Political Science* 6: 233–256.

———. 2007. "Why Is Structural Reform Stagnating in Mexico? Policy Reform Episodes from Salinas to Fox." Paper presented at the annual meeting of the American Political Science Association, Chicago, August 30–September 2.

Lemarchand, Rene. 1972. "Political Clientelism and Ethnicity in Tropical Africa: Competing Solidarities in Nation-Building." *American Political Science Review* 66: 68–90.

Levi, Margaret. 1996. "Social and Unsocial Capital: A Review Essay of Robert Putnam's *Making Democracy Work.*" *Politics and Society* 24 (1): 45–55.

Lipset, Seymour Martin, and Gabriel Salman Lenz. 2000. "Corruption, Culture, and Markets." In *Culture Matters: How Values Shape Human Progress,* eds. Samuel P. Huntington and Lawrence Harrison. New York: Basic, 112–124.

Little, Walter, and Antonio Herrera. 1996. "Political Corruption in Venezuela." In *Political Corruption in Europe and Latin America,* eds. Walter Little and Eduardo Posada-Carbó. London: Institute of Latin American Studies, 267–285.

"Llega a labastida la sombra." 1998. *Proceso* 1110 (February 8): 66–72.

Loaeza, Soledad. 1999. *El partido acción nacional: la larga marcha, 1939–1994.* Mexico City: Fondo de Cultura Económico.

Lomnitz, Claudio. 1995. "Ritual, Rumor, and Corruption in the Constitution of Politics in Modern Mexico." *Journal of Latin American Anthropology* 1 (1): 20–47.

López, Jaime. 2002. "Acceso a la información pública en el combate a la corrupción." *Atatl* 3 (June): 3–5.

López-Ayllón, Sergio, and Hector Fix-Fierro. 2003. "'Faraway, So Close!' The Rule of Law and Legal Change in Mexico, 1970–2000." In *Legal Culture in the Age of Globalization: Latin America and Europe,* eds. Lawrence M. Friedman and Rogelio Pérez. Palo Alto: Stanford University Press, 285–351.

López-Cálix, José R., Mitchell A. Seligson, and Lorena Alcázar. 2009. "Does Local Accountability Work? Tracing 'Leakages' in the Peruvian 'Vaso de leche' Program." In *Corruption and Democracy in Latin America,* eds. Charles H. Blake and Stephen D. Morris. Pittsburgh: University of Pittsburgh Press.

López de Nava, Claudia Berenice Cano, and Leticia Hortensia Gutiérrez Viggers. 2004. "Efectos de la corrupción en el control de gestión en departamentos de instituciones públicas." IX Congreso Internacional del CLAD Sobre la Reforma del Estado y de la Administración Pública, Madrid, November 2–5.

López Presa, José Octavio, ed. 1998. *Corrupción y cambio.* Mexico City: Fondo de Cultura Económica.

Loria, Cecilia. 2001. "La transparencia de vida, transparencia vivida" *Para Leer Sobre Transparencia* 3 (September–October): 5.

Lozano Gracia, Antonio. 2001. *La fuerza de las instituciones: poder, justicia y seguridad pública en México.* Mexico City: Editorial Planeta Mexicana.

Luken Garza, Gastón, and Virgilio Muñoz. 2003. *Escenarios de la transición en México.* Mexico City: Editorial Grijalbo.

Luna, Matilde. 2004. "Business and Politics in Mexico." In *Dilemmas of Political Change in Mexico,* ed. Kevin J. Middlebrook. London: Institute of Latin American Studies, 332–352.

Mabry, Donald J. 1973. *Mexico's Acción Nacional: A Catholic Alternative to Revolution.* Syracuse, NY: Syracuse University Press.

Magaloni, Beatriz. 2003. "Authoritarianism, Democracy, and the Supreme Court: Horizontal Exchange and the Rule of Law in Mexico." In *Democratic Accountability in Latin America,* eds. Scott Mainwaring and Christopher Welna. New York: Oxford University Press, 266–305.

———. 2006. *Voting for Autocracy: Hegemonic Party Survival and Its Demise in Mexico.* New York: Cambridge University Press.

Magaloni, Beatriz, and Guillermo Zepeda. 2004. "Democratization, Judicial and Law Enforcement Institutions, and the Rule of Law in Mexico." In *Dilemmas of Political Change in Mexico,* ed. Kevin J. Middlebrook. London: Institute of Latin American Studies, 168–197.

Mainwaring, Scott, and Matthew Soberg Shugart. 1997. "Conclusion: Presidentialism and the Party System." In *Presidentialism and Democracy in Latin America,* eds. Scott Mainwaring and Matthew Soberg Shugart. New York: Cambridge University Press, 394–439.

Mainwaring, Scott, and Christopher Welna, eds. 2003. *Democratic Accountability in Latin America.* New York: Oxford University Press.

Manion, Melanie. 2004. *Corruption by Design: Building Clean Government in Mainland China and Hong Kong.* Cambridge: Harvard University Press.

Manzetti, Luigi. 1994. "Economic Reform and Corruption in Latin America." *North South Issues* 3 (1): 1–6.

Manzetti, Luigi, and Charles Blake. 1996. "Market Reforms and Corruption in Latin America." *Review of International Political Economy* 3 (4): 662–697.

Manzetti, Luigi, and Carole Wilson. 2006. "Understanding the Nexus of Corruption, Economic Satisfaction, and Confidence in Government." *The Latin Americanist* 49 (2): 131–139.

———. 2009. "Why Do Corrupt Governments Maintain Public Support?" In *Corruption and Democracy in Latin America*, eds. Charles H. Blake and Stephen D. Morris. Pittsburgh: University of Pittsburgh Press.

Martínez, José. 2004. *CONALITEG–Vamos México: Corrupción de estado, el peón de la reina.* Mexico City: Benemerita Universidad Autónoma de Puebla.

Martínez Miranda, Marisela. 2000. "Rendición de cuentas y fiscalización del gasto público." Paper presented at the conference "Aportes para fundamentar el análisis y las propuestas sobre presupuesto y rendición de cuentas en México," Mexico City, September 28.

Martínez Puón, Rafael. 2002. "Las políticas de la OCDE en la reforma de la administración pública y la lucha contra la corrupción en México." VII Congreso Internacional del CLAD Sobre la Reforma del Estado y de la Administración Pública, Lisbon, October 8–11.

Mauceri, Philip. 2003. "Globalization, Social Capital, and Democracy: The Andean Region in Comparative Perspective." Paper presented at the annual meeting of the American Political Science Association, Philadelphia, August 27–31.

Mauro, Paolo. 1995. "Corruption and Growth." *Quarterly Journal of Economics* 110: 681–712.

———. 1997. "The Effects of Corruption on Growth, Investment, and Government Expenditure: A Cross-Country Analysis." In *Corruption and the Global Economy,* ed. Kimberly A. Elliott. Washington, DC: Institute for International Economics, 83–107.

Maza, Enrique. 2007. "El rancho de Fox y su dolorida justificación." *Proceso* 1613 (September 30): 14–15.

McCann, James A., and Jorge I. Domínguez. 1998. "Mexicans React to Political Corruption and Electoral Fraud: An Assessment of Public Opinion and Voting Behavior." *Electoral Studies* 17 (4): 483–504.

McFarlane, Anthony. 1996. "Political Corruption and Reform in Bourbon Spanish America. In *Political Corruption in Europe and Latin America,* eds. Walter Little and Eduardo Posada-Carbó. London: Institute of Latin American Studies, 41–64.

Meier, Kenneth J., and Thomas M. Holbrook. 1992. "I Seen My Opportunities and I Took 'Em." *Journal of Politics* 54: 135–155.

Mendoza López, Alberto A., Alfonso Moreno García, and Dante Acevo Anonales. 2005. "Las responsabilidades administrativas de los servidores públicos." *Bien Común* 125 (May).

Merino, Mauricio. 2007. "The Challenge of Transparency: A Review of the Regulations Governing Acccess to Public Information in Mexican States." In *Evaluating Accountability and Transparency in Mexico: National, Local, and Comparative Perspectives,* eds. Alejandra Ríos Cázares and David A. Shirk. San Diego: University Readers, 19–66.

Michener, Greg. 2005. "Engendering Political Commitment: The *Grupo Oaxaca*—Expertise, Media Projection—and the Elaboration of Mexico's Access to Information

Law." Paper presented at the annual meeting of the Southern Political Science Association, New Orleans, January 7–9.

Middlebrook, Kevin, ed. 2001. *Party Politics and the Struggle for Democracy in Mexico: National and State-Level Analyses of the Partido Accion Nacional.* San Diego: Center for US-Mexican Studies, University of California.

———. 2004. *Dilemmas of Political Change in Mexico.* London: Institute of Latin American Studies.

Miller, Arthur H., and Ola Listhaug. 1999. "Political Performance and Institutional Trust." In *Critical Citizens: Global Support for Democratic Governance,* ed. Pippa Norris. New York: Oxford University Press, 204–216.

Miller, Rory. 1996. "Foreign Capital, the State, and Political Corruption in Latin America Between Independence and the Depression." In *Political Corruption in Europe and Latin America,* eds. Walter Little and Eduardo Posada-Carbó. London: Institute of Latin American Studies, 65–95.

Miller, William L. 2006. "Corruption and Corruptibility." *World Development* 34 (2): 371–380.

Mishra, Ajit. 2006. "Persistence of Corruption: Some Theoretical Perspectives." *World Development* 34 (2): 349–358.

Mitchell, Kenneth Edward. 2001. *State-Society Relations in Mexico: Clientelism, Neoliberal Reform, and the Case of Conasupo.* Burlington: Ashgate.

———. 2005. "Building State Capacity: Reforming Mexican State Food Aid Programmes in the 1990s." *Oxford Development Studies* 33 (3–4): 377–389.

Mizrahi, Yemile. 2003. *From Martyrdom to Power: The Partido Acción Nacional in Mexico.* South Bend, IN: University of Notre Dame Press.

Mocan, Naci. 2004. "What Determines Corruption? International Evidence from Micro Data." Working Paper no. 10460. Washington, DC: National Bureau of Economic Research.

Molinar Horcasitas, Juan. 1991. *El tiempo de la legitimidad.* Mexico City: Cal y Arena.

Monge, Raúl. 1998. "En el gobierno de Espinosa en el DF hubo corrupción y caos administrativo." *Proceso* 1110 (February 8): 33–35.

Monge, Raúl, and Ricardo Ravelo. 2001. "La corrupción, asunto de seguridad nacional." *Proceso* 1275 (April 8): 28.

Montinola, Gabriella R., and Robert W. Jackman. 2002. "Sources of Corruption: A Cross-Country Study." *British Journal of Political Science* 32 (1): 147–170.

Moore, Molly. 1998. "The Pen May Be Mighty, But in Mexico It Gets Bodyguards." *Washington Post,* September 7.

Morales, Cesareo. 2001. "Los costos de la corrupción." *El Economista,* April 29.

Moreno, Alejandro. 2002. "Corruption and Democracy: A Cultural Assessment." *Comparative Sociology* 1 (3–4): 495–507.

Moreno-Jaimes, Carlos. 2007. "Do Competitive Elections Produce Better-Quality Governments? Evidence from Mexican Municipalities, 1990–2000." *Latin American Research Review* 42 (2): 136–153.

Morris, Stephen D. 1987. "Corruption and the Mexican Political System." *Corruption and Reform* 2: 3–15.

———. 1991. *Corruption and Politics in Contemporary Mexico.* Tuscaloosa: University of Alabama Press.

———. 1995. *Political Reformism in Mexico.* Boulder: Lynne Rienner.

———. 1999. "Corruption and the Mexican Political System: Continuity and Change." *Third World Quarterly* 20 (3): 623–643.

———. 2003. "Corruption and Mexican Political Culture." *Journal of the Southwest* 45 (4): 671–708.

————. 2008. "Disaggregating Corruption: A Comparison of Participation and Perceptions in Latin America with a Focus on Mexico." *Bulletin of Latin American Research* 27 (3): 388–409.

————. 2009. "Corruption and Democracy at the State Level in Mexico." In *Corruption and Democracy in Latin America,* eds. Charles H. Blake and Stephen D. Morris. Pittsburgh: University of Pittsburgh Press.

Morris, Stephen D., and Joseph L. Klesner. Forthcoming. "Corruption and Trust: Theoretical Considerations and Evidence from Mexico." *Comparative Politics Studies.*

Muller, Edward N., and Mitchell A. Seligson. 1994. "Civic Culture and Democracy: The Question of Causal Relationships." *American Political Science Review* 88 (3): 635–653.

Nacif, Benito. 2004. "Las relaciones entre los poderes ejecutivo y legislativo en México tras el fin del presidencialismo." *Política y Gobierno* 11 (1): 9–41.

————. 2005. "Congress Proposes and the President Disposes." In *Mexican Governance: From Single-Party Rule to Divided Government,* eds. Armand B. Peschard-Sverdrup and Sara R. Rioff. Washington, DC: Center for Strategic and International Studies, 1–26.

"Narcopartidismo 'militante.'" 2007. *Proceso* 1614 (October 7): 32–34.

Nef, Jorge. 2001. "Government Corruption in Latin America." In *Where Corruption Lives,* eds. Gerald E. Caiden, O. P. Dwidedi, and Joseph Jabbra. Bloomfield, CT: Kumarian, 159–173.

Nieto, Francisco. 2004. "Demitificando la corrupción en América Latina." *Nueva Sociedad* 194: 54–68.

Noonan, John T. 1984. *Bribes.* New York: Macmillan.

Nye, Joseph S. 1967. "Corruption and Political Development: A Cost-Benefit Analysis." *American Political Science Review* 61: 417–427.

OAS (Organization of American States). 2004, 2005, 2006. *Report to the OAS Committee of Experts.* Washington, DC.

Ochoa León, Sara María. 2005. "Corrupción y contrabando en el sector textil en México." Thematic Report no. 5. Mexico City: Cámara de Diputados, September.

O'Donnell, Guillermo. 1994. "Delegative Democracy." *Journal of Democracy* 5 (1): 55–69.

————. 1998. "Horizontal Accountability in New Democracies." *Journal of Democracy* 9 (3): 112–127.

————. 2003. "Horizontal Accountability: The Legal Institutionalization of Mistrust." In *Democratic Accountability in Latin America,* eds. Scott Mainwaring and Christopher Welna. New York: Oxford University Press, 34–54.

OECD (Organization for Economic Cooperation and Development). 2000. *Trust in Government Ethics Measures in OECD Countries.* Paris.

Oldenburg, Philip. 1987. "Middlemen in Third World Corruption: Implications of an Indian Case." *World Politics* 39 (4): 508–535.

Olivera Prado, Mario. 2003. "Corrupciómetro internacional, hacia una nueva medición objetiva de la corrupción." *Revista Probidad* 24 (September).

Olvera, Alberto J. 1997. "Civil Society and Political Transition in Mexico." *Constellations* 4 (1): 105–123.

"100 jueces bajo investigación." 2006. *Milenio Semanal,* January 16.

Padgett, Humberto. 2002. "Reina corrupción en verificentros." *La Reforma,* October 1.

Paldam, Martin. 2002. "The Cross-Country Pattern of Corruption: Economics, Culture, and the Seesaw Dynamics." *European Journal of Political Economy* 18 (2): 215–240.

Panizza, Ugo. 2001. "Electoral Systems, Political Systems, and Institutional Quality." *Economics and Politics* 13 (3): 311–342.

Parametria. 2004. "La corrupción en las vialidades del DF." Mexico City. http://www
.parametria.com.mx/escartaprint.php?id_carta=27.

Parás, Pablo. 2007. "Unweaving the Social Fabric: The Impact of Crime on Social Capital." In *Reforming the Administration of Justice in Mexico,* eds. Wayne A. Cornelius and David A. Shirk. San Diego: Center for US-Mexican Studies, University of California, 323–348.

Pardinas, Juan E. 2007. "Felipe Fox y la sociedad civil." *Reforma,* July 15.

Paternostro, Silvana. 1995. "Mexico as a Narco-Democracy." *World Policy Journal* 12 (1): 41–47.

"Percepciones de la población de la Zona Metropolitana de Guadalajara." 2002. Guadalajara: Centro de Estudios Estratégicos para el Desarrollo, Universidad de Guadalajara, July.

Persson, Torsten, Guido Tabellini, and Francesco Trebbi. 2003. "Electoral Rules and Corruption." *Journal of the European Economic Association* 1 (4): 958–989.

Peruzzotti, Enrique, and Catalina Smulovitz, eds. 2006. *Enforcing the Rule of Law: Social Accountability in the New Latin American Democracies.* Pittsburgh: University of Pittsburgh Press.

Peschard-Sverdrup, Armand B., and Sara R. Rioff, eds. 2005. *Mexican Governance: From Single-Party Rule to Divided Government.* Washington, DC: Center for Strategic and International Studies.

Peters, John G., and Susan Welch. 1980. "The Effect of Charges of Corruption on Voting Behavior in Congressional Elections." *American Political Review* 74: 697–708.

Pharr, Susan J. 2002. "Public Trust and Corruption in Japan." In *Political Corruption: Concepts and Contexts,* eds. Arnold J. Heidenheimer and Michael Johnston. New Brunswick, NJ: Transaction, 835–862.

Phelan, John. 1960. "Authority and Flexibility in the Spanish Imperial Bureaucracy." *Administrative Science Quarterly* 5: 47–65.

———. 1967. *The Kingdom of Quito in the Seventeenth Century: Bureaucratic Politics in the Spanish American Empire.* Madison: University of Wisconsin Press.

Philip, Mark. 1997. "Defining Political Corruption." *Political Studies* 45: 436–462.

———. 2002. "Conceptualizing Corruption." In *Political Corruption: Concepts and Contexts,* eds. Arnold J. Heidenheimer and Michael Johnston. New Brunswick, NJ: Transaction, 41–57.

Porter, Michael E., Augusto Lopez-Claros, and Klaus Schwab. 2005. *The Global Competitiveness Report, 2005–2006.* World Economic Forum. New York: Palgrave Macmillan.

Porter, Michael E., Jeffrey D. Sachs, Peter K. Cornelius, John W. McArthur, and Klaus Schwab. 2002. *The Global Competitiveness Report, 2001–2002.* World Economic Forum. New York: Oxford University Press.

Porter, Michael E., Klaus Schwab, and Xavier Sala-I-Martin. 2007. *The Global Competitiveness Report, 2007–2008.* World Economic Forum. New York: Palgrave Macmillan.

Posada-Carbó, Eduardo. 2000. "Electoral Juggling: A Comparative History of the Corruption of Suffrage in Latin America 1830–1930." *Journal of Latin American Studies* 32 (3): 611–645.

Power, Timothy, and Mary Clark. 2001. "Does Trust Matter? Interpersonal Trust and Democratic Values in Chile, Costa Rica, and Mexico." In *Citizen Views of Democracy in Latin America,* ed. Roderic Ai Camp. Pittsburgh: University of Pittsburgh Press, 51–70.

Presidencia de la República. 2001. *Plan Nacional de Desarrollo, 2001–2006.* Published in the *Diario Oficial de la Federación,* May 30.

Przeworski, Adam. 1995. *Sustainable Democracy.* New York: Cambridge University Press.

Przeworski, Adam, Susan C. Stokes, and Bernard Manin, eds. 1999. *Democracy, Accountability, and Representation.* New York: Oxford University Press.

Ramírez Cuvas, Jesús. 2005. "IFE: la prueba de fuego" *Masiosare,* July 3.

Rauch, James E., and Peter Evans. 2000. "Bureaucratic Structure and Bureaucratic Performance in Less Developed Countries." *Journal of Public Economics* 75: 49–71.

Ravelo, Ricardo. 2000. "Diagnostico del equipo de Fox: la PGR, descompuesta." *Proceso* 1247 (September 24): 22

———. 2007. "Poderoso y protegido." *Proceso* 1614 (October 7): 28–31.

———. 2009. "Capos, los verdaderos jefes de la SIEDO." *Proceso* 1681 (January 18): 12–16.

Reames, Benjamin Nelson. 2007. "A Profile of Police Forces in Mexico." In *Reforming the Administration of Justice in Mexico,* eds. Wayne A. Cornelius and David A. Shirk. San Diego: Center for US-Mexican Studies, University of California, 117–132.

Rehren, Alfredo. 1997. "Corruption and Local Politics in Chile." *Crime, Law, and Social Change* 25: 323–334.

Rendón Corona, Armando. 2001. "Representatividad sindical y representación del Congreso del Trabajo." *Estudios Políticos* 27: 249–291.

Reyes, Leonarda. 2004a. "Mexico: Corruption Notebook." In *Global Integrity Report 2004.* Center for Public Integrity. http://www.globalintegrity.org/reports/2004/2004/country9fe7.html?cc=mx&act=notebook.

———. 2004b. "Mexico: If You Don't Cheat, You Don't Advance." In *The Corruption Notebook.* Washington, DC: Center for Public Integrity, 176–187.

Reyes Heroles, Federico. 1999. "Values and Corruption: Changing Private Attitudes." Paper presented at the conference "Transparency and Corruption: Trends in Mexico," Mexico City, November 4–5.

Rivera Sánchez, José Abel. 2004. "Cambio institucional y democratización: la evolución de las comisiones en la Cámara de Diputados de México." *Política y Gobierno* 11 (2): 263–313.

Robinson, Mark, ed. 1998. *Corruption and Development.* London: Frank Cass.

Rocha, Oscar. 2005. "Civil-Military Relations and Security Policy in Mexico." In *Mexican Governance: From Single-Party Rule to Divided Government,* eds. Armand B. Peschard-Sverdrup and Sara R. Rioff. Washington, DC: Center for Strategic and International Studies, 185–229.

Rodarte E., Mario. 2007. "Mala regulación y falta de transparencia como promotores de la corrupción." Presentation at the seminar "Transparencia, Confianza Ciudadana e Instituciones." Mexico City: Instituto de Acceso a la Información Pública del Distrito Federal (INFODF), October 25–26.

Rodrigues, Fernando. 2004. "Brazil: A Protected Elite." In *The Corruption Notebook.* Washington, DC: Center for Public Integrity, 37–42.

Rodríguez, Victoria E. 1997. *Decentralization in Mexico: From Reforma Municipal to Solidaridad to Nuevo Federalismo.* Boulder: Westview.

Rodríguez, Victoria E., and Peter M. Ward. 1995. *Opposition Government in Mexico.* Albuquerque: University of New Mexico Press.

Romer León, Jorge. 2005. "Índice latinoamericano de transparencia presupuestaria 2005: resultados para México." Fundar (October). http://www.fundar.org.mx/indice2005/docs/paises/ReporteMexico2005.pdf.

Rosas, Guillermo, Federico Estévez, and Eric Magar. 2005. "Are Non-Partisan Technocrats the Best Party Watchdogs Money Can Buy? An Examination of Mexico's *Instituto Federal Electoral.*" Paper presented at the annual meeting of the American Political Science Association, Washington, DC, August 31–September 3.

Rose, Richard, and William Mishler. 2007. "The Gap Between Experience and Perception of Corruption: An Empirical Analysis." Paper presented at the General Conference of the European Consortium for Political Research (ECPR), September.

Rose-Ackerman, Susan. 1999. *Corruption and Government: Causes, Consequences, and Reform.* New York: Cambridge University Press.

Rosenberg, Tina. 2003. "The Taint of the Greased Palm." *New York Times,* August 10.

Rothstein, Bo, and Dietlind Stolle. 2002. "How Political Institutions Create and Destroy Social Capital: An Institutional Theory of Generalized Trust." Paper presented at the annual meeting of the American Political Science Association, Boston, August 29–September 2.

Rowland, Allison. 2003. "Assessing Decentralization: What Role for Municipal Government in the Administration of Justice?" *USMEX 2003–04 Working Paper Series.*

Rubio, Luis, and Edna Jaime. 2007. *El acertijo de la legitimidad: por una democracia eficaz en un entorno de legalidad y desarrollo.* Mexico City: Fondo de Cultura Económica and Centro de Investigación para el Desarrollo.

Sampford, Charles, Arthur Shacklock, Carmel Connors, and Fredrik Galtung, eds. 2006. *Measuring Corruption.* Burlington: Ashgate.

Sánchez González, José Juan. 2004. *Reforma, modernización e innovación en la historia de la administración pública en México.* Mexico City: Instituto de Administración Pública del Estado de Quintana Roo and Miguel Ángel Porrúa.

Sandholtz, Wayne, and Mark Gray. 2003. "International Integration and National Corruption." *International Organization* 57 (4): 761–800.

Sandholtz, Wayne, and William Koetzle. 2000. "Accounting for Corruption: Economic Structure, Democracy, and Trade." *International Studies Quarterly* 44: 31–50.

Santoro, Daniel. 2004. "Argentina: The Tango of Corruption." In *The Corruption Notebook.* Washington, DC: Center for Public Integrity, 6–13.

Schatz, Sara, Hugo Concha, and Ana Laura Magaloni Kerpel. 2007. "The Mexican Judicial System: Continuity and Change in a Period of Democratic Consolidation." In *Reforming the Administration of Justice in Mexico,* eds. Wayne A. Cornelius and David A. Shirk. San Diego: Center for US-Mexican Studies, University of California, 197–224.

Schedler, Andreas, Larry Diamond, and Marc Plattner. eds. 1999. *The Self-Restraining State: Power and Accountability in New Democracies.* Boulder: Lynne Rienner.

Schlesinger, Thomas, and Kenneth J. Meier. 2002. "Variations in Corruption Among the American States." In *Political Corruption: Concepts and Contexts,* eds. Arnold J. Heidenheimer and Michael Johnston. New Brunswick, NJ: Transaction, 627–643.

Schmidt, Steffen W., Laura Guasti, Carl Land, and James Scott, eds. 1977. *Friends, Followers, and Factions: A Reader in Political Clientelism.* Berkeley: University of California Press.

Schneider, Ben Ross, and Blanca Heredia, eds. 2003. *Reinventing Leviathan: The Politics of Administrative Reform in Developing Countries.* Miami: University of Miami Press.

Scott, James C. 1972. *Comparative Political Corruption.* Englewood Cliffs, NJ: Prentice-Hall.

SECODAM (Secretaría de la Contraloría y Desarrollo Administrativo). 2001a. *Acuerdo nacional para la transparencia.* Mexico City.

———. 2001b. *Plan nacional de desarrollo, 2001–2006.* Mexico City.

———. 2001c. "Primer informe." Mexico City.

———. 2001d. *Programa nacional de combate a la corrupción y fomento a la transparencia y el desarrollo administrativo, 2001–2006.* Mexico City.

———. 2002. "Segundo informe." Mexico City.

SFP (Secretaría de la Función Pública). 2004. "Mexico." Report presented to the 6th meeting of the OAS Committee of Experts, Washington, DC, July 26–30.
———. 2005a. "Mexico: Final Report." Report presented to the 7th meeting of OAS Committee of Experts, Washington, DC, March 7–12.
———. 2005b. *Transparencia, buen gobierno y combate a la corrupción en la Función Pública.* Mexico City: Secretaría de la Función Pública and Fondo de Cultural Económica.
———. 2005c. "Questionnaire on Provisions Selected by the Committee of Experts of the Follow-Up Mechanism for the Implementation of the Inter-American Convention Against Corruption for Analysis Within the Framework of the First Round." Mexico City: Secretaría de la Función Pública.
———. 2006. "Acciones recientes en México en la lucha contra la corrupción." National progress report presented to the 9th meeting of the OAS Committee of Experts, Washington, DC, March 27–April 1.
SEGOB (Secretaría de Gobernación). 1983. *Renovación moral de la sociedad.* Mexico City: Talleres Gráficos de la Nación.
Seligson, Mitchell A. 1999. *Nicaraguans Talk About Corruption: A Follow-Up Study.* Washington, DC: Casals.
———. 2001. "Transparency and Anti-Corruption Activities in Colombia: A Survey of Citizen Experiences." Washington, DC: Casals.
———. 2002a. "The Impact of Corruption on Regime Legitimacy: A Comparative Study of Four Latin American Countries." *Journal of Politics* 64 (2): 408–433.
———. 2002b. "The Renaissance of Political Culture or the Renaissance of the Ecological Fallacy?" *Comparative Politics* 34 (3): 273–292.
———. 2002c. "Trouble in Paradise: The Erosion of System Support in Costa Rica, 1978–1999." *Latin American Research Review* 37 (1): 160–185.
———. 2004. "Victimization Scale." In Transparency International, *Global Corruption Report 2004.* London: Pluto, 307–310.
———. 2005. "The Latin American Public Opinion Project: Corruption Victimization." In Transparency International, *Global Corruption Report 2005.* London: Pluto, 282–285.
———. 2006. "The Measurement and Impact of Corruption Victimization: Survey Evidence from Latin America." *World Development* 34 (2): 381–404.
Serra, Danila. 2006. "Empirical Determinants of Corruption: A Sensitivity Analysis." *Public Choice* 126: 225–256.
Shadlen, Kenneth C. 2004. *Democratization Without Representation: The Politics of Small Industry in Mexico.* University Park: Pennsylvania State University Press.
Shirk, David. 2004. *Mexico's New Politics: The PAN and Democratic Change.* Boulder: Lynne Rienner.
Shirk, David A., and Alejandra Ríos Cázares. 2007. Introduction to *Reforming the Administration of Justice in Mexico,* eds. Wayne A. Cornelius and David A. Shirk. San Diego: Center for US-Mexican Studies, University of California, 1–50.
Shleifer, Andrei, and Robert W. Vishny. 1993. "Corruption." *Quarterly Journal of Economics* 108: 599–617.
Silva, Carlos. 2007. "Police Abuse in Mexico City." In *Reforming the Administration of Justice in Mexico,* eds. Wayne A. Cornelius and David A. Shirk. San Diego: Center for US-Mexican Studies, University of California, 175–196.
Skidmore, Thomas. 1999. "Collor's Downfall in Historical Perspective." In *Corruption and Political Reform in Brazil: The Impact of Collor's Impeachment,* eds. Keith S. Rosenn and Richard Downes. Boulder: Lynne Rienner, 1–20.
Smallman, Shawn C. 1997. "Shady Business: Corruption in the Brazilian Army Before 1954." *Latin American Research Review* 32 (3): 39–62.

Smith, Michael L. 2008. "Explaining Corruption Perceptions: A Cross-National Analysis of 15 Countries." Paper presented at the annual meeting of the Midwest Political Science Association, Chicago, April 3–6.

Smulovitz, Catalina, and Enrique Peruzzotti. 2000. "Social Accountability in Latin America." *Journal of Democracy* 11 (4): 147–158.

Soares, R. R. 2004. "Crime Reporting as a Measure of Institutional Development." *Economic Development and Cultural Change* 52 (4): 851–871.

Soreide, Tina. 2006. "Is It Wrong to Rank? A Critical Assessment of Corruption Indices." Working Paper no. 2006-1. Bergen, Norway: Chr. Michelsen Institute.

Spector, Bertram I., ed. 2005. *Fighting Corruption in Developing Countries: Strategies and Analysis.* Bloomfield, CT: Kumarian.

Staudt, Kathleen, and Irasema Coronado. 2007. "Binational Civic Action for Accountability: Antiviolence Organizing in Cd. Juárez–El Paso." In *Reforming the Administration of Justice in Mexico,* eds. Wayne A. Cornelius and David A. Shirk. San Diego: Center for US-Mexican Studies, University of California, 349–368.

Subero, Carlos. 2004. "Venezuela: With Me, or Against Me." In *The Corruption Notebook.* Washington, DC: Center for Public Integrity, 365–372.

Swamy, Anand, Stephen Knack, Y. Lee, and O. Azfar. 2001. "Gender and Corruption." *Journal of Development Economics* 64 (1): 25–55.

Taylor, Michael C. 1997. "Why No Rule of Law in Mexico? Explaining the Weakness of Mexico's Judicial Branch." *New Mexico Law Review* 27: 141–166.

Teichman, Judith A. 1996. *Privatization and Political Change in Mexico.* Pittsburgh: University of Pittsburgh Press.

Thacker, Strom C. 2000. *Big Business, the State, and Free Trade: Constructing Coalitions in Mexico.* New York: Cambridge University Press.

Tirole, Jean. 1996. "A Theory of Collective Reputations with Applications to the Persistence of Corruption and to Firm Quality." *Review of Economic Studies* 63: 1–22.

Tranparencia Mexicana. 2005. "Integrity Pact Sheds Light on Mexican Electricity Tender." In Transparency International, *Global Corruption Report 2005.* London: Pluto, 43–49.

Transparency International. 2002a. *Corruption Fighters' Toolkit: Civil Society Experiences and Emerging Strategies.* Berlin.

———. 2002b. "TI Press Release of the 2002 CPI." Berlin.

———. 2007. *Global Corruption Barometer.* Berlin.

Treisman, Daniel. 2000. "The Causes of Corruption: A Cross-National Study." *Journal of Public Economics* 76: 399–457.

———. 2007. "What Have We Learned About the Causes of Corruption from Ten Years of Cross-National Empirical Research?" *Annual Review of Political Science* 10: 211–244.

Ugalde, Luis Carlos. 2000a. "Theoretical Framework." In *The Mexican Congress: Old Player, New Power,* eds. Luis Carlos Ugalde and Armand B. Peschard-Sverdrup. Washington, DC: Center for Strategic and International Studies, 1–19.

———. 2000b. *Vigilando al Ejecutivo. El papel del Congreso en la supervisión del gasto público, 1970–1999.* Mexico: Instituto de Investigaciones Legislativas, Cámara de Diputados, and Miguel Ángel Porrúa.

———. 2001. "Presidencia débil ¿congreso fuerte?" *Proceso* 1287 (July 1): 30.

———. 2002. "El debate sobre la corrupción en México." VII Congreso Internacional del CLAD Sobre la Reforma del Estado y de la Administración Pública, Lisbon, October 8–11.

Uildriks, Niels. Forthcoming. *Mexico's Unrule of Law: Human Rights and Police Reform Under Democratization.* Lanham, MD: Lexington.

United Nations. 2002. "Civil and Political Rights, Including Questions of: Independence of the Judiciary, Administration of Justice, Impunity." Economic and Social Council.

US Department of State. 2004, 2006. "Mexico." Country reports on human rights. Washington, DC: Bureau of Democracy, Human Rights, and Labor.

Uslaner, Eric. 2004. "Coping and Social Capital: The Informal Sector and the Democratic Transition." Paper presented at the conference "Unlocking Human Potential: Linking the Formal and Informal Sectors," Helsinki.

Valverde Loya, Miguel Ángel. 2002. "La corrupción en México y el entorno internacional." VII Congreso Internacional del CLAD Sobre la Reforma del Estado y de la Administración Pública, Lisbon, October 8–11.

Van Rijckeghem, Caroline, and Beatrice Weder. 2001. "Bureaucratic Corruption and the Rate of Temptation: Do Wages in the Civil Service Affect Corruption?" *Journal of Development Economics* 65 (2): 307–332.

Velasco, José Luis. 2005. *Insurgency, Authoritarianism, and Drug Trafficking in Mexico's Democratization.* New York: Routledge.

Vilas, C. M. 1997. "Inequality and the Dismantling of Citizenship in Latin America." *NACLA: Report on the Americas* 31 (1): 57–63.

Waisser, Ronén. 2002. "De México para el mundo: conferencia México contra la corrupción." *Revista Probidad* 20 (September). http://www.probidad.org.sv.

Warren, Mark E. 2004. "What Does Corruption Mean in a Democracy?" *American Journal of Political Science* 48 (2): 328–343.

Weaver, R. Kent, and Bert A. Rockman. 1993. "Institutional Reform and Constitutional Design." In *Do Institutions Matter? Government Capabilities in the United States and Abroad,* eds. R. Kent Weaver and Bert A. Rockman. Washington, DC: Brookings Institution, 462–482.

Weber Abramo, Claudio. 2008. "How Much Do Perceptions of Corruption Really Tell Us?" *Economics: The Open-Access, Open-Assessment E-Journal,* 2 (3) http://www.economics-ejournal.org/economics/journalarticles/2008-3.

Weiss, John. 1996. "Economic Policy Reform in Mexico: The Liberalism Experiment." In *Dismantling the Mexican State?* eds. Rob Aiken, Nikki Craske, Gareth A. Jones, and David E. Stansfield. New York: St. Martin's, 58–77.

Weldon, Jeffrey A. 1997. "Political Sources of *Presidencialismo* in Mexico." In *Presidentialism and Democracy in Latin America,* eds. Scott Mainwaring and Matthew Soberg Shugart. New York: Cambridge University Press, 225–258.

———. 2004. "Changing Patterns of Executive-Legislative Relations in Mexico." In *Dilemmas of Political Change in Mexico,* ed. Kevin J. Middlebrook. London: Institute of Latin American Studies, 133–167.

Wesberry, Jim. 2004. "Obstáculos institucionales que limitan las funciones de los organismos gubernamentales de combate a la corrupción en América Latina." Colonia Tovar, Venezuela: Centro Latinoamericano de Administración para el Desarrollo (CLAD).

Weyland, Kurt. 1998. "Politics of Corruption in Latin America." *Journal of Democracy* 9 (2): 108–121.

Whitehead, Laurence. 1989. "On Presidential Graft: The Latin American Evidence." In *Political Corruption: A Handbook,* eds. Arnold J. Heidenheimer et al. Edison, NJ: Transaction, 781–800.

———. 2000. "Institutional Design and Accountability in Latin America." Paper presented at the annual meeting of the Latin American Studies Association, Miami, March 16–18.

———. 2002. "High Level Political Corruption in Latin America: A 'Transitional' Phenomenon?" In *Political Corruption: Concepts and Contexts,* eds. Arnold J. Heidenheimer and Michael Johnston. New Brunswick, NJ: Transaction, 801–818.

Williams, Mark Eric. 2001. *Market Reforms in Mexico: Coalitions, Institutions, and the Politics of Policy Change.* Lanham: Rowman and Littlefield.

Willis, Elisa, Christopher Garman, and Stephan Haggard. 1999. "The Politics of Decentralization in Latin America." *Latin American Research Review* 34 (1): 7–56.

World Bank. 1999. "The Fight Against Corruption: A World Bank Perspective." Stockholm: Central America Country Management Unit, Latin American and the Caribbean Region, May 25–28.

———. 2001. "Controlling Corruption: Towards an Integrated Strategy in Latin America." Paper presented at the 10th annual International Anti-Corruption Conference, Prague, October 8.

———. 2007. *Democratic Governance in Mexico: Beyond State Capture and Social Polarization.* Washington, DC: World Bank.

Wuhs, Steven T. 2008. *Savage Democracy: Institutional Change and Party Development in Mexico.* University Park: Penn State University Press.

Xin, Xiaohui, and Thomas K. Rudel. 2004. "The Context for Political Corruption: A Cross-National Analysis." *Social Science Quarterly* 85 (2): 294–309.

Yarrington, Doug. 2003. "Cattle, Corruption, and Venezuelan State Formation During the Regime of Juan Vicente Gómez, 1908–35." *Latin American Research Review* 38 (2): 3–28.

"A Year Later, Slain Councilwoman Symbolizes Frustrations in Fight Against Mexican Corruption." 2002. *Associated Press,* September 6.

Zamora Briseño, Pedro. 2007. "Amistad lucrativa." *Proceso* 1618 (November 4): 12–14.

Zaniartu, Mario. 1996. "El contexto humano de la corrupción." In *Eficiencia, corrupción y crecimiento con equidad,* ed. Aula Abierta de Ética. Bilbao, Spain: Universidad de Deusto.

Zepeda Lecuona, Guillermo. 2004. *Crimen sin castigo: procuración de justicia penal y Ministerio Público en México.* Mexico City: Centro de Investigación para el Desarrollo and Comisión Federal de Electricidad.

———. 2007. "Criminal Investigation and the Subversion of the Principles of the Justice System in Mexico." In *Reforming the Administration of Justice in Mexico,* eds. Wayne A. Cornelius and David A. Shirk. San Diego: Center for US-Mexican Studies, University of California, 133–152.

Zovatto, Daniel G. 2000. "Political Finance in Latin America: Comparative Study of the Legal and Practical Characteristics of the Funding of Political Parties and Electoral Campaigns." Paper presented at the annual meeting of the International Political Science Association, Quebec, August 1–5.

Index

access to information law, 101–102, 110; constitutional provisions, 120, 128–129; state laws, 56, 70, 131. *See also* transparency, and IFAI

accountability, 18, 233; and civil society, 57, 65–66, 69, 72, 76, 79, 234; in congress, 54; demands for, 3, 22, 50, 192, 211, 223, 226, 232, 238; and democracy, 6–7, 9–10, 17, 27, 50, 52, 63, 231, 235; downward or reverse, 50, 52, 62; and federalism, 47, 49, 55; horizontal, 6, 9, 21, 27, 33, 36, 70; institutions of, 120, 229, 234; in the judiciary, 41, 43, 45–46; and Klitgaard´s equation, 212; and local governments, 48; measures of, 243, 245; and political culture, 223–224, 230, 232; in the press, 192; societal, 6, 43, 48–49, 214–215; under the old regime, 2–3; vertical, 5, 9, 21, 36, 77, 214, 234

Acosta Lugo, Nahum, 109, 261

Acuerdo Nacional para la Transparencia, 101–103

AFI (Agencia Federal de Investigaciones), 106, 108, 121, 127

age: impact on participation in corruption, 170–171, 173, 176; impact on perceptions of corruption, 147–148,151–152, 176; impact on

perception of change, 154, 156; impact on the consequences of corruption, 158

Ahumada, Carlos. *See* video scandals

Aldana Prieto, Ricardo. *See* PEMEX

Alianza Civica, 36, 59, 64–66, 70, 79–80

alternation in power, impact on corruption, 26, 49, 51, 142, 144, 152–156, 160

Amigos de Fox, 28–31, 100, 124, 189, 191, 221, 253–254

anticorruption campaigns, 2, 4, 85,122

ANUIES (Asociación Nacional de Universidades y Institutos de Educación Superior), 68, 73

aregional.com, 68, 80

Argentina, 8, 37, 80, 146, 211, 220, 241

ASF (Auditoria Superior de la Federación), 33–37, 40, 53–54, 88, 120, 130, 234, 251–252, 257, 261–267

audits, 33, 37, 48, 52–54, 66, 74, 93–94, 98–100, 102, 110, 119, 129, 130–131, 189, 234, 251, 267. *See also* ASF; SFP

authoritarianism, 3, 62, 211, 224

autonomous organizations: within government, 25–26, 33, 40, 49, 51, 102, 107, 111; within society, 3, 6, 40, 58, 63

About the Book

Has the fundamental shift in Mexico's political system away from single-party authoritarian rule had any impact on the pattern of corruption that has plagued the country for years? Is there less or more corruption today? Have different types of corruption emerged? If so, why?

Stephen Morris addresses these questions, comprehensively exploring how the changes of the past decade—political, structural, institutional, and even cultural—have affected the scope, nature, and perception of political corruption in Mexico. More broadly, his analysis sheds new light on the impact of democratization on political corruption, the conditions that make effective reform possible, and the limits of an institutional approach to understanding the corruption equation.

Stephen D. Morris is professor of political science at the University of South Alabama. His numerous publications on Mexico include *Gringolandia: Mexican Identity and Perception of the U.S.* and *Political Reformism in Mexico: An Overview of Contemporary Mexican Politics,* and he is also coeditor (with Charles T. Blake) of the forthcoming volumes *Corruption and Democracy in Latin America* and *Corruption and Politics in Latin America.*